The Metamorphosis of Self

Political Charms

Looking at Life on the Outside
while Enjoying Life on the Inside

Book 10

k. e. leger

ζ

Also by k. e. leger

ζ

Novels:

Answers
Answers Awakening
(A rewrite of Answers)

Poetry Collections

Shadows of A Life Series—
A Lone Journey
A Mother's World
A Fight from Within
The Invisible Conquest

The Denial and Isolation of Self—
(Book 1) Guiding Self into the Hands of Silent Abuse
(Book 2) Political Charms: Looking at Life on the Outside while Denying Life on the Inside
(Book 3) An Eagle's Flight—America's Story in Rhyme:
Looking at Life Back There while Stuck in Here
(Book 4) Feeding the Monster—Fixing What Is Not Broken in American Education
Looking at Life on the Outside while Denying Life on the Inside
(Book 5) Anger's Deflected Course—The Emotion Turmoil—
Silent Abuse to Physical Abuse...Physical Abuse to Silent Abuse
(Book 6) The Silent Abuse Survivor's Guide—Fighting Anger
Bargaining Self into Sanity
(Book 7) Silent Abuse: Scream NO MORE!—
You're in Depression. You're Not Losing Your Mind. You're Just Doing the Time.
(Book 8) The Metamorphosis of Self: Accepting It Wasn't Your Fault
(Book 9) The Metamorphosis of Self: A Delicate Walk
Fighting to Separate Anger and Codependency from Self

For Judy Wallace

ζ

COVER DESIGN BY k. e. leger

Library of Congress Cataloging in Publication Data
Leger, Karen Elaine, 1969-
The Metamorphosis of Self Political Charms
Looking at Life on the Outside while Enjoying Life on the Inside/k. e. leger
Library of Congress Catalog Card Number:
Copyright© 2018 by Karen Elaine Leger
Layout, Design, and Editing by k. e. leger

ISBN 9781723817625

FIRST EDITION

Contents

ζ

~Constituted Leader~

leading selflessness—constructive and healing
our Lord's† gentle test–
be humble in living, humility's *certainness*
be teachable in learning, share with the rest

unconditional—lessons of loving
all people's oneness, God's† way of leading–
enact inclusiveness, follow His† teaching
—enjoy all's closeness

spiritual everlasting success–
begin by serving, think of you less–
others as *being*—don't be envious
begin sharing the truth of righteousness

learn on a daily basis
–good character growing, keep striving–
grace raises from nothingness
–self-denying creativeness

remember the beginning—great-leader making
no inheriting from hierarchy's nest
–better in growing, answering Jesus Christ's† test–
others you're loving
of God†, you're learning—for all, you're serving

forget world greediness, imitate God's† teaching
start leading through righteousness
then all soon follows your quest

(September 15, 2013)—*In this world the kings and great men lord it over the people, yet they are called friends of the people—Jesus Christ.*—Luke 22:25

A little prayer for our leaders on this beautiful Sunday morning.

After studying the *Bible* and writing about past U.S. Presidents (I've written a chapbook about the lives of the first 31 thus far and have several on the history of this great country.)
[Since this writing, these chapbooks have been changed.]

I've come to believe that this here land is the land of *milk and honey.*

It was shown to us at the most perfect time: When a people wanted, needed a land where they could freely worship the Lord. We built this country on our beliefs: *God comes first.*

We elect leaders to adhere to what this country was founded upon.

Along the way, many of us have forgotten this. It's not hard to see how this happened.

It's the oldest story in the book: Lust, greed, power, envy, jealousy.

These are the tests we're put through. Which road we travel is entirely up to us.

When an elected leader chooses the wrong road, they forget that they bring a people with them. This is where *"Constituted Leader"* comes from.

The quote I chose to lead into this poem speaks volumes.

Since we elect our leaders, we tell them that we are putting our trust into them to do what's right, hence, *friends of the people.*

We have always been a trusting people because we believe in our faith and that which made this country great.

Just to make my point clear: The United States of America has the largest volunteer military in the history of the world! That, in itself, speaks volumes about its people and our beliefs.

When the highest of our leaders disregards that faith, they also disregard that trust, but we are so convinced that what our forefathers put before them is so powerful that no one would dare deceive us so strongly that they would destroy that which we are built on.

It's a very big brick to chew on.

Let's get simple for a moment.

I always write about my personal life.

I feel confident in sharing, not for attention, but for the paradox of it all.

I was married for 19 years.

I put all my faith in it that we could survive anything.

We took a vow in front of God, promised our forever, then built a life: Had children, invested heavily in the financial part, built a home, invested every minute of our lives for it.

I trusted it beyond measure, trusted that our friends and family (those who stood with us as we pledged our love before God, those I dearly loved and trusted beyond measure as well) would insure that we kept that promise we made no matter what.

I thought about giving up here and there, but continued to fight because of my beliefs.

[x] was my *leader*, but I was blind, lost in the trust that *this too shall pass* and before I knew it, it was gone. See where I'm going.

Think on a bigger scale now.

We, as a people, have taken a vow.

To our country, we are married.

Our *Constitution* is our wedding certificate.

The moment of conception on this here land, we slid on that ring.

Our leaders are our partners.

We put all our faith and trust into them believing that our investments...our time, our money...is safe because we've taken a vow before God.

Our leaders (our partners) place their hand on a *Bible*, and before us and God, raise their right hand when they are sworn in pledging to honor our relationship in good times and in bad, in sickness and in health, until death due us part (until their term is up).

They swear to protect us, to honor us, to obey us.

If you recall, Obama used Lincoln's *Bible*.

It was housed in a glassed case.

It was not taken out of that glass case.

Correct me if I'm wrong.

See where I'm going.

To be an honorable leader, as Christ says, you have to remain humble at all times (honest), even in the face of adversary, even when you're fighting the evil that awaits (greed, lust, envy, jealousy, power).

When you stop fighting evil, you become evil. It's that simple. Jesus saw evil first hand.

He experienced His closest friends, those who swore alliance to Him, turn on Him when He needed them the most.

In divorce, I've experience this, too.

Are we divorcing our country?

I ask this because it seems that a large number of us are turning on our *Constitution*: Our beliefs, our own way of life.

Like those who turned on Jesus: One actually hung himself because of his shame; like the spouse who turns away from his marriage: Because of shame and guilt, they ignore or run away from the other, they align themselves up with haters because they are alone and can't admit they are wrong; a large number of Americans are turning away from their country by denying what they are doing, by placing blame, instead of looking at themselves (because of the larger scale of shame they would have to face), by running and hiding behind something or other, by burying themselves deeper into their lies by pushing for more laws against their own people, by making alliances with the enemy to have something to hold onto because they feel totally alone in their own country, so they turn against their own people: The people who are trying to make them see that they are on the wrong side.

Just something for you to think about.

Sometimes, the things that happen in our personal lives mimic things happening on a much larger scale.

The people of Germany believed in their marriage, too, even when their towns were being gated and isolated.

An emotional, spiritual, and physically abused spouse does the exact same thing: They hang on to their belief that *this too shall pass*.

God gave us this country.

Are we so willing to give it up because of shame that we may be wrong?

Just wondering....

ς

See, the Lord is coming with fire, and His chariots are like a whirlwind; He will bring down His anger with fury, and His rebuke with flames of fire. For with fire and with His sword, the Lord will execute judgment upon all men, and many will be those slain by the Lord.—Isaiah 66:16-17

~

(March 20, 2017)—I'm currently editing this book and some of it was written four years ago.

Today, there's a new President in office and the same old strife exist.

As I moved through healing from the anger stage of the five stages of grief, I continued to concentrate on politics.

As I stated in *Anger's Deflected*

Course—How to Recognize the Emotional Turmoil—Silent Abuse to Physical to Physical Abuse to Silent Abuse, I didn't get divorced until August of 2013.

I didn't leave my hometown until September of that year.

I did a lot of things to keep me busy.

Politics has always been one of them.

And through the years that follow 2013, I continued to write about politics.

When you are a teacher, when you are a disabled veteran, when you are just surviving, you tend to focus on a lot of things you always focused on.

I included all my political writings from 2012 until 2017 in this book.

I haven't focused so much time on politics this year, but there is still concern in me to which way the people are going.

In any sense, I've learned that the anger stage continues if you continue to be around strife.

It's very hard to let the anger go.

More on this part of the healing later in another book.

For now...I keep it moving forward.

I had no idea what to write about for this book's introduction.

As I was editing, it became clear.

I wrote the following in 2012.

It pretty much sums up how I was feeling...all my frustrations and where they were pointed at other than the [x] during that year and the coming years.

Sometimes, when you go back there, you have to let things be as they are.

So, I'm letting this *Facebook* post be my introduction to this book.

We don't always survive the stages of grief perfectly.

All that matters is that we survive.

~

(June 3, 2012)—There's a posting to the right of my screen that ask: Do you love the *Constitution*?

There are a little over 140,000 clicks for like.

I'm a tad bit disappointed in that number. What the hell!

This is the United States of America, right?

I think I'm in that country...born and raised, as did every single generation in my family extending as far back as [when] the Choctaw Indians began their existence. I'm a native.

The *Constitution* of this country is very important to me as is the fundamentals of *freedoms* my ancestors have enjoyed since the inception of this great country.

I have listened to all the arguments on both party sides and I firmly agree with Washington when he stressed the point (as he stated in his farewell speech, which I reprinted in my first political book titled *Denial and Isolation of Self: How We Guide 'Self' Smack into the Hands of Silent Abuse* (*Political Charms: Looking at Life on the Outside While Denying Life on the Inside*)) that this country has no place for parties.

I [also] firmly agree with Washington when he made his argument in his final farewell speech that this country should never get involved with other countries because once you do, then the invasion will start and continue until there is no more *free* America!

That argument was made over 200 years [ago] and it has come to pass.

How wrong we are to have allowed this craziness to go this far!

All these lawsuits and debates are useless.

If you can sit there and read your *Facebook* page without once noticing that question: Do you love the *Constitution*?

And, not once, feel obligated to click the like button, then I know that you do nothing to protect the *freedoms* in this country.

I'm 43 years old and my children have less freedom then I did.

It was unheard of [when I was a teenager] to have the government tell you that you have to wear your seat belt, that at 18 years of age you can die for your country, but you can't have a drink, that you can't legally drive on your own until what age is it now?!

That you are forced by the government to buy flood insurance and if you don't FEMA (the fucking government) has the right to go into your bank account and take it!

That a cop can legally scratch your fucking window up because your tint is too dark!

What the hell are you sitting on your ass for?

By the time your children's children are of age, they won't be able to buy a gun without having to send the registration to some international organization, let alone have as many Christian children as they want, or cross a state's line without needing papers!

Ever been to Europe...that is what is happening here.

Looking back at the 2008 election....

Have you ever witnessed a presidential candidate who could not prove he was actually born in the U.S.?

Have you ever witnessed the need to question such a thing?

Have you ever witnessed a U.S. President bow to a king?

You are fools for letting this get this far.

You have every right to take back your country with force...I've never studied, read, or witnessed a time in the United States of America's history where it was laced so heavily with cowards.

The U.S. never backs down...never!

But the Tea Party movement (all was in their rightful place as true Americans) have failed, have proven my previous sentence to be true.

The present leader of this country (I will never call him my President...never!) should have been impeached...read the description in the *Constitution* to what constitutes an impeachment...obviously they don't teach this in U.S. schools anymore!

There was enough to charge him and fully impeach him.

Just by going around and calling the very country he leads arrogant is an impeachable charge.

But no...you let it go as so many parents let their children get away with everything because they are so afraid to whip them thanks to the Clintons!

When are you going to be proud to stand up and take your hat off and sing our National Anthem and feel proud to click like when asked: Do you love the *Constitution*?

Enough said...I'm one pissed-off American, and I vow to continue being pissed off and will fight with everything I have to let all of America know that I am an American by my given birth right and I will remain one!

And that I have earned my place here!

~

(November 25, 2017)—Nothing much has changed, except for the person in the White House.

ζ

Get wisdom, get understanding; do not forget my words or swerve from them. Do not forsake wisdom, and she will protect you; love her, and she will watch over you. Wisdom is supreme; therefore get wisdom. Though it cost all you have, get understanding. Esteem her, and she will exalt you; embrace her, and she will honor you. She will set a garland of grace on your head and present you with a crown of splendor.—Proverb 4:10-19

~

The following, written in 2012, are in alphabetical order for the exact dates in which they were written was not recorded.

~*Codes of Ethics*~

NRA's breath—accepting nothing less than a hunter's very best

place your hand on your chest child, woman, man— stand behind our crest:

upon your land, I'm an invited guest welcome me again for my honorable conduct, always my quest behind gun safety—I stand avoiding accidental death others in my band, abides by my friendly jest

game laws—regulations set
I won't bury or ban
I won't detest—including my guest
–upon my humble request, my insistence met

with a steady hand
not off to the right, not off to the left
straight down the middle-
leaving no mess, for I studied at a desk
–a firing-ranging fan, leaving all I can
for a clean kill—I can easily dress

supporting conservation-
I demand, protecting the good-hunting nest
for the future clan—of america's breast

as a hunting vet'—I will pass the pan
–an outdoor-sportsman debt
to our country's youngest pets-

have good attitude, a positive fest
learn like the rest, put your skills to the test
–don't be a pest—put others in duress

follow these gentle commands
be our rep'
passing a graceful hunter's pledge
you can bet–
hunting won't be a contest, but a fest'
–you'll be glad—you hadn't slept

~Dream One~

I questioned You†...what happens if I do
writing this here...Your† view
what to expect by writing it

I questioned You†...weeks waking up
to an empty morning dew
–then the message from You†...
offering a clue

like a bug on the wall–
me in an interview, words not heard
–I just knew—criticisms due

the message from You†...*be not afraid*
mixed-heart's roux—continue to do
this writing from You†
a message—to the red, white and blue

~Dream Three~

again a questioning dream—
my doubts stream
I want to scream—all this writing
–this political-religion scene

my heart does wean–
what will happen if I don't heed
to You're† scribing gleam

weeks upon weeks I plead
then Your† message—picked my weed

standing at the local store
as people go in, can you be so mean
this money—evil's deed—don't use it

I plead, but they ignore my plea

this money, the mark it screams
we can trade—eggs, food, clothes

but they continue–
they ignore my scream

Your† answer—it seems to me
a heavy price, if I don't heed

a world-order currency
foregone democracy
Your† name—they'll not redeem

~Dream Four~

doubts plague, I'm out of line, but I beg

please, clear my mind
give me a sign—if I don't heed
–is this your design

again and again–
weeks my question binds
then Your† message, a dream's clear find

a concentration camp, lying in a ditch
all those I love, in a clear line
hands tied, waiting to die, me they find
I think—they're being kind
chosen for the kitchen line
–watching all die
as I'm allowed to stay alive

how vast a punishment
how vast a sign, is my work so divine
why me—this scribe's line

wasted time—I'm so incline
writing this rhythm
seems all—Your† messaging design

~

(June 3, 2012)—There's a posting to the
right of my screen that ask: *Do you love the*
Constitution?
There are a little over 140,000 clicks for
like.
I'm a tad bit disappointed in that number.
What the hell!
This is the United States of America, right?
I think I'm in that country...born and

raised...as did every single generation in my family extending as far back as when the Choctaw Indians began their existence.

I'm a native.

The *Constitution* of this country is very important to me as is the fundamentals of *freedoms* my ancestors have enjoyed since the inception of this great country.

I have listened to all the arguments on both party sides and I firmly agree with Washington when he stressed the point (as he stated in his farewell speech which I reprinted in my first political book titled *Denial and Isolation of Self: How We Guide 'Self' Smack into the Hands of Silent Abuse (Political Charms: Looking at Life on the Outside While Denying Life on the Inside*) that this country has no place for parties.

I, also firmly agree with Washington when he made his argument in his final farewell speech that this country should never get involved with other countries because once you do, then the invasion will start and continue until there is no more *free* America!

That argument was made over 200 years ago and it has come to pass.

How wrong we are to have allowed this craziness to go this far!

All these lawsuits and debates are useless.

If you can sit there and read your *Facebook* page without once noticing that question...*Do you love the Constitution?*...and, not once, feel obligated to click the *like* button, then I know that you do nothing to protect the *freedoms* in this country.

I'm 43 years old and my children have less *freedom* than I did.

It was unheard of when I was a teenager to have the government tell you that you have to wear your seat belt, that at 18 years of age you can die for your country, but you can't have a drink, that you can't legally drive on your own until what age is it now?!: That you are forced by the government to buy flood insurance and if you don't FEMA (the fucking government) has the right to go into your bank account and take it!

That a cop can legally scratch your fucking window up because your tint is too dark!

What the hell are you sitting on your ass for?

By the time your children's children are of age, they won't be able to buy a gun without having to send the registration to some international organization, let alone have as many *Christian* children as they want, or cross a state's line without needing papers!

Ever been to Europe...that is what *is* happening here.

Looking back at the 2008 election....

Have you ever witnessed a presidential candidate who could not prove he was actually born in the U.S.?

Have you ever witnessed the need to question such a thing?

Have you ever witnessed a U.S. president bow to a king?

You are fools for letting this get this far.

You have every right to take back your country with force...I've never studied, read, or witnessed a time in the United States of America's history where it was laced so heavily with cowards.

The U.S. never backs down...never, but the Tea Party movement (all was in their rightful place as true Americans) have failed, have proven my previous sentence to be true.

The present leader of this country (I will never call him my President...never!) should have been impeached...read the description in the *Constitution* to what constitutes an impeachment...obviously they don't teach this in U.S. schools anymore!

There was enough to charge him and fully impeach him.

Just by going around and calling the very country he leads *arrogant* is an impeachable charge, but no...you let it go as so many parents let their children get away with everything because they are so afraid to whip them thanks to the Clintons!

When are you going to be proud to stand up and take your hat off and sing our *National Anthem* and feel proud to click *like* when asked: *Do you love the Constitution?*

Enough said...I'm one pissed-off American, and I vow to continue being pissed off and will fight with everything I have to let all of America know that I am an American by my given birth right and I will remain one, and that I have earned my place here!

~*'If' Entitlement*~

closer to presidential elections
all looking for self validations

political machines—playing games
calling each other names
their *what ifs*—no longer sounding lame
the supreme court

holding the deciding fork

changing the *constitution*
–without retribution

while the american people
idle by, ignoring her found principles

a five-to-four-chief-justice vote
amerian life—rewrote

health-care–
now executively controlled
the i.r.s. holding the bowl
snuck in tax–
on every american household

a *what-if* summation
God's† ways—put up for execution

new abortion insight–
laws passed in the night–to kill outright
–a new constitutional right

a new sign for the picketing line–
the u.s. government will pay in kind
human existence—redefined
–nothing but *perfect* you'll find

suicide—protected by law
without one thought of misery's flaw

no more dreadful moans–
replaced the dead with human clones
–pure body-chemistry zone

exact duplicate–
illusion's wondrous gift
absent, one missing piece
only God† gives to you and me–
souls—our ability to feel *free*

instead of loved ones returning home–
you'll get a robot of flesh and bone

God's† words thrown away
man and woman—no longer the way
america's government has the final say

it's great to be gay

male in male, negative to negative
female in female, positive to positive
–*marriage* guarantee

science no longer in the gray
confusion gone astray
gender—no longer to be

God†-given rights—thrown away
life, liberty, pursuit of happiness

–just memories of yesterday

the *what-if* blight
americans' forgotten *will* to fight

presidential elections–
preserved-political self-validations

liberals and conservatives–
playing games—a country re-named
–a *constitution* maimed

God's† laws become afterthoughts
–His† words no longer heard

united states shown its fate
ruled by hate—its people in sedate

the *what ifs* quickly redefining it
until she'll become just a myth
–history to gossip with

Appearance
▪*Facebook* (June 29, 2013)

~*Isaac*~

on God's† demand
death—at a father's hand
trust—if you can
His† message sent to man

sent back in rain bands
over southern land
showing His† mighty *I am*
–mixing up norm's brand

a turning, twisting lamb
slow-moving strand
–fooling its most trusted fan
taking on a three-day stand
day and night—don't you understand
He† added mystery
to an already freezing pan

cold winds, low pressure
mouth's whispered–*I'll be damn*

thinking, we were in a mighty jam
–never question—His† bigger plan
as mouth's then whisper–

thank you ma'am

only a day, our lights were banned
on God's† demand
belief—at our heart's hand

trust—if you can—His† message–
sent to—the sins of man

~*Morphined Leader*~

addict yourself to fame–
this leadership game
manipulate their brain–
innocence, you'll drain
–they'll fit your frame
then power, you'll gain

tyrannical bells rang
millions lost in vane

to hitler's lighted flame–
prosperity claimed
to stalin's bang, power came
through mao tse-tung's stain–
me-first politicians sang
atilla th hun built his name
–a population—sliced and hanged
hussein's power strain
I-am-god aim—vespasian did proclaim

this past-powering band
taught how to stand–
the greatest liars playing hand
–hypocrisy's neat little pan

nothing to blame—excuses in a can
breaches of faith, all the same

explanations—they easily brand
they quickly learned the game
so easy to sustain–
the simple-minded man

–immediate-need strand
deceitful men find lame
they simply control, tame–
take over the land

today's modern-technology train
daily-tv clan
too easy—take-over manipulated brain

aggressive-schmoozing game
persuaded—favors to gain
playing the favorites' hand
–fairness and equality—too lame

playing to personalities–
money in the hand—easy way to fame
deception's lane–
truth so easy to drain hypocrisy's gland

a saying, doing migraine
leaving the train
without a meaningful hand

wanting the fame, living through *vain*
–barely walking with a cane

as their people are drained
become tamed–
suffering pain without complain
not seeing their manipulated brains–
have fallen to the flame of the insane

~*Slanted*~

sound off, beat the drum
add to—this liberal-media fund
of definition—there is none
here's a pun, just for fun

an african-safari run–
pleasurable hut—went two sons
of tycoon donald trump

fact's bleeding crumb
mainstream's media-slanted strum

they went and killed some
enjoyed shooting their guns
their aftermath stunk, paraded-prize stunt

liberal-change for the good–
the fact-rolling drum
listen—here it comes

african hunting—rightfully welcome
africans need the funds

come hunters come
trophy-kill pun—villages' loaded trunk
after a kill's final thump

having money by the ton
protection-groups punt
leaving readers, confused and drunk

their lost facts, creative writing undone
lies sealed in hum-drum
–how lazy and dumb

serious hunters—these sons of trump
–remembering where they're from

for it's made what they've become–
honest and hardworking
–under whatever sun

with strength they've won–
facts speak louder
then the lie-inventing slums

~*Stick This*~

in 2012 america's history–

slowly shelved

macdonald wrote in the sixties–
the turner diaries

if you haven't read–
you're lost in your head

banded by the government
underground—went its shipment
if you don't know why–
bow your head—sigh
here's a comparison
killing america's son:

a dictating president–
around america—wrapped a tight skirt

today's handled puppet
america's *constitution–*
declared rubbish dirt

people-controlling black shirts
enforced dictated rules

destroying america's birth
over thirty czars
people voting—they did not flirt

required i.d.'s–
swipe with your every step
your location—tight records kept
or to jail you're set
–today's controlling net

driver's license, social security cards–
federal government's controlling deck

government's further dip–
land-rights stripped
can take it, with a bullet in a clip–

today's radical fit, liberal activist–
protecting animal *rights*
global-warming plight
national forest–
spreading government ownership

like the british
before america elevated–
charge-every-home mandate

americans completely sedated
every gun confiscated–

today a paralleling spouse
heading—this branding mouse

larry bneuer–
assistant u.s. attorney general

head of the justice department's
criminal division
u.s. senator diane feinstein
–just to name two

bills passed by the house
–over thirty for view
sit in the puppet-controlling senate
ignoring for clout
stashing-bills, refusing to view

second amendment to stew
here's your clue–

to take all guns
stripping from american sons
to eat, to protect—they reject
–the n.r.a. fights
this controlling inject

...enduring gun registration, giving bureaucrats the
power to 'decide' what guns 'law-abiding people' could
own based on government's ever-changing notion of
'need'....

bneuer arrogantly said

illusions fed, with muslom-lovers in bed
no need to beg
just on more penetrating leg

operation *fast and furious–*

blame americans–
make it contagious, plant the illusion
mexican cartels—perfect intrusion

americas the *cause*—smuggling weapons
aiding this criminal action

the truth should make you sore–
make you take arms
against this muslom gore

the u.s. government carelessly ignores
this mexican-opened door

musloms blending in–
their true intentions soar
their slow penetration, slow destruction
of america's core

here's the score:

america's health–
deciding death and wealth
from cash to checks, to check cards–
mandatory—government-dictated
driver's-license requirement
–have insurance or face indictment

the *constitution* again ignored

american people's money–
increased taxes for federal luxury
everything bought
–sneaking-under-the-radar bunny

freedom of religion broken down
turned to folklore
time no longer marked
before Christ†, after death––changed to:

you can only guess

from an atheist breath–
muslom's-pushed-islam dart

their next tack––watch your back
the *second amendment*–
the hardest to crack–
slow-destructive trap
using cartels and drubs
a hunter's slug––their illusive club

to override america's
most scared instrument–
they know the stakes' involvement

the only country in the world–
every american boy and girl
their constitutional rights
protecting self outright
to eat without a fight
ownership, multiple guns in every home
sealed tight

to implement control
musloms *have* to destroy this hold

if you want to be *free*
then you have to see
who's actually in the lead
–pushing this controlling seed

if you don't want to be
then just let it feed

remember, please
many, many years––they deceived
their slow-moving-in sneak
their politically-correct deed
education––american children now weak
green zones, global warming
–land-rights to keep

years it took––baiting the hook
laws passed, just have a look

america's *constitution*–
they slowly cooked, rights already took

their patience you fail to see
waiting, within, they creep
solidly––their planted feed

america, they tend to defeat
then we'll no longer be *free*
musloms––to force their creed

just read history–
their intentions will weed
–through illusions and deceit

~*Time-Out*~

see under the sun–
destruction of our *free* son
rights coming undone
–silent little muslom

plainly in london––very sight of a gun

so injurious to the mental health of the young

olympic-shooting fun, *free*-ticket drum
–off limits for all of them

here's a ripe one–
in 2011 orlando, florida's
t.s.a.-beach bum–
teenage girl detained not for fun
no alarms undone
just her purse––a design of a handgun

more than some
to attack america's *freedom*
students expelled, wearing n.r.a. t-shirts
–against this new world's forum

free speech, rights for protection
in the last decade–
america's entire *constitution*
quickly being broken
–is it *political-elite* dedication
or is it something else within

take a time-out, breathe deep within
this inserted saturation–
see who's implication
see who's satisfaction
is really heading this destruction

let the air slowly out, stand up
instead of mere negotiation–
take some kick-ass action

(September 4, 2012)––I wrote a lot about
what was happening in the news the pass
couple of years. My politics run deep.
I have many books put together on various

subjects in the news.

It makes my blood boil when someone is fined, suspended from school, forced to conform because it makes someone *uncomfortable.*

If families can condemn each other, fathers and mothers can walk away from their kids without being fined or arrested, then don't tell me I can't wear my tie because my *crosses* offend you.

Get the hell out my country if you can't allow others to be individuals!

Any person who has ties with foreign countries has *no* right to have any say so in this country. Period.

That's where *"Time-Out"* came from.

I haven't posted a lot of my political writings, but I think it's time to show my ass when it comes to this truth of mine.

Condemn me, try to silence me, ignore me.

You will never win because when it comes to my voice, always remember: She is loud, she is fierce, she is a true heart, which can never be contained.

Love your country.

Stand up for your beliefs.

Wear that damn tie.

If they try and stop you, you have a law that protects you: It is call discrimination!

It's time to use it!

~*We Must Stand*~

it is two thousand twelve
two hundred thirty six years
since a hand full of men
set aside their fears

–for a king in england
had total control of this land here
a king who lived in royalty
by collecting heavy taxes
giving our land to his kin
reinforcing his royal ring
red coats came, raped our women
took our homes, killed our men
then more taxes—added a heated flame

brave men
who had no country of their own
not just lawyers–
but farmers and merchants
together decided
america was *their* home

they wrote, they signed–

without being forced
a declaration–
telling england they will die
if they had to
but *no more* would they hide
to england, they said their adieu

england wouldn't give up so easy
it took years—arguing, negotiating
when these brave men
stopped shedding tears–
knowing many would die
they wouldn't give in
and came their revolution—leaving us
two hundred thirty-six years
of *freedom*

what have we done to honor them

praised them with monuments
read of them in books
their pictures, we stare and look

not good enough
for what they gave up

imagine writing a declaration today
ordinary men, coming together
declaring to...instead of england
to their own government–

no more—we declare we will not stand down
we have dried our tears
no more shall we live in fear
we have negotiated enough
our lives, we're willing to give up
we'll take arms
shutting down our warning alarm

do you have the courage
risking all that you own
signing your name
standing with other brave men
behind a declarational marriage

are you willing to pay the price
like those brave men, sign your name
knowing you could be hanged
sign your name—not for fame
but only to be *free*
as those in 1776 chose to be

how far do your negotiations have to go
before you see—the repeating of history

those seated in d.c.
have become what england used to be

to maintain their royalness blood
higher taxes pays a king's ring

those brave men didn't ask why
didn't even try
they grabbed a pen and signed
knowing tomorrow—they could die

~*Trivial*~

what do you see, what do you see
islam and christianity

who's the savior, which one's *free*
who speaks love, who speaks heed

what do you see, what do you see
islam and christianity

who will walk, who will cease
who will struggle, who will lead

what do you see, what do you see
islam and christianity

one full of demons, one full of He†
who will give in, who will pray to Thee†

~

(July 9, 2012)—Okay...done enough reading for the night.

Just finished commenting on some liberal B.S. bickering about the government.

I'm so sick of hearing the complaints!

Why don't they just gather with the guns and take over D.C. and put it all back to how it should be?

Has America turned into a nation of cowards?

For a veteran, it's sick to watch...even sicker to read about.

This poet will just sit back and record their stupidity for other generations to laugh at!

On with the show: I think I'm going to work on some sort of schedule tomorrow.

If you got any pointers on organizational skills, I would be really glad to hear them.

My time slips by so fast, before I know it, it's midnight...have got to get to bed earlier.

~

(August 9, 2012)—The point of expression is to be able to voice your opinion, be it happiness, anger, frustration, etc., and enjoy the boundaries of *free* speech.

Well, I think Obama is having his way with suppressing this once enjoyed *freedom*.

I wrote on here my opinions of frustration and anger just to have it thrown in my face by my family.

It seems that *freedom* of speech is only allowable when you make others look good, but speaking the truth and writing about how things really are is forbidden.

I'm the same person I've always been.

Just because others change doesn't mean I have to change as well.

I've learned this year that all love has its boundaries.

You cross that line and you're out the door.

My mother is the only person I've ever met that sets her boundaries, and then tears them down as quickly as they are built.

I love her with all my heart, and her arms are open when I need to cry.

Everyone else can love you one day, and then hate you the next. I never truly hate.

I try to look pass it and feel love.

I get angry and disappointed, but never do I truly hate.

My *Freedom of Speech* has been suppressed and used against me by the ones I love the most and that's not how life should be.

We should be able to enjoy all of our *freedoms* without suppression, especially, by the ones we love.

Yes, Obama has gotten his way and his message is clear.

There's no such thing as speaking the truth and having honor or writing criticism about anything.

Everyone has to be equal or you're an outcast, even by the dearest ones to your heart.

Yes you can has become equality without individualism.

~

(September 29, 2012)—Comments required: This morning on yahoo news it is reported that Delaware has made it illegal for parents in that state to whip their kids.

I'm curious about your thoughts.

My daughter asked me is this constitutional.

I think this is going too far, way beyond being unconstitutional.

The government is reaching its hands way too far in the cookie jar by dictating more judgment calls on us.

Are we not smart enough or responsible enough to take care of ourselves anymore?

Don't give me that *some people just need to be told what to do*...you'll lose that argument with me.

When is enough going to be enough?

~*A Beacon*~

do you hear it–
ring, ring, ring—liberty does sing

through the tiniest notion
–every vocation, each unique
imagination—one nation
stands for liberation
she's not a simulation
she's reality's verification–
there's ramifications if tied by dictation

do you hear it–
ring, ring, ring—liberty does sing

no unification of nations
can match her situation
no militant formulation
can undermined her creation

she has limitations, push her motivation–
her wrath's determination
unveils against aggression

do you hear it–
ring, ring, ring—liberty does sing

all look upon her manifestation
for *freedom's* not suppression
it's an awakening sensation
unmatched by any's validation

she is *liberation*
the *beacon-of-hope* rendition
to all oppression–
she is the united states of america
under God†–she *is* one nation
to the world's population–
she *is* their mandation–

being *free* is God's†-given
human condition
not under bureaucracy regulation
not under controlled restriction
but through the *self's* desire
for *liberation*

do you hear it–
ring, ring, ring—liberty does sing

~

(December 15, 2012)—Enough of this

bitching: As I was reading my *Facebook* news today, I came across a post by [friend] and I couldn't keep myself from responding.

After I reread my response several times, I felt it most important to repost it here on my own page.

You can agree or disagree, but the facts still remain.

Here's my response: Our founding fathers in establishing the Judicial Branch had the perfect idea.

They had lived in times where innocent people were assumed to do crimes and were punished, many by *immediate* death, before any investigations were done to prove if they actually did the crime or not.

By simply looking guilty or not liked by the town or being at the wrong place at the wrong time or having Christian beliefs, they were automatically assumed to be guilty.

Before the 1980s, many innocent people spent most of their life-time behind bars for something that they didn't do.

The Judicial Branch was established for one sole purpose: To protect the innocent.

Greed is the sole reason that it's not fulfilling the desires of our founding fathers.

An example: A man can walk up to two people and butcher them (O.J. Simpson) and get away with it, but a woman (me) gets a ticket and the threat of being arrested because her husband's goats broke down a fence and grazed in the pasture next door.

The sole blame: The American people themselves who sit back and play video games, watch movies, drink and have a good time, busy themselves by buying stuff, play on their cell phones and computers all day long and refuse to take a stand against a government that they were given the right, the responsibility to control, not the other way around.

I, myself, have spoken many times to people about what's been happening with our country and I have been silenced by their pity remarks, and then completely ignored because [according to them] *I run at the mouth.*

American people today refrain from talking *politics* because it's not *sociable*! making it easy for corruption and abuse to take place.

The old saying *who's watching?* comes to mind.

From pay-offs to under-the-table deals, the Judicial Branch is corrupted beyond repair.

It doesn't stop there.

Our founding fathers designed a system of checks and balances to ensure that one branch wouldn't overpower the others and would not get out of control, and they were also given the responsibility to ensure that neither of the branches step out of bounds.

They were given the responsibility to ensure that all follow the laws written by a group of men who personally experienced tyranny at its best.

All this has failed because the American people failed to do their job.

It is our responsibility to ensure our government is honest, honorable, loyal, and doing the jobs they were hired to do.

We have become a business that has let our

employees run the company, instead of us, the employers!

The result of all this slacking: The victims have become the criminals and the criminals have become the victims.

The only way to undo this is for the American people to stand up and say *no more!*

Remember the Tea Parties and their outrageous signs: *Next Time We Come With Guns.*

Our founding fathers gave us the right to take back our government if it became out of control, too big, and corrupted.

We were given the very right to use force by means of arms if all else failed.

I would never encourage a civil war or blood to be spilled on American soil by its own people, but how many mass killings, how many more regulations, laws, rules, ordinances will the government be allowed to place on us before we say enough!?

How much more foreign influence (like [*seven*] presidents who don't have enough experience at being an American) will it take for Americans to stand up and take action?

These mass killings give this liberal-run, foreign-invaded government more ump to instill more laws, regulations, rules, ordinances on us making it easier for them to gain more control over our every day lives.

The sad part is that no one seems to willingly want or have enough courage to open their eyes wide enough to see that their way of doing this undermines us without our involvement.

Hint: They tend to go straight to the gusto while our people mourn and are vulnerable.

A man kills and gets rights.

A woman gets a ticket over a goat grazing in a pasture and has no rights. Where's the logic?

Where's the reason?

The last [four] years should have taught America one lesson: Talking and negotiating will work no more!

God is hanging in the balance.

Christians are already being persecuted by slander because of Him.

How far are we willing to go before we Christians are persecuted by the guillotine just because we believe in Him?

If He were still present in our schools, in our courts, on our TVs, the events of yesterday would have never happened.

If parents and teachers were allowed to do their jobs with Him in their hearts, yesterday would never have happened and we would not be having this discussion.

It's the conservative, Christian Americans, especially, those of us who's had family fight for the small amount of *freedoms* we still have left, to say *no more* and take action to right the wrongs of the oppressive-liberal cronies.

If you can't do that, if you continue to be the coward and curl up on your [chair] and watch as your *freedoms* are being stripped away, then stop bitching and accept the results.

I'm so sick of all this talk, talk, talk and no action.

As I've always believed: *Actions speak louder than words!*

That's what the next generations will see, not the bitching or griping or negotiations or the legal B.S...no, they'll simply study our actions.

It's up to you which legacy you're willing to leave behind. Good day. Karen E. Leger

ζ

Therefore, rid yourselves of all malice and all deceit, hypocrisy, envy, and slander of every kind. Like newborn babies, crave pure spiritual milk, so that by it you may grow up in your salvation, now that you have tasted that the Lord is good.—1 Peter 2:1-3

~

The following, written in 2013, are in the order in which they were written.

~*Zulu*~
(The Plantation)

always keen to learn new
coming, straight from the scene
who can argue—truth it seems–
an ignorance issue
african-amerian—not at all on cue
like north america–
africa is a continent too

hold on to your seat, don't come unglued
through history lessons
these facts—you already knew

towns are the homes of the zulu
like down the bayou, not a continent
–understood by so few

the honorable tribe of zulu
held together with virtue
hard-working crew
take pride in all they do
–refer to themselves as *colored*
call themselves black–
they wouldn't dream
for they earn their keep
like american white people do

they despise black americans
their message overdo

what is this brew–
their question often leaks
what's these *handouts*–
black americans seek
taking from their government
what the working population reaps
–why do american blacks devalue

lincoln *freed* slaves—way back in 1862
a date—the whole of africa

knows well too

slavery through the world—still continues
why the slave-rotting attitude
–don't they know the truth

coming from the mouth's of the zulu

black americans should be grateful
living on american soil–
adds to any life's value

why don't black americans
understand the entire stew–
all *americans* descend from other views
coming together—share
the same north-american
continental avenue, to become one crew

americans to nourish that seed
honor, pride, hard work
to their *united* nation, they should feed

the zulu's review–

why milk dry the very country
who freed you, why the bad attitude
where's the gratitude
why screw the very hand that rescued
–set free—a people—renewed

yes, the zulu carries a hating streak
for those calling themselves–
african-americans on every street
for the african continent–
carries no claim for *a people*
who to their homeland—can't be true
stealing revenue
that doesn't belong to you

a powerful zulu truth
black—a label's tissue
a solid color of nothing–
no tribe, no home

colored means solid glue
many shades to speak
many shades to see
placing honor where it's due

knowing where you belong–
understanding the right things to do

their message clear–

slavery ended in 1862
now americans–
through and through
protect this institute
with honor, pride–
build your loot

instead of being your own prostitute

~*Bits and Pieces*~

bits and pieces is all I can say
bits and pieces—I feel a bit dismay

with our every day, an enemy of the state
continues a strategic game of *bourre*
that began long before yesterday

too much to speculate
too much to say *too late*

a stealing of an independence day
making serious headway
beginning with those we educate–
a dumbing-down-promised engage
soon takes its shape

the minds of the young–
a dissolving decay—so easy to dictate
when threatening to take
the federal dollars away

in the enemy hands–
those who educate, quickly did play

in a parallel-forming ray
entertainment used to saturate
elevate *game* day—remold the clay
importance in buying—conveyed
the *economy,* after all, has to be repaid

even on sundays–
take the place of Yahweh†
–material worth to splay

arrogance does portray
guilt—the gangway
beginning-deception's chassé
against each other—gainsay
–courage will easily break

bits and pieces is all I can say
bits and pieces—I feel a bit dismay

confusion solidly placed

homeland security is in the gray
building a secret résumé
–executive branch protégé

why the armor-tank-weaponry matinée
stripping d.o.d. to a mere negligée
what's their entrée
what are they trying to defray

answers to questions delayed

bits and pieces is all I can say
bits and pieces—I feel a bit dismay

federal health-care hearsay–
an american pompeii
trampling a thanksgiving day
back-to-the-stone-age toupee
–with just a bunch of words to say

federal-government-shut-down heyday
not just for a day
–parks owned by the state–
unmanned café
loads of land on the tray
–it's a bit of an overplay
but let's do it anyway

welfare recipients put at bay
enough time opens to disarray
a little game of russian rouler

playing-on-fear holiday

let's disarm every state
hey—we found a way

a mass-killing sauté
an eight-year survey, numbers out weigh
the history of the united states

all an illusive sway
a *now-you-see-it-now-you-don't* opaque

bits and pieces is all I can say
bits and pieces—I feel a bit dismay

a further mind-blowing exposé–
post-traumatic-syndrome foray
–a temporary-mind-gapping state
victims of traumatic events, abuse, rape–
overcome by a therapeutic interplay
made a *permanent* mental state
on gulf war veterans—placed
there's nothing to debate
–purchasing-new-weapon divorcée
a brilliant-controlling parlay
on the private-citizen forte

add in a bit of climate-change sway
maybe a bit risqué
maybe a seeming-soothsayer way
keeping actions at bay
–words is all they can say

bits and pieces is all I can say
bits and pieces—I feel a bit dismay

an ingenious plan put in place

the perfect recipe to slay–
the great *united* states

just a quick survey–
this inside-coupd' etat
seems just a bit outré
maybe a little cliché

but hey, who's actually holding the cashé
a government designed not to rule
or the people of the united states

bits and pieces is all I can say
bits and pieces—maybe we should pray

Appearances
▪*Facebook* (October 9, 2013)

ζ

If anyone teaches false doctrines and does not agree to the sound instruction of our Lord Jesus Christ and to godly teaching, he is conceited and understands nothing. He has an unhealthy interest in controversies and quarrels about words that result in envy, strife, malicious talk, evil suspicions and constant friction between men of corrupt mind, who have been robbed of the truth and who think that godliness is a means to financial gain.—1 Timothy 6:3-5

~

The following, written in 2014, are in the order in which they were written.

~Bi-Monthly Scheme~

greed consumes all living things
we're doomed—giant-corporate schemes
makes me want to scream

your maze of clouds–
let me say it out loud

it's a scheme—a monster of greed
just upgrade my program and leave me be

I've taken the time to buy
sat *alone* for hours learning–
trusting you without a sigh

new computer, new system
my precious program's explosion–
outdated—price inflated

plugins, drivers—you halted my dive
causing me stress, my sleep deprived

now pay monthly—use programs online

–give it time—money, money, money
I'll pay three times, four times its price
–I won't get a cd that's mine
you've connived, found a way inside
to rob me blind

–halting my creative side

~*Theory*~

watch, watch—in the tv
read, read—on the net
listen, listen—through the radio

what's for real, what's to forgo

developed homeland security
believe, believe—f.e.m.a. helping me–
I see a dirty deed

lessons of barnum baily
mock, mock—jokes on me

newly built facilities
doubled-barbed wires facing in–
secured quite heavily

scary, scary—what's so deadly–
we'd cage for *free*, maybe zombies–
viruses to the contrary
flue vaccines—no chance of escaping

just experimenting
words keep saying

ants from forestry—bodies empty
nerves projecting, continuously moving
spices added to injury—a little rabies
making what's empty, pretty damn angry
covered in sores—completing the ugly

total brilliancy–
adhering to constitutionality
attacking a domestic enemy
white lab coats—in the making

no using military–
on lands of this country
take their money—reroute
build a new security, heavy artillery

a country's tactical facility
under noses—a people so trusting

no real need–
taking guns owned privately
the enemy—preparing
it's win—biologically

science-fiction reality–
is it just theory

executive order's bravery
–the gracious heart of tom clancy

creative thinking—even in the movies

always predicting
an undercover warning–
without actually saying
what's really coming

watch, watch—in the tv
read, read—on the net
listen, listen—through the radio

what's for real, what's to forgo

history repeats history
different means of delivery
woolen eyes sunken deep
–in all entertaining

(January 18, 2014)—In this particular set of books in my series, I've been writing about what I hear, see, and read in the media.

History is one of my most favorite subjects and recording what is becoming history is most exciting.

I told you I write about many subjects...I wasn't kidding.

I live, most of the time, outside the box.

Life is very interesting to see it from the outside.

If you come here to just be hyped up, you'll be disappointed.

I'm here to touch every emotion you have, not just one or two.

Yes, I may piss you off...that's okay.

Stick around, my world is just beginning and I love my country as much as I love my happiness! Be open to all things.

If you shut your mind down to one or two, then secretly, you are shutting yourself down to many.

As a journalist, I was taught to not be bias, but to be objective, so, I take everything into account and write about them. Enjoy.

Think...the most important gift God gave us, our mind and *free*-will.

Being well-rounded is very important.

As a writer, I re-define the meaning of that.

~*Men of Ungods*~

new men of times—crossing lines
living selfish rhymes
–sharia law—they'll easily applaud

wives they left—you'll find
commitments, there's flaw

lies, be careful, they'll easily tell in kind
they'll connive—in the back—claw

off them, turn the fault

yes, new men of times—crossing lines
they'll kneel in a pew, lie to me and you
while making the sign of the cross

be careful, they secretly back sharia law
when their need–
control women—they feel they lost

for them, no heavy cost
notice their actions—it's all about them
this new time of ungodly men–
narcissus sin
crossing lines—living in selfish rhymes

(May 17, 2014)—I did a lot of research on what Sharia Law is about between the years 2009 and 2011. It's a scary thing for women.

It enraged me how many men in America have converted to Muslim to push this law in our country, but that's not why I wrote this.

At least, not all the way.

[x] had acted insulted when I called him a Muslim. I still don't know why.

I call it like I see it.

Muslim men have a right to pawn off their women to their friends, beat their women, their women are last to eat and last to be thought of. Sounds familiar to me.

Too familiar.

In court in ---- Parish, Louisiana (that's in the United States of America), the court ruled in favor of [x] who said I fell, even though I had pictures of the bruises he put on my skin.

Bruises.

A size [nine]-steel-toe boot print on the inside of my thigh where he held me down, so he can beat on my head.

The court believed his lie: I fell.

That's Sharia Law if ever I saw it, and the women in this country do nothing, but ignore it.

Here in the South, it's *let the family take care of it...hush-hush!*

Some of my family and friends completely ignore me because I'm so outspoken about domestic violence. Why?

Don't they know that women have been liberated in this country? I know I have.

No man will do this again to me, and no woman will go without knowing what [x] is capable of. Period.

It's up to us women who were treated this way to speak out and prevent Sharia Law from coming into this country full force.

Enough is enough. Concealed weapons.

You bet your bottom dollar this chick will be having a permit.

You bet your bottom dollar if I feel threatened in any way, I will use it.

Enough is enough.

It's time to hold these selfish, un-Christian men responsible for their actions!

Not one man that I, personally, know stood up for me. Not one.

That tells you right there the seriousness of this problem for women. My father didn't.

My son didn't. My brother-in-laws didn't. No one.

They ignored it like it didn't happen. It did. (It happened to me: Bruises on my skin, [three] times in my marriage.

For some women, it's an every-day thing.

Some women have their faces punched in.

I was lucky on that, but a bruise put on your skin by the man you trust is still a bruise, is still domestic violence.

I should have left after the first time.

I was the fool for staying.)

If it has happened to you, don't let it go ignored. It will happen again. I assure you.

If not the physical, the mental.

These men will use something (trust me... something) that you did against you to control you. They do not have the right to do that.

Period.

Love the skin you're in because you are worth it.

~*Let Buildings Be Buildings*~

is it not brick and mortar–
do you see flesh and bone
is your altar really His† home
is it not in your heart, He's† left all alone

for in brick and mortar
there is praise and song
for something deeper, one is left too long

sitting in pews, praising a restless throne
in its baskets–
your money eagerly thrown

hearing its bells bong
wondering, if you really belong

walking its isles–
you temporarily postpone
judgments, drunken merriments–
in customs you're grown
laws and traditions of man–

your false-happy zone

fitting in—you're drawn
a mocking, careless clone–
drowning in food and drink
condemning the weak and mild
preaching false pretenses—you're prone

ignoring the hurtings' moan
pretending to be better—strong
not seeing your own sinful tone
not seeing the seeds you've sewn
you're careless grip—all wrong

yes, you enter a building of stone
a place you call His† home
praising Him† with song
–once the hour is gone
you reenter your false-happy zone
wondering why all seems wrong
–you're left feeling all alone

(January 25, 2014)—I'm not a preacher.
I wouldn't dare step into that role.

I do have my faith and it's always been
strong even when I, myself, was weak.

I opened the good book and read passages
from Isaiah and this one stuck out—*These
people came near to Me with their mouth and honor Me
with their lips, but their hearts are far from Me. Their
worship of Me is made up only of rules taught by men.*

Powerful for me because I've always
believed God does not exist in a building.

He exist in our hearts, and as individuals
we must seek Him for our own personal
journey.

We all have our sins and going to a
building to confess does not relieve us of
our burden unless we seek our own personal
redemption in our hearts where only He
understands and can forgive.

For me, listening to men preach about their
own interpretations of the good book is not
the same as in my understandings of what
each passage means to me.

I've never been really good at following
the rules of men.

So, when I say this, it's true to my
character.

Sure, it's nice to sing and see our friends
and family all sitting in one room, but we can
get that at funerals and weddings, too.

From my point of view, if you attend a
building to worship the Lord and exit the
building leaving Him behind, then what's the
point.

That's where *"Let Buildings Be Buildings"*
comes from.

Isaiah speaks to the people of Jerusalem,
but doesn't his words reflect on us as well?

Doesn't his warnings tell us something
today? To me, they do.

When you attend a worship gathering, at
least for me, in a building where there are
no idols on the walls, no asking for money, a
place where it's all about Him, then it's worth
getting dressed up for.

When you attend a worship gathering and
tears fill your eyes unexpectedly and you
just can't hold back, then there's something
extremely powerful taking place and it has
nothing to do with the building!

When you attend a worship with others in
a room, then leave and willingly (*free*-will)
bring Him along, then it's all worth the trip!

Love the skin you're in and don't forget
Him along the way.

Comments
▪(Friend) Very nice.
▪(Friend) ♥

~Faithfulness to the Rebellious~

history is history—written in parables
solutions—there are no mysteries

deep within the word–
let His† voice be heard

generation after generation
commanded dictation

teach my children

pass it on
every father—in every home
give up your hands—in trust
remember God's† mercy

when stubborn, rebellious
nations lost their faith
–the men of ephraim
turned their backs—obedience lacked

forgetting words of wisdom
no one taught them:

*a divided sea—its waters standing tall
cooling their days, lighting their nights
giving comfort through it all
when thirst came—rocks split, water poured
without any dams to stall*

they were grateful
as God's† hand appeared—then silence–

allowing His† people
to find their own way

without anything to take
beggars and sinners were to make–
testing God's† word
forgetting what they heard

feed us—prove to us
if you want our trust

anger filling His† heart, He† couldn't part

again through rocks–
water once more stocked
birds covered the sky
grain came from the Most High†

they still didn't see
all around them—there was He†

they weren't grateful
just part of a moment
then back to their ways
spiteful and sinful

only in times of grief
did they really believe
only in times of need
He†—did they seek

they used His† name
righteous—their game
for cliques and fame

God† still remained
when He†—they blamed
anger—He† restrained

again and again, forgetting His† love
forgetting His† power–
how He† saved them
from the perils of egypt
test after test—God† in a contest

until anger consumed, jealousy and rage
closing His† generous door
–handing them to the sword

then a sudden release–
anger ceased
enemies—God† beat
rejecting ephraim–
leaving them on their own
–He† would not enter their home

the faithful—judah, david, jacob
tribes guided by His† hand
moved forward—they were never alone

~*Money's Deity*~

this forcing way of control
has all in a bowl

trying to survive, trying to stay alive

the devil's claw has a flaw
greed on top of greed, selfishly-laid seed
makes us all heed

phone, internet, tv, electricity
gas and rent fee

without it—we're put on the street
without anything to eat

trying, trying, trying—selfish men
abandon families
–lost in their own insecurity

women just surviving
trying to stay healthy
basic necessities, without any security
hope bidding to seep—praying

God† set me free

greed on top of greed
all protecting money
–evil's coring seed, running on empty
just one more night—this bed to keep
instead of out on the street

(May 30, 2014)—Oh! the webs we weave.
I have a new neighbor down stairs.
Another scorned woman.
This apartment complex is full of them.
Their story...most of them: They called their
[x] out and they were attacked physically and
emotionally because of it!
So, they left.
This complex (40 acres of it, with over 900
units...the largest in several states) is the first stop
to a large number of scorned woman on their
way to their next life.
We are all forced to leave our homes
because of the constant manipulated B.S.
caused by our [x]'s. That's fact!
We are all struggling because of lust and
greed. That's fact!
We are all struggling because of the denial
of a failed manhood. That's fact!
"Money's Deity" is the summary of that.
A woman's moral dilemma: Stay and deal or
leave and deal.
The lucky ones have a man who truly loves
them no matter what.
The rest of us just survive all because of

greed in one form or another.
Those of us surviving are worth it for
some lucky man who will gain a woman of
strength no matter how you look at it.
I so love the skin I'm in...poor or not...
because I'm worth it.

~*Dramatized Society*~

what is this—society we live
when middle schoolers, sex is ideal
fathers pretend, family isn't real
broke homes—quiet your moans
move on—this—your life
anyone can steal

what is this—plague of brokenness
anger lives in the very young
–acting out *what* they're from
no discipline in their homes

turn it around—the first to eat
adults, no longer authority's feed

age pulls back—minds that lack
faces not slapped
adds to a society full of crap

then the questions arise
what happened to civilized

what is this—society we live
killing dogs, outweighs, a child unborn
–doesn't it put us—back into the barn

where's all the adults
who's really at fault

where does authority lay
when children no longer play

~*Lessons to Place*~

civilizations disappear
do you hear a changing world
–lost in a techno swirl

if you put it out to the universe–
read carefully your every verse

all your pinned up fears
repeated over and over
–it'll come true my dear

your inventing twirl—dramatic hurl
stirring up unwelcomed dirt
day-dreaming through cinema–
reality's danger, you do flirt

robots—mechanical-minded gears
earth separating
leaving mankind in the rear

disease-spreading curl
killing every boy and girl
bodies waking up, while in a hearse
all for quenching
drama's ever-ending thirst

dry your tears
you're awakening your worse fears

this pretending maze
putting the universe in a whirl–
it'll all come back
in a reality-driven twirl

without intentions to hurt
all the same—yes, drama's driven flirt
becomes reality's desperate thirst

~*Coureurs de Bois*~

meanings have changed
–a bit deranged, going for fame
generational-crazed game

a mixed breed, family tangled
forced strangle—flipped in mind
grab whatever passion to find

results of twisted seeds
crazy—tightly hidden—not easily seen
–a sinner's reprieve
outsiders—left to grieve
intelligent minds
bypassing that intertwined deed

seeing too much, maybe they're touched
given gifts—a real runner's rush
enough–
to leave, settle where they can breathe

they become outted–
strangers to places born
for they saw, they felt
this inside buried wrath
this entangled web

–secrets—years of years
inter-family brawls
setting their own laws

the coureurs de bois—remain the same
living without change
handling its own—in the raw

becoming more and more—deranged
hiding hidden fangs
'til that *one*—says it out loud
revealing what's within–
coveted clouds—spoken aloud

no matter how good
the revealer once stood
–floating about—living in doubt

once it's said–
quickly, they're pounced dead
thrown out—by this tightly coveted clout
made to feel—anything but real

yes, the coureurs de bois–
once they pounce
–the revealer ousted—ignoring fully
pretending they never lived
their clouded of covet—closes
returning back to their hidden world
living in a spirited-drunkened swirl
without one once of guilt
for they've squashed
that *damned-crazed-lying bird*

their story-laden air
smothering truth's words–
what was heard, what was written
just turds—from a crazed mouth

once again to hide
secrets buried deep inside

yes, go against their stride
you'll surely left to die
never getting an answer—to why
as they raise their spirit-filled glass
you, gone at last
their laughter spilling everywhere
sucked back inward
drowning in ego and pride
for they can continue
living in their generational-buried lie

(October 26, 2014)—I travel places most don't want to go.

Although, I simply adore my home: Where I'm from, there are things that I must say.

Agree. Don't agree.

It's not your place to judge, nor is it mine. I record. I write history.

My work speaks its own.

I'm just the instrument.

That is the curse of the writer.

We reveal what we see for the simple sake of revealing.

There's no intention on hurting anyone.

That's not what writing is about.

That's not what any writer is about.

We seek truth, and I would guess 90%, if not 100% of the time, what we reveal is the truth.

That's why many writers are criticized, estranged from their families, their hometowns.

Many women writers in the past have committed suicide for they could no longer handle their gift or what it brings out in people.

Yes, the thought has crossed my mind as well. It is normal. Don't worry. I'm pass that.

I now understand why I was given this gift.

I now understand why I must write the things I write.

It's not for any of us to decided what is expected, where our journey must go.

The big Man will damn well make sure that our journey continues.

He *will* take away *all* that stands in the way. Believe me, I'm am testimony to that!

I have been greatly criticized for my work.

It is only the beginning. This I fully know.

The *Freedom of Speech* in any form has been granted to us for a reason.

Free-will...God's most precious of gifts to us must be adhered at all cost.

For those of us who record what we see during our lifetime, tells those who come after us—*Please, listen...don't keep making the mistakes.*

Hundreds of years have gone by and still things are remaining the same because ears are refusing to listen, minds are refusing to learn.

Oh, technology is making its way...but humanity isn't.

[x] once texted me—*Take it down!*

Meaning some of my work on here.

Those words came from a man I believed to have the same values as I: The one most important: *Freedom of Speech.*

I guess I should have known better.

My lessons by way of him are still forthcoming.

He is now *protecting a woman from her abusive [x]-boyfriend!* Imagine that.

The mind can get lost beyond our comprehension.

It is only those who are separated from the

evils of life who see truth...it's those who are given a responsibility to teach, to show, to tell, even when no one is willing to listen.

Our lives are already paved.

Our journey has to be followed. It's sad.

It really is.

When your truth is held against you by every one you thought loved you and would have your back, but I understand.

The lessons are clear.

My son came to visit.

His attitude has not changed.

His character and morality has changed.

I am not impressed. I love him dearly.

I miss him.

I gave my speeches as I have done to the other two before him. To no avail.

I'm a mother.

Part of our job is the lessons we teach.

I'm my children's friend second, their mother first.

There are times when our children will hate us for the decisions we must make.

It's called hard love.

When a child is raising themselves, when they spend more time with people other than their parent, when they are subjected to lies and fake, a mother's heart is torn.

At 11 p.m., [x] came and picked up my son because my son *texted* him.

There is no parenting there.

My son was upset by what I had to tell him...a mother mothering as she is supposed to do.

When you are the friend, instead of the parent first, the child loses.

I see it every day in the classroom with broken homes and kids caught in the middle.

—I'll be your friend. I'll give you what you want. You don't have to go with her.

It's a sad, sad world.

This is just one of many examples of how our culture is failing.

It is easier to ignore and oust the person living by truth than to admit wrong.

I am not a perfect person, but I have raised my children to have open minds, beautiful hearts and to strive for everything they desire.

I did not raise them to be liars, drunks, stealers, bullies...that's not my doing.

It's sad how people take one year of broken and make it about your whole life.

The culture I left behind I am no longer proud of. I am ashamed.

Actions speak louder than words.

Today, I accept what's underneath my skin.

I have empathy, compassion.

Those I left behind do not.

To write about some of the things I do, brings me to tears. The realization of it all.

Those who truly love understand why it must be done.

Those who do not see it as betrayal, see it as only about them. It is not.

It is written to teach. So learn.

Stop the hate.

Stop assuming it's all about you.

See it as a collective lesson and help make life better. Help make humanity better.

I am not the first to write about these things.

No, I am not, but it seems the lessons have not been learned.

Truth...when my son called [x] to come pick him up, [x] should have said—*No, you will stay there until the morning. She's your mother.*

Instead of keeping my son from me and I have to ask for visitation, [x] should have him here willingly every other weekend and every holiday, but that is not the case.

There's no empathy, no compassion, no taking responsibility.

It's a continuous cycle of hate, spitefulness, pure meanness.

It's a continuous cycle of avoidance.

Intelligence exist you know...just saying....

~*Know This: You Can't Hide*~

it takes a will—a strong, deep will
to swear an oath, raise your hand
say the words—knowing–
sit behind a desk or be put to the test

but to think death—not even close
to your pride's depth
–honor and courage
that inside-roaring fest

in training, it builds—that inside strength
yelling cadence—top of lungs
bypassing sore
there's just something deep in heart
putting reality—that possible surety
way out of mind

just march on, passing in rhyming song

tears in my beer

clinging to *betsy*
that colder-than-steel *joe*–
war's lover—letting all else go
excitement grows
that next-to-perfect marksmanship hole

the pride, the honor, worn on the outside
striding in a parade's high

then it comes—properly schooled
all those gearing rules
embedded in a *warrior's* head

a permanent place to show face
put to the rim, all that's been interlaced
–masked and cammoed lace

even as you see, comrades hauled away
boarding planes, new issued gear
still—no fear
from reality, you casually steer

even when you're on your way
boarding a plane, new issued gear
still, no sincere
'til dust covers your boot
comrades in arms, you feel no harm

then comes the moment
along side your head, a bullet's whistle
grazing by—no time for shy
no time for good-byes
no time to kneel down
beside your friend–
for months, closer than kin
lies still—a moment's rush

no time for even a touch–
keep moving, put it quickly behind
forever trapped in mind

'til that day, returning–
to what others call the norm
where *pretend* lives on
no one hears the sounding alarms
living in but not quite–
burying the silenced storm

doing anything, keeping it hidden
a place so forbidden—altering mind
the only type of kind
–a drawn, deceptive line in order to say

I'm fine

but it'll come one day
–that sealed, locked door
will blow a raging explode

the more you hide, the more it strives
the more you suppress, the more unrest
–duress—the more anguish
enjoys, in you, its glamorized fest

it'll be hell—sit and tell
expunge this raging spell
out of honor—comrades who fell

release the smells—let go—the sounds
yell, scream, cry, but don't hide–
it all—covet—deep inside

gain the strength, dig deep from within
say it—find peace in it
let it all out—out loud—shout

this is not what I'm about!

you'll release this dis-ease
find the peace, stop the constant bleed
no longer having to heed
to war's endless need, to be your creed

you'll then—stand—breathe

this is me—I am free

(November 7, 2014)—I am a soldier. Always.
I did not get sent in harm's way.
I did not experience death in the perils of
war. I have seen those go off to war.
I have seen the blank expressions of
reality's wake.
I have listened to those who have been
there.
I have sat with the aged veteran, many of
them, and listened. Listened.
Their experiences are profound.
From World War II and beyond, I've have
listened.
I have experienced the hidden silence.
I have seen its unwavering hold on the
most honorable of men and women.
Last night, I had an experience that
touched me deeply.
"Know This: You Can't Hide" came from
that experience.
Not all men are bad...words that have been
told to me many times. Correct.
Not all men are bad.
Many veterans, especially, men, are
labeled harshly. People fear them.
Many of them are tatted up, they drink
heavily, they lose themselves to drugs,
nightlife...many leave the humbling path of a
righteous life for a more soothing one.
One that offers them some sort of security.

One that offers them the chance to forget what they have seen.

Many refuse to talk about it.

They bury it and it eats them up inside.

A soldier of war: Not just a military soldier, but also policemen, firefighters, doctors, teachers... those who protect and serve...have a strength beyond measure.

They see the evils of life, and yet they continue on in any way they can.

Their truth is dark.

You don't want to see it, let alone experience it.

You say you understand it, but you really can't.

Unless you've seen, heard, smelled, felt the chaos of death, you can't possibly understand what swarms in their minds, their hearts.

Many run, and they keep running because they don't want to relive, they don't want to face their demons.

I know exactly how that feels.

Thoughts of writing a book on my experience with silent abuse...knowing I'll have to relive, I'll have to face my own demons...scares me to death.

No, it is not easy and I keep finding other things to do, so I don't have to for the moment.

Cleaning my apartment, rearranging, sorting through, playing on *Facebook*... anything, but what I have to do...face the demons, tell the story.

I'm beginning to see that in order to move on, to heal...those demons must be faced.

The story must be written. How?

I still haven't a clue.

The same goes for a Veteran of War.

They need to tell their story, but they can't even figure a starting point in which to release their burden. How can they?

When those who haven't experienced it, don't have a clue...not even close...of how to be able to understand their truth.

A Veteran of War is a very special individual.

Those who protect and serve for the better of mankind are not just doing a job, but a necessary one. Thank them.

Protect them in return.

Try...just try to get through to those who are running.

It's hard, but, sometimes, they need you, even when they firmly believe they do not.

~*Aged Ink*~

I sit, I watch—age turning the clock
arms laced with ink, of the old and weak

once they were strong
a place in life—they belonged

when wars were fought
guns—ammo brought—lives spared
a time when it didn't matter to care

once they were young
bad boys having fun, toting a gun
living life in the sun

somebody's son, released to the world
to come undone
sex and *freedom*, wild at random
chasing and running
lost in a world—mixed criticism

returning from war
adrenaline still their star
wondering who they are

adding more ink
to feel the void of their warring heart
searching for ways not to feel
locked in a jar

their heads screaming
their hearts dreaming
time and time again
returning to memories streaming
hurting others—not feeling

just moving without thinking
lost in their minds
not knowing, how to draw the line

as age creeps in, the ink becomes dim
their faces grow old
to youth, they no longer can hold
finding their hearts alone
still not knowing, where they belong

just memories—where they got that ink
without reasons to think
old and shattered
wondering what really mattered

~*Step Back*~

step back, what do you see
chest board pieces moved strategically
–a careful study—piece by piece
under your eyes to see

without seeing an enemy
without seeing the deed

step back, what do you see
–for one minute—stop, breathe
look around—sea to sea
are you that naïve, easy to deceive
is it that hard to conceive
–gone of nobility—famine and disease
corporational greed—piece by piece
right in front, for you to see
step back, what do you see

a fathom freeze, a war politically
–turn off the tv, there's no need to sneak
the trojan horse, ready for its siege

step back, what is it
that you need to see, to believe
to stand for your creed

it's so much ease, to delete
move on, than to see—believe
what's already there for you to see
piece by piece—head on a block
chop, chop, chop
–the icy of the coming freeze

Appearances
•*Facebook* (November 20, 2014)

ζ

*Therefore, since we are surrounded by such a great cloud
of witnesses, let us throw off everything that hinders
and the sin that so easily entangles, and let us run with
perseverance the race marked out for us. Let us fix our
eyes on Jesus, the author and perfecter of our faith, who
for the joy set before Him, endured the cross, scorning
its shame, and sat down at the right hand of the throne of
God. Consider Him who endured such opposition from
sinful men, so that you will not grow weary and lose
heart.—Hebrew 12:1-3*

~

The following, written in 2015, are in the order
in which they were written.

~*Doc's Excuse*~

don't diagnose what you don't know
don't do it for show—if it's fibro–
years of torment, years of ailment
–then it's a possible go

don't try to be a hero if you don't know
–you just don't know
don't let money ruin your growth
fibro doesn't easily show
it's a hide-and-seek foe
many test, many needless

–ruling out other crows
is the best way to go

don't make fibro the way to go
if you're too busy to see flow

don't diagnose what you don't know
don't do it for show—if it's fibro–
years of torment, years of ailment
then it's a possible go

~

(January 13, 2015)—This article was shared
on my page last night and it disappeared.
I am re-sharing it with some serious
points that are questionable and I'm appalled
that the *New York Times* allowed it to be
published at all.
I'm not the best writer in the world, but
come on, give me a break.
Using big words and fantasy phrases does
not constitute good writing, nor does it justify
adding strife where strife isn't needed.
There is no race issue.
Stop trying to make it one.
Onward: (Article) *'When Will the North Face
Its Racism?'* published as an opinion in the *New
York Times* on Jan. 10, 2015...interesting...I have an
opinion of my own directed to the author and the
New York Times!
1. The author, Isabel Wilkerson, refers to *black*
Americans as *African-Americans,* then talks about
gaining *freedom* in their *own* country.
Well, which country is that?
Africa, last I checked, is a continent and
America is a country.
The *country* in which Wilkerson is obviously
referring to is *America,* so why confuse it with a
continent?
I wish everyone would just stop this particular
nonsense.
No matter your color, if you're born in
America...guess what?: You are an American!
Please leave the continent of Africa out of the
equation...it is silly at best!
2. Wilkerson's use of the term *state-sanctioned
violence* in referring to the South during, I am
assuming, the slave years, if you look at the true
meaning of the term, it does not fit. Not even close.
The Jim Crow laws were unconstitutional and
unfair, but as a decedent myself from a mixture of
races: Black, Indian, French, German, etc., the French
and Indians were treated bad as well.
The white man only saw the *white man.*
Have people forgotten what the Irish went
through or the Indians or the French or the
Vietnamese?
It's time the record was set straight and we all
stop living in the past.
To me, the only reason mindless people keep
bringing this up is because they want to keep the
chaos, they want to keep the anger because it sells.

Greed: *The root to all evil.*

Please read the following for the correct meaning of what exactly *state-sanctioned violence* is.

I think Wilkerson had a brain fart on this one and the chief editor of the *New York Times* was sleeping when this article passed his desk.

Shameful!

(http://www.academia.edu/1437336/The_Full_Weight_of_the_State_The_Logic_of_State-sanctioned_violence)

3. Black Americans didn't go North just because of the Jim Crow laws.

Before the Civil War, they were promised *freedom* which included housing, jobs, etc.

The federal government decided after the war that they would not follow through with their promise leaving many former slaves starving in the streets because the plantation owners, which most ran their plantations fair, were forced to *free* their slaves.

Correct me if I'm wrong, but they had no choice but to force these now *free* blacks to leave the only place they knew, the place that sheltered them and fed them.

Many plantation owners gave their former slaves their last names in order for these now *free* Americans to find jobs.

So, the black population was left on their own angry, penniless, homeless.

Jobs were scarce in the South so many moved North looking for a home and work.

Aside from competition for employment, there was also competition for living space in the increasingly crowded cities. While segregation was not legalized in the North (as it was in the South), racism and prejudice were widespread.

After the U.S. Supreme Court declared racially based housing ordinances unconstitutional in 1917, some residential neighborhoods enacted covenants requiring white property owners to agree not to sell to blacks; these would remain legal until the Court struck them down in 1948. Rising rents in segregated areas, plus a resurgence of KKK activity after 1915, worsened black and white relations across the country. The summer of 1919 began the greatest period of interracial strife in U.S. history, including a disturbing wave of race riots. The most serious took place in Chicago in July 1919; it lasted 13 days and left 38 people dead, 537 injured and 1,000 black families without homes.—from http://www.history.com/topics/black-history/great-migration.

You can go to the above cited page, which I easily found for more information about the hardships my black-counterparts had to endure in the North during the *Great Migration* as they call it.

Wilkerson fails to acknowledge that the White House had slaves, as well as General Grant, the entire time the North was destroying the South during the Civil War.

4. The [third] paragraph states—*In matters of racial injustice, the South has been the center of attention since before the time of the Civil War, but the North, with its shorter history of a mass black population, has only more recently dealt with the paradox of an enlightened ideal coexisting with racial disparity.*

Really? WTF?

Excuse my *unlady-like* expression.

Would someone like to explain this to me?

Especially, the last [two] lines of this, then Wilkerson writes, same paragraph—*The protests have become a referendum on the black condition since the Great Migration. 'The protests are beginning to wake people up to the idea that the problems are not only there, but have been obvious all along,' the historian Taylor Branch told me. It feels like the South in the 1950s.*

What the hell?

An article in the *New York Times* and Wilkerson writes...*the historian Taylor Branch told me.*

Where did she attend college exactly?

I know [my professor] at [university] would have yelled at me and my paper would have bled if I would have wrote something like that!

5. The next paragraph gets worse—*...that African-Americans now live in every state of the union. They were seeking political asylum within their own country in what was, in effect, one of the nation's largest and longest mass demonstrations against injustice. It was barely recognized for what it was at the time, arising as it did organically, rather than from a single leader, much like the protests today. Both migrants and protesters were pleading with the world to take notice that something was terribly wrong in the places where they lived.*

Let me point out the obvious—*...that African-Americans now live in every state of the union....*

What?

I'm a bit confused about this statement—*...They were seeking political asylum within their own country....*

Really?

This was actually published in the *New York Times*?

The rest of the paragraph just threw me for a loop—*...arising as it did organically, rather than from a single leader...migrants and protesters were pleading with the world....*

How exactly were they pleading with the *world*?

Someone please explain to me....

6. Next paragraph—*...a caste system ruled the south....*

Really?!

A caste system is a class structure that is—*determined by birth. Loosely, it means that in some societies, if your parents are poor, you're going to be poor, too. Same goes for being rich, if you're a glass-half-full person.*

I just typed in *caste system definition* and there it was! Amazing!

Please take a look at what a *caste system* actually is: (http://www.mrdowling.com/612-caste.html)

In the same paragraph, Wilkerson writes—*Those conditions forced most every black family to consider the best course of action to feel safe and free. 'Where can we go,' a black woman in Alabama wrote in 1902, 'to feel that security which other people feel?'*

I am a woman so the first thing that popped in my head when I read this was the struggle women in general went through.

So, I typed in *women's right to vote* and it took me to: http://www.archives.gov/historical-docs/document.html?doc=13&title—*19th Amendment to the U.S. Constitution: Women's Right to Vote: Passed by Congress June 4, 1919, and ratified on August 18, 1920, the 19th Amendment guarantees all American women the right to vote. Achieving this milestone required a lengthy*

34   k. e. leger

and difficult struggle; victory took decades of agitation and protest. Beginning in the mid-19th century, several generations of woman suffrage supporters lectured, wrote, marched, lobbied, and practiced civil disobedience to achieve what many Americans considered a radical change of the Constitution. Few early supporters lived to see final victory in 1920.

So tell me, do you feel like French, Indian, Creole, etc., women felt safer than black women?

Just wondering....

7. The next paragraph—*Generations later, police killings of African-Americans occur as often as twice a week for at times mundane infractions and at three times the rate as for whites, according to conservative estimates from recent studies....*

What studies?

In this whole entire article, there's a lack of justification (citing) to where Wilkerson got her information; and she continues to use the term *police* too loosely.

I worked with the police in many different forms in my life...Military MPs, customs, narcotics investigators and always...*always* there was a large population of black officers.

So, is Wilkerson saying that black officers are just as prong to kill black people as white officers?

Would that be considered racism?

Just wondering....

According to http://www.naacp.org/pages/criminal-justice-fact-sheet, the *Criminal Justice Fact Sheet* was published in 2012 stating—*African Americans now constitute nearly 1 million of the total 2.3 million incarcerated population.*

But when I Googled to find the ratio of police killing blacks compared to that of whites in 2014, the top sites all were directed towards police killing blacks...race...race...race!

My last teaching job was at a 95% black middle school.

The main goal of the educational god*s—Write the bad students up, write them up, write them up, so we can get them out. Where do they go?*—I asked.

No one could give me an answer.

I have an answer—*On the streets to fight for their lives.*

When you have a 14-year-old black student robbed at gun point come to you scared, what do you do? I wanted to help.

Do you know what the school did? Ignored him!

The problem: *Uneducated, poor, angry young black men.*

(We'll stick to black since Wilkerson fails to talk about the other colors with the same problems.)

They are angry because they see the greedy taking the money they need and lining their pockets, instead of buying computers and helping these kids out.

So, they are pushed out on the street.

What's out there?

With no education, no money...the easy route or the only opportunity: Selling drugs, robbing, stealing.

Give me a break!

This has been going on for years and when these children grow up and cause strife, the police are blamed, the teachers are blamed.

The parents: Go on without being held accountable.

The legislators and educational gods: Go on getting richer and doing nothing.

Who ends up the victim of a bullet or the guest to one of this countries many prisons: The poor, uneducated, angry black child that everyone just left behind because of selfishness and greed!

No Child Left Behind has made the education institutions a joke!

This program as well as affirmative action and many others has just given the government or the American *regime* more opportunities to suck up our hard earned tax dollars and make themselves richer. Go figure....

A good example: In just my state, Louisiana, our parents voted to allow casinos for [two] reasons: Education and improve our roads.

I am 46 years old now and the education system has not improved, but gotten worse since I was in school and this law passed. Where's the money?

Anybody out there wondering...hmmm...guess it's just me!

8. Wilkerson then describes black *migrants* as *the refugees from the South shared the same dreams as the immigrants who stepped off the ships at Ellis Island, huddled masses yearning to breathe free.* Refugees? Really?

Uneducated, mindless journalist made that same mistake when hurricanes tore up New Orleans.

Refugee—A person who has been forced to leave their country in order to escape war, persecution, or natural disaster.

I just Googled *refugee definition*...that easy!

During the hurricane aftermaths and that word was used over and over, I kept asking the air—*What country are they going to exactly?*

I have yet to get an answer!

Wilkerson then writes—*One of the few contemporaneous studies in the early years of the migration, published by the Chicago Commission on Race Relations in 1922, surveyed Southern migrants to determine why they had come north and what they had hoped to find. The migrants responded:*

Freedom in voting and the conditions of the colored people here. Freedom and chance to make a living. Freedom and opportunity to acquire something. Freedom of speech, right to live and work as other races. Freedom of speech and action. Can live without fear, no Jim Crow.

That's coming from *Chicago* of course...if you haven't noticed all the corruption seems to be coming out of Chicago.

If they would have polled women of all colors, as well as Creoles, the Irish, the French, and the Indians, guess what, they would have gotten practically the same response.

9. The following paragraph I've seen in several places, not just in Wilkerson's article, and she did not cite it...isn't that interesting since the *new* educational gods keep pushing the kids to cite everything without even explaining what the hell *citing* means?

It was a measure of how dire conditions were in the South that the Great Migration continued into the 1970s. When it began, 90 percent of all African-Americans were living in the South. By the time it ended, nearly half of all African-Americans lived elsewhere.

I typed in *Great Migration* and pulled up this particular web page—http://www.history.com/topics/

black-history/great-migration, which stated—*By 1970, when the Great Migration ended, its demographic impact was unmistakable: Whereas in 1900, nine out of every 10 black Americans lived in the South, and three out of every four lived on farms, by 1970 the South was home to less than half of the country's African-Americans, with only 25 percent living in the region's rural areas.*

I wonder why there's so much information on blacks in America and where they *migrate* to and not so much on other races like Orientals, French, Germans, Irish, Vietnamese, etc.

Is the migration of the Mexicans and Moslems being so carefully documented as the blacks are?

I personally live in the South.

I went to school at the time they integrated.

My high school still had separated dances in 1987.

Of course, not by the students' choice, and at the same time, our school was voted one of the best race-relations schools in the South.

Do you want to know why?

Because we were treated equal.

Race wasn't pushed down our throats.

If we didn't want to sit together, we weren't forced to.

We were allowed to find our friends (black, white, whatever color) on our own.

We didn't have *Affirmative Action* or political correctness or *No Child Left Behind* B.S. forcing our teachers to dumb-down our lessons.

No, instead we were challenged to the max.

We didn't have to sit in classes where *inclusion* was mandatory and we had to put up with disruptive, slow-learners who didn't know how to sit still and kept our teachers flustered from bell to bell.

No, those students were sent to special education where the teachers there were properly trained on how to deal with such behavioral problems. We were allowed to be *us*.

We knew we all weren't equal and we were taught if we wanted anything in life, we had to fight for it.

We learned how to compete and if we lost, we lost. That was a part of life.

I lived in ---- Parish, Louisiana.

We had but one, still do, high school.

My senior year there were over 200, I think, seniors. We were 80 to 70% black. That's right.

Any questions?

From coming from a background like that, leave us the hell alone. It's that simple.

Stop adding color to the equation.

We are Americans. It's that simple.

Stop comparing the North to the South.

We are Americans.

Start putting your energy into why the schools systems are failing our young.

You want to make a difference, start with the kids.

Articles such as this...books such as the one Wilkerson is making money off of is not the answer.

All this race crap is pretty much started by people with no life and have nothing better to do.

I'm sure Dr. King didn't see it this way.

I'm sure he didn't die for this.

I'm sure he wanted a world where no one saw color. *Period*!

Down here in the South...we are just about bored to death hearing this. I'm Karen Leger.

I'm not white. I'm not black. I'm not creole.

I'm not Cajun. I'm not French. I am all of them!

I am personally sick of the forms with check boxes for all these nationalities and races, but none for mine.

Why don't you go make a big stink about that, instead of starting mess (as the kids say) and raising tensions that are not called for?

Thank you very much for reading.—http://www.nytimes.com/2015/01/11/opinion/sunday/when-will-the-north-face-its-racism.html?_r=0

~*God's† Intellectual Surface*~

tell me—do we learn
when a bullet is shot
when anger, argument–
plague a congressional floor
is it love—the ambitious sought to adopt

when a country is built
on intelligence, the love of God†
was its intention—always for it to flop

is it all make-believe—just a plot
–for greed's jackpot

is it easier to settle in facades of lies
focus on gossip
play games, dance the foxtrot
then to untie corporate knots–
ask how they pay for
those elaborate yachts

is it better to be simple
spend time in shops
settle for pawn shops, fix the coffee pot
sit around all day on a well-worn cot
–think not

does it make you feel powerful–
smoking cigars, drinking scotch
planning the lop
of those refusing to be mere robots

tell me, as your child becomes just a dot
in unfathomed plots–
is it easier to call truth
conspiracy whoops
as logic happens, right before your eyes

it's all there—clop, clop
workshops after workshops
–warnings in snapshots
words booming from hip-hop
right there, all around—the out crop

the surface—right on top
intelligence given by God†
–what has you in such a knot
are you just a heterodox
too afraid to turn truth's knob

I just wonder how long it'll take–
to see the paradox
that's taken years to concoct
hidden truth—causing people to die
as the clock goes tic-toc, tic-toc
their courage, risks taken
secrets unlocked
continuously going unnoticed—blocked
for you'd rather sit on your buttocks
as intelligent minds are robbed
as a corporate disease–
parallel to smallpox
unravels—without you taking stock
having courage, lay dying–
shell-shocked
realizing you had the power–
a gathering of mobs
to pull the triggering shot
–these corporate-government slobs
you *had* the option to stop

~*Bacon*~

I'm so confused
someone, please, pop my fuse

from the laws of God†
isn't it written in the *bible*
–didn't really know
the koran followed it so close

eating split-hooves forbidden
testing the population–
was it before or after
God† sent His† son for validation
giving a lesson—testing temptation
as hypocrisy spread–
burying souls in self-made prisons

they didn't listen—they failed–
in the thrones of waters
they were nailed

prophecies awakened
sending His† son—God† into flesh
washing original sin through baptism
–leaving man two conditions:
free-will, love unconditional
simple principles

not found in any temples

so how is following one sermon
meant for a season
and not another meant for absolution
–justify any spiritual ambition

the bigger picture's observation
plainly reveals man's intentions
it's all for acclimation–
seeking power through false affirmations
never really gains God's† confirmation
of a grateful nation

enjoy your man-driven communion
while I sit here in appreciation
–gratification
of God's† given emporium–
food to be eaten—preventing starvation–
as part of the non-hypocritical
population

go on, jack up those prices
support your isis

I'll just sit here, thank God† for my life
then drink my coffee, eat my bacon
as you continue living in damnation–

guns, murder, rape

preaching a religion—lies and demons
soaked in blood and hate–
false proclamations
–ignoring what God† really had to say

(January 16, 2015)—Raising [three] children
is not easy when it comes to finances.
I always looked for the bargain.
Pork was always the cheapest.
Steak was always too high.
It's easier to raise pigs than cows.
My dad raised a pig every year, so I know
what it takes to raise a pig.
Now, today, wild hogs are every where.
God ensures us that we will be fed.
He gives what we need for in the *Bible* it
says the earth is plentiful.
No one should be hungry.
I think it odd that now pork is almost as or
more expensive than beef.
The price of bacon is overwhelmingly
ridiculous because if anyone knows what it
takes to raise a pig, they know it's much less
expensive than raising a cow.
It's not the farmers raising these prices.
I see that now.

An article I read this morning titled *'Oxford University warns authors not to write about bacon, pork to avoid offending Muslims'* by Jessica Cashmar was the basis behind *"Bacon."* Give me a break! Really!

So, I had to look further into this issue.

In an article titled *'Oxford University Press dismisses reports of ban on pork and pigs in books'* by Ewan Palmer [The Oxford University Press (OUP) Publishing Director, Jane Harley]

...said—*To address children's learning needs, it is important that they also reflect the cultural context in which children are learning. In the U.K., we take it for granted that we would not include references to sex, violence, or alcohol in our textbooks; to do so would be considered inappropriate and offensive to many.*

In order to make an impact around the world, there are other sensitivities that, although not necessarily obvious to some of us, are nonetheless extremely important to others. While we should be mindful of these cultural sensitivities, a healthy dose of common sense is also required. Cultural taboos must never get in the way of learning needs, which will always be our primary focus.

So, for example, a definition of a pig would not be excluded from a dictionary, and we wouldn't dream of editing out a 'pig' character from an historical work of fiction. We also maintain entirely separate guidelines for our academic titles which are relevant to scholarly rather than educational discourse.

Harley added the company must consider how to avoid references to a range of topics that could be considered sensitive in a way that does not *compromise quality, or negatively impact learning.*

An OUP spokesperson added—*Our materials are sold in nearly 200 countries, and as such, and without compromising our commitment to educational excellence in any way, we encourage some authors of educational materials respectfully to consider cultural differences and sensitivities.* [End of article quoted]

Do you see what I see? I see side-stepping.

She says they can print about pigs, but what she doesn't say is that they can't print about eating pigs. Do you see it?

I had read in other places how this *man-made religion* is forcing changes in history.

In all my schooling as a young girl, I don't recall studying about Muslims, period!

Or Islam!

In my young child's books a couple of years ago, there it was...incorporated into our history! I found that really interesting.

This article above is from the U.K., but it should be a warning.

Changing history is already happening in school books around the United States of America. I find that interesting as well.

Suppressing truth and adding what *they* want our children to know is going far and beyond what this country stands for.

I call this a breach in contract.

Which contract is that?

Oh, you know the one that farmers, bankers, salesmen, some legal fellas bitched and gripped over for a number of months after winning a war against their former mother country.

They kind of all willingly signed this contract and a country was born standing for none other than *freedom.*

That document would be the *Constitution of the United States of America*!

Remember studying about that?

Today, they barely cover the whole document.

I think Oxford University, an institution that has been admired by many a writers, has fallen in disgrace.

Controlled by radical people who are not a religion or a race or a culture, but a political regime out to kill, maim, rape, and destroy... all very evil.

Common sense, what this lady talks about in the article isn't so *common* after all.

Common sense would be to fight against this evil, not give into it, and stay honest and true to history.

Thank of that U.K. as you sit down and enjoy that freshly fried bacon!

Here in America: Think hard to why the pork prices are so high!

Over $3 here where I live for a cheap pack of bacon.

When my children were young, before all this Muslim crap...$1.75 for the same pack not on sale, and my question is to why the American people aren't raising questions about this?

~*Swinging of Branches*~

tattle-tale, tattle-tale
you're all going to hell
sinking down the well
oh! silly baby, don't yell

you crept in–
thinking you'd tip the scale
but they grabbed you
yanked your little innocent tail
charmed you—dined and whined
knew all your details
where you were frail

you didn't even need
to be hung like a whale
just add a little ale and a cat for sale
there you go—easy blackmail

don't bewail—the threats assail
you'll easily sail
if you don't rock the entail

oh! the trap of travail
to the chief—all hail
in your boots—quail
they got you, my little dovetail
they snuck in like a snail
covered you with their coveting veil
try to prevail, you, they'll easily curtail

tattle-tale, tattle-tale
you're all going to hell
sinking down the well
oh! silly baby, don't yell, cry and wail
–just admit you're weak
fell under their bale
put your own self up for sale

~*Swinging of Roses*~

rumors spread—bring them out–
you're easily dead

mind games in the fed
white house full of beds
boredom quickly spread
mixed in tightly-woven threads
innocent blood bled

rumors spread—bring them out–
you're easily dead

oh! the missing of untouched flesh
secrets of the pledge
gather them—collect
young toys—smallest of sex
caught in an incomprehensible web
–one you'd never suspect

caged-up little pets, caught in nets
grooming them to stay wet
mindless little jets
stripped of all self-respect
servants of masters—hidden in sheds

rumors spread—bring them out–
you're easily dead

dots to connect—avoid civil unrest
a carefully placed embed

easy to misinterpret
–manipulated side-step

oh! this awful defect, never a breadth
from the beginning—a bisect
keeping all in check
waiting for the ebb—elect, elect, elect
all a preselect, locked upon objects
mere subjects—push alone—directed
'til the enmesh
–by the likings of untouched flesh

mind-boggling head
now injected—no where to start fresh

rumors spread
bring them out—you're easily dead

the unsuspected architect
plans gone unread
not even proof read, stripping knowledge
–by ways of youthful flesh

fear of the crypt, debunking the alleged
truth—easy to shred

rumors spread
bring them out—you're easily dead

as the intersected in churches' genuflect
stamped forehead–
generation to generation
bred, bred, bred

elect, elect, elect—bisected
the obvious neglected–
the carefully laid thread
the stripping of innocent flesh
robbing of every homestead
–plans of perfect

suspicions—off with the head
an illusion's effect
as the masses live on meds
entertainment's deflect
truth seekers—mere hotheads
branded for dead

your little ones—hold tight—protect
be careful who you text or you'll be next

~*Mad Mic*~

give me a class
my handicap, like witchcraft
out the door—I'm about to dash
rather bash
mad mic's continuous upgrading path

what's all these tabs
what about this new patch—and that
I'm going mad
can't you make something to last
instead of added pieces–
that leads to crash

hours and hours—sitting on my ass
on your behalf
I'm building—a not-so-soft wrath
shape this—app that
here's a hatch, there's a latch
wrapped up in this downloading batch
filling in more grabs
with more and more crap

this degree-held sap
can't understand all your jargon syntax

sorry to be such a hag
but what am I suppose to tag
what about all this updating stash
–how to understand all that

am I just to accept—sit back, relax
I'm a skeptic–
how do I know this new batch
overnight—
new to my programming format
is not someone's mask
sneaky little tom-cat
sucking-up bureaucrat
–sliding in to hack

this is all beyond my grasp
with all this upgrading pizazz
money-sucking hold-fast

how are the masses, not willing to ask
explain the details—give me all that
I'm a big girl, I can handle the sass

is this all some cyber trap
spying, easy trespass
just a complicated, invasive wiretap
–big brother's easy snatch

or are you really rooting for my craft
helping to lay my path
for success in a bag

mr. gates I need answers to all that
for all these file tabs, are driving me mad

my little working prefab
needs detailed descriptions–
please, explain the math

for me, what's a good match
in this webbed map
what can I scratch, the riff raft I can ax
without causing an anthrax attack
so I can rest easy, relax
knowing mic's not really mad

I can laugh—feel totally secure–
my craft can sail smoothly
on a clean knowing-all raft
without worrying that some evil gaff
can sneak in—grab
through all this automated shag

and all my time
blown up—in a single—technical crash

~*Cyber Nut*~

over forty years in the know
absolutely nothing, do I really know
my brain not on fame, but on each frame
click, click, click—read, read, read
as I visit places, without any faces
just back-link tracing, back-office lacing
ad posting for *free*—not even knowing
where I'm supposed to be

page after page, what about this new age
drive, drive, drive—traffic the rage
leads everyone craves
what is real, what is fake
nothing about it is fast
my brain just has to last
this new class, takes out all the sass

read, read, read—click, click, click
the only way to know
on life, you have to shut
to be a cyber nut
–hope you don't get lost
in this linking rut

~*Gamble*~

I'm investing this money
–international honey
I'm leaving it to God—why not

I fear—it's deep inside
mixed with excitement—I have to trust
–put my feet in, without ruckus or fuss

a gamble on international levels
–what marvels!
bringing people together

in-spite of country, government, weather
–a blending—helping one another
helping to become survivors

I'm jumping—all the way
putting trust in actions
instead of mere words

yes, I'm terrified, but who am I
if there's no try
leaving *what ifs* at the door
I may fail, I may fly
taking a gamble—a giant leap–
on my dying bed, I won't have regrets
I made it or failed
–I'll have stories to tell

~*Brain of Kill*~

what's all this
–God's† clinching His† fist

mass-killing fit, are you not seeing it
evil placing its grip

can you stop it—the mind's sinking ship
lost in the devil's niche
wanting to own it

what's with this, you're seeing all this
are you going to fight it
how can you stand it—all this evil shit

wake up—absorb it
this mind-driven nip, people all around
losing grip, to this evil slip
a curse's whip, america in dip
–sucked-up little twit

God's† watching *all* of it
you can bet that clip
–something to promise
He'll† come to fix, He's† already done it
–a past in fit, lost in evil's mix

oh! yes, you can bet on it
He's† shown how much of it
He's† willing to miss
–over look too much of it
He'll† have to come rid us of it

continue your losing grip
invaded mind, the devil's throwing brick

continue living, breathing in all this
–avoiding involvement's hip

He'll† surly come to fix, not in hate's lip

rather in love's kiss—evil to rid
–for human's lost in weak
instead of stand—get a grip
rathering watch—sit

yes, you can bet
He's† clinching His† fist
waiting, watching *all* of it, absorbing it
His† beautiful artistic create
falling, tumbling—turning to waste

stand—get out of sit
or watch His† fixing grip
His† mighty hand—powerful, big
–rather large kind of pick

go back in history
understand His† *enough*
well...He† truly means it
don't test it—you'll lose—be stripped

read His† words–
understand meanings of it

stand—get out of sit
or waddle your wit—evil's grip
sinking minds in barbaric

He'll† come—all of it—fix
you won't like it

He† won't tolerate much more of it–
you handing over His† gift

it's *free*-will's nip–

stand, get out of sit
or see His† way of fix

(July 24, 2015)—The killings here in place
brought on *"Brain of Kill."*
I'm tired of all this murder.
This country needs to wake up and see
what's happening.
History is a good place to start.
We should be intelligent enough to learn
from our mistakes. I don't see that happening.
History does repeat itself.
I posted yesterday on my personal page
some educational information on the
tectonic plates off the coast of Oregon and
Washington and how their movement will
lead to a mass destruction of that part off the
U.S.
It would seem with all the killings and
rage, people would wake up to humility and
intelligence (knowledge given to us...I would
imagine to test us to see if we can indeed learn

from past mistakes).

So far...well, you see what you want to see, and the good man upstairs sees all.

~*M.A.P.*~

in a new world, I've tapped
a part of m.a.p.—in—I'm zapped

avoiding every nap
no more sleeping cat
in all its hope—I'm wrapped

I now wear this extra hat
forget negative—no time for all that
my time now sapped
I'm building my m.a.p.
wearing its cap, no longer feeling flat
click some ads, buy some credit packs
I'm becoming–
my own wealth-building rack

my mouse, my computer–
yeah, no longer a hibernating bat
into the world-wide-web
–following the marketing pack

learning every bit of that
so, go on sit back—relax
while your boss—in your back—stabs

I'm all into m.a.p
taking care of my own back

yeah, it's just like that
watching my money build to fat

~

(January 27, 2015)—I have known for years that sooner or later I would have to buckle down and learn the marketing industry if I'm going to sell any books that I write.

Well, the time has come and I'm learning fast how all this drive-traffic-to-your-*website* thing works.

The marketing industry works like the stock market does.

In the stock market, you buy shares in things like gold, corn, and bacon, then you watch the prices, which tell you when to buy and sell.

Your money is the *traffic* and those people who own that gold or those crops are banking on you to buy their product in order to make money. Farmers depend on this to survive!

The marketing industry's stock is traffic!

By *traffic,* I mean if you have a store like Macy's and you want people to shop there, well, you have to advertise and those people who come buy at your store are *traffic.*

So, in terms of cyberspace, if you have a website and you want people to visit it and, hopefully, if it peeks their interest, they will buy your product or service or attend some event you are a part of, you have to have a means to advertise and get that *traffic* to your site.

Traffic has become a product like corn and bacon!

You now can buy stocks of traffic and make money doing it!

To the basics: In order to get traffic to your website and purchase what you offer, first you have to get the word out that you even exist.

Ask anyone who owns a brick and mortar business how hard that is just in a small town.

Now think of just that aspect of owning a business in a globe market!

A website business is a whole new ballgame!

I have spent years trying to figure this *new business world* out. Years!

I spent so much time on this that my kids renamed my study the *bat cave* because I spent long, long nights working on my books and trying to get an understanding of this web-page-traffic-marketing thing.

From an author's point of view, it's even harder!

Steven King said in the early 2000s that authors would, eventually, have to master this new way of thinking if they wanted to survive in the publishing world because they would, eventually, be responsible for their on advertising and marketing, if they wanted to sell any books.

Well, his prediction has come to pass!

The internet marketing world is a very interesting and fast-paced entity.

When you enter it, you learn just how vast this world is, but also how connected we all are on a *global* scale.

I haven't designed a web page yet for my books.

I'm not even close to figuring out how I want it. I don't need to right now.

I've learned that first I must learn this new world or I'll just be sitting there lost in cyber world like a piece of lent floating in the air.

So, I have been in training, learning the

ways of this cyber world of advertising, marketing, and how traffic is moved.

I have fought this.

I didn't want to be a *seller* or a *marketeer*.

I just wanted to be a writer. Yeah, right!

My thick-headed self has learned the obvious: In order to be a best-seller, you first have to be a *seller*! Go figure!

In the process of my learning experience, I have also learned that while one is marketing their business and learning the trade there's money to be made.

So, I have joined my first [two] prospects: Or as the marketing world labels it: I have started my first [two] businesses!

You will start seeing my post on these [two] businesses and how they are working for me.

I have no idea where I'm going, but I do know I want my writing to spread the globe, I want to inspire every woman on the planet.

I know: Big aspirations!

Well, we don't exactly get anywhere with small ones now do we!

In order to accomplish my goal, I need to become a marketeer as well as a published writer. That's just plain, stupid facts.

So, a *Wordpress* blog is in the near future and my spreading the word about the businesses I've joined.

More about them later.

As a writer, I've been learning that I need to look at my work as a business and in order to grow my business, I have to become a businesswoman.

Well, 2015 is the year of the business woman.

I will share my education with you as I go.

Maybe, what I'm learning can help you with your business.

Of course, I'm a born writer and teacher, so it makes perfect sense that I would want to teach.

P.S. One other thing I've known always, but just didn't act on is that you have to invest in order to make money.

I've always looked at that idea like this: *Yeah, right. You have to be rich in order to invest!*

That belief has been blown out of the water for me. At least, for now.

~

(October 2017)—A lot of what I did write about online marketing I did not include in this book.

Several of the companies I talked about no longer exists and I was new at all this online business stuff, so the learning process for me was lengthy and does not benefit you by being included here.

The poetry work I've included because of its relevance to the journey of recovery.

~*Bonding of Nations*~

I've seen so much–
three years buried in lost trust
mixing—evil, friendship, love's touch
but this—this—marketing world's rush
bonding nations, a like-minded crush

God's† way of saying

*girl, you can't just hush–
there's a whole world
yearning, hearts to be touched
by a pen's carefully placed brush*

so I picked up my pen
wiped off the dust
–inspired by this bunch

missing sleep, even lunch
to read every word—see every ad
a world brought together without fuss

learning and work
dedication—over-coming every crutch
helping one another
building dreams, through hidden seems

wow! what a rush!—bonding of nations
through a key-board's touch
without lust, without a warring fuss

bring it—I'm in–
on all these marketeers
I have an unending crush

(February 22, 2015)—As I learn the marketing world, I realized the two businesses I'm in, just looking at their titles alone, are about bringing together the world.

I didn't really realize that until this morning. God has His ways, doesn't He!

That's where *"Bonding of Nations"* comes from.

It is very inspiring to see so many nations, in all their languages, seek the same thing...it is a small world after all.

Love the skin you're in and never stop seeking your dream!

~*Work is Work*~

what are you waiting for

your pants laden with dirt
–for someone else
your callused hands flirt

don't you come first
aren't you more important
than making another a millionaire
–shouldn't you matter

take a leap of faith
search for more out there
than just that dirty shirt

why is working online—so out of line
–where's your hunger, your thirst

for getting out of worse
improving your life
affording the better dessert–
isn't it time—reevaluate your worth

work is work–
for someone else, for yourself
nothing good comes easy
–without work's insert

instead of just being a clerk
working on another's turf
–while they go play golf
go fishing, take fancy trips
treating you like a jerk
you, their little jailbird
throw them a curve, build your own turf

join an online network
scrap up pennies
roman wasn't built in a day
you the millionaire—you do deserve
–a little hard work
you'll make their toes curl
–for you'll get all the perks!

Appearances
tumbler (February 23, 2015)

~*Propaganda's Sword*~

you can't lose faith
over what's written today
people will say—anything to sway
do anything to make you stray

let me lead the way
–words for you to bathe
a non-believer will hit his knees
beg and plead for God† to see
keep troubles away
when life doesn't go their way

when they bleed
when family they need to feed
they pray—even when they lie
they close their eyes, praying not to die

don't let doubt darken your way
the devil's here to slay
it works in manipulative ways
to blacken your day

you must be strong
protect yourself from this harm
you'll pass your storm
just pray, keep faith
God's† listening, watching
–a test is paved
it's your choice—*free*-will
to either weaken to evil's deal
or truly see God's† alive—real

~

(March 18)—Note From A Working Girl
(read): I'm learning all this internet business one
step and one day at a time.
I didn't watch every single [business] video
before I did anything. I should have. I just dove in.
I've already made a ton of mistakes.
I can see [*sweet man*] slapping my hand if he had
a chance. I plow on. Why quit?
Tomorrow is a brand new day.
Having fibro makes it hard at times and I have to
walk away to get my perspective, but I'm learning.
[Online business] is great and I'm so proud to be a
part of this [it].
I also have my writing, marketing, advertising,
now [online business], plus my health and family
issues to deal with. I'm working and working hard.
Today, I put the [online business] to work with
my pages and domains thanks to [*sweet man*] and
his great videos and guidance (I finally sat down and
watched them!).
I have been in this online business adventure
since Jan. 24.
My personal business is a lot more than just
[online business] and all the rest and it's taking me a
lot of thinking to pull it all together.
My *Facebook* account here, my *Google+*
account and my website will all blend because of
the hours I'm putting in behind the scenes.
My dear friend and sponsor, the *sweet man,* and
I went some rounds because I took my frustrations
out on him.
No, he's not my friend on here because I deleted
him.
Now, I have to earn his trust back, but I owe him
a lot for introducing me to all of this.
He knew I was capable, but I didn't.
I'm still learning and now I'm listening...one
thing the *sweet man* said was my downfall.
He was right.
When the *sweet man* presented all of this to me,
I began to have a vision, but things were moving
too fast for me.

I didn't like the website we had built and I knew, as a teacher, I had a lot to learn.

So, I quit the website and just let it hang there for a while.

I have been slowly redoing it into the vision I have for it.

As frustrated as my dear friend has been with me, I'm finally seeing through his eyes: Business... it's a whole new world for me.

I didn't know I could actually *park* a website until tonight.

In fact, I have learned a lot tonight from [online] tech guys.

I was on chat with them until their chat closed, then on the phone with them until about an hour ago.

If you want to do something and you want to succeed, then you have to take the initiative and learn for yourself.

No one is going to hand you everything.

When I get into something, I want to learn everything. At times, I have to step back and think.

When something good is happening, it can't be rushed.

Now I see where the *sweet man* was taking me.

It took mistakes, aggravation, frustration, losing a friend, and wanting to quit altogether, but, then a lot of prayer got me to realize that nothing gets done unless you work and work hard.

I have my domains in place for the [my website] and one of the domains is ----.

Yes, that's my old website name.

I tested it out in [online], worked perfectly.

I tested it out in [online] and was brought to this website that questioned my honor. I was furious.

No one questions my freaking honor!

I did comment on their site my concerns about the legitimacy of who they were because it looks cheap...so, scam or not?

When I see things like this I want to rip heads off, but I shouldn't be surprised.

Anything worth doing takes work and those who aren't willing to do the work or put up capital, well, they fall by the wayside and yell *scam* or some B.S. like that.

Any worthwhile business takes some kind of capital to grow it.

Believe me, there is no magic fairy dust that will make it just appear.

I never met a business owner (of the brick and mortar type) to be given anything in order to start their business. Have you? The same goes here.

If you want my opinion, no business is legit if it requires little to no work.

No business, and all those screaming scam or fake or some *crime* B.S., well, those are the ones who are lazy and don't want to apply themselves to make their lives better. So, go on screaming.

(I may be a little off on the price, but to get a [major] franchise, a turn-key system, a system of duplication, you pay somewhere of over $45,000 or more.

Do you see my point?)

For me, I stand 100% behind [online business] and everyone who is a part of it, and according to the [online] tech guy who *googled* me, (yeah, while I was on the phone with him) I'm right on track.

He found my *Google+* page and was over-the-top impressed.

With all the work I'm doing on my website and all the questions I had for him, he was stunned when I said I had only been in the business since Jan. 24. I owe that to the *sweet man*.

He took a leap of faith. I'm glad he did.

You won't have anything of value unless you put some elbow grease behind it.

My daddy taught me that.

All the negative going around about [online business], all the nay-sayers, only leads to one thing: [Online business] coming out on top.

They are in their infancy.

They are relatively new.

Everyone wants to crash the *new* party.

With over 100,000 (correct me if I'm wrong) people now involved in [online business], I can't see them crashing any time soon.

As for me, I'm just starting.

I'm here to change lives.

I'm here to help people change their lives for the better by showing them, even if they are disabled or with little money, they still have a chance to be somebody. How about you?

I ask all the nay-sayers: What have you done? Networking rules! [Online business] rocks!

~Colorless Birds~

a failed adhesion
—mixed-hypercritical damnation
of all the hysteria–
the misunderstood mystery
–hundreds of years
still shed tears, still darkened fears

what was fought so hard for–
doesn't seem we came too far
even living under the same stars
color—keeps bringing us back
–justice lacked, white—black
heresy in a broken-down shack

tackle the government
–greed's endowment
keeping that stupid war's enlightenment
taking it's very commitment
–back to days of judgment

where are the colorless birds
–haven't you heard
that war ended in a blood-soaked swirl
leaving this mixed-race girl
in a confused swirl

–still an uneven world
lost in racial twirls

we're still paying tokens
–what was broken
thought to be fixed—all should be mixed

still backwards—the clock tics

years and years—suffered pain
what did we gain, it's just insane
still playing this black-white game

didn't *king* die for a simple dream

to live in a time where there is no color

just people—where each other
given no time to smother
—no matter skin color
you're still my sister, my brother

honoring a man's life
doesn't give war the right—
to bury the dream
—words he openly screamed
leave hatred and difference behind
to each other—be kind

it's just time—*stop* banking on race
look into each other's face
—see beauty's lace
of God's† amazing grace

(October 20, 2017)—*It's never too late to live happily ever after.*—Author Unknown

God doesn't see color. He sees love.
He sees joy. He sees honesty.
He expects that of us as well.
What will you decide to see?

A relationship with God is the most important relationship you can have. Trust Him and everything will always turn out fine.—Author Unknown

Can you feel it?
The emotions of this piece.
Each time I read *"Colorless Birds,"* I get thick in the throat.
It was written April 15, 2015.
That says a lot about *change*.
How sad are we!
I watched a video last night about a *brown* boy (who I will name Tom) who was raised by a *white* mother.
He never had any problems with the law.
He was raised like I was raised.
One day, he and a *white* friend was pulled over. He was searched first.
The *white* friend had a bag of weed on him. Tom did what I would do.
When the police began to search his vehicle, he asked to see a warrant.
I know that police can search if in the moment there is probable cause.
The bag of weed was.

Tom did what any young person would do. It was innocent.
The police ganged up on Tom and beat him to almost death.
I forget how many stitches he had to have after all was said and done.
The other boy was not touched.
Another video I watch last night was that of another *brown* boy...man.
He just pulled out of his driveway when pulled over by the police.
He had to show license and registration.
He kept asking what did he do wrong.
Do you know what the police told him?
He was pulled over because of his air freshener hanging from his rear-view mirror.
Something we all do from time to time.
The officer told him it was *obstructing his view!* I never got pulled over for such a thing.
How is it obstructing our view?
Today, I sat down to continue my work and *"Colorless Birds"* was the first work of the day to edit. The *Sweet Man*.
I worry about him.
I don't handle my worry good at times.
I handle it with anger.
I'm not giving up on myself or him.
No matter what I say. It's just how it is.
Society is fucked up in so many ways.
This isn't just about the president now in office.
This is about our government as a whole.
They have failed.
We should be *one* nation under God.
They have slowly stripped us of God.
We are divided.
Only...only I'm in love with the other half... if that's how you want to call it.
Why all the anger? Why all the hatred?
How does a person's color change the way you see their heart?
Or do you ever get that far?
Personally, I'm not going to let society dictate to me who to love or what to believe.
I believe in *God*.
I believe that everyone has the right to be loved.
I believe that true abusers need to be dealt with.
I believe that those who've experienced racism should be forgiven for their anger and loved, and showed that they are just people and their skin color doesn't matter, it's what they, too, believe that matters.

46   k. e. leger

I believe we bleed the same color.

I believe we make babies the same way.

I believe that we die the same way in that final moment.

I believe Jesus did *not* believe in *different*... at *all*!

I believe that unconditional love truly means that you love no matter what.

I may sound like a hypocrite and I have been called one to talk about unconditional love, and then dismantle the only [x] I have.

You are right to believe that, but you are wrong. I never wished the [x] to die.

I never would do that.

I never wished harm on him.

I would never do that.

I just called him out on his shit.

There's a big difference in all of that.

If he was in danger and I was the one there to save him...I would have to give my life for him, would I? Yes. He's still a human being.

I'm not totally insane.

Maybe half way...but only half way.

In anything, my very first thought is what God will do to me if I do this, or do that?

That's a very heavy price going against what my Heavenly Father wants from me.

That's how we all should think.

I hope that all those people who hate because of someone's skin color come to terms with themselves and what God wants from them before they die.

That there is a heavy mark to wear on a heart. A burden that needs to be lifted.

All of our ways are different.

Not just the color of our skin.

You've all learned to drink from the same fountain. You didn't die because of it.

The same goes with shaking hands and hugging and loving.

The only thing you do by doing these things is adding light to a darkened world.

Do you realize how much light can be added if everyone thought this way? Wow!

It would be so bright, we'd have to wear sunglasses all the time because the joy would be so loud! I love you.

You are a stranger to me. I still love you.

You may hurt me and I may retaliate because I'm stubborn that way...but only for a little while because that's just my heart.

I may be bitter about some things.

That's okay.

I'm a child of God and a work in progress...

always improving myself for the love of everyone else because I want to.

On the subway, on the bus, in the grocery store, in church, in the courtroom, on the train, on the plane, look around.

Really look around.

Take it all in, then take away the color.

What do you see?

~*Disrespecting Bliss*~

how can they help, when anger's dealt
a job—life put on a shelf
a calling beyond self, helping all else

why can't all see–
some bad eggs, doesn't overflow the sea

uniforms worn with pride—outside *I*
good suffering for bad
ends in just a fad
when truly needed—we'll all be had

à cussing and screaming–
over-engrossed ego and *self*-demeaning
–responsibility you should hold–
not making yourself seem bold
in front of a screen

to protect and serve—haven't you heard
they come when called, equality in all

when peace is disturbed, let them serve
in public—we all deserve
harmony and peace

–you join the disrupting herd
you, too, fall
showing your *self* a hypocrite
not a deserving gift

for when trouble—on you—doubles
it's only a guess
you call—they come to arrest
ease your burden, truth in certain
–on you, they don't close the curtain
respect—you're sure to get

so why turn the card
when you become a part, of what's hard

you fail to see, the bullet they'll take
for your sake
–never warranting a turned back

stop adding problems
–ease the momentum
law and order—protecting us all

disorder and crime—wallet's barely lined
still, working 'round clocks
so you can sleep, in dreams to keep
your family—safe and sweet
praying to survive the day–
make it through the night
so, they, too, at dinner tables
take their seat
their families—see—safe in peace

(April 16, 2015)—I saw a video yesterday that led to *"Disrespecting Bliss."*

There was a woman who had drank too much and caused a disruption in a restaurant.

Law enforcement was called to keep the peace.

The woman seemed to have been initially fighting with her sister.

Just cussing each other out very loud in a public place.

A third person, a man, who was part of their company, was filming the incident.

The cussing and disrespect was unbelievable.

The policeman, who was first to arrive, was trying to keep the peace, and he finally had to get into the woman's face because she turned her yelling and cursing towards him, then the sister of the woman joined in with the same kind of verbal attack towards the officer, and because the man was filming, everything was recorded openly.

The man accused the officer of shoving the woman when the officer began escorting the woman out of the restaurant.

The officer did not shove the woman.

He barely placed his hand on the back of the woman like us mothers do when we're trying to get our children to move along a little quicker.

The man filming just kept cursing out the officer with total disrespect, then tried to get other patrons in the restaurant to film and take pictures of the incident.

The faces on those patrons was understandable.

They were in *awe* of this guy.

Clearly, the officer was doing his job to keep peace in a public place.

The officer had to warn the woman that if she continued, he would have to arrest her.

She continued.

Outside the establishment, both the man filming and the sister continued with their extreme verbal attack, egging the situation on.

The drunken woman's behavior got even worse when the arrest was taking place, so the officer had no choice but to call for backup.

As the backup sirens approached, the man filming and the sister began to slowly lower their verbal stance. I thought that funny.

The woman didn't, and she refused to allow the officer to handcuff her.

He had to take control of the situation by forcing the woman on the hood of his police car in order to handcuff her.

The entire time this was taking place the sister and man kept screaming—*take your hands off her, what is she being arrested for*—etc., etc. I thought this amazing!

The woman, drunk, was clearly disorderly in a public place.

She was clearly warned if she continued, she would be arrested.

She clearly resisted arrest.

She clearly put herself in the position where force was indeed necessary.

Need I say more?! I am a vet.

I worked for the 42nd Military Police in the Army, and then for Louisiana State Police Troop I while in the National Guard.

I saw first-hand how the uniform affects the human brain.

I clearly saw how people react to authority figures.

I clearly saw first-hand how people don't want to take responsibility for their own actions when the law is finally called.

I have been put in positions like this myself.

The passing of blame is unbelievably astonishing to see.

Point: There has always been corruption in law enforcement.

There has always been corruption in every single type of organization that you can name!

With today's technology, it's recorded and placed on the internet for all to see...mostly from the point of view of those offending.

My question here: Why is everyone so focused on making our law enforcement personnel look like the enemy and not the government officials who are elected and stealing our money and adding laws behind our backs, etc., etc.?

Those who decide to become police officers sacrifice the greed of money just like soldiers do to protect you and me from harm.

Is that too hard to comprehend?
These people do not make a lot of money.
Do you comprehend that?
They put their life on the line every day to protect you and me!
Do you comprehend that?
When you call, they come!
Do you comprehend that?
Yes, as I said before, there are bad eggs in every organization.
In American politics, they make tons of money!
Have you ever seen a politician living in a mobile home or a house falling down around their ears, drive old cars, their kids going to public schools, or struggling to feed their families every day? Well, have you?
Have you ever seen a politician put on a bullet-proof vest just to survive the day so they can see their families at night?
How many times have you seen an officer of the law travel by private jet or have a limo pick them up to go to work? Well?
I'm waiting? The answer is: Never!
Wake up America!
Dealing with an officer of the law with anger, hate, cursing, etc., only warrants them to become defensive because that's their job!
Things can escalate pretty quickly in a simple *disturbing of the peace* call.
They *have* to be prepared and they *have* to, sooner or later, take control of the situation, sometimes, having to use force in order to do that.
What is so freaking hard to understand about that?
I lived in Germany for [three] years.
I witnessed their police take down a drunk.
In 1988, when I was there, they had the right to use their batons to beat the crap out of you if you resisted or continued the disruption!
The officer I watched in the video handled the circumstance with grace and had an extreme gentleman-like character.
If I were him, I would have arrested all [three] of those individuals for the total disrespect and the egging on of the disturbance.
All the bad eggs cannot diminish the *good* law enforcement guys and gals out there!
If this continues, all it's doing is putting their lives in more danger every day.
Think about that before you bash someone who sacrifices being wealthy to protect you.
Use your energy wisely.
Go after the real perks of the world, then you'll be making *real* a difference.
Just saying....

~*Suffrage of Greed*~

america's government—over the top
   –dispersing its whim
forgetting Him†—who handed over
   lucky's four-leaf clover–
   land of milk and honey
–sucked dry by worshipers of money

   manipulations and illusions–
      propaganda at its best
   –you believe, they deceive

common sense—thrown over the fence
   taking every cent
–squeezed from the people's vent
without dropping one little hint

      it's easy you see–
   controlling you and me

      instill the fear
   mix up words people hear–
confusion sets, race-war bets
   –flying in private jets
   keeping all in guess–
   as more money they get

   while you and I just let–
      ignoring the conquest
   sitting in front of tv sets
–a country in silence, muffed by ear bugs
   glued to phones and laptops
youtube genius, war-game finesse
   the newest movies
   –damn! we're so blessed

   'til we get that paycheck

oh! wait—stop holding your breath
      direct deposit–
seeing government's sneaky little hands–
      a little less

who really pulls up that pay-stub fluff
   user names and passwords–
      almighty internet
   –who really keeps track of that!

   how about that income tax
all those laws passed—behind our backs

and oh! so fast—sneaky little i.r.s.

did you vote, did you give them the *go*
to take more of our doe

trillions of dollars—red-coded flow
lining pockets
sent to countries we don't even know

america's government in monopoly-
controlling its lot—ignoring God's† gift-
land of milk and honey
a country drying up
slowly flopping—turning to slop
its people failing to stop
—as politicians continue to reap its crop
leaving all at the bottom-
not paying attention
how they're being controlled-
by a simple penny-for-penny chop

Appearances
•*Facebook* (April 17, 2015)

~*Vacuumed*~

truths in secret—this very depth of me
—enjoying pleasures of naughty
keeping young—heart, mind and body

no! it's not a fault
it's what lies deep within me-
this burning sexuality
satisfying my man's wantings
losing himself in my world
—deep inside privacy's pleasurable swirl

it's buildings of flirtation
letting imaginations run wild
while mixed in crowds
hearing each's silent hunger-
growing desire's howl

then these lyrics through voices seep
placing this beauty in cheap
—destruction in a rhythmus beat
canceling out romantic-
that which leads to my world in secret

explicit lyrics exploiting-
my adult-play of private
turning passionate desires-
what makes me on fire
to a moment's pleasure-
disposability in bore
—a bitch degraded to whore

your open sass saps-

a continuous caging of me
—my value and worth—burying deep–
what's left of me to keep

through all my struggles–
my sought-after respect
years spent in tears
—I finally came out in clear

only to be re-speared–
displaced in mixtures of death
through tapping and rapping–
songs sung for money
—stripping all mystery
financing bling and private jets
pushing me again to *back*–
repetition of history
—always leaves *serious* in misery

oh! that silly delusional freud-boil–
forcing worlds to see mere toys
—deceptional, deceivable troy
lyric's exploitational text–

play don't spoil—emotions sealed in foil
when that heart starts its swirl–
avoid its cost—get up, zip up, get out
smash it to soil

games lyrics shout

don't you even hear
—over this massiveness of ego
as lyrics flow–
understand seeds being sown

have there any concern
the paths being burned
—where words, in stone, set

there's much more here
than this inner goddess being smeared–
listen close dear, listen loud and clear
here's something to learn
maybe a little—things will turn
respect soon earned:

all around here
little me's live in mixed fears–
wanting, no, needing
to belong, not be alone
—opened and eager ears
lyrical *gems*—they proudly sing along

their basic communication-
needing to be what they hear
lyrical-driven impressions-
give direction

when they lack important's gratification

song's sung and they believe–
lyrics demanding they shouldn't be
simple and innocent temptations
–but bold and wide-open invitations
pleasing erections to getting attention

starting younger than teens
going *all in*—blends *fitting-in*
these once innocent little me's
stripped of being a young, desired dream
–forgetting boys should respect all parts
forgetting truth of hearts
adhering instead to emotionless texts–
lyrical details glamorizing sex

young boys seeking a man's needs–
mesmerized by songs sung
words screaming–
all those hidden parts exposed
gone innocent kisses on noses
rip off those pantyhose
better yet, short skirts and bare toes
–then you'll be in the *know*

lyrical messages sent
embedded, driven
spreading through schools
just to *fit-in*—living in code
text to sext to pics in nude
bold yet answered request
fitting-in to *hanging out*
knowing what to expect
knowing what it's about
–without having to ask out loud

yes, songs sung—demean my worth
but my little me's surf
believe every word–
avoiding horror's of alone
feeling they must play along–
they dismiss being a teen
innocence of *sweet*
turn to sexy—open all up
fill young boys' cups
–give in to sex—explosions in text
–yearned attention they get

all 'cause songs preach
through lyrics—teach
sex no longer out of reach
court and date—no need
young boys fulfill easily
desires they seek

a little play, a little sway
learning from words sung
–they just get their way

all these little me's
–stripped innocence of *sweet*
gone self-worth's seed

while teaching the deed–
money-sought technological ingenuity
producing status of celebrity
building fancy homes
buying more expensive stuff
getting a little high—a little more drunk
words sung, explicit videos strung
exploiting what should be left to fantasy
–adult-only mystery

forgetting the sacredness of *me*
–abandoning passion's imagination
bleeding my life in tough
causing alone, broken bones
shattered homes, tears running in rough
respect, handcuffed—thrown over bluffs

forgetting my little me's
–innocence vacuumed up
dating turned to immediate expectancy
spread those legs, for this 'hard'—beg
then gone, left for newness of next
realization's over-flow
–hearts scattered on the flo'

explicitness makes me less
messages lessoned—all my little me's
their lost self-respect
–one day grow into me—woman

time moves, doesn't stay–
after burn, they'll turn and say

my secrets you've stolen
disregarded—placed on display
for greed's gain, my mystery you drained
sucked up my worth in a vacuum of insane–
turning sex into a teen's 'fitting-in' game

they'll realize all that *fun*
left them a bun–
lost in anguish, self-blame and shame
–without any responsibility
by those mouthing the words—claimed

explicit sex-filled lyrics
pleasing moralless crowds
–ends in comings of reality:

buried in money

–lacking a serious, loving honey
even broke and lonely
thinking a little too late–
all those little me's turned to women
wishing for naughty again–
a man to kiss, enjoy secrets of play
wishing–
they could change their yesterday
while courting fatherless babies
trying not to hate
–as they struggle through
seemingly endless, tiresome days
silently praying *one day...one day*

Appearances
•*Facebook/Google+* (May 18, 2015)

~*Undermined Reality*~

taking God's† words–
using them to be heard
you're just a turd—lost in a troubled herd

in each person lives—heart, soul, mind
in each person breathes
free, will, unconditional love

to use it to benefit anything in *self*
you just assume lock yourself
on a shelf

being liberal—avoids true principle
if you can't be an example
a disciple–
then you're just a ripple—a pimple
to be popped
for God's† true stance, you chopped
forwarding your own cup

all people have a dance–
their circumstance is *not* substance
to forward your branch

pay attention to your prance
for God's† words–
were not written to rearrange
–an open invitation to re-interpret
according to your will

take time—be still
forget re-inventing the wheel
listen—stop forgetting
self and unconditional love
stop incorporating your liberal belt
stop misinterpreting *free*-will

all have a price

all must answer to Christ†
–you don't roll the dice
His† will—how we live, how we die
is our only right
in Him†, our only light

~

(April 29, 2015)—*There is no better time to be an entrepreneur.*—Author Unknown

Being an entrepreneur: I read somewhere that you have to separate your business and your personal life.

On *Google+*, I can do it a little, but every where else I can't.

My business is my life...all that I see, smell, hear, touch, know...I'm a poet, a writer first. I'm also a very slow turtle!

Moving on a journey I don't yet know where it's leading, but I'm going....

If it makes me money, if you read me or not, if I crash and die tomorrow, I'm still going.

When we let our journey be just about money, then we lose the idea of the entire journey.

I'm slowly becoming an entrepreneur.

I have my hand in a few more pots then I need presently, but they're in the pots all the same. Personally, I'm not about money.

I am about building.

That's a good thing for me because I don't have any money and I am building from ground zero, so there's plenty of room to spread.

I'm a good writer, but I'm not a good communicator.

I can write you a novel that can make you cry or a poem or two that will have you thinking for days, but my communication skills suck and I chase people away because of it.

As an entrepreneur, you need to know your weaknesses and your strengths.

Being a lousy communicator is a strong weakness of mine.

I'm working on it, losing friends along the way, but gaining ground for *self*.

I'm learning the most important lesson: Be you!

If I tell people I'm horrible at communicating and they still leave, I guess it doesn't matter who I am, they will leave anyway.

So, don't let others judge who you are, *and* don't let their silly judgments stop you from chasing your dreams.

Just keep plowing...like me the slow turtle, you'll get there sooner or later.

~

(May 23, 2015)—There should be a special day to recognize military wives.

When their husbands go off to war or training, there's no every-day contact.

How do they do it?

Every second, every minute, every hour, my heart pounds and my thoughts run wild being away from the one I care for; steadily, sending stupid messages that to any normal person would sound crazy, but that's anxiety and stress reacting, a lot of it due to fibro and my past, and all I can do is hope he still understands because he's been there before with me, and hope that his heart is strong.

How do military wives do it so much?

So, I want to salute military wives on this Memorial Day weekend.

They deserve a medal for their hearts, their strength.

Thank you to *all* military wives who have endured, and those still enduring when their husbands are gone. Thank you so much.

~

(June 25, 2015)—My response to a video and comment about a white guy being arrested peacefully compared to white officers arresting black men in the past.

I agree with you.

I have a thought: Is the brutality shown to a black man by officers country-wide or is it all coming from a certain region?

I worked for the police all during my military time and some while a civilian.

I've seen cases where the officer had no choice but to get physical.

Where I'm from (---- Parish, Louisiana) a young white officer was gunned down during a pull over or house call due to drugs.

He was standing by his car and shot to death. No physical force was taking place.

As a military person (police schools teach this as well), standing alert and prepared at all times is part of the job.

You are taught to react fast.

When things go wrong, they go wrong fast.

Many officers have died when not reacting fast enough or trying to keep peace.

Maybe, this particular guy was well known and the officers knew what to except, and you can see in the video that the guy arrested didn't resist in anyway, and there were enough officers standing around that if things changed, they would have taken him down by force.

I've heard stories about raciest cases.

I'm from the south, but working with Troop I here and seeing the precautions they take is astounding when I see in other areas when an officer has to take extreme measures, they are blasted.

Seeing it first hand, and then watching videos and people's assumptions is stupidity at its best.

You don't know or understand the circumstances involved.

If any reasonable doubt exist that a suspect could *possibly* cause harm to an officer, he/she will be ready at the slightest wrong move by the suspect to take him down.

You can't draw conclusions without knowing every single fact about an arrest.

A person who goes to school and pledges to protect also knows that he/she may not come home one night.

When I put my hand up in the air and joined the Army, I knew that I swore to protect no matter the cost.

A police officer doesn't make a whole lot of money, but still they take that pledge.

People need to stop making accusations without facts.

People need to stand and fight the *system of government* and not the individuals out there putting their lives on the line every day.

I'm not black.

I am still scared when I have to face an officer. Why?

Because it is drilled and drilled into our heads that a person in uniform is to be respected and feared.

The fear is put there to maintain order.

If people don't understand that, then they lack common sense.

Think about seeing a patrol car on the side of the road.

When you see it, you automatically check your speed.

Do you know that a lot of the cars are empty?

They are put there to make you check your speed.

Everyone should be happy to see a cop unless they are in trouble.

I get nervous and shaky every time I ever

get pulled over for a traffic violation.

It's just my nature, but, instead of being rude and disrespectful, I am nice.

If you get rude, guess what, that officer will become immediately on alert and ready to take you down. Know the difference.

Men tend to be more hot-headed than women. It doesn't matter their color.

So, black or white, you get disrespectful, they're going to get ready for a physical confrontation.

If you don't settle down and you keep adding to the flame, then all force will be used against you.

It is totally up to the individuals on how they *want* to be treated.

Keep getting irate and disrespectful and you will keep getting treated like a criminal.

That's just common sense.

Show respect and you will get respect.

All this bashing officers is just a governmental-people control deal.

Every one should read history books, and then you will see what is happening.

I don't have the time or patience to teach here.

This is the whole problem with education... the government is forcing teachers to teach the wrong freaking things.

History...not important anymore.

It's a shame.

God...not important anymore...that's an even bigger shame.

This...*all* this tension has absolutely nothing to do with race.

The wool has been pulled really well over American eyes. Shame.

~

(June 27, 2015)—Are y'all paying attention?

The federal government does not have the right to dictate to the states!

It is a choice if a state wants to pass a law to allow gay marriage to be a legal option or any other law.

It is not the right of the federal government to impede on that right of *choice*.

I'm just a pea in a big field...what the hell is wrong with the American people?

You have a right to decided for yourself.

They cannot force laws on us!

When will this end?

Comments

•(Friend) I thought the *Constitution* said it's a state affair not a government one...I am so confused how this passed...again the *Constitution* is compromised

•(Me) The *Constitution* has been compromised beyond reason. There's reason on top of reason to impeach going on since the first year in office...wouldn't you say that in no other time in history has the [three] branches gone so unchecked?

It's almost like someone, some group, some other country has taken over already and is slowly revealing itself.

I can say for a fact: This is not the country I raised my right hand to protect.

When Louisiana is ready to break away, I stand 100% behind it.

•(Friend) Go get'em guys.

•(Friend) Here's a different viewpoint that might explain some of the craziness happening in Washington.

Gonna be hard for some people to believe this...but, from what I see, it's the only thing that explained to me what the heck is going on...

https://youtu.be/9VDlxMr70a4

~*The Imagining Law*~

it's been said before, it'll be said again

you dream it, you imagine it
you receive it

put before eyes—time after time
end-of-the-world rise
zombie-living kind, world-order jive

keep seeing it, keep imagining it
you'll soon experience it

it's just how it goes—the universe flows
don't think it so?
you're not in the know—give it time
its reality's head, soon to show

~*Fear's Premiere*~

think too old dear, really? is that sincere
–that dream lurking in back
your anguish is its fact
–here's a little tit for tat

othmar ammann—for sixty years
buried in that very sack
a swiss-born engineer
immigration—he volunteered
the united states—his new frontier

new york's port authority's
chief engineer–
for seven whole years then to director
–advancing his career

a dream lingered in the rear
an architectural shakespear
–his heart sincere, holding back tears
'til no longer he could endear
forgetting all those years
–new york's cavalier

to himself, he became a musketeer
put his dream in gear

a bridge-designing mountaineer
verrazano-narrows
delaware memorial—wat whitman

just a few—he calls dear

his last twenty-six years
he threw out fear
let his dreams become his spear

listen to that inner ear
it's never too late—to hear it clear
it's all up to you dear
live in a massive-emotional puppeteer
to hear—adhere—or bust it wide open
whatever age
take that dream—out of the rear
live it—loud and clear

~*Trees for Hanging*~

my wavering stagger for truth–
is this a goof
–or somewhere—hidden in heirs
is there proof

temptations rage
back there—those slave days
continuing on—secrets enroot
–separation's compute

sacredness in grassroots
honor thy family—there's no dispute

oh! ways of heirlooms
how many swung in tribute
–tradition's savaging institute

picked out grooms—*do-as-we-say* salute

oh! sweet, sweet perfume
from broken up boots to bathing in loot
family into family—men in suits
women in costumes

all in absolute or risk *deplume*

in that there, buried deep
in a witches' brew
secrets masked in voodoo

give some room
to this little guessing gloom

population mixed in color, why the flute
unless here lies a little truth

passion's virtue
beginning with adam and eve–

oh! sweet child—a fact undisputed

add mystery to the purlieu
–a people *free* of tradition's noose
caught in the mix of truce–
soul's caught in family's roost
hiding of *self*—an inside fuse
burning to let loose, so goes this profuse

these dark skins infused–
beautiful maidens, caught in valor's tomb
–awakened by masculine's repute
men unscathed by passed-down ooze
no forced bridegroom, no forced tribune
–away from majority's rule

he sees her beauty's glue
forbidden's home-brew
she opens the vestibule
his untamed whoop
–nothing she's used to
his passion not subdued—wild and *free*
–she becomes a bit skewed
needing him, wanting him

in comes the snafu—way pass taboo
too many rendezvous, too much passion
–can no longer conceal in recluse
too much gratitude
too high a magnitude to elude–
any outward, revealing mood

questions confute, traditions perfuse
on her, lies burdens of proof

within the tightly screwed capsule
–privacy in ridicule

sometimes, a beating's coop
even incisive cesspool

whatever's expected goo
coupled with an investigative woo

saving skins—*turning on you*
his secret's in view, suffers the impute

charges infused
in comes—the sudden swoop
no trial, no lawsuit
from open-fire—shoot
to a human battue, to a torturing spew
–a leeching zoo
to the trees for hanging—wahoo

year to year, century to century
burying truth—passion's woo

a family's collude–
remains—her in restitute
rebuilt-brain coot
seemingly to pain—immune
her heart buried in gloom
a cold, empty tomb, living life in delude

her secret—her fortitude

how many swung in tribute
–tradition's savaging institute

oh! the hidden of truth
how many men—holding the noose
children produced in secret rendezvous
with mystery's bloom

secret's roost—heated precludes

the cowards live loud
shrewd and snood
unable to seduce passion's truth

those living in truth
–abused—stuck in servitude
suffered the ridicule
lived with rule after rule
–never needing to prove

year to year, century to century–
their passion subdued
only in secret—coming unglued

to the outside, they're just voodoo
anger's brew—the boog-a-boo
a bestrew coming after you

on the inside—lies truth
in the witches' brew
–where trees for hanging
many swung in tribute
continuing on, secrets enroot
their passion—to be reduced
hidden in made-man truth

year to year, century to century–
living in destitute
struggling for truth's moot
persecute, prostitute, substitute
little by little—winning the refute

to the beautiful maiden–
he, without fearing a noose
becomes her groom

a solemn salute
those who fought in solitude

I'm not confused—passion's woo

explains well, a coward's
whoop-de-do witches' brew

today's sweet, sweet perfume
mixing skins' debut–
no longer living in taboo
no longer living in tombs
no longer trees for hanging
contributors

there's better things to do
like enjoying the fruits
of ancestors who gave a hoot

~

(July 9, 2015)—*Positive thoughts are not enough. There has to be positive feelings and positive actions.*— Author Unknown

I said my peace today.

To experience true peace and *freedom,* you have to turn off that stuff that constantly talks with anger and hate.

I thought long and hard about what I wrote this morning.
[What I wrote appears in Book 9]
By-passing the issue solves nothing.

I suffered abuse and immaturity for way too long to be silent about everything that I don't agree on. Speak up.

You want positive change, then you have to do positive stuff.

You have to stand for something always.

When you strive for a positive outcome, you may have to suffer a bit, but if you are doing it with a positive attitude like *this will help people or I want to inspire*...then you are living in the positive.

There's this saying in the *Bible* that if you see something wrong taking place and do nothing about it, it is a sin even if you are not part of the wrong. Isn't that something?!

Make changes.

Make them in a positive way.

Live for positive change.

Say what you have to say, then move on.

Those who continue on the hate issues... they may have some money or make you think they have money...that is easy to do, make you think they are happy. They aren't.

Move on.

Strive to make your life, and that of your family, better.

If others around you don't like your new direction...walk away. Turn the hate off.

Love yourself.

You are beautiful no matter what others

say.

~

(October 2017)—I wrote the above passage in 2015 and meant it. I didn't adhere to it.

I still had a ways to go in understanding my anger.

—Posted an article about the Confederate Flag

I have been ignoring all the ignorance and crap out there surrounding this flag.

Today, a tipping of scales for me.

[Dear entertainer] and your dear husband: You are bought out.

It is obvious, and every song I have enjoyed by the two of you, I am deleting.

This flag stood for *freedom*.

If you do not know the history of this country, like most people who attended any school system in this country for the last 30 years: You have been dumbed down. Welcome to the society of ignorant.

When you declare you are going to buy the rights for a flag that belongs to a part of this country (a people) so no one can merchandise it, you are trying to control: Hence, bought the fuck out!

Congratulations, you entered the elite spectrum like so many other *celebrities* that live off the sufferings of other people singing songs, preaching their woos like we are supposed to bow down to you or something.

You are nothing more than an entertainer. Period!

The tarnished history of this flag was brought on by none other than the carpet beggars later the kkk (Union).

You know nothing of the history of your own country, which shows your ignorance is so many areas.

Go on...use your money for a stupid cause... that's all celebrities are good for.

(I bet you bought into the gay marriage thing, too...it's only a wild guess...ha ha.)

I have my rights to stand up for this flag.

If it weren't for those who fought under this flag and the truth behind it, I wouldn't be here.

Neither would be my *sweet man*.

If it weren't for the Indians, the French, the blacks who sacrificed and survived, paving my way to *freedom*...I wouldn't be able to enjoy the fruits of knowing my *sweet man*, and because of your stupidity, the black man breeds anger, stripping them of their natural gentlemen-like qualities...go on, keep doing what you're told... Lord help us when the ignorant can actually think for themselves, I almost forgot the elite can't have that!

They'll strip you of your status and you'll be back on the streets peddling your silly songs, buying your food from the dollar store!

Oh, how silly of me to even think it.

When I got divorced, everyone said move on and leave the past behind you!

That's only [three] years ago.

You silly people are still stuck in something that happened hundreds of years ago.

What the hell is wrong with you?

Freedom of Speech...who the hell cares what the kkks say!

They are idiots and you stoop down to their level making yourselves idiots as well.

This flag does not represent murder, slaughter, etc.

It represents a people fighting for *freedom* of *free*-will, the ability (as our forefathers intended) to decide for themselves and iron out their problems on their own. Yes, people died.

Thousands of them, but...but...that's the cost of *freedom*. Answer this: Are you *free*?

Hmmm...I wonder why....

Those of you trying to control the *will* of those who fly this flag are going against everything these men stood for.

So, what others say and do gets under your skin! So!

A country like this was built, so those people can say and do what they want, as well as yourself.

Those who shed blood to build this country intended for those that follow to have that right without question.

The puppet in the white house...if he's going to put all the kkk names on a national terrorist list, then I expect to see every member of the black panther group on there, as well as every member of the *crips* and every other hate group (black, white, green, purple...it doesn't matter) on this very same list.

If not, then he is racist...choosing color over the principles of *freedom's* actual meaning...deciding on his own what is and isn't!

Just like he did with the dictatorship of gay marriage.

That's the purest meaning of the word racism and the purest example of dictatorship and the purest example of what entails the rights of the people of this here country to demand an immediate impeachment.

As to the point that I usually am.

[Entertainer] (however you spell your name) is that hair on your head your natural *black* hair or is it hair from a white-skinned person (what is known as weaves).

Just asking because if you are so proud of your heritage, then why mask it with the hair of the very people you hate.

Go on little missy, tell me I'm wrong!

If you want to blend...freaking blend and stop picking and choosing!

You either want no color or you do want color. It's called *free*-will...your choice!

Trying to have your cake and eat it too never really works out. Trust me on that one!

Hypocrisy runs in heaps in this country and you are part of it. You sing songs.

Leave it at that and take your money and help the poor.

White, black, Hispanic, and every other race... shut your mouth when you don't know what the hell you are talking about. It's that simple.

You are an entertainer...nothing more.

A bought entertainer at that.

Oh, please continue following your bosses and be their puppet...it's only evil and you played into their hands just like a good little molded piece of clay that you are! Laugh, laugh.

Applaud, applaud for being so weak-minded.

A majority of us are sick of hearing about these stupid, mindless causes. They only breed hate.

They are not of God.

At this time, (and I am a Veteran!), I'd rather live under this flag, then the one you live under because you only want to destroy the country I served.

I have zero respect for anyone who tries to control the *freedoms* set forth in my *Constitution*.

Money is the source of all evil.

That there is in the *Bible*.

Maybe, you and your hubby need to sit down and get some Jesus.

Impeding on the rights of others is a sin.

You are impeding on my rights.

Go ahead and buy the rights of this flag...be my guest.

Just a reminder because if your mother taught you about the Lord, you obviously have forgotten His truth and He *is* watching your every move.

While you continue to screw up in spite of His name, my little southern butt will fly this damn flag in spite of you because that's what rebels do.

I am a rebel [in a confederate heart]!

A rebel sticks to their principles and they cannot be bought.

I stand for truth not greed as you my dear little entertainer!

Put that in your little hoffa (however you spell that stupid shit too) pipe and smoke it!

To all those out there sick of these kinds of people...hands up.

I sit with my *sweet man*, hold his hand, kiss his lips, talk and smile with him all because of those who fought under this flag.

Color doesn't exist.

The hate of these people is a pure sin and they all need some church and not the kind of church served up in man-made buildings.

They need to sit in silence with the Lord and talk to Him...and, and, listen to His word for a change!

Point: There are still many peoples in this world suffering in slavery.

Point: Human trafficking.

Apparently, these *celebrities* are *all* for that kind of stuff or else they would be putting all their efforts and resources in stopping this prostitution of the human being, instead of focusing on mindless stuff such as gay marriage and dishonoring of this flag.

From watching videos of their musical *intellectual* property, it is easy to see they see women, especially, as a simple pet.

[Message to singer continues....]

Congratulations...you talk against a history (that history that if not have happened, you wouldn't be here) and at the same time promote an even worse present. Take the role of a teacher any day.

Go ahead. That is if you're smart enough.

Go see what your musical intellectual property has caused.

P.S. The federal government...oh, that would be the Union for those still living under the hate of the past (Lincoln and Grant had slaves in their homes at the exact same time they were burning down the south and killing not only the southern white man, but the Indians, the French and the blacks! and you celebrate them both...how ignorant of you!).

The Fed is what you should be voicing your big strong musical talents against.

Oh, I forgot you have zillions of dollars and forgot just where you have come from...bought out!

That almost slipped my mind.

Oh, those federal tax breaks must be goooood!

Can't impede on that. Can we?

Point in reference...you're so blind to the reality of truth that you use your status to influence what you really know nothing about.

I bet you know nothing about the Irish or the Indians or the French...shame.

Lil' Wayne...when he talks about his years in New Orleans...please listen to him. He can teach you a lot.

When the Union forced the plantation owners to set their slaves *free*, the federal government promised them jobs, homes, etc.

The plantation owners knew different, so they gave their former slaves (they were forced to kick them out to the street because of the federal government!) their last names and money. What did the federal government do?

Not a damn thing!

They reneged on their promise, hence, young boys like Lil' Wayne, had to suffer living in slums, and, hence, the anger that bred in the hearts of these good people.

Get your freaking facts right.

The only thing that's totally wrong with this entire nation is the traditional secrets that they hide behind (the masking of truth)...you see only the surface of the truth, and without even trying to see the secrets, well, that makes you all the more ignorant.

Go on sing your silly tunes, use your bought money and fight for your cause...there will always be another and another...when this country begins to shed blood on its soil again because of your stupidity, tell me, which country have you chosen to run to?...because that's what cowards do...they yell, scream, get as much attention as they can, so they can play the silly victim role, then when the shit hits the fan...they freaking run. I'm a proud veteran.

Tell me...did you stand the wall? Nope!

You are just a soaker of what those died for you to have.

(I had ancestors on both sides fight in the Civil War, as well as in every other battle this country fought in.

My principles are inherited from a long line of people (French, Indian, black, etc.) who stood for freedom!)

Do me a favor and get the Lord way down deep in your soul as you buy your next fancy house (50,000+ square feet of wood, nails, etc. can house at least 20 families who are currently living in slums like Lil' Wayne grew up in), or a silly pair of shoes ($300 can feed how many people, children who are eating one meal a day at school!)...or snort that white shit up your nose (so you can forget the actual unhappiness of your life because money cannot buy it, but you thought it could!)...He's watching and you will have to pay the price for your actions not I or anyone who flies this flag! Only you!

Me...I'm holding to the original meaning of the Confederacy. *Freedom*. Exactly what Dr. King wanted.

(I bet he's rolling in his grave!)

I bet you don't know that history either...sad!

Comments

•(Friend) The true history of this country no longer fits the lie that has been perpetrated on us by those who wish to destroy us from the inside out. Don't fool yourself, the media is their puppets.
•(Friend) The media is their puppet.
•(Friend) You do know that was a fake article about ---- and ----? Fake news article reports musicians ---- and ---- are purchasing the rights to the Confederate flag in.----.
•(Friend) Even it is fake, those who read it are impressionable either way.
•(Me) Okay....that's friends there...Thank you ----!
I hope that is true because I didn't read any article.
That was a news announcement on the radio!
So, it's not me checking facts if this was a hoax...and that is scary! Speaking from the media student stand point of view...we are in a shit load of trouble if the radio is just broadcasting crap that they heard and turning it into fact (false facts)! So, who am I to believe? Or, is the true fact...that these singers and their crew figured they screwed up and twisted the tale to be a false article report to fit their needs?
I question them all these days because apparently the media aren't doing their job!
P.S. And the singers just want us poor dumb folks to believe in them, so we can go spend money we don't have on their music, so greed overpowers moral stability and they still get the dollars and can do whatever they want like speak on subjects they know nothing about. Brainwashing of society at its peek!
The Lord is watching...that's all that us commoners have to say about it!

~

(July 10, 2015)—*The problem with the world is that the intelligent people are full of doubts, while the stupid ones are full of confidence.*—Author Unknown

I'm on a roll today.

I guess because of all this ignorance and I have had a lot of thinking time since my computer's been in the shop.

I use to self-doubt myself all the time.

I was actually told by one of my professors that if you didn't have self-doubt, then you need to worry. I never worried.

My focus on the political spectrum lately is a serious matter. You don't have to read me.

That's *free*-will...choices...I like that.

If you do read me, I don't B.S...I've done enough study to be able to not self-doubt when it comes to my *freedoms*, my children's *freedoms*.

Cornell University has a great website with the entire *U.S. Constitution*.

It's easy to read and you can really see what D.C. has been doing behind your backs.

All those *ad-ons* were done behind your back and without your vote.

You can also see how the *Madison Papers* greatly influenced judicial decisions.

(Meaning: Instead of referring to the *Constitution* for the proper decisions, decisions were made based on the *Madison Papers*, which were written by Madison and Hamilton. Hamilton was a sleaze.

He was not very happy that he couldn't run for president because he was not born on U.S. soil, and, this is what my intelligence tells me, he saw that the *Constitution* was way too tight. The *Madison Papers* are interesting.

Loop hole after loop hole...easy ways to penetrate and weaken the *Constitution* from the inside out.

Washington didn't much agree as he warned that a [two]-party system would crush this country.)

Go ahead and take a gander at Cornell's website. I bet you'll be in a little shocked.

I was.

Madison wasn't sure of the writing of those papers...he was the smart one.

Hamilton was all ego...full of self-confidence!

Madison didn't stick to his guns...self-doubt. He was a good man, but not a warrior.

When we let self-doubt dictate our moves, we short-change ourselves, and those around us.

The ones full of self-confidence are the slick ones (they'll have your money before you can turn your head).

Those are the ones to be careful with.

It's good to have self-doubt...makes you think before you act, saves you some money, too, but don't self-doubt to the point where fear controls your every move.

Being afraid of doing something is good, it's because you have excitement mixed in there.

Don't let it hinder you to the point where you are too afraid to try new things (that's what *getting out of your comfort zone* means).

It's okay to have a little fear, a little self-doubt, a little self-confidence, a little pride... that's [four] very important things.

If you possess them in [four] equal parts, then you have balance.

You can train yourself to have this if you have God as your teacher...never leave Him out. Good luck.

Comments
•(Friend) It's true!

—Posted a WBRZ video with the caption—
Thousands gathered at the capitol grounds in South Carolina Friday morning to watch the Confederate Flag be removed.

And so it begins...U and S and A....

Comments
•(Friend) I hope this brings positive to the nation....
•(Friend) This was done because of a white guy shooting up a black church and killing [nine] black people...well then...what is gonna happen now. http://www.thepcmdgazette.com/black-guy-shoots-up-church....
'Black Guy Shoots up Church Killing 4 then Abducts his Wife and Kills her' hepcmdgazette.com
•(Me) I'm just a small-town country girl! What do I know?
They are seeking their claws into our asses through race!
They tried to do it by killing all the kids in the schools.
That didn't work! Really!? Race is the only issue we ever had! Ever! How else to break such a country, but to go after their weakest point! Open your eyes!
Yes, when it comes to this kind of thing, I speak.
God is watching...I know this much!
•(Me) That's not the way it will go.
There's nothing positive about dictating what a state can and cannot do and it's worse when you do it to a people.

You cannot change history. You learn from it.
Germany keeps those camps over there open so visitors can go see truth.
You don't see the people there hating on Jews or Germans because of this. It's a reminder. A powerful reminder. I know.
I personally visited one. It did happen silly people.
It will happen again!
That flag stands for many different things to many different people. The liberals have no right impeding on these beliefs, nor do they have a right to dictate what a monument means to a people and who can have one and who can't.
If you think stripping God from schools, the courtrooms, ball fields, now the stripping of this flag and the dictatorship of gay marriage is all they will do, you have another thing coming.
Wow, how blind can a people get?
Oh, I forgot, the Jews, they were walked to the gas chambers believing to the end that they were going take a shower!
Imagine that! One little right at a time.
One little brain-washing implantation at a time.
Just a slow stride making the people believe it's for their best interest...that's exactly what Hitler did...took him years.
Oh, did I mention that he went after the students, too.
Dumbed them way down.
I believe he changed a little bit of history while doing so!
In my own country...amazing, and it's *all* happening right before our eyes!...there are thousands and thousands of papers and books written about this subject.
Of course, in 2007, I taught at a private school.
Ninth graders who had never heard of what Hitler did.
They do now because I showed them and made them read *Night*.
I think more people need to go buy this book (oh, public libraries... you can read it for *free*) and learn a little bit about how easy it is to brain-wash a nation! Just keep sitting down and let it happen.
Don't scream when they bust your door open and confiscate your material possessions, shot your brother, rape your sister, make you wear a symbol on your arm, brand the traitors with hot irons, oh, forgot the new technology of inserting chips in our arms, they already implemented the debit card, which tracts every move we make...hello! Big brother is already here...and it's okay!
Yes, of course, it is. It keeps the criminals controlled.
Sure...Hitler already used that tactic, but in another way because he didn't have this technology...my, my, my...and one big wow!
Commentary based on a *YouTube* news cast titled '*Tomi's Red, White, Blue & Unfiltered Final Thoughts the Slaughter of 4 Marines by Another 'Mohammad''*

—I posted this in March 2012.
[Didn't copy the quote.]
None of these questions were answered.
None of them. Still no impeachment.
Why is that? I don't hate. I seek truth.
I'm an American and a soldier.

I am a mother, a sister, a daughter raised from a background that extends far beyond this country actually becoming a country.

I have ancestors who fought in every battle...for *freedom* here and abroad.

I was raised to question.

I hold a B.A. in Mass Communication (print journalism), I was a teacher (high school, English, civics, business, speech, math, science, advanced writing composition).

I have always been a student of history because of my father.

I have studied in debt the lives of the first 32 U.S. Presidents writing a chapbook for each one.

Never has a President's history been questioned. *Never*!

Have we overlooked one of the most important aspects of being the leader of our country because of the color of a person's skin?

Have we downgraded ourselves that far to not stand as a people (a *united* people) and ensure that our *Constitution* is upheld, that those demanding to change it is released from their duties, questioned for their loyalty.

We used to call these acts against our *Constitution treason.*

(Remember that word: Punishable by death because we stuck together as a people and refused to allow anyone to destroy what was left to us by people who risked everything, so that we can be *free*!).

Several U.S. Presidents have been brought up for impeachment for much smaller accusations...much, much, much smaller... Clinton for having sex in the White House with another woman! How silly of us...!

Yet, everything since 2009 has been overlooked. How can that be?

Fact: We used to be a Republic, but the Electoral college changed that (bet you don't even know what that is...it's illegal by the way!

So is the forced issue of having to have a driver's license, but that's peanuts no one cares about...we just conform! Say *okay* like the good little children we are!)

That made us a democracy.

We are *not* a democracy if you actually read the definition of the word.

What are we?

We *are* now a socialist nation.

We have been for quite some time now.

Don't believe me...get out your dictionary! *Read*!

We are in the controlling stages of socialism...the next stage: You pick unitarianism, totalitarianism, militarism, and they are a few others that are just too nasty to mention....

Just saying...decide now because it's coming if you like it or not.

I don't watch the news these days.

Don't need to.

I posted this article back in November 2012.

If anyone has the intelligence to read it, can you tell me how off-base he was?

All of you marketing out there.

All of you who listened to that *gracious* speech about starting your own business that came from the White House...history actually teaches us about the human condition and what it is capable of.

People like me can talk and talk, but if no one is listening, then what's the point.

The penny shows...Roman's way of

masking the reality of what was *really* going on.

No one on here answered my question about that big *trade* agreement some of those nasty corporations across the globe signed this month.

I bet you have never heard of it...shame!

The online money...that's the push for a unitarian money...that was predicted.

It's happening.

All this money moving through online businesses...have you *really* checked out where the money is flowing in and out of?

I have. I am not here to weaken your drive.

You should chase your dream no matter what, but be careful along the way.

It really pays for you to do your homework, check out every single aspect of a company before you sink in your money (check where the money flows...that's really important), understand fully what the product or service entails, and don't fall for just anything; *and* pay attention to the happenings in your country.

Banks can go bust quickly when a country begins to fall.

Ask the *Romans*...they didn't have time to react...and all of it happened while the commoners where being *entertained*!

True story there!

—Medical Insurance, no one can sum it up better than Trump.

*Let me get this straight...we're going to be gifted with a health care plan we are forced to purchase and fined if we don't, which purportedly covers at least ten million more people, without adding a single new doctor, but provides for 16,000 new IRS agents, written by a committee whose chairman says he doesn't understand it, passed by a Congress that didn't read it, but exempted themselves from it, and signed by a President who smokes, with funding administered by a treasury chief who didn't pay his taxes, for which we'll be taxed for four years before any benefits take effect, by a government which has already bankrupted Social Security and Medicare, all to be overseen by a surgeon general who is obese, and financed by a country that's broke! What the hell could possibly go wrong?—*Donald Trump

Okay...still waiting for my computer...my dad is a fan of the Trump!

That shocked the hell out of me knowing his voting history.

He was Reagan's #[one] fan!

Even campaigned for him.

So, dad has me curious on this issue.

I read earlier of a quote the Trump made about his daughter...it was a compliment, but to us Southerners, a rather disturbing one.

Now this quote, which I absolutely applaud. He has his own money.

He's not scared to speak his mind and say it like it is.

He knows business and how to get out the red, but he's a *big* corporateer.

So, any body want to share their impressions?

~

(July 17, 2015)—Posted a WOWK13 News cast with ---- about a young boy stopped by police.

My friend shared this asking for opinions.

I read only two of the many comments on her page and got red-hot pissed.

You do not have to comply if you have not broken any laws! Sorry.

This young man was not angry, he didn't curse, yell, scream. He was not rude.

It's simply the officer did not like a young boy knowing his own rights.

You can tell by his arrogance.

I've been put into situations like this with students and when I said something that was wrong and my students corrected me, I got a little testy with them.

I had to ask myself *why?*

In this kind of situation, what this young man did, was correct.

We don't want to fear the law.

I have a lot of friends that are cops.

They are good people.

They do have some really nasty people as cops, too. That's in all professions.

A number of years ago there was a cop in our area where I'm from who first made a woman drive her car way off the road, then raped her, then went to a bank and held all the women hostage and did nasty things to them, killing one of them point-blank to force their compliance.

I had a cop come to my door to give me a ticket from [x]'s goats and I refused to sign the ticket. He got hustle with him.

I had to raise my voice to make him understand that I wasn't going to sign the paper.

He commenced to yelling and screaming at me.

I did file a complaint learning I was the [fourth] one to do so.

He is no longer on the force...so I'm told.

This boy filmed it all.

These are bad cops and they acknowledge

that by admitting out loud that the boy knew his rights!

So, if this was a black kid, would they have hit on him, arrested him, treated him worse?

In my experience in the military working for MPs and in the civilian sector working with detectives, it is the force that has to insure that their workers remain professional at *all* times!

The *chief* of their force is the main problem.

If he/she can't insure the public that their force will not bring harm to the community in *any* way, then the burden should rest on them.

These cops brought harm to this kid...lucky for him that he was raised with a good, strong mentality.

If it were another person with a weaker, *skiddish* mentality, then things could have gone wrong, seriously wrong.

Their chief is responsible for their behavior out in public as well as themselves!

This goes to show you that they don't have a good leader.

I can say a good leader matters here the most.

One day, I ran out of gas on the very top of the ---- bridge.

That damn bridge sways and is scary.

I had my children in the car and groceries and there's not much room to open your door up there.

A cop came and parked behind my car and suddenly this great, hulk of a black man opened my door startling me a bit.

I was *skiddish* because of the height we were at, the shaking of the bridge, the big mac trucks zooming by, etc.

I had a small car at the time and this guy was big.

He bent down and smiled at me, his white teeth shining brightly eased my mind.

He came to drive my car off the bridge while the cop behind me pushed a little on the car.

So, I got out and went to the passenger seat.

When he got in and we were all ready to go, I was so relaxed because of his pleasant character.

On his shirt, read *Chief of Police, ----, Louisiana*!

Yes, the Chief himself came to drive me off the bridge! It all comes down to the boss.

This young man has every right to file suit on these officers, not only for scratching his car, but mental abuse.

Sorry, that's just the way it goes.

After all, he has it on tape.

If he's not willing to go that route, he has the right to get the names of every officer that was there and file a written complaint.

If he lives in the area, put the complaint in the newspaper and have other people start watching the behavior of these officers of the law and file written complaints about them constantly.

If there's no complaints, then how will the boss, if they have a good boss, know; and, if there are no complaints, then how will the rest of the public know at election time when they need to know if the boss is good enough to get reelected?

You never give up your rights to comply!

You be polite and nice, but never give up your rights.

There are actions to take if you are treated in any unfair and/or illegal manner!

As an American citizen, you are obliged to execute those rights!

When they are impeded...there are steps to take!

Take them, even if it inconveniences you for a while.

It all starts with those willing to stand up for themselves against those who have no respect for this country or the *Constitution*!

Comments

▪(Friend) I normally don't get involved in discussions like this because as you said in your opening comments, I get *red-hot pissed.* I agree with many things you have said, however, this young man is ridiculous.

Yes, he may be well within his *constitutional rights,* which I did give years of my life to protect and defend, but does he really give a hoot about his rights or is he just like every other smart ass across the country that is trying to get their [five] minutes of fame?

It's real simple, the officer came up very nicely and asked him to put his window down...throughout the history of this country when a police officer asks you to do something...you do it!

While I was in the Marine Corps, I was an MP and I can guarantee you that if someone would have acted like that with me, my very first question would be...what are they hiding?

The whole problem with this country is people have no respect for real authority anymore...instead, we have turned into a *gimme* society and will listen to any *authority* or *expert* that gives us what we want...the others, well, we treat like this young man treated this officer that was just trying to do his job...which [by the way] was getting drunk drivers off the road to keep everyone else safe.

What kind of sober person is going to start acting like he did at a DUI check point?

The kind that twists and bends words written over 200 years ago to fit their own agenda and make a mockery of what this country was actually founded on.

Keep in mind, when the *Constitution* was written, everyone was on the same page, they didn't know that some 200 years later there would be a surplus of crooked politicians, judges, attorneys and regular smart ass people that would bend, twist and mold their words into what they want it to be.

•(Friend) The whole problem is how cops think they can intimidate people...when they have not done anything wrong.

•(Me) I apologize. I just read this today.

I've been ignoring notifications while writing.

Thank you first off for you service. I agree with you here.

You make a very fair and intelligent argument and, yes, you have a great point of view.

If you ask me, honestly, how I feel about the mess of this country, I can write for days...I have been writing poetry about it all because it fascinates me to the core. It's all confusing at best.

The point I made is good and the point you made is good.

How are we to act when there's so much confusion?

I don't think an MP would ever get hostel like the officer in the video did and I don't think not one military person would refuse to roll down their window for an MP.

In the civilian world, things are a bit different.

I've been faced with rude officers of the law and I've been faced with kind-hearted officers of the law.

As things get worse here, how are we to tell the difference who will be kind and who will be arrogant and hostel?

If I were young today, I'd be afraid of anyone in uniform because of all the things that's happened in the last [eight] years, then on the other hand, speaking from a mother and former teacher, the young are arrogant and smart asses to boot (not all of them) because of the destruction of family unity and the disappearance of faith in schools and at home.

The things the young can watch without problems on the internet is unbelievable!

In my opinion, what I said above about it all falls on what kind of boss the officers have.

If you look at the big picture, 200 years ago our founders didn't anticipate the kind of leader we have today to even have a chance at sitting in that chair in the oval office.

I'm sure they are rolling in their graves!

They gave us the right to retake our country if we felt our rights were being taken and if greed became the flag.

No one seems to care about anything anymore, except what they can get...selfishness at its core.

This is a whole different world from the one I grew up in.

Sad to say.

I just wonder what kind of world will the children of my children have to face?

•(Friend) Yes, Karen, I, too, could go on for days and days about how much of a mess we are in.

There are so many things wrong today, where would we even start to fix it?

You touched on a point that I have thought for a very long time about our youth! I could go on for days just on that.

In any event, I feel that if more people would just start using the common sense that God gave them, that would be an awesome start! Very few will do that though, which will leave the rest of us pulling our hair out. Thank you for continuing to use yours.

☺I hope you have a great day

•(Friend) (just my opinion)...I was raised to have respect for the law. My dad was a veteran of the U.S. Air Force and the National Guard, then went on to retire as captain in the ---- Police Department.

My dad's first cousin was Chief of Police.

That's how me and both my sisters were brought up.

You obeyed the officer. Always.

Personally, I don't find it an annoyance at all.

It was a DUI check point

My own philosophy is, if you don't have anything to hide, why all the *secrecy*? Why not just comply?

It's quicker and easier than all the crap he gave the policeman. Why make it harder for himself?

All he did was waste his time and the cops.

Just because the *Constitution* gives you the right to be an asshole, doesn't mean you should be.

That guy kind of reminded me of my oldest when he was in his teens...he'd do everything in his power to keep from doing what we'd ask him to do...spending [three] hours fighting from doing something that would take him no less than 10 minutes to do. Boom...done. ☺

~

(July 21, 2015)—A real open letter to the American public.

Oh, the *trickable, deceivable, entertainable* you!

Reading the poetry I wrote on politics back in 2008-2011...all the predictions...all of them that

FOX news was condemned for (go Bill and his crew back then...at least, some of us were paying attention!)... they have come to pass or happening now.

How silly to be so blind.... Basically. Obama.

You're a failure.

You failed at protecting this country.

You deserve a full-public impeachment, but I don't think you'll get one because of your skin.

You brought enough shame to it already and I don't think those with the same skin want any more shame brought to it.

You are a failure, and more people have died as in murdered, as in mass murdered on U.S. soil during your reign, then any other president in our history except for the 9/11 attacks.

(Look it up if you don't believe me.)

You are the blackest hole in our history and it's still continuing.

Shame to the American politicians walking by your side and seeing first hand your inability to lead, to protect and doing nothing about it because their pockets are being lined with blood-soaked dollars.

I was pissed when those seals were killed on a secret mission, which only a hand few knew their location (one of those was, of course, you, Obama)...oh, the sweet ties you have with the bad guys.

(I read part of your book about your beliefs... you clearly stated, in your own words, that you hate America!...Hitler did the exact same damn thing.

In my opinion, you are a disgrace to this flag!)

Yes, I said that out loud. I'm an American.

I have the right to say that...I have a right to demand an impeachment!

You are a traitor in every since of the word and people have died because of you!

Your job is to keep America safe, especially, from foreign people.

Your job is to keep the enemy from coming on American soil.

We put our trust in you and you failed!

Mass killing after mass killing and the enemy is here! On American soil!

It is your job to keep them off our soil!

After all, you are the Commander-In-Chief of the military.

So, that means soldiers, on American soil, are being killed under your watch!

You clearly have failed!

(Of course, with zero experience and absolutely zero military training, how in the hell are you supposed to know what to do?)

Reagan knew what to do!

He took no prisoners and brought our people home! What have you done?

You brought the enemy here! Shame!

Absolute disgrace!

By any written testimony on what a traitor is... you, my dear, are a traitor flat out!

I'm so pleased to see someone else willing to say it like it is.

Sooner or later, something is going to give.

American People: These idiots came here to pick a fight and if you don't see it...my God, you are as blind as the Jews were!...are you just going to sit on your ass and not do anything about it?

I suggest you start buying up the guns and bullets before they force a stop-buy.

Anyone remember what stop-lost was?

Clinton unconstitutionally forced that one on us during Desert Storm (sort of like the draft...yea, just like the recall of soldiers back to duty).

They did that one legally by sneaking in, very, very tiny print, mind you, on our contracts that when we signed up (volunteered) for [three] years, we were actually signing (enlisting...volunteering) for [eight] years. Yep.

That's how they got around the no more draft laws.

They, meaning the federal government, can do anything they please when it benefits their pockets or their private agenda.

(Anyone doubting the world-order myth now?)

They don't care about you at all!

Watch your backs.

Obama is Muslim by birth, he has Muslim ties down to his shoelaces and he's inviting all this icicles to our country...I'm sure giving them a *free* ride.

(That Hussein guy, who killed all his people that led to the Gulf War...I bet you didn't know that he got his education right here in ----, louisiana (U.S.A.) at ----!

Gullibility runs a muck in this country!)

Yeah, blind America, while they have you deeply embedded in the race war they created...Obama is sneaking in his pals.

Y'all really don't believe in all this race horse shit do ya? How naive!

It's just a ploy to keep you busy.

They know how to allude you and you so easily buy into it.

Take your head out your ass and start paying attention.

These *icicles*...they work in cells.

I have a bunch of these Muslim-looking people living right here in my complex.

I'm not judging, but God does say the enemy easily tricks us...and we are so *trickable*.

Y'all sure do love y'all sports and games now do you...*trickable*!

I really suggest you start paying attention.

Like I said before: The Jews believed they were going take showers right up until the gas came raining down on them.

Illusions work.

Obama and his cronies have really become masters at using them.

They're making you into fools right under your noses...hate to say that.

I love y'all, but wake up...he's moved them in while y'all were bickering about mixed marriages (there's reasons for everything...do you really think he just forced *dictated* everyone to agree on the gay-marriage issue just because he likes gays...controversy keeps you busy so you aren't paying attention to the *real* agenda!

Haven't you learned that yet of this administration?!) and *race-hate* because of statues and flags and cops.

How silly to be so blind and ignorant and not see what's really going on!

This is the best time to be a writer.

I'm enjoying writing about the show while you sit on your ass and play video games, watch movies, play sex games, deal with broken homes, financial problems, bad cops, good cops, race, gays (all mess brought on by government impeding on our religion and rights, and dictating to media on what to say!) etc., etc... boy, the penny-games of the Romans.... people are so freaking gullible, and they are so ignorant of the past that they can't see past their own noses, while they just keep on sitting there enjoying the entertainment designed to keep you distracted!

At this point in the game, I'm so glad to have been born in Louisiana...we are really known for certain things; and the swamps... well, we know them too well and how they work...it's kind of easy to survive crazy icicles.

Of course, (I bet you don't know this either... we do) they were training their little war ships in our bayous...they didn't think we were watching...we were watching their every move.

You don't really fuck with deep south Cajuns...so, I'm in a good place.

What about you?

Like I said before...it's only the beginning.

Don't believe me.

Keep sitting there...at least, you can't say you didn't get a warning.

How many more have to die for you to wake up? Just saying....

~

(July 25, 2015)—*The further a society drifts from truth the more it will hate those who speak it.*—from *.984* by George Orwell published in 1949.

Big brother.

At that time, there was no way to even imagine the possibilities.

The Turner Dairies was another warning published in the 1960s, which was actually black-listed by the federal government!

Imagine that!

It always amazes me at the brilliance and

genius of writers who warn and no one pays attention.

I went for my walk today and thought about all the things happening in my home town. Funny, isn't it?

Yes...I said, funny, isn't it?

[I totally respect and mourn for those who are suffering here.]

[Note: October 2017—I am referring to the theater mass shooting that took place five minutes from where I lived in Lafayette, Louisiana.]

While doing so, I have to look at the bigger picture; and there is a bigger picture.

This has happened to how many *other* home towns across the nation during this president's reign?

Are you not paying attention?

Are you seriously going to sit there and tell me this is, yet another accident or incident and they are not...I repeat...not...related? really? Are you that blind?

There's absolutely zero connection?
Really?

(How else are you going to attempt to disarm the most privately owned gun population in the world? Seriously, y'all need to wake up and soon!)

One article states the gunman was *mental*... of course. (Haven't I heard that one already?

How many times have I heard that one already?)

...then a question was posed to our governor about *gun control*...of course.

(Haven't I heard that same question posed to other governors? How many times already?

Do they really think Louisiana...home of the Cajuns, French, Creoles are going to give up their guns? No, dear nut cases...we will buy more.

Bet you behinds on that!

Here is the wrong...I repeat...the wrong place to pick a fight...oh, one more thing: Texas is our friend!

Not good for who ever is behind this!)

...on top of that, these people claiming to be of a church-going type are coming here to protest the death of people stating that those who died *aren't* Christians so the devil had to take them....

(What kind of church did they make over there on the east coast?...that is from where they are coming? Correct?)

...of course, (isn't that funny...in the *Bible* it clearly says do not judge...only God can judge)... aren't they judging?

I'm curious to know what they practice behind closed doors and what book they are studying because it is clear to me that they are not studying the *Bible,* nor are they living God's way?

Those of us pointing these things out are not trying to scare you...we are not scandal mongers or any of that sort.

We are smart and we call it like we see it.

Besides, there's a ton of physical evidence to back every single thing we say.

Yet, you, apparently, can't see the truth.

Orwell had it right back in the 1940s.

So, hate me. I welcome it.

I won't deviate from the truth. Not one bit!

I'll be meeting my maker and tour His universe, His heaven, my home after I leave this world...and nothing will stop me!

The way it's looking...I won't have much time waiting in line to get in...think really hard about that one!

When is enough going to be enough? Just saying....

~*Yclad*~

in faith—stay
vulgar, ignorance—cast away

live in light's way
voices come—protect your way

hear, hear—today
hypocrisy is hypocrisy
it's not your matinée to sway

only you, your individual attaché
you need to obey

in faith—bathe—no one can penetrate
when God's† your main deejay

your test may cause some weight
–keep the faith—you're a work of clay
–a simple, little pâté
a life-building résumé

it's okay—be a little risqué
your faith, paves your way

don't adhere to man's way
–that'll only bring a bit of pompeii
delay—your *thanksgiving* day

the only entrée, your only needed sway
of the words Jesus†—be the protégé

had to say—faith can never be passé
when you're open–
faith—your main forté

(August 7, 2015) ...*When you are brought before synagogues, rulers and authorities, do not worry about how you will defend yourselves or what you will say, for the Holy Spirit will teach you at that time what you should say.*—Luke 12:4-12

I've been listening to all the B.S. being

reported these days.

I guess that's where *"Yclad"* comes from.

The word *yclad* means clothed.

If we are honorable in our faith, then we should not worry.

That's what the above verse means.

By *honorable*, I mean true.

You can say you believe in God all you want.

You can say you pray all you want, but if you are not in it with all of your heart, then you are not with God. Period.

The strife that comes into your life are tests. You must learn from the tests.

The tests are sent to you for several reasons: Your faith is too surface, God is preparing you for something greater, etc., etc.

It's that simple.

I learned this through many, many hard, hard tests.

You have to clothed yourself in God.

How do you do that? Simple.

Read the *Word*, but not just read the *Word*...think about what you've read.

Take one passage at a time and think how it relates to what you're going through.

The message is there.

All you have to do is put all that ego, pride, greed, man's law...put all of that out of your mind.

That's when the message opens itself up to you. You are no different from me.

You have as much heart and soul to conquer the demons in your life as I have.

You just have to allow yourself to be true in heart. Most people live on the surface.

They don't dig deep into who they *really* are.

A lot of us who have traveled through the darkness understand this fully.

So, pay attention to your *I*.

Pay attention to what you are feeling.

If there's confusion, doubt lingering...then the only...the only one who can help you is God. Trust me on that.

You can go around saying you don't believe in His existence all you want.

Go ahead. Be my guess. *Free*-will.

He gave that choice to you.

As things continue down the road of *not changing*...then, maybe, you will understand these words I say.

May God bless you on your journey.

Always adhere to your faith.

As the passage from Luke says, if you get arrested or have to face greed-sucking entities, why worry?

If your faith is true in heart, then God's hand will lead your way. That's just fact.

Love the skin you are in. You are beautiful.

The whole world is at your feet...it's yours.

You only need to keep your faith in front of everything in order to get your piece of it.

Love yourself. Love God.

He's got your back...trust me on that one 100%!

~*Kalpa*~

not seeing the beginning
not knowing the ending
placing hopes in mañana
trusting in our Messiah†

passing each era, avoiding hysteria
not having any perfect formula
excepting the enigma

etcetera, etcetera
ignoring warnings of academia
living life through cameras
casting selves in self-driven cinemas
breathing then spitting drama
getting stuck in dilemmas
joining in—all the hoopla
without thought, a paying of karma
not seeing the opening–
boxes of pandora

side-stepping—attentions given–
all this mania
played-out orchestras
thrown-out history—lost to dementia

instead extravaganza—sought, chased
whatever it takes, life in fantasia

eyes moved—closed
avoiding the intended *magna charta*
for comings, unions in combined agenda
–an imagined utopia

patiently waiting—add its stigma
well-financed *persona non grata*
seeping propaganda

as butts on sofas, in well-worn pajamas
sipping vodka, caving into inertia
oblivious to the casanova
laughing, joking—it's all just paranoia

'til comes the gala—ribbons and bows
realization's diploma
penny—dollar show

eyes, ears, minds–
drowned in the aurora
now sitting—caged nostalgia
lost in a silenced opera
for lost hope in our Messiah†

(August 15, 2015)—I'll let you figure it out.
Have any questions, ask. Have a good day.

~

(August 22, 2015)—*Robbery in progress. Better
go online and see how civilians think we should handle
it.*—Author Unknown

There are no words...the world is going
mad and, at least, when I dial 911, they come.

I accidentally did that while walking about
a month ago.

They called me back and I assured them I
called by accident because my phone is set
up to do so that if I just need to push a button
to get them, I can, and that I was okay.

Not [five] minutes later several patrol cars
were circling the park where I walk to be
sure...now...that's standing a wall.

For those mindless people who have not
stood a wall...*I have stood the wall*!...I pray
they come when you call.

In fact, I *know* they will come because
the people honorable enough to stand a wall
and take liberal crap...even when you bash
them without knowing the *why* behind their
actions...have hearts.

So sick of this B.S....I read a post from one
of the guys on my author page and he said it
right...where's all the *good* news.

He said, referring to black men...but it does
pertain to *all people*...there are good men out
there who do good work, charitable work...
where's the articles on that, where's the
videos on that?

I so agree...where's *all* the grownups?

~

(August 23, 2015)—*This is America: We eat meat...
lots of bacon. We drink alcohol...lots of beer. 'We' speak
American...a form of English. We circumcise our boys, not
our girls. We love our guns and 2nd Amendment. We love
freedom to pray to God, not what you demand. Like it or
leave it...Now.*—Author Unknown

I saw a school banned *all* flags...even the
U.S. flag. A school...what does that tell you?

I think a lot of people will sooner or later
say enough is enough.

God has always been a forefront of this
country. I think He's getting to that point, too.

Our most powerful weapon is God.

That's what the founders of America *truly*
believed without thought.

It seems He's testing this country.

Asking the simple question—*Do you
believe?*

Hate is hate.

If you hate, there's something missing in
you.

To deny God is like denying your need for
water or air.

Answer this question: If someone put a gun
to your head and said—*If you love, believe in God I
will pull the trigger.* Would you say—*YES, I believe, I
love God?* Would you?

That's a tough question for some.

It shouldn't be.

Ignoring this problem is not solving this
problem.

Those out there saying it's right to kill
an unborn child, it's right to *not* believe, it
is right to treat people bad, it's right to hurt
others because they are not *your* kind of
people, it is right to ignore the good and seek
the bad...they are just fooling themselves.

I know. I've been there.

Love is a beautiful thing, but it is not God's
love if you are selective. Just saying.

When Moses sought the promised land, he
was up against some bad ass people.

God said—*Believe and you won't be harmed.
Believe!*

Moses didn't personally get to see the
promised land because his faith was shaken.

Doubt over took his strength to put *all* in
the hands of God. We are only human.

Our faith does get shook up a bit here and
there, but to totally *stop* believing...sad.

It's Sunday. Not the day of rest.

That's Saturday, but it is a day the people
chose to pray, think about what matters most.

I don't attend church. Stopped years ago.

I, instead, think of God and all that matters
to me and pray in my own way.

So many confusing issues on the world
plate today.

The only thing that really matters is love.

It's so simple yet many just don't get it.

They'd rather hate.

Word of advice...the devil is out to destroy
all that is in God.

Everyone is easy targets if they don't have
the truth in their heart and they don't believe

that truth. It's your call...*free*-will.

—Why is this? [Didn't record the quote.]
I'm so confused on this issue.
This guy's right.
It doesn't matter color of skin.
Killing is killing.
So: If I'm black and you're black and I shot you, it's okay, but if I'm white and you're black and I shot you it's not okay...where's the logic?, *and* why is this happening.
I'm with this guy...sick of it all.
Everyone needs God!
Crime is crime no matter color of skin, no matter what someone does for a living.
Enough already!

—Posted an article titled: *Breaking: Shariah Law Gets Banned by Alabama...Muslims Are Going Crazy* by conservativetribune.com

This is *America*...why is Sharia law even being discussed?
Why should it be up for vote to be banned?
It shouldn't even be in this country.
Sharia law is evil! Pure evil.
To even discuss it is maddening at best.
Alabama shouldn't have to worry about this B.S...*Alabama* is in the *United States...* hello?

~*Spontaneous Sarcasm*~

I have this thing—ya know–
living inside me

ever so often, it's gotta ring
it overrides—this inside *gentle*–
coming out like a raging bull
with a little *fuck you*
calling it out, for all to view

it doesn't like *sucking* shit in
nor dealing with idiots
who live in pretend

some folks relate
to academically-laden
perfectly-said crap—I tip my hat–

sure, I can go there
if to sleep, you want to be

nah!—holding back–
that's how tensions build
faces get slapped

sometimes, this inside bitch
just needs to scratch this burning itch

it's those times, when *fucking* polite
just saying it out right
ya know—how ya feel and shit
gets the notice, gets ya fucking heard
puts those truly lost, in this here world
–in a bit of a swerve

give it a try–
watch those pretenders of *good* citizens
stumble into mumble—then avoid you
'cause, damn! the truth fucking hurts

that's how saying it like it is—truly fits
sending this bitch to–

I don't give a shit

~

(September 11, 2015)—Restoration Proves Power—*Lead out those who have eyes, but are blind, who have ears, but are deaf. All the nations gather together and the peoples assemble. Which of them foretold this and proclaimed to us the former things? Let them bring in their witnesses to prove they were right, so that others may hear and say, 'It is true.'*
'You are My witness,' declares the Lord, 'and My servant whom I have chosen, so that you may know and believe Me and understand that I am He. Before Me no god was formed, nor will there be one after Me. I, even I am the Lord, and apart from Me there is no savior. I have revealed and saved and proclaimed—I, and not some foreign god among you. You are My witnesses,' declares the Lord, 'that I am God. Yes, and from ancient days I am He. No one can deliver out of My hand. When I act, who can reverse it?'—Isaiah 43:8-13

Thoughts? Seems pretty clear to me.
Think about this passage as we think and remember the events of 9/11.
Still...still...nothing has changed.
Still...ears are listening, but not hearing....
Still...still eyes are open, but not seeing.
There is but one God. None before Him. None after Him.
Still...still you go against His word. Silly. Really. You are still blind.

—*Sometimes, people are beautiful. Not in looks. Not in what they say. Just in what they are.*—Author Unknown

My good night kiss to you: All who said a *Thank You* to a service member today.
I thank them, too.
We are only *free* as long as someone stands the wall one way or another.
If you haven't stood the wall, for one reason or another, showing your support like saying a simple *thank you* or helping a service member who faced a bullet get back on their feet without showing pity, or showing kindness to a family (a mother and child) who paid the ultimate cost for *freedom*.

The smallest gesture...a smile, a hand shake, a cooked meal, a paid bill.

Just something. Makes it all worth while.

Freedom has its cost.

Those who paid it are *all* those who did that smallest of gesture...you stood the wall or you supported the wall...you, my friend, stood for *freedom*...and, that's worth everything. God bless and you are welcome.

Comments
▪(Friend) I posted on my page, but I'm going to thank you personally on your page.
Thanks for doing all you did for this country and our *freedom*.
I hold you high on a pedestal for your bravery in all that you went through for us.
If I could at this moment, I'd give you a huge hug...and thank you face to face.
I wish I could do something to help suppress what you fight with everyday. Since you were a service to me and this country.
I'd like to be of service to you if there is anything I can do for you.
Love ya, Karen. Tons of respect to you.
▪(Friend) Amen

~

(October 3, 2015)—Posted an article titled *Trump demands $5 million donation to vets to appear in next CNN Debate*

Didn't Trump get Ford to change their minds about Mexico?

I believe I read that somewhere.

He's not even the official Republican candidate yet. Hmmm....

American young men and women go to a military recruiter, check this one out and that one out, then choose *on their own* if they want to join and which branch to join.

Sure they get paid.

Sure their medical and housing is taken care of while on active duty. Sure.

They *volunteered!*

Not one soul forced them to join. Not *one*!

A small paycheck and housing in return to signing that dotted line that says you are pledging to protect the United States of America with your *body*.

That means...for all those liberals who do *not* support vets...*all* veterans said they *would* take a bullet for *you*! Many have!

Trump's support for veterans of this country is right on cue.

You can't have a *free* country if the military is forced to protect it, now can you? No.

Free means exactly that *free*.

Without an *all* volunteer military, then you don't have a totally *free* country.

Don't you get that? Trump is for *freedom*.

The current White House staff is for control, *more* control...do you get that?

I hold a degree in journalism.

We were taught to be objective in all articles.

These journalist who are being bias *are not doing their job period*!

They are simply bought and not real journalist at all.

A *real* journalist remains objective no matter what. That's just fact.

Thank you Nicholls State University for teaching me that!

(My errors are my own and not the fault of who taught me.

I take my own error-credits, thank you very much.)

~*Lacking of Common's Sense*~

guns and shooting—who's horn tooting
bases in fooling

stripped morals and values–
simplicity of fooling

give the right tools
–young minds drooling
hungry for the right food
feed, feed, feed
simple manners, simple rules
then in civil—guns wouldn't be used

teach the youth, good hearts breed sooth
when God's† view–
subconsciously pursued
–or ignore the biblical roux
sit—believe political goo
waddle in lute
as fools, liberals continue their woo–
playing that agending flute

oh my! oh my!—why add fuel
–falsifying truth
take heed—what common sense can do

untangle this mute, reseal real's glue
return to roots, times unmatched–
to today's patronizing zoo

oh! the total of fools
common sense given the hoot
the unnecessary duels—morals, values–
teach them, teach the youth
sack this political-agending hoot
keep those guns
–put back in schools
God's† point of view
then pulling those triggers
will get a second view

oh! what fools—not seeing truth

killing on streets just continues
when taught sexual poop
instead of knowing what to do
when rude—anger's mood
cloud's the view

so sad, creating this agending goof
new's generational roof
lacking simplicity, lives to devalue
buckling in—politicians so cool
pick up that gun—shoot, shoot, shoot
unspoken messages
new breeds of young
not knowing what else to do

~

(October 29, 2015)—Okay, *Facebook* peeps...I heard all the hoopla about [high school] this morning.

I have a child that goes there, and like some of my friends my age who also have children there, our health matters and is affected by things we hear involving our children.

If you don't know the *facts*, please don't post hear-says.

If you hear something that worries you and it involves the law: i.e. shooting, guns, etc., on the campus of one of the schools our kids go to... call the police station, get the facts, then post the *facts*!

Do you realize that if I had read someone's status that screamed—*there's a shooting at ---*—and I had a heart attack and my child lost his mother it would be because you posting B.S. and not *facts*! Just saying....

~

(October 31, 2015)—Posted an article titled *The Clinton Body-Count* by whatreallyhappened.com

Okay this is interesting.

I guess if we all repost this, we'll all in up dying mysterious deaths, and this family is in the White House. Unbelievable!

From running drugs with Barry Seal to murder! WTF is this....

Do you want this to continue?

It's up to the American people!

I guess they are going to follow me, too.

I guess they are going to follow all of us.

I guess they going to kill everyone who gets in their way....

I hear Monica L is now working on Hillary's campaign.

So, according to this list here, Mena, Arkansas is where it all started...there's books written on all this.

All these people here are dead! *Dead*!

And we sit there and worry or talk about silly local politics...this is major and she's running for U.S.A. President!

The Clintons + Murder...?

Read this...OMG!

~*Fists of Rage*~

all this mockery
you're spreading all this treachery
–lost words in head
pounding each other
'til meanings are dead

don't you see
you're fighting all that's *free*

all this hype—over simple colors
–lost little flowers
missing what's truly right
not letting the light guide
–holding on tight—evil's constant blight
letting it consume, war's raging fumes
taking on names—a person, a group
seeking glory, fame
without calling His† name
–all adds up to the same
a filling of an empty cup–
lose of hope and love
history's forever returning glove
without adding new's page
over and over, round and round
backwood's burnings—fists of rage
buried—locked in steadfast's cage

laugh, laugh—blood-soaked bath

children are children, guns and knives
taking each others lives
deep in darkness' gloomy night

without hearing God's† words
lessons go unheard
oh! little history, not much of a mystery
lost in worlds of fools—avoiding truth
so emptiness, you can rule

oh hear! hear! oh hear!
brought on self-sustained fear
this coming together–
language-blended world
a chance for peace

instead, the spread of dis-ease
fists of rage
locking up each other—self-made cage

all blind—this here Divine†
seeking only *self*
or a clique's helpless little vine
–avoiding truth
oh! precious little fools
sit down, sit down—drool
over none—you rule—illusions come
in all sorts of pretended fun
it is only in the setting sun
that you find the truth of *One*†

~

(November 14, 2015)—*Your work is to discover your world, and then with all your heart, give yourself to it.*—Author Unknown

I wonder why when I talk about abuse I don't get much feed back. Are you afraid?

Does it bother you?

You shouldn't be and it should.

We try our best to avoid the negative that's in the world, but it is all around us.

If we don't acknowledge it, it will sneak upon us and consume us. Paris. Sad.

The invasion video I shared is our reality.

Coming together as a nation to fight abuse and the hate is what we should be about.

You choose to ignore the wrong that happens beneath your nose every day.

You choose. Why?

Is it because you feel helpless, so you join the ranks of those who just ignore? Ignore.

Yeah, that's a *key* word.

The ones who do wrong like to ignore.

They like to place blame.

They like to hide their secrets and make those who speak truth look silly.

Well, hmmm...on my political site I ran back in 2010, I spoke a great deal about this *invasion,* if you want to call it that, by the Middle East. I wrote many poems about it.

Hmmm...what do you think now? Curious.

Hmmm...you live your world among the entertainment like the Romans did while their government destroyed their country.

Hmmm...professors back in 2009 wrote about this and the similarities to the U.S.A.'s economy.

Hmmm...playing all those games, watching all those movies, playing on all those phones.

Fun isn't it?

The *penny games,* but in a different form.

The world is still happening.

Do you think they will stop at Paris?

Do you think they will just take over Europe and be done with it?

Hmmm...play, play, play...the world still spins.

While the enemy is making plans, you are playing, and people who warn you are just scare-mongols.

Well, Europe doesn't think so anymore.

I guess they will just have to invade us like they are doing in Europe before your eyes are open. Shame.

Abuse comes in all sorts of packages.

Ignore the one right in front of your face, bigger ones come along. Shame.

Just saying....

Comments
•(Friend) Some things just hit me like a brick in the face...and...it makes me smile.
•(Friend) So true.

~

(November 17, 2015)—Damn...the whole *south*! That's what I'm talking about. No.
[Didn't record quote.]

This isn't hate.

This is keeping a country safe in a time of turmoil. You don't add fuel to fires. Never.

We have enough issues in the states.

We don't need another.

All outside the U.S., you must understand our position here. Coming elections.

Terrible politics.

Fighting wars we don't need to be fighting.

We have had enough. I know I have.

I believe it's time for change is a good way. This is not it.

For those outside, if you don't understand this, then that is natural.

You shouldn't understand, but trust us here.

We do know what's best.

We accept people here who truly need it.

We don't want more crime.

We promise safety, we do have to deliver.

People here that don't want to be here, should leave. It's that simple.

Christ lives here.

All those who say He doesn't, they are lying to protect their image.

We are a Christian nation.

If your religion or government allows the beating of women, the degrading of women... you are *not* welcome here.

That's *why I don't want these people here.*

We were built on Christian values.

You can't destroy that. We won't let you.
Yes, it's that simple. Good night.

—*It is what it is. Accept and move on.*—Author
Unknown

You think they'll listen as they sync their
cell phones and think they're all bad ass
gathering their intel? Let's try it: *It is what it is!*

That's right. We are *Americans*. I'm worse.

I'm an American *woman*. The scorned type.

A bitch when she's pushed. I like that.

Oh, there's a whole bunch of us here.

We stand with our men when goings get
tough.

Not a good combination when we are *all*
pushed. *We* have values. A lot of them.

Oh, I'm even worse.

I'm an American southern woman. Ouch!

That means I not only have a gun, I have
attitude.

Oh, there's a whole bunch of us down here.

I'd think twice about coming here.

I really would. Just saying....

Can you see it?: They hurrying up to type
on their phones—Question the bad ass American
southern woman.

People are so fun....

Comments
•(Friend) Add one northern native American with Irish blood gone
south. I think to add all the other fears as well.
I love my grandfathers blood in veins. Can explain another day.

~*Blind*~

hear, you deaf—look, you blind and see!

wanting to see good–
reading a good book
watching movies, tv, news
glued to computers and cell phones
avoiding what should

*who is blind, but my servant
and deaf like the messenger I send*

so greater—blinded, walking crusaders
lessons still unlearned
pages repeatedly burned—avoided truth
hindered messengers made into fools

*who is blind like—the one committed to me
blind like the servant of the Lord†*

wanting to live in the light
sucked in by fears of the night
what is wrong, what is right
shadowed by all in plain sight

*you have seen many things
but have paid no attention*

your ears are open, but you hear nothing

something we cannot fathom
–what already happened
so long ago, repeated history in flow

*it pleased the Lord†
for the sake of his righteousness
to make his law great and glorious*

to begin again—a new start–
praise His† name
knowing all's not the same
honoring *difference* without hindrance
so more came, not for glory or fame
not for suicide or game
–just for the glory—glory of His† name

*but this is a people—plundered and looted
all of them trapped in pits
or hidden away in prisons*

a fight for independence
worthy and honorable
behind the indifference
waited a silent evil—so small
seemingly so trivial—still—it waited
as those of ancient israel
held their rebel—waiting, waiting
they have become plunder
with no one to rescue them

*they have been made lost
with no one to say—'send them back'*
—Isaiah 42:18-22

they didn't know then
words—unwritten, unspoken
nothing offered—the first—lost
quenching evil's thirst
–not knowing better or worse
lying there in waste
slaves buried in caves

'til one—just one—listened–
giving courage, showing them the way

just one—eyes open
heart heavy—ears listening

setting a precipice, things still to come
long days, after they succumbed
repeat in malice
evil—waiting in indifference

years, years, years
patience without fear
that group—that one group
fighting, fighting, fighting

honoring His† name

oh! so in—evil rejoins the game
setting in motion, constant twisting–
on-going commotion, slowly stripping
glory of His† name
greed—pure gain
inside—mocking insane

evil's upper hand
understands weakness of man

oh! how it seeks the win
sinking of sand, pretends of *friend*
drawing, pulling—way down deep
fighting, fighting—deception's little seep
slowly, slowly over His† glory
laying in waste
curling up—sad little weep

oh! how it shouldn't be
gone blind—open in see
for this time around, dance little clown
written, spoken, still, Him† forsaken
still, deaf, blind—warnings left behind
lessons already earned, again, as foretold
to gallows—hung, shot, burned
endings of same, forsake His† name
on shelves, go on!, pre-order those urns

(November 19, 2015)—I don't think I need
to explain.

~*So Many Things*~

so many things bring plague
so many things said–
in minds—constantly fed

as high winds—birds reject
as a racing thoroughbred breaks its leg
as car wreaks leave stiff-necks
–common threads—all to accept

so many things adds to a single breath
so many things misdirect

from a simple mind–
to a well-studied architect
from a four-course meal–
to a plain ole omelet

so many things pass each sunset
so many things haven't happened yet

as a plug goes in a socket
–different voltage, same ole experience

so many things placed in bet
so many things start as mere concepts

moonlights, sunsets, cigarettes, rockets
bracelets, toilets, no matter the interpret
proper etiquette, stockings in fishnet

mechanical gadgets, angering riots
open voices, top-secret

so many things misread
so many things cause bloodshed

germs to disinfect, detours to deflect
different dialects
projects, projects, projects
something incorrect
some kind of prospect

stay dry, get wet

so many things to forget
so many things to dread

all common threads

all ends with empty pockets
six-feet under–
the yes or no—satin-laced caskets
–without anything else to get

(November 20, 2015)—*Nobody cares if you dance
well. Just get up and dance....*—Martha Graham

Do you really believe you are so different
from everyone else? Well, do you?

I've seen so many things as so many others
have.

I've experienced so many different types of
people, but in the end, they are the same.

It doesn't matter where we came from,
what color our skin, if we're rich or poor or
somewhere in between.

In the end, we all end up in the same
predicament. Dead.

As I get older, this certainty gets closer and
closer to my face that I should fear it. I don't.

As my mother drove me home from
dropping off my [rental] truck, I stared out the
window and began to cry.

I said to no one in particular—*I just don't want
to be.*

I turned to my mother's *why* and told her
what's the point? I meant it in a way.

Nothing has changed.

It's the same ole, same ole.

The world always seems in chaos.

The Jim Jones craziness.

The man who shot all those people from

that university tower, then killed himself all those years ago. The Holocaust.

The Twin Towers.

All those deaths: Theaters, schools, universities, on the street, in homes, in cars.

History that just keeps happening over and over. Why?

Haven't we learned anything from anything?

I've come to the point in my life that I wish to write and love.

I don't want to hear people's ridiculousness.

I don't want to be around negative commotions.

I don't want to keep screaming the same ole thing over and over.

Get over yourself and live your life.

Is this normal for a person [three] years from being 50 years old? I wonder.

I really do.

I often ask: Where are all the adults?

I think I missed the memo that went around 20-30 years ago that warned us that when we hit what they called *adulthood*, we really won't experience anything different, except it's okay to have a baby and get married.

Nothing much changes from childhood it seems, except the size of our clothes.

I thought, leave it to me to over-think, but I did think that adults did things to help better the world, they helped you when you get lost, they helped you when you didn't understand things, they helped you respect and love, they were honest and decent.

I haven't experienced much of that.

What have I actually experienced?

People hiding from truth.

These so-called adults lying about life to cover up their wrongs, pretending to be someone they are not.

These so-called adults lying and making other people's lives look bad because they can't face their own reality.

All children wearing adult clothes.

That's what I've experienced.

I always wondered about people much older than me.

You know the kind with gray hair.

I have never encountered an irate person with total gray hair. Have you?

This always awed me.

I think I'm beginning to understand why.

They already know.

They've seen it all and they have learned *what's the use...we all die.*

If that's the lesson they have learned that makes them so mellow when all their hair is gray, then I welcome it. Gone the stress.

Gone the hypocrisy.

Gone the idol worship of the almighty dollar. Gone the ignorant.

Gone the jealous, arrogance of people.

Gone the shifts of blame.

Gone the stupidity.

They already know which way the wind blows when it comes to all of this.

Maybe, that's the true beauty of age.

It doesn't matter what sets us on fire, we all die. We have no choice now do we?

At this stage in life, believe or not, for me anyway, things are simpler.

It's easier to rule the wicked out.

It's easier to see the games people play.

It's easier to understand the reasons behind the things people do.

Do you know how I came to this *indifference* way at looking at life?

By experiencing the same exact thing, but in a different environment and at a faster rate.

Only the second time, I saw exactly what was happening, I understood what was happening and I let it happen 'til the final card was dealt knowing and fully understanding why the end would happen the way it did and the exact fault of it all.

That's a strange thing to experience, but it happened all the same.

Is that what they mean by gaining wisdom? Maybe. I don't really know.

I just know that being aware of something is better than being in the dark. Age.

It's a good thing if you think about it.

At this stage of life, I think the best things in life are the simplest things in life like holding the hand of someone who truly knows you: You know that person who fully understands *why* you need that coffee in the morning, *why* you aren't very communicative in the mornings, *why* it's okay to walk around the house without any clothes on, *why* it's okay to grab that person all naked and slow dance in the middle of the kitchen without a single sound around.

That's what life is about.

Its meaning in true form. So, live.

Don't just breathe...live

Experience the *real* of life.

As my good friend told me last night when

I asked her how to date: Be yourself.

The best answer anyone could ever give me. Be yourself. I will.

Love the skin you're in.

Comments

•(Friend) Older, stranger how once we reach a certain age [and] we hate the fact we are getting older.
Yep, we will try anything to keep getting...older. Time.
It slips away in a day. It slips away in the night.
The only thing that changes time is to have someone to share it with, but you must take the time in order for them to give the time.
Until then...it will continue to slip away in the day, and slip away in the night.
A younger man will run hard and fast and become weakened and careless and make mistakes chasing a woman.
An older man will walk because his age and wisdom says, who he is chasing is not getting any younger.
•(Me) Good night. Thanks for these pics. They are great.
•(Friend) Good night! You are very welcome.
•(Friend) I am different...and I may not die.
I am a Capricorn...I am stubborn.

~

(November 25, 2015)—[This should be a news article in itself.

The damn news just reports on the wrong damn things.]

Okay...for you people living in the United States of America who think Germans should leave their country and hand it over to Syrian immigrants (I can't believe someone actually has to say all this stuff out loud!).

Someone has to!...damn...me and my over-verbal, educated stance! Find...I'll do it!....

History lesson...we had Ellis Island, which heavily screened those who immigrated to this country.
(That would be America for those who don't read anything more than short tit-bits on the Net.
Hint: Knowledge is key.
Those short tit-bits actually add up to zero.
Just saying....)

Do you really think people just came here to America like they are doing to Germany?

Ellis Island may be closed, but heavy screening isn't.

I hear Obama is trying to ban and overrule all of this *normal* heavy screening. Why?

Germany is only an [eight]-hour flight to New York. Hmmmm...interesting.

Do you know the *why* behind this heavy screening?

OMG...clarity...to keep the spread of disease out of our country! Hello.

Common freaking sense anyone?!

Every *clean* country has this.

Hmmmm...must be the reason they are *clean*! Black plague anyone?

From personal experience, while working for the 42nd Military Police Group (headquarters for all military police in Europe... oh! it apparently doesn't exist anymore...strange isn't it?), when American soldiers would come train in Germany, they couldn't return to America with one iota of dirt on their gear.

I know because as an E-4, I had the privilege of telling a Major to clean his shit or he couldn't get on the damn plane!
(Yeah, I felt powerful...and that's a feeling no soldier ever forgets! Ever!)

Another history lesson that's not so old: Clinton (the male one and a black-mark on U.S. history) handed over military base after military base...just handed them over to the German government.

Taylor Barracks (where I lived and worked) was one of them.

Do you know the amount of money the U.S.A. put into these places? Clinton handed them over!

Closed them!

Germany was under our protection, but clinton (oh, law-school chums of the Obamas (more black marks on American history) before anyone actually knew any of them) took that away...why?

When I stopped working on my political page before my personal strife in 2011, Germany was up to [six]% Muslim population. Do you see where I'm going?

It's been a warning. No one listened.

Professor after professor had video after video on *Netflix* (I can't find them anymore...wonder why?) about how Islam was determined to take over the world...not just Europe...the world.

The videos showed how wide-spread their killing-machine was and how fast they were continuing to grow and the *why* behind it.

No one listened.

Those who were trying to get the truth out...oh, most of them are dead!
(They were moslems by the way.
You know that insider shit.
Insiders know the *actual* truth because hmmm... *they are on the inside*!)

Why? Hmmmm...that's a curious thing.
Isn't it?

I guess the Holocaust really didn't happen as Islam wants the world to believe.

I don't know...I didn't have the term *Islam* in my history books. Did you?

It's in there now. Hmmmm...wonder why?

Isn't that to do with some religion...man-made?...oh, I'll get to that later.

Come on...I'm waiting to be corrected... hmmmm...Germany is about the size of Rhode Island (I may not be exactly accurate on size, but you get the picture...get your world map out yourself) and they say *10 million+* of these Syrians are moving there. *Over 10 million!*

That's a *lot* of people for a place the size of Germany who has a *German* native population of their own!

[Sort of like when Columbus brought the English to America and decided to *keep* it and slaughter nearly all the native population...they don't exactly elaborate on that in history books, now do they?

The video I posted on this subject tells a different tale. Hmmmm...curious how that works!]

So, all you liberals, as mentioned in the article I posted about how the Germans should abandon their own country, please, tell me your answers to the following:

1. Why are these Syrians immigrating to Germany?

2. What does Germany have that they want or need?

3. Why Germany? Really. Europe is very large. Should I post a map of Europe for you to fully comprehend the basis of this particular question?

4. How is Germany, this small country, suppose to accommodate all those *extra* people?

Over 10 million...am I missing something?

5. What's so wrong with their own country...that is Syria...right? Yes, they are in a civil war.

Well...many countries on the continent of Africa have been through the same.

So have those in Europe and Asia, and, and...oh, yeah, we, the good ole U.S. of A. (that would be on the continent of North America) had one of those damn things, too. Yes, hmmm...when was that exactly?

I don't think American citizens immigrated out.

Oh, damn, they stayed and fought for their beliefs...some losing everything they had, including loved ones, and still stayed!

Imagine that! So, answer #[five].

I bet you can't.

6. That leads to this: Why are we involved in a *civil* war?

I can see helping France...they helped us win the Revolution.

Did anyone come help in our civil war? Hmmm...I don't recall.

Did we even know that *Islam* existed?

Did we care? Hmmm....

We supposedly went to war in 1990 (November, was it) that Desert Storm (war) was declared, over a genocide.

After all, Muslim (Islamic) Hussein slaughtered his own people, tested chemical warfare on his own people.

(No one questions this or wonders why was he testing this type of weapon...hmmm...it was just *find the chemicals!*

Like, really, he or anyone in his regime was gonna tell ya! How silly that would be! They hate Americans.

Really!)

Then it was said that Iraq was stealing oil.

Is that a reason to go to war? Hmmmm....

We lost sons and daughters fighting these people, then we stayed to *keep* peace. Really?

Obama *fired* freaking American military generals because they didn't agree with us being their.

7. Here's one for you: Has any other United States President ever *fired* a freaking military general?

After all, they didn't get to the rank of *general* being naive or dumb or having a *lack* of experience (oh, yeah, that's Obama...U.S.A.'s 'elected' Command-n-Chief!)

Please answer this because Obama didn't just *fire one!* My last count was *three!* Hello? *Why?*

8. If we are to separate church and state, you liberals are *always preaching* this, then why are we involved in a religious war? Really!

Islam is supposed to be a religion...of course, of the man-made type...that's still *church*...so, why is our *government* involved?

I'm listening...my ears are wide open for you to reply...Hello? Separation of *church* and *state?*

If we can't combine the two in our own freaking country, why the *hell* are we combining them in another freaking country who obviously *hate us?*

(Oh, that would be Americans!

Us I mean, if you didn't catch that one.)

9. Which leads me to...if we can't practice Christianity in our schools, if we are forced to remove crosses and framed *Ten Commandments* from *official government* buildings, if Christmas can't even be a part in *official government* buildings, if our text books can't teach about Christianity, then why, oh please tell me, why it's been Muslom this and Muslom that, Islam this and Islam that every where since this man *took* over the office of the United States President?

How many Presidents came before him?

I don't know...45, 46, 47...why has this become an issue with this one? Please enlighten me.

Would it be because he *is* Muslom?

Would it be because he *is* Islamic?

Hate does breed hate. Just saying....

Oh yeah, could it be the *keep-people-dumb* syndrome?! Almost forgot that one.

The man *did* write a book about how much he *hates* the United States and, yet, still gets *elected*...and suddenly his ideologies don't matter (our ideologies are really the bases of who we *truly* are as individuals!) and his skin color does; *yet* [eight] years later there's race this and race that...people distrusting law enforcement because of skin *color* (oh, the very people who are trained to keep us safe)... sounds a lot like someone picking our (that would be Americans again) pockets, then trying to pick a fight when we question them about the theft.

The warnings went unnoticed.

People playing their games and not reading... by-passing that stupid little book about the hatred of America and his Muslom/Islamic love...and went on and *elected* the man to the highest office in our country!

(That book was actually really important when it comes to the character of a person running a race for U.S. President)

Bam! Played!

10. Here's another for you: If you get so rowdy on safety (which you do)...lawsuits after lawsuits on the *direct relations* of this drug and that drug and ailments, and this building material causes this and that, and *hot* freaking coffee burns, and *organic* this and *organic* that, and this health issue and that health issue, then why, oh please tell me, why would you even suggest opening the doors to millions and millions of immigrants without *knowing* exactly why they are abandoning...really...their own

freaking country? Why would Germany?

Shouldn't we like send in scientist and examine the place before readily saying—*Come on in?*

Just curious...I mean over *10 million* people leave their country over a civil war? Really?

And they aren't going to hurt anyone? Really?

Odd...that's just my take...10 million...wow... that's like an army or something....

Of course, it's obvious that you liberals are *okay* with killing innocent people.

You have pushed and pushed for the killing of babies in the womb. I get it.

Somewhere down the road, way-back-when down the road, some rich daughter got pregnant... hence, the war on abortion began.

(I guess the immediacy of the family name being scorned by-passed what truly matters like the first command *Thou shalt not kill.*

Go figure...the things selfishness and greed do...just saying....)

So, I can fully understand that you don't mind people who are well-known for their Christianity-hate killings (around the world) to come here to the United States (a place where the *majority* of the population believe in Jesus Christ and God!

For those *not* in the know...that's Christianity in a nutshell) or go to Germany...a country who has suffered enough at the hands of Hitler, who also (by the way) wrote a book before *put* into office about how much he hated Jews.

(Over [six] million he killed before we got involved and swore it would never happen to those people again!

You may not know this, but a lot of you (liberals that is) have had great-grandfathers and great-grandmothers die while freeing Germany and her allies...oh, a lot came home, too.

Maybe, check those family relics...might be somewhere hidden away in the attic somewhere...I'm sure you'll find the reasons to *why* those of us against this immigration B.S. are screaming and yelling!)

Oh, I almost forgot...that business with all those Jews being killed and tortured—didn't happen.

Never mind...forget looking...gosh, I forget so easily!)

11. It's coming...wait for it...wait...here it goes... so, you are going to accept the fact that when these people make it here to the United States of America and act all nice, shake hands with you, you might even get hugs for your wonderful hospitality...making you feel all bubbly and all... they are patient.

They'll wait until you are completely sucked into their B.S.

History shows how patient they are.

I guess you didn't read about that either.

Oh, well...then *bam*! It will happen. Believe it.

The *bam* will come when they begin their *real* reason for being here and start taking your freaking shit, killing your daughter etc., etc...you know... all that gory shit that you didn't see coming (but was warned about over and over), you are just going to easily hand it all over without yelling—*Wolf?*

Right?

I mean, come on, this cause and that cause...it's never ending.

So, if Germans have to give up their country because these *immigrants need* a place to stay, then you're going to leave America, too, and give up your country, so they can take it as well?

That's what that article said. Right?

Or, is it just my pissed-off self seeing this and no one else?

Please enlighten me...I'm anxiously curious!

So? I mean...read history.

There *is* a such thing as good and evil.

This is fact...repeated over and over in history.

Hitler and his pals (the Holocaust is the best example for simple minds) were the evil, and America, Germany, France, etc., were the good.

(Oh, damn, there I go again forgetting the Holocaust didn't actually happen!

Forgive me...I'll try not to forget again!)

Brainwashing is so damn easy.

It's actually scary!

You know the last guy I was with....

(Relax....this is simplicity at it's best, so maybe, you'll understand just how easy it is to brainwash.

If you can't get this, you're a lost cause...just go on and open your doors, burn all your shit, kill your family and slit your own throat 'cause all the Christians...you turn evil on them, they are going to use the power of good on you...just saying...read the *Bible*...that's all I can tell ya!)

...he...well...long story short...in order to cover his ass told this story to this woman he knocked up of how him and I had zero contact for [five] months when he was seeing her, then me the very next day for those [five] months.

Didn't matter how I thought about the lie... just as long as she believed him.

He went to such great lengths as to have this woman believe that I had the capabilities of making up realistic text and phone records (how? is all I can say to that one).

He ignored all the facts and had her totally believe that those entire [five] months I just dreamed up in my head. Really.

I was honest, gave her the evidence... whatever she needed because the lie was done and so was I.

(As I always say, you should make amends...I tried).

Still...some have a knack for talk.

The vulnerable have a knack for believing anything they are told when there is no other way out or they have themselves up against a rock and hard place (as the old saying goes), and that's just in a simple relationship.

(Yeah, the woman truly believed him...still does.)

Think what it takes to bleed a people (meaning...brainwash).

I did this paper in college on brainwashing through advertisement.

It's so easy to brain-wash a people through

simple advertising.

Take a government...a country....

[October 2017—I later learned the *woman* in the relationship I mentioned here was the one making up the story.

I can't even tell you how close this simple misunderstanding resembles what's been happening with Russia since the elections.

Manipulation...the core of evil!]

Read Elie Wiesel's *Night*...scary stuff right there...yet...it never happened.

At least, that's what Islam wants everyone to believe!

Oh, they kill in the name of some god... that's what I hear anyway...so, it's *apparently expected* that we trust, believe in them.

Any culture that beats and rapes their women, cuts freaking hands off of kids for stealing or runs a car tire over a child's hand for stealing (we give ass-whippings...if that!), kills professors for teaching truth...is *pure* evil!

Wake the hell up...these people aren't *immigrating* any where...this all puts a whole new meaning too *blind*....

Ten million+ people up and decide to leave their country. Really? All at once?

They *all* going to the *same* country?

They *all* have the *same* agenda?

All 10 million? And you rally for them?

And *again* the German people have to fight for their very lives...just like ole times.

Right? Is it *just* the Germans?

Does this add up for anyone other than Islam? Oh and Obama?

Just an observation of a veteran soldier, a mother, a former teacher (I guess I would be on the chopping block!...being all educated and shit!)

They get Germany...hmmm...they have already infiltrated the continent of Africa, now the continent of Europe...hmmmm... seems like there's one more *big* one to get... well...is Asia still...don't tell me, I don't want to know.

I don't know everything, but I *do* know this much: I want to leave *promise* to my children... not strife, famine, and/or death by the hands of evil because they believe in Jesus Christ.

No one *kills* for God. *No one!*

Please, answer the questions posed here.

Personally, I don't believe Germany is a stopping point and I'm gonna stay my happy ass in the south where when it comes down to the wire no matter if we like each other or not: Outsiders are just that...outsiders.

Just saying....

[October 2017—For some very deep personal reasons explained in Book 9, I moved out of the South to Nevada.

I still believe that if strife broke out here in the U.S. (as in any kind of invasion), the South *is* the best place to be!]

[October 2017—Explanation of the following part follows.]

[I purposely did *not* cap certain words in this because I hold zero respect and that's just my little writer's rebellion going on.

I spell Muslom the way I do because that is the original spelling.

The reason they changed the *o* to an *i* was because they had such a bad reputation and they needed to disassociate *murder* from *Muslom*, so some *brilliant* mind thought that changing the *o* to an *i* would be suffice.

It didn't dawn on them that *Muslom* and *Islam* would *always be one*!

You can't change that association by changing a letter...sorry, life just doesn't work that way; hence, *murder* will *always* be part of the game!

So, I'll just stick to the original because I don't conform very well!...and I'm not afraid to admit that being that I don't conform very well brings me little friends and much strife...and God *is great all the time*.

I'm Karen E. Leger and I approve of this message!]

[All grammatical inconsistencies were *mostly* corrected for the publication process.]

~

(December 8, 2015)—Trending Topics: This may seem like a radical statement, but according to American history and the way in, which its laws are set up, it's right on cue.

When a people is at war, declares their intentions, you don't exactly invite them in until they have settled their issues.

It's not rocket science. It's common sense.

For all those protesting...screaming *wolf*, here's a little bit of knowledge that you actually need to have: Laws in the United States of America were made to be *free* of passion.

People in this country are forgetting this simple rule-of-thumb when it comes to this country.

Look at the craziness with the gun issue, the police, now with this group of people.

[I didn't record the article.]

I keep seeing it over and over.

Instead of thinking with your head, many of you are thinking with your heart.

Free of passion means leave the heart out of it. That's how you keep being *free*.

Didn't you get that?

You don't invite people who are at war and threaten to kill you into your house, do you?

Just wondering....

~*Warnings of He†*~

He† told you—
matthew, mark, luke—all of them—
His† words passed through

you don't see, you fail to heed
He† told you exactly what to do

nation against nation

that wasn't a notion
some off-the-wall notation
not even an observation

famines and earthquakes

various places, not any continuous wake
guesses you make
warnings—failed to take

handed over—local councils
persecuted in *synagogues*
standing before *governors and kings*

does any of it bring bells to ring
muslim buildings–
one by one—added to catalogs

at the door, remove your shoes
bow to the east
their death-of-the-west songs
they openly sing

their only disciple
blood-shed-forced fog creating detours–
after-death-sexual fling
by-passing Jesus'† warning sting

false prophets to appear
instill horrifying fear
perform great signs, miracles to deceive
oh! the webs to weave

–if that were possible
oh! His† words—to the point
illusions will anoint
man's created bubble
stripping from the very cradle–
reality's actual steeple

His† warnings so plain
to ignore—just insane

the sun will be darkened
and the moon will not give its light
the stars will fall from the sky
and the heavenly bodies will be shaken

politics isn't His† deal
teachers of the law and
pharisees, you hypocrites!
my kind of cadence–
natural occurrences lost to ignorance

ask your demon-like mind
what could possibly
smother the sun's line
hide a full-moon's shine

so simple, His† warnings
so blind—that of man-kind

His† riddles throw you off
leaving you stuck in the middle

–apply surgical staples
raising hundreds of cattle
preparing baby bottles
driving tanks, firing rifles

oh! so smart, yet not able to read
His† simple riddle

stars so bright, from a sky, breathing fire
heavenly bodies, oh! how they'll shake

the perfect world, He† did make
oh! those tectonic plates
around, around, around
so slow goes their pace
push, push, push
there goes liquids in crates
up, up, up to the face
–grounds create—push, push, push
oh! how much force
can that pressure take

all these things have to happen
oh! just wait, coming is the day
slow, fast, slow

My† words will never pass away

His† small warnings
–firework show—pop, pop, pop
generations of flow
giving you a chance
–duh! you still don't see the dance

for every reason, changes of seasons

don't frown bay-bay, He† did warn
straight up—words He† did say

be ignorant, be brave
it's all up to you, which road you'll take

(December 9, 2015)—God is the best listener, you don't have to shout nor cry out loud because he hears even the silent prayer of a sincere heart.

As always my question each morning: What are we going to write today?

I'm kind of *free*-styling now since I've reached my life goal of writing 3,000 poems before I'm 50. (Actually, this one makes 3,047!)

So, with my goal accomplished, of course, comes the publishing of books, but everything else I write is whatever He wants of me. That's just how it is.

So, this morning I opened *The Daily Bible In Chronological Order 365 Daily Readings* *(New International Version With Devotional Insights to Guide You Through God's Word)* and I landed on pages 1448-1449 and I kept reading through page 1451.

Matthew, Mark and *Luke*...pretty powerful words.

And the gospel must first be preached to all nations....

I met a young man on here *(Facebook)* a couple of days ago and I had a few minutes to chat.

He's from out of the country and he said that he likes what I preach and reads me every day. *Preach.*

I don't really like that word.

I guess because I'm not a preacher, and I told him that I wasn't a preacher, just a writer, then he said to me that I have changed the direction of his life because of the things I write. That caught me off guard.

He brightened my whole day.

Actually, it's been sort of brighter ever sense.

I haven't had time since that conversation to converse again with him, but I will soon enough.

I don't like to be told I'm preaching because I'm not really. I'm a student of life.

Always have been.

I was also, and I guess have always been, a teacher.

I speak all of the time about our gifts and how important it is that we use them.

God gave them to us for a reason.

With me, I don't know, I'm just putty in His hands. Guide me and I shall follow.

I live *outside* the box most of the time.

I'm very open to things and I see the logic and the stupidity.

My [fourth] grade English teacher has been on my mind a lot these days.

I don't know if she is still alive today.

If she is, I hope she knows how great of a teacher she was.

If you want to throw race in there...as everyone does...she wasn't white (the [two] best English teachers I every had were black...I think I actually got my sense of style from those [two] ladies).

Anyway, she drilled into our heads two words (one a daily basis, I might add) common sense.

She'd say—*Common sense is not so common after all.*

That was always after someone in the class messed up.

That lead to the entire class writing a page or two or three filled back and front with those two words...over and over and over.

It may sound horrible, but actually that was the most brilliant punish work...ever!

When I hear *stupid* coming at me, those damn [two] words creep into my head.

I can actually hear her saying them.

She was a beautiful woman, always smartly dressed, and when she would say those [two] words, one hand flew to her hip and the other automatically went to a *L*-shaped form and that pointer finger went to shaking.

She'd bend her head just slightly, not a hair would fall out of place, and her eyebrows kind of pushed her forehead skin into [three] or [four] lines, which sort of transformed her lady-like, everyday appearance into drill-sergeant status.

When this event happened, not a pen, not a scratch, not a peep could be heard, except for those [three] or [four] forehead lines rising to the occasion. Effective! Boy, was it!

My common sense tells me to listen, adhere to my gift no matter what others say, which is—*that'll never sell or no one will read poetry or no one will buy one let alone five or more of continuous poetry books*—all that doesn't matter.

It's doing the gift that matters.

Here's how I see it: I trust Him.

He trusts me that I'll do the gift, then, in return, I trust Him again to do what needs to be done with what I produce as a result of this gift. Does that make sense?

If it doesn't, then you're probably not an artist. Just joking....

"Warnings of He†" was the result of my readings this morning.

I write what comes to my heart.

You don't have to agree. Nope.

The warnings were still said.

Free-will...you have the choice to believe or not. I'm just a messenger...of sorts.

You make your own choices of what to believe and what not to believe.

For me, so far, He's kind of helped me out...a lot!

So, I'm going to stick to my guns, follow the good book and trust in God.

He's not brought me astray thus far.

Oh! I've veered kind of, but with prayer, there I go exactly where He was leading me.

I pray.

He answers me by providing what I need in order to do what He wants me to do.

It's that simple.

So, *do* I shall continue, and this I can tell you with absolute certainty: That devil thing... damn that's a weak ass MF.

Every time that damn evil whore comes and tries to mess things up, the power of God stumps, you hear that, stumps the hell out of it! I've seen it.

(No, silly, not literally...it's an experience that you just can't deny...it's an *experience*!...get that one right, okay?!)

Trust. Believe in what you're doing.

When things are going good, you are on the right path.

If things get thrown out of whack, stop and pay attention...something's astray with your path. Hear. He's there. Ask. Be patient.

He doesn't work on our time.

We kind of live on a fast moving clock that doesn't exist, I have come to learn, in His world...which, of course, is all the universe.

Patience, and...yeah, it's okay to cry in frustration. You're not a weenie.

Cry if you must.

Yeah, that's okay, then snap the hell out of it and get back on track.

Love the skin you're in.

You are worth every step you take.

~

(December 10, 2015)—*We must reject the idea that every time a law's broken, society is guilty rather than the lawbreaker. It is time to restore the American precept that each individual is accountable for his actions*—Ronald Reagan

[I'm reposting my last comment on my post concerning *Common Core*.

I think it's that important.

I don't know, maybe, it's un-American to actually know America.]

Okay, I know [friend]'s issue personally and it's not with me.

That is why he deleted me...I would like someone to please post these statistics for me because I would really like to see them.

Expressing your opinion and/or facts on *Facebook* is the way of the world.

When this medium is mentioned more than several times during a Presidential debate, then I would say *Facebook* has become somewhat important in the great scheme of things.

So, this would not be called bickering to someone who actually listens to the news and reads the news as well as history.

I said I was straight up.

This is straight-up debate and sharing... getting the word out.

If you can't handle the fire, then step out the ring. [Friend] has spoken.

He can't handle the fire.

I'm used to being deleted and/or blocked.

No offense taken or given.

I'm going to talk anyway.

Here's the bottom line: If the American people don't speak up, then folks like [friend] will just run this country further into muck.

That's just fact.

Point: President Bush (the second one) went to ground zero personally and immediately.

He stood on the rumble, his shirt sleeves folded back and tears fell from his eyes.

He landed Air Force One in New Orleans for Katrina and waited for local government to invite the federal government in. They declined his immediate offer.

This isn't made up stuff people.

The Republican President before him, that would be his father President Bush followed through on Reagan's plans because he was President Reagan's (Oh, the Republican President before him) Vice-President.

Both of these men didn't take shit from anyone. That's just fact.

The prior Republican Presidents of the United States of America were combat soldiers and had the experience required to make the call.

[October 2017—Bush two wasn't a solider. I got this fact wrong.]

They are also both business men and had the experience to make the call.

There were several policies under the second Bush that I didn't totally agree on *No Child Left Behind* and the *Patriot Act*.

I've come to accept the *Patriot Act* after reading his book. Have you read it?

As a former teacher, I've come to despise the federal government's hand in any type of education.

Clinton takes office (democrat) and we're at war! No experience to make the call.

Arkansas was practically run into the ground.
No experience. I was a soldier under this man.
Okay, I served. Done. [Eight] years of crap.
He gets almost impeached for having sex with
another woman *in the White House!*

So much for family values and morals!,
then Obama...*Common Core* is just a tip of
the fireball that he let out on this country...
and educated people are *still* supporting him.

Unbelievable.

I was a kid when Reagan was in office.

My folks were around my age.

They spoke out. They voted.

We knew what was happening every
second of this great President's [eight] years.

We didn't have to question his Vice-
President. He left some sort of stability.

How much debt are we in now?

How many courts in this country thus far
have incorporated Shari Law?

How much *passion* has been allowed
to seep its ugly head into law-making
decisions? *A lot!*

How many killings, mass killings on
American soil have occurred since Obama's
taken office?...more than under any President
thus far and he constantly preaches about
taking the guns...*passion* inserted into every
speech, instead of enforcing the *law*!

As his job entails.

This is not to mention the simple—like his
smoking habit that our children watch.

Reagan was a smoker, but he thought of
the United States children and took up jelly
beans.

I should mention the first lady deal here.

Every first lady up until the Obamas was
respectful, dressed accordingly knowing that
they stood as a *role* model for our young.

Need I say more on this issue!

I speak out and loud because now I'm my
folk's age and it's my turn.

My folks didn't have *Facebook.*

They had town meetings and company
over. Today, do we do company?

No, a lot of times you bring up politics and
you're shunned. These are all *facts!*

So, please, if you read this, which most
won't because it's not quick and fast...because
society as a whole (education) has been
brought down to an ability to only read one
or two lines!, but can sit through hours of
football and freaking reality crap that's not
even reality, but full of fake everything and
cursing and sex.

That's why Obama hasn't gotten impeached
yet because no one really cares (the majority)
about the facts or why we have this *free*
country.

Everyone is too busy buying, being
entertained, bitching at the wrong things
to know that they have the right to fire the
freaking President as well as Congress!

Delete me.

Please if you are among those kinds of
people. I stood the wall.

Those who support Obama (who stood
on a Muslim wall and wrote a book before his
Presidency about how much he hates America...)!
are the very ones who would rather have their
daughters raped, all their worldly possessions
taken by force, their throats slashed during
the night as a bullet passes through their wall
and hits their baby in the head!

Common sense is not so common after all.

Or, maybe I just have it wrong and, as *all*
democracies of the past, America's finally at
its end.

Knowing me, I'll go out kicking, clawing,
and screaming. That's just me.

Comments
▪(Friend) You are speaking so much reality and the saddest part is
you are right.
People will only read one or two sentences in to be off on something
else.
They forget what it is to actually obtain knowledge, to truly do
research, truly read, taking the time to let....[rest of comment was
cut off]
▪(Me) You are welcome.
I'm going out with the notion that no matter what, I tried.
I may not be doing it with a political banner, or a gun, but I do have
my pen, keyboard and paper.
If anything, I'll be considered more of a documentarian.
My voice, long after I'm gone, will shake its head from side to side
and say—*Here's why your country went down hill. Here's why
American children were dumbed down and the 'penny' games took
over. Now learn from the mistakes.*
Will we still have a country after I'm gone? I sure hope so.
At least, for my children's sake. I can be bias when it comes to them.
They already have less *freedoms* than I had.
As I had less *freedoms* than my parents had.
I feel sorry for their world. I really do.
I guess if I were a guy, they'd listen.
Or some young sexy blond in a short skirt with boobs busting
through the buttons.
Even my dad wouldn't listen when I first began writing about all the
political wrong going on back in 2009.
Now, he won't even debate because he knows he has to admit I was
right and he was wrong. To each their own.
I'll adhere to your compliment and keep on writing like the ignorant
just doesn't exist because, actually, they don't in my world.

~

(December 15, 2015)—To all the newbies
here on my page: This is not a hate page, but if
you're Islam, just leave because I guarantee you
will not like me.

If you beat or have beat on women or in any
way abused them, I guarantee that *you will not like
me.* So just delete me.

I don't go around checking facts about you.

I'm a Christian. That means I love God.

I love everything about what He is and stands for.

I also love my country...not necessarily the people who run it and I will stand against them if ever I need to protect my country.

That would be America.

So, if you're liberal and you believe Islam is peaceful, that we should *all* kill babies, divorce is good, God is not real, our children don't need to learn about Him, our children should learn about sexual orientation instead etc., etc., then you go against all of my principles, delete me now...I really have no beef with you, but I'm loud and really I don't have any left-over hankies to dry your tears when I offend you; and I'm not for sale and/or for grabs. Thank you. Merry Christmas.

God is great *all* the time.

[There are some warriors who will stand up, not in hate, but in the protection of what *is all good*.

Evil is easy to spot once you learn what it looks like.

Are we in a crusade? Just curious....]

Yes, it's happening!

—Posted an article titled *President shuts borders, closes mosques, except...*by allenbwest. com

I have many sides and my political side is one not to be reckoned with.

France...thumbs up!

I hate the fact that Obama's picture is on this article.

He is a Muslim who doesn't care about this country...that would be *America*!

France President is the one who has the balls to do what is necessary to protect its people, and many will continue to go on and say—*There is no threat.* Shame.

Let the icicles come to Louisiana...damn!

I'm hell not converting.

I'm hell not paying them any z taxes and they sure ain't going to kill me.

So, I guess there's only one option.

Merry Christmas icicle people.

Scare tactics don't work here.

We just shoot and take names later.

Sickening. Just sickening.

God be with you, people of the *Book*, God be with you, because He's sure not with them the evil naysayers that they are.

P.S. I think they want to pick a fight with the wrong damn people if you don't mind me being blunt about it.

—Posted articles titled *Swedish govt in panic after ISIS letters give [three] days to convert to Islam or be decapitated* and *Muslim ex-Illinois Guardsman pleads guilty in Islamic State plot* by jihadwatch.org

[Second] time today, reporting about Sweden!

This is how Sweden is getting rewarded for being kind and allowing the poor women and children refugees into their country!

Wake up America! WTF.

This is not a Christmas joy to see.

Who gives this icicle group authority to put such demands on people who are not of their kind?

I think that Trump is right on the money. Hail Trump!

Ban, ban, ban...get them out this country! Corner them in their own country.

The audacity!

~Drunken Tavern~

oh! awaken, see—warnings posted
still time remains–
avoid this coming ravaging
of spiritless locus

open those back doors
breathe in fresh air
see the fields of green
more souls kind—not mean

fill the heart of *free*, choices at markets
exchanges' guarantee, labor for money
in safe harbors—you sleep

open doors, screened—see *free*
walking in streets, smiles in happy
hands in greet, fresh produce to eat–
safe from disease

see your mother and wife
sister and daughter–
sincerely yours to keep, willings in *free*
not scorned and raped, no knife to face
–doing what's right, in God's† pure light

oh! slam that *drunkened* hate
that which comes to sedate
–with their heartless blade
they've come to change
your nation's fate

those closing doors—sealed tight
curtains drawn, blocking out the light

oh! let the air in *free*—breathe
many spilled words in deceive
careful—spoken to mislead

ten simple commands sent by He†
a sober man clearly understands
only in He†, nations stay *free*

(December 18, 2015)—*When all these blessings*

and curses I have set before you come upon you and you take them to heart wherever the Lord your God disperses you among the nations, and when you and your children return to the Lord your God and obey Him with all your heart and with all your soul according to everything I command you today, then the Lord your God will restore your fortunes and have compassion on you and gather you again from all the nations where He scattered you....— Deuteronomy 26-30

My journey led me to *Deuteronomy* this morning.

I don't know this as total fact, but I've heard that many dismiss the *Book of Deuteronomy* all together. Shame.

If you read the entire book, you might understand the happenings of today.

There are many people out there warning that we are at the end of times.

I don't believe we are at the *end* of times, but I do see why these people are frightened.

I talk often about history and how often it repeats itself.

I do question often if we are not in the mince of another crusade against evil.

It's really silly to say my last statement is a guess or part of some *scare* tactic.

The happenings in the world are clear.

If you don't see them, you are not paying attention.

All those that I read who's talking about the *end* of times are actually familiar, in some way, with the words of the *Bible*.

I was told that you can read any passage in the *Bible* a thousand times and each time it has a new meaning. I can understand this.

In *The Daily Bible In Chronological Order 365 Daily Readings (New International Version With Devotional Insights to Guide You Through God's Word)*, commentary by F. LaGard Smith put out by Harvest House Publishers Copyrighted 1984, the chapter concerning the Book of Deuteronomy titled 'March 7 Conquering A Land (ca. 1400-1100 B.C.),' subtitled 'Renewal of the Covenant,' the commentary that begins the chapter is—*With this restatement of the laws completed, it is an appropriate time for the Israelites to reaffirm their covenant with God, just as they had done at Mount Sinai when the law was first given [this is referring to the Ten Commands handed down to Moses].*

It is not a covenant to be taken lightly, for along with God's promised blessings go the promised curses, which will be imposed for breach of the covenant.

Breach of the covenant will occur when breach of the laws occurs; and breach of the law can easily occur, for the law handed down from God through Moses is the most comprehensive, radically different, and morally demanding law that any nation of people has seen to this time.

Isn't that interesting?

I was born and raised here in the United States of America.

Throughout my schooling, learning the history of how this country came to be was the most important lessons.

Through each grade, 12 years, there was always something we had to memorize, to understand from the *Pledge of Allegiance*, to the *Gettysburg Address*, to the *Declaration of Independence,* etc.

Along with that, outside the public school system, I learned the *Ten Commandments* and the history of how that came to be.

It was a normal upbringing for all American children no matter one's race.

We *all* learned the same thing.

If we went to public school, no, we didn't go to a class during school hours to learn about God.

We did start off each day by saying out loud and together the *Pledge of Allegiance* and a prayer.

It wasn't some brainwashing tactic.

It was just a way to begin the day with *grace*.

In today's world, the screams and yelling about prayer in schools baffles me a great deal.

If you take the *Bill of Rights* (which is the beginning of the United States of America's *Constitution* [which is a set grouping of laws, which the founders of this country put together and all agreed on.

A constitution for any group, states that these rules are jointly agreed upon for all to follow as a whole and besides these *united* rules, each entity can also create their own rules they jointly agree on, but those who agreed on the constitution governing the whole doesn't have to follow] and the *Ten Commandments* and compare them, then you see how closely they match.

Is this a coincidence? No.

The founders of the U.S.A. knew the value of the land they were in.

Though those who came before our founding fathers made a lot of mistakes when they discovered this land, the founding fathers knew and understood the value of what they had.

Those *founding fathers* (as we refer to them all...the first group who signed the *Declaration of Independence*, then years and years later, the second group who developed and signed the *Constitution* that governs this great country) were ordinary men who came together and with much debate made the most extraordinary decision during this particular time in history to include the laws of God into the laws of their new country.

There's no debate here. This is fact.

Not religion, but God played an important part in the beginning design of what would become one of the most powerful countries in the world. That wasn't an accident.

If you read history and do the comparing, the same thing happened to Israel all those years before.

You can look at the U.S.A. and Israel in all the different lights as you want, but the realization of the reality of both countries is the same: Both made a covenant with God.

For the U.S.A., the evidence is in the way the founding fathers designed the *Bill of Rights*, as well as the *Declaration of Independence,* to match the laws handed down to Moses, the *Ten Commandments*, thousands of years before.

You can argue this point until you are blue in the face, it doesn't change the facts.

Put these documents side by side, tear them apart until your clothes fall off in shriveled little rags, the facts will always remain the same: *The U.S. Constitution* in it's original form with the *Bill of Rights* match the *Ten Commandments*.

Our founding fathers made a covenant with God: Live in righteousness: Honesty, courage, love, hope, *free*-will, unconditional love, and in exchange they were given the fruits of a land which has, indeed, proven to be far beyond anything these men could have ever dreamed of.

The reason that is is because they *chose* to adhere to their beliefs, that of which fall to their faith in God.

Though many questioned their faith and that of their fellow law-makers, they all came to see the honor in what they were doing, hence, leaving us with a solid foundation.

It is only political-agendas and greed that these beliefs have been twisted in selfish ways that we find ourselves divided today.

The facts speak for themselves.

You can go to Cornell University's website and read the entire *Constitution* including all the additions (which the people didn't ratify) if you want to second guess me. It's all there.

Every single thing that was twisted to fit a political agenda that the people did not agree on.

This country was built on a foundation of Christian beliefs.

Sure, throughout our history, there have been a lot of torments like the wars against the natives and blacks and women.

All of this began based on passions.

It took a while, in fact years and years, for passion to be removed in order for the pure facts to stand by themselves.

Our founding fathers didn't give us a straight-up recipe for perfect.

That wasn't their intention.

What they did give us was the bases for the recipe: The one main ingredient (the most important) was that we *free* ourselves of passion before making judgment. We lack a lot in this simple area.

So much so that it does take us years before we see the facts *free* of passion.

As our history has proven, that's okay as long as the end result adheres to the original ingredient.

We are all just human.

Perfect is not how God made us, hence, not how our founding fathers saw us.

They knew we'd make mistakes.

They knew that innocent blood would be shed.

I'm sure many who put down their signatures on our country's most important documents spent many a long, sleepless nights debating with themselves and with God not exactly knowing what lies in the future, but praying that what they seal would give us the leverage to handle anything.

Haven't they succeeded thus far?

We have the tools which we need to see *free* without passion.

The *Bible* is part of this country if you like it or not. If you believe in God or not.

It has gotten us this far. Hasn't it not?

So, in saying all that (not opinion, but fact), in all that's happening in this world and knowing the history of this country, the history of man-made religions, it is apparent to what is happening today.

You can look at it however you want, but we are in a huge test.

I see the United States of America as a fruit given to us by God.

We can keep it fresh or we can let it spoil.

It's entirely up to us, its people. *Free*-will.

If you actually read the *Bible,* then read history books of all the wars, the lands, the people involved in such wars, you will see the constant battle between good and evil.

In the history of the United States, minus the corruption of greed (corporate and political), you see how America has always fought for the *good* of man. Why stop now?

As I see it, today, we as a people are in the fight our founding fathers knew would one day come.

They have given us the tools, which we need. How we use them?

Well, that's entirely up to us.

Are we going to fight for the *good* of man and keep the fruits or are we going to let *passion* take over and let evil win?

It's a decision we all have to make as

individuals whatever our individual beliefs are, then come together as a united people and act upon it.

There's always a war between good and evil.

Blood has always been shed in order for *good* to prevail. Always.

Look back in history and understand which entity (good or evil) prevails and is rewarded.

It doesn't take rocket science to understand the answer.

May God always be with you in your decision making and your life.

~

(December 20, 2015)—Posted an article titled *4-Star Admiral: Obama Acts 'The Part' Of A Muslim, Muslim Brotherhood Has Completely Infiltrated US Gov't*—www.truthandaction.org

When I had my political page *keleger. org*, I put all of this on there and had two full-bird colonels tell me that I was right on the money.

That page was hacked over and over again and I was even offered $5,000 in its beginning stages to shut it down.

When my personal life went up in smoke, I abandoned the page, but continued writing on the matters at hand. Shame on America.

Shame.

Obama wrote a damn book before taking office that he hates America.

Shame on Americans for not taking that seriously. Wake the hell up.

Or go on ignoring the facts.

The choice is yours.

God did give us *free*-will.

You *freely* choose to ignore...when they come here or when they get the call to strike, don't go cry wolf and beg those who believe in this country to protect your sorry ass.

That's all I have to say.

Truth has run à muck and lies have taken its place.

The *Bible* warns of this...oh, I forgot the *Bible* is being replaced by the *Quran* (is that how you spell that evil book's name?)...January. I make 47.

Off to purchase my weapon of choice.

I'd rather be prepared than some dumb-ass crying—*Oops, I forgot we had that 'right'!*

~

(December 30, 2015)—*There is no evidence that he ever attended or worked for any university or that he ever sat for the Illinois bar. We have no documentation for any of his claims. He may well be the greatest hoax in history.*—Matt Patterson, *Newsweek Magazine*

[This part in brackets was copied with article from a private page, but we thought it was good enough to reprint with article: Matt Patterson and Newsweek speak out about Obama. This is timely and tough.

As many of you know, *Newsweek* has a reputation for being extremely liberal.

The fact that their editor saw fit to print the following article about Obama and the one that appears in the latest *Newsweek*, makes this a truly amazing event, and a news story in and of itself.

At last, the truth about our President and his agenda are starting to trickle through the protective wall built around him by the liberal media....]

—By: Matt Patterson (*Newsweek* Columnist—Opinion Writer)

Years from now, historians may regard the 2008 election of Barack Obama as an inscrutable and phenomenon, the result of a baffling breed of mass hysteria akin perhaps to the witch craze of the Middle Ages.

How, they will wonder, did a man so devoid of professional accomplishment beguile so many into thinking he could manage the world's largest economy, direct the world's most powerful military, execute the world's most consequential job?

Imagine a future historian examining Obama's pre-presidential life: Ushered into and through the Ivy League, despite unremarkable grades and test scores along the way; a cushy non-job as a *community organizer;* a brief career as a state legislator devoid of legislative achievement (and in fact nearly devoid of his attention, less often did he vote 'present'); and finally an unaccomplished single term in the United States Senate, the entirety of which was devoted to his presidential ambitions.

He left no academic legacy in academia, authored no signature legislation as a legislator, and then there is the matter of his troubling associations: The white-hating, America-loathing preacher who for decades served as Obama's *spiritual mentor*; a real-life, actual terrorist who served as Obama's colleague and political sponsor.

It is easy to imagine a future historian looking at it all and asking: How on Earth was such a man elected president?

There is no evidence that he ever attended or worked for any university or that he ever sat for the Illinois bar.

We have no documentation for any of his claims.

He may well be the greatest hoax in history.

Not content to wait for history, the incomparable Norman Podhoretz addressed the question recently in the *Wall Street Journal*: To be sure, no white candidate who had close associations with an outspoken hater of America like Jeremiah Wright and an unrepentant terrorist like Bill Ayers, would have lasted a single day.

But because Mr. Obama was black, and therefore entitled in the eyes of liberal dom to have hung out with protesters against various American injustices, even if they were *a bit* extreme, he was given a pass.

Let that sink in: Obama was given a pass—held to a lower standard because of the color of his skin.

Podhoretz continues: And in any case, what did such ancient history matter when he was also so articulate and elegant and (as he himself had said) *non-threatening*, all of which gave him a fighting chance to become the first black president and thereby to lay the curse of racism to rest?

Podhoretz puts his finger, I think, on the animating pulse of the Obama phenomenon—affirmative action.

Not in the legal sense, of course, but certainly in the motivating sentiment behind all affirmative action laws and regulations, which are designed primarily to make white people, and, especially, white liberals, feel good about themselves.

Unfortunately, minorities often suffer so that whites can pat themselves on the back.

Liberals routinely admit minorities to schools for which they are not qualified, yet take no responsibility for the inevitable poor performance and high drop-out rates which follow.

Liberals don't care if these minority students fail; liberals aren't around to witness the emotional devastation and deflated self-esteem resulting from the racist policy that is affirmative action.

Yes, racist.

Holding someone to a separate standard merely because of the color of his skin—that's affirmative action in a nutshell, and if that isn't racism, then nothing is, and that is what America did to Obama.

True, Obama himself was never troubled by his lack of achievements, but why would he be?

As many have noted, Obama was told he was good enough for Columbia despite undistinguished grades at Occidental; he was told he was good enough for the U.S. Senate despite a mediocre record in Illinois; he was told he was good enough to be president despite no record at all in the Senate.

All his life, every step of the way, Obama was told he was good enough for the next step, in spite of ample evidence to the contrary.

What could this breed if not the sort of empty narcissism on display every time Obama speaks?

In 2008, many who agreed that he lacked executive qualifications nonetheless raved about Obama's oratory skills, intellect, and cool character.

Those people—conservatives included—ought now to be deeply embarrassed.

The man thinks and speaks in the hoariest of clichés, and that's when he has his teleprompters in front of him; when the prompter is absent, he can barely think or speak at all.

Not one original idea has ever issued from his mouth—it's all warmed-over Marxism of the kind that has failed over and over again for 100 years.

(An example is his 2012 campaign speeches, which are almost word for word his 2008 speeches)

And what about his character?

Obama is constantly blaming anything and everything else for his troubles.

Bush did it; it was bad luck; I inherited this mess.

Remember, he wanted the job, campaigned for the task.

It is embarrassing to see a president so willing to advertise his own powerless-ness, so comfortable with his own incompetence.

(The other day he actually came out and said no one could have done anything to get our economy and country back on track).

But really, what were we to expect?

The man has never been responsible for anything, so how do we expect him to act responsibly?

In short: Our president is a small-minded man, with neither the temperament nor the intellect to handle his job.

When you understand that, and only when you understand that, will the current erosion of liberty and prosperity make sense.

It could not have gone otherwise with such an impostor in the Oval Office.

—Matt Patterson—*Newsweek*

ζ

What causes fights and quarrels among you? Don't they come from your desires that battle within you? You want something, but don't get it. You kill and covet, but you cannot have what you want. You quarrel and fight. You do not have because you do not ask God. When you ask, you do not receive because you ask with wrong motives, that you may spend what you get on your pleasures. You adulterous people, don't you know that friendship with the world is hatred toward God? Anyone who chooses to be a friend of the world become an enemy of God.—James 4:1-4

~

The following, written in 2016, are in the order in which they were written.

~*Vices to Break*~

she fights, history reveals her fright
—over and over, her life put into strife
religion used as stripes striping her rights
for ego, pride—darkening her light

holy books' truth—vaporized–
changed to idealize
her to be ostracized, at the rolling of dice

God† gave her to man, a gift in the night
brightening of lights
adding spice—knowledge in paradise
to man's uneventful life

centuries, centuries
ego-driven homicide–
destroying her life—husbands, sons
peeling her layers–
standing there, watching her bleed
holding a killer's knife

her knowledge sealed in formaldehyde
through man's driven genocide–
death in the night, burying her in hide
where she wails and cries
so man's wrong turns to right

centuries, centuries—change mystified–
her rights seem untied

equal seems amplified

it's all propagandized
way down deep inside
where truth lies—a mask is verified

to man, she's just trite
an instrument in subsidize
man to gratify—she deprived
seen only as a device
a material-like vice
easy to sacrifice without thinking twice
blaming her
for man's weaknesses outright

God† bless the man, standing in the light
seeing her *might*, breaking the vice
that sees her as a mere device

God† bless the man–
who stands by her side
instead of ahead, pushing her behind

God† bless the man–
who, to the ground, throws the knife
builds her in height
sees how high she can fly

man, who *beside* her, stands
sees clearly words of Jesus Christ†
peace in the light
for all, *equal* in right

(January 8, 2016)—*Dear men: You might think she wants your car, your money, and gifts, but the right woman wants your time, your smile, your honesty, your effort, and you choosing to put her as a priority.*—Author Unknown

If you are on my personal *Facebook* page, you know I'm currently reading *I Am Malala* by Malala Yousafzai, which is a true account of her life in Swat, Pakistan when the Taliban took over her country and on October 9, 2012, she was shot in the head by the Taliban for speaking out on the rights of girls to be educated. She was 15 years old.

She is the youngest recipient of the Noble Peace Prize.

(If you have not read this book, please do. You won't be disappointed.)

I'm not at all equaling my experience to hers.

It is far from being equal, but I do think it's rather interesting the year in which both of our strife took a turn for the worse. 2012.

It is also the same year in which *Proof of Heaven* was released, which is a true account of a neurologist's account of his near-death experience in which he learned during his after-life experiences the two things God gave us to have: *Free*-will and unconditional love.

Yes, these events couldn't be more interesting. Coincidence? You decide.

Last night, after reading Chapter 14 in Malala's book, I pulled out the *Bible* and reread the *Revelations*. It struck me hard.

The *Revelations* talk about *false prophets* over and over.

I don't think it's a coincidence that after the 7.6 earthquake in Pakistan in 2005, the Taliban had their hands on thousands of orphan children and turned them into evil soldiers.

In a way, what happened there during that period follows the *Revelations* really close, but, then again, so did the events that happened during the Holocaust...not as close, but somewhat similar.

Do I believe the world is coming to an end? No.

I have written a lot about events in the *Bible*.

I hope that I haven't misrepresented any of it.

Malala says that many misrepresent the *Quran* because it's first version was written in old Arabic, which few understand.

This makes me see my own misrepresentation of their holy book.

Her story also shows me how things are misrepresented when it comes to Muslims.

As she writes her story, she often refers to God in the same way as all Christians do.

This surprises me, but I welcome the surprise.

As I read Malala's words, I see the difference between Muslims and Islam.

There is a *big* difference.

My apologies are deep for this misunderstanding.

I am a learner always and I never tire of it.

No one should ever tire themselves from learning as the world is always changing and manipulation is easy.

Seeing the truth through it all is often not.

I often ask questions, but get no response, even though I have over 2,000 people from around the world on my personal *Facebook* page.

Reading first-hand accounts of world events is far better than reading news because you see it from the eyes of someone who has been there during the horror.

You come to a more clearer understanding in differences that aren't so different at all.

Night by Elie Wiesel gives the same vibe.

He was also 15 during his experience in the Holocaust.

As I read Malala's book, it's like reading *Night* all over again, but in a more detailed, horrifying view of suppression and damnation.

I don't know how you see these two events.

I can only tell you how I see them.

I see them as warnings.

Not the end of the world.

Two *false prophets* who came from nothing, gaining power so simple and easy.

These thoughts led me to *"Vices to Break."*

When my mind wonders to the ideals behind suppression, I can't help, but to look closer to home.

Why are women still put on the back-burner? You may not see it, but it is so.

Here's an example: A woman working in the South.

I have a [four]-year college degree, plus courses beyond that. I spent 11 years in the military, yet, my teaching salary, at its highest in 2014, was $42,000.

My day didn't just end when school ended.

I often stayed up way past midnight planning lessons, reading books, and grading papers.

I don't have any other example, so I will use [x] for this example. Zero college. Zero trade school.

Zero military.

At the time of our divorce in 2013, he was making over $70,000 a year.

He worked for a company that repaired boats. I worked to educate children.

Put *all* aspects of traditional beliefs aside: Which is more important: The education of minds or the repairing of boats?

Point: You can't repair boats unless you have some type of education.

Am I wrong?

Do you see where I'm going with this?

I saw this not only in the education field, but every where else.

Women are treated different.

They are seen in a lower mind-set.

After I was separated, I saw even worse.

A man could move from one woman to the next and this is looked at as normal behavior.

A woman on the same path is viewed as a whore. A man can cheat.

A woman who questions this behavior is beat, abandoned, scorned.

A woman has children (her body suffers the pain and disfigurement), raises them, takes care of the house, the yard, the cars, the bills (most of the time), the shopping, everything, and, in today's world, works [eight-plus]-hour days, and she is expected to take care of her man as well.

A man works, comes home, here and there fixes things around the house, the yard, goes to the camp, has a boat, has other toys, drinks with the boys, expects to be pleased by his wife, but doesn't go the extra mile to please her.

(Of course, you know this doesn't apply to all men...this is just a general forum of what I have seen.)

In my case, I've spoken with a lot of women after my strife...a *lot!*

After the ending of the relationship, they are blamed. For what, I have no idea.

They are ostracized, especially, when they demand the truth, they demand to be faced, and/or they speak out about what happened.

I love it now when I hear the word *drama*.

I now know exactly what it means.

This is in America!

When you read about accounts of what women have to face in other countries, you almost...*almost*...want to feel blessed for being somewhat *free*.

We are *not free* here in America.

Here in the South, nope.

People don't want it to be talked about.

That *hush-hush* syndrome.

Do you see all that a woman does?

(One paragraph up) and she is still not appreciated or respected.

There are some very good men out there.

I have a few very close men friends and I hear their voice. They are honorable.

Their minds are open and they are willing to set their prides aside when they finally get a good woman to walk by their side.

I admire them so much.

I first met these men as a hoping for them that I'd date them. No.

That wasn't the reason I met them.

God was showing me that there are, indeed, good men and these particular men would always be my friend, but they were not meant for me.

They were just meant to show me what a good man is. I value them.

I have said before that I'm often directed

to books when I question my work and the direction in which it is going.

As I'm reading this one, boy do I see the importance of my work.

Treating women badly, silencing them, making them feel unimportant in a subtle, silent manner is just as if you put a bullet to their head. I try not to treat people this way.

I'm very vocal if not in voice, in message.

I'd rather tell a person, get it off my chest, address a problem.

I'm, a lot of the times, blunt in text...not in person. Why?

Because I'm able to see their eyes, their expressions, their humanism.

In text, bla, bla, bla....

At times, I fear thinking no man will ever want a woman who speaks her mind so loud.

At times, I just want to go quiet, then I think back to the time when I was quiet and what happened because of that *quietness*.

I'm no longer afraid to show my aggravation because I'm thinking of who I am and what I've been through.

Never again, even when fear grips me of the loneliness I must face, will I let the fear control me.

Women: Getting along with a person is totally different from bowing down.

If a person ever makes you feel guilty about anything, blame of actions is being passed onto you.

(This may seem odd, but you have to see the similarities to this: The Taliban got the support of women by playing on their emotions telling them that they were precious and should be protected at all cost.

The women began seeing this *false prophet* as a knight in shining armor.

After he won them over, he instilled Shari law...read about that, then tell me how *precious* Islam thinks women are. It was all a lie!)

Knowledge is everything.

Understanding yourself is very important.

Knowing your worth is very important.

Not your material worth.

Your spiritual worth.

I'm sticking to the fact that a woman, especially, women over 40, should never give up what makes them happy for another to be happy.

Women *deserve* just as much as men do.

I keep seeing these messages—*If they don't make time for you, they are making time for someone else, and no one is too busy to include you in their life if they really want you there.*

I saw things as a child that I swore would never happen to me as an adult.

It happened all the same because a woman doesn't see it when she's in it. I know now.

I saw it a couple more times since then.

As a writer, writing books about abuse, I have realized that if something is at the forefront of your mind, it will keep coming to your life.

So, putting all else aside and finishing this work has become the most important thing in my life. Truth: I don't want it anymore in my life.

The same goes for all women.

If we all get this thought in our mind that we are all worth having knowledge, being treated as equal in the workforce (respect and pay-wise) is a must, being respected by men is key, we are not the blame for everything, then, maybe, things will change throughout the world.

Love the skin you're in because you are worth it.

Comments

•(Friend) You should not say, men. Maybe, say, certain kinda guy? Maybe?
What I find very confusing about a woman is this...the ones that show the most cleavage gripe about guys that send pics with their shirt off. Mixed signals...always mixed signals. My favorite saying! Say what you want, but want what you say, and if you're not getting what you are looking for, change what you are looking for.
Men don't operate with, on, off, on, off, maybe, kinda, sorta.
We just work on...are we good?
•(Me) Men are just as confusing.
At this point in my age, see work published today, I'm throwing up my hands and just concentrating on me and my work.
I fear it, but I'm reverting back to the old ways of courtship.
I've experienced all the news ways and they hold no water.
So, if I end up 50 and alone...so be it.
After the discussion with my parents, the body, eventually, fails us, but the heart goes on. Going after the heart is the best way.
That's how it was when I was growing up.
The body comes after the heart is won.
Women are careless these days, I'm one of them, to think it's our job to win the heart of a man byway of the body. Wrong.
It's the man's job to win the heart of the woman byway of her heart.
•(Friend) Yes, some woman are very careless, (I find they are the ones most ready).
The ones that think too much...those are the ones, I talk about that confuse me. They say, but don't do. Old ways of courtship?
Explain that one. See, that confuses me.
If you mean chase someone, gonna open the eyes a bit, guys over 45 don't chase. Men have to be fed past that age. Why?
Because, by then, we don't want to guess anymore...we wanna know. Do you want me or not is what we look for.
Too much work...this chasing stuff.
Is easier to go rent a chick for the night.
I read someone's post earlier and they said, easier said than done, on the part about just give up. I wish I could just give up. Ha!
Men being confusing? Maybe, the men you choose are confusing? And that may be because the ones you select are of your, steadfast, criteria
As I had stated other times...change your criteria...then...you will see a man less confusing.
Most older men, not old little boys, would rather have a woman first. Scars here and there become sexy conversations.
A bit of sagging, not a good word, feels tender, warm and more soft, and *more womanly.*
Sensual, provocative, luring, she knows how to touch, feel, be tender, yet...*kill your ass in bed.*
Woman now, (40s), want *tats*, and us grown men want a body that is proven and, for damn sure, more interested in a brilliant mind to boot.
Why do you think young guys, including old boys are so attracted to an older woman?

So, if you end up 50 and alone, then my point was made.
A lot of older women (past 40), go back to wanting those men, (old boys). When I was in my thirties, I dated several very young ladies. They wanted older men. Why? Experience and security.
What they were really getting, (myself included) were old boys, then all of a sudden, they turn 30 and their preferences changed.
When women, (not all) turn 40, plus they want that bad boy, (old boys) again...now all of a sudden, that physical becomes important to them.
Yeah, yeah, they want all the other bells and whistles, too, but...they want that *bad*...and if that is what ya want...well...see you at 50.
Real men don't wear pink...real men do love Jesus, and real men love real women. You know I keep giving you *top-secret* stuff.
I could be hung for telling dude secrets...and, geez, it would be so much more interesting using a phone communicating stuff like this...I know I would understand more of what you are saying. ☺
•(Me) Did you read my work I posted today? I'm a poet.
It doesn't mean every single thing I write about is about *me*...a lot are, but a lot are *in the moment* emotions that I tend to grab a hold of and use it the best way I know how, then the moment is gone, the work is written and the feeling disappears.
That's me in a nutshell when it comes to my writing.
I went through that *bad*-boy deal.
That part comes after the divorce and a woman is searching for anything to cover up what's hurting.
It goes on for a while until the weight lifts and she's sitting there *free*. Not wanting anything much at all.
I'm not going after no man again.
I guess those boots are going to have to find me, cross themselves, then wait for me to trip over them because that's the only way he'll find me. I'm tired of lies and betrayal. I have fibro.
It's a whole ball of mess and I don't really want to explain it again.
I figure the guy who's truly into me, he'll learn everything he needs to know.
Many of us women who have been through the darkness, we don't know what *real* looks like.
I know, personally, I think I find it, they like the pretty me, then they get to know the inside me and disappear. Happens all the time.
I've known three loves in my life. I guess I should be lucky.
They didn't love me the same. So, I, personally, give!
Over-45 women have enough of the boys.
Over-45 women have enough of the players, the lies, the deceivers, the manipulators, the abusers, the egos, the pride.
Over-45 women want truth, a good lover who's into her and not just himself, someone they can depend on, not money wise, emotional wise.
They need to know that if they fall on the floor and can't get up, that man who said he's *real* is going to gently pick her up without criticizing her or bringing her down because she stumbled and lose her balance.
Over-45 women are pass the stage of *sexy,* even though they can be sexy.
They want a guy who takes the time to really get to know them, but...but they aren't going to fall in love with a guy on the first or second or even third date.
I'm sorry...for me, a guy's going to have to work for it.
I, and I'm sure a lot of women feel this, gave to enough with no return to match. So, I'm alone at 50.
It's better than being with an abuser or someone who really can't handle the fire that comes with the package.
I know I can satisfy a man.
I'm very confident in that, but for that *one* to satisfy me...that's the one I want.
If not, I'd rather be alone at 50 if you want me to be honest.
•(Friend) All I can do is smile...always nice to smile.
•(Me) Yes.
•(Friend) My favorite is the last line...equal in right. Yes.
I read this. I liked it. As usual ☺ .

~*Warriors of Knowledge*~

knowledge is key, if you want to see
learn from history—don't repeat
go—teach
take the weak—set them *free*

~

(January 6, 2016)—As an educated woman, I know the privilege it is to have the education that I do.

Every woman in the world should have this privilege, should not be mocked by men, should never be hushed, should be respected beyond anything other than God.

Places where women are denied, those are the places where lack of everything exist.

I'm reading 19-year-old Malala Yousafzai's book. I adore her father.

In Swat, their home in Pakistan, he was an educator and Malala was his first born (not very accepted for a *girl* to be first born...those there wouldn't fair well here in America!).

He fought corruption a lot there.

To show a little about his character, which I would love to have witnessed:

The other principals took paying bribes for granted, but my father argued that if all the schools joined together they could resist, 'Running a school is not a crime,' he told them. 'Why should you be paying bribes? You are not running brothels; you are educating children! Government officials are not your bosses,' he reminded them; 'they are your servants. They are taking salaries and have to serve you. You are the ones educating 'their' children.— Ziauddin and Malala Yousafzai from in *I Am Malala* by Malala Yousafzai.

Comments
•(Friend) Go get 'em Karen.
•(Me) Go get who?
•(Friend) Great Malala.
•(Friend) She's my villager.
•(Friend) Karen, you are not just gorgeous, you have a sharp mind!
•(Me) Thank you very much.

—You want to know how easy it is to brainwash a nation, read *I Am Malala*.

I think it'll open up your eyes since it is modern times, and since many have forgotten how easy it was for Hitler to do it.

Fazlullah, a 28-year-old idiot who's only education was the lowering and raising of a local bridge in Pakistan, became their Hitler in 2005, using the earthquake of that year to spread his falsified ideology.

Malala's father's response to a teacher leaving to work on Fazlullah's building:

Your prime responsibility is to teach the students, replied my father.

No, I have to do this—said Nawab Ali (the teacher).

My father came home fuming.

If people volunteered in the same way to construct schools or roads or even clear the river of plastic wrappers, by God, Pakistan would become a paradise within a year, he said.

The only charity they know is to give to mosque and madrasa (which are 'charity schools' to teach militant skills).

Her father's great!

His response to her question to why the Taliban didn't want girls to be schooled was— *The pen is mighty.*

A wise man.

Free women aren't afraid to speak or write.

If you buy any book this year, buy this one.

Malala has started the Malala Fund which—*...believes that each girl, and boy, has the ability to change the world and that all she needs is a chance. To give girls this chance, the Fund aspires to invest in efforts that empower local communities, develop innovative solutions that build upon traditional approaches, and deliver not just basic literacy, but the tools, ideas and networks that can help girls find their voices and create a better tomorrow.*—from *I Am Malala* by Malala Yousafzai.

I always found that it's better to get a person's first-hand account, then to believe what is told through news broadcast and articles.

I've tried many times to get first-hand accounts through this medium, but always a fail.

Malala's account is truly amazing and horrifying.

No one listened to her father who spoke up about the ignorance going on around him.

Everyone was sucked into false preachings of idiots.

They didn't believe it could happen to them as the Germans believed it couldn't happen to them.

The same is when you're directly in the mask of abuse and find out later what had happened to you.

You're completely dumbfounded.

These people believed, then when it was time for the true mission of Fazlullah to be known, *wow* is all I can say.

History repeats every where. Get this book.

Read it, then stop being lost in the mask of false and see the truth or, like those in Swat, Malala's village, you'll lose.

Knowledge is everything.

~

(January 9, 2016)—Reposted an article titled *'Texas Passes Law Permanently Banning Muslim Sharia Laws'* by *Zionica.com*

Why do we even have to pass legislation on this? This is the United States of America.

We have a federal *Constitution* and state *Constitution*.

Voted for, passed by, for the people by the people.

We *should not* have to even choose *should we/shouldn't* we when it comes to other countries laws. *No.* No, and *hell no!*

You want to practice *your* country's laws, hello...*go back to your country!*

It's that simple. There's no need to explain.

You come here...*you give up your country's laws* and follow *all of ours!*

That's why *you must learn to speak English!*

How much more of this crap do we have to take?

~

(January 14, 2016)—*How Barack Obama is the Jackie Robinson of American politics: One was the first black major league baseball player, the other the first black president. Both men were insulted and unjustifiably opposed at every turn, but kept their dignity and grace and never sunk as low as the bigots. History judged Robinson's haters harshly, just as it will soon judge Obama's.*—Author Unknown

God be with me for saying what I'm about to say: This picture was shared by a friend to me.

I replied back, even posted my reply on the link that shared the picture.

This disturbs me a great deal.

One is a baseball player.

Did you hear that *baseball* player.

One is a United States President.

I beg your pardon to those agreeing with this picture. There is a big difference here. Big.

Does anyone know who Warren Harding is? He is white.

He is considered, up until now, the blackest mark on United States' history.

Do you know why?

Don't bother...I'm going to tell you.

Congress was shady. Big time.

He was going to rat them out.

It's that simple.

Here's what one internet site says about Harding—*He died while crossing the nation on a train tour during his third year in office. After his mysterious death, it was discovered that Warren Harding had been involved in several adulterous affairs and that his cabinet was severely corrupt. Many historians consider him one of the worst U.S. Presidents.*

Everything in this little paragraph is not true.

He died after the train ride which took him, before a mysterious stop along the way to Alaska, after he then went to California.

After becoming ill, he was seen by several university doctors in California who said he had food poisoning.

He was in a hotel alone with his shady wife when he died.

I say *shady* because she burned all his papers before calling in his death.

I read many things about him, never about *adulterous affairs.*

His cabinet and his wife played him like a

puppet, oh, Congress was heavily involved in that sex, drinking scandalous out-of-sight, out-of-mind, back-door political way of doing things.

So much so, Harding was going to testify against them.

Oh, right after his trip to Alaska.

His death was ruled as a heart-attack.

There are many other stories like this in our colorful history.

The *mysterious* deaths really get me.

Why don't they just say *murdered*?

Because they were.

If they weren't, then they would know exactly how they died and it wouldn't be labeled *mysterious*. Strange how that works.

I went bowling with a liberal from New York. I told him I didn't support Obama.

He asked me to explain the wrongs he'd done.

Doesn't anyone read or, rather, study the *Constitution of the United States of America*?

I don't need to sit here and teach anyone anything.

I'm part of the greatest nation that there has ever been. I love its history.

It hasn't always done the right thing, but when genocide shows its ugly face, my country has always faced it head on.

My country was started on the ideals of a country where anyone can practice *freely* their religion. That's right.

All those who weren't natives came here because of religion.

Over the years, we have come to respect all religions, except those that believe in killing us.

No, that doesn't fair too well with us.

If you studied American history and its politics, you see when the corruption began and why.

I stopped my poetry books on the U.S. Presidents with Coolidge.

Yes, I will publish them.

I couldn't stand the corruption anymore.

I couldn't stand the lies. The greed.

I may finish. I may....

Warren Harding served this country as its President from 1921 to 1923.

He's consider the blackest mark on this country's history.

All the faults were placed on him.

Of course. He was dead.

Obama surpasses anything blamed on Harding.

Obama, as president of this country, is our Commander-in-Chief.

Though overlooking the severity of the usage of *under-qualified* when it comes to this position and referring to Obama, as Commander-in-Chief, he is sworn to protect his people.

He is given the sword and shield and heads all those standing the wall to protect and defend.

Without going in detail to anything else he's done wrong...he failed to protect and defend. He failed.

How many people died on American soil in mass killings under his command?

It's nothing to do about guns.

Guns didn't kill anyone.

Guns can't pull its own trigger.

People killed people.

All those people died on this soil because the Commander-in-Chief didn't do his job.

He didn't honor anyone with grace.

He failed to attend funerals.

He went on vacations instead.

His wife failed to dress properly and be the lady that this country honors and deserves.

He can't even make a decent speech without teleprompters.

I heard one...ummm...ummmm.

When asked by the American people to show proof of his birth, what happened there? That's just simple, mindless stuff.

I ask everyone...really?

We always had a government separate of church and state and this guy brings religion as a forefront, and it's acceptable. Why?

He brought race back up to the forefront.

Why? Etc., etc., etc. Truth.

No one wants to hear because the color of a person's skin, you're willing to forgo your *freedoms*, your inheritance? Really?

You compare the life of a United States President to a baseball player.

Are you serious?

Where's the logic, the brains?

I'm ashamed of some of my countrymen.

Let me end this with a simple lesson in logic: A baseball player (white or black...disgraced or honored) throws a damn ball, then hits it with a damn bat.

A United States President (white or black) leads the most powerful country in the world.

P.S. The difference between haters and people who are criticizing because of the wrongs a person does: Education.

   Oh, that would be knowledge along with the fear of God! Class dismissed!

~Labored Hands~

sitting behind desks, staring at screens
not having to think, brings on sink–
undermining, humanistic dreams

imprisoned behind walls–
cubicled little stalls
halting individual thoughts
living without reason
–not moving one inch
without boss-directed instruction
tears apart what dreams do call

leaving it all, computers with decisions
absent a soul
brings minds to complete fold
lost is time—human connection
by-way, programming direction
laboring hands, no longer, that of man
leaving him wondering
exactly where he stands

(January 27, 2016)—*Out of the current confusion of ideals and confounding of career hopes, a calm recognition may yet emerge that productive labor is the foundation of all prosperity.*—from *Shop Class as Soulcraft* by Matthew B. Crawford

~Personal's Touch~

I pump my own gas
the window shield—bugs in mass
there's a bucket, sometimes, none at all

no tip to give from my pocket
for just the smile, that personal attendant
who used to give it for nothing more–

raise my hood
my oil, my water, my wipers
even air in my tires, insuring my safety
–knowing this caring service
me, I'd resurface—again and again
'til my name—by heart—learned
where I'm from, experiences in life come

understand frustrations
as life moves on in mail
inviting invitations
christmas-card validations
hung behind cash-register walls
of a job well done

I so miss that station, that attendant

my car, the specialty
but my world, the better in receive
personal touch's attention

~Of Craftsmen~

starting in nothingness–
thoughts form, images born
slowly into something
through maddening storms
that *something* starts to begin

from nothing to anything to something

not needing to prove
nor anyone to soothe—just caught in *do*

our humanistic side–
bettering another's life
–tangible and alive
working, shaping—engineering in vive
bringing in light, harmony and peace
as visions awaken in see

not needing to explain, just point a finger
of a well-worked hand

a physical thing—woven and crafted
taken in kind, patience—mistakes
doing-over, starting again
'til perfection's end

leaving behind
what's been imagined in mind

nothing to anything to something

~Artisan's Virtue~

what are you, surround by such new
–thrown together in masses, conforming
sitting around—waiting, searching
ideas—someone else's
flowing, individual spirits in erosion
with all this *seeking* commotion

minds of artisans hold true to *self*
paving roads
–a different set of cards dealt

avoiding apps of commercial
–holding *self's* principle
going beyond reasonable–
artisan's think in logical

how will this help–
apply *inward* direction
avoiding mass productions–
minds laid out

stacked nice and neat, shelf after shelf

the *different*–
artisan's unwelcomed sentiment
plows through, seeing beyond new
takes what's there—desires in view
making life better
for the likes of me and you

~

(February 8, 2016)—*Congressional Black Caucus. Congressional White Caucus. Congressional Asian Caucus. Congressional Latino Caucus. Oh, I see...but everyone else is racist, right?*—Author Unknown

No offense to any color cause I'm far from being racist, but this makes a lot of sense.

Why does any race need this if we are all children of God?

The Cajun french and the native Americans were treated unfairly, too...you don't see them singling themselves out. Do you know why?

Because when we say we have faith in God's power...we actually mean it.

We don't need greed and pride to work for us. God does!

—Posted historical and modern pictures black and whites holding confederate flags.

When someone crosses me, I will stand up for myself.

Sorry, surviving a narcissist does that to a person.

So...to the gentleman who rudely criticized one of my friends on here, not to mention *me*...history has it's complications.

The American Civil War was one of them.

Example: The owner of Oak Ally actually took his slaves to Texas so the northern aggressors wouldn't kill them because that's what they came here to do...burn our ancestors homes and livelihood down and kill as many confederates as they could including slaves who weren't even fighting while the ignorant President, at the time, as well as, the ignorant general of the Union army, had *slaves* in their homes!

That's *fact! Historical facts!*

Yeah, you don't hear about any northern places being burned, do you?

If you don't know this, then, maybe, you should come down south and ask.

I know some plantations here where *still* ancestors of slaves work the land...in Louisiana...I don't know about other places.

I don't live there.

I live in Louisiana where we have our flaws, traditions that need to be broken, but respect for each...we have.

A lot of our foods came from the mixing of our french, native American (sorry...I wrote Indians earlier...my mistake), and black cultures.

This Confederate flag stands for the preservation of *our* heritage.

Just because it doesn't represent yours, does *not* give you the right to try and strip us of ours!

We don't go up there and try to strip you of yours. We've had enough.

The kkk animals did not originate from the south.

What do you think the carpet beggars came here for...to penetrate us and bring us to our knees. They almost did!

Hence, the kkk...people here in the deep south...we are not white.

We are mixed...and quite enjoy this label. Don't insult my friends.

We preserve our culture at *all* cost.

The traditions we need to overcome and change, trust me, we will deal.

This is my heritage. My war flag.

The same as these men here.

You can throw that they *made their slaves fight*...all you want.

They wouldn't decorate a *slave*...now would they?

I know what it takes to get awarded in the service. *You have to earn it.*

These men I celebrate.

They stood up when cowards ran.

They knew truth when others twisted it.

Their families suffered as my french and native American ancestors suffered.

You can't win here.

You lose when you tried to dis my heritage.

I pose this question to *all* those who dishonor my heritage: *Did you ever stand for anything other than ridicule those who stood for freedom?*

~

(February 12, 2016)—Posted an article titled *'Are Your Chicken Nuggets From China?'*—from *huffingtonpost.com*

Okay! Yeah, no politics on my page.

Right! This is getting out of hand.

This article...this is *not okay*!

Please read, then share!

If you are from Vietnam, please comment!

I had my nails done in December by a very intelligent Vietnamese.

She recently graduated from L.S.U. as a bio-chemical engineer.

She did nails to pay her way through college and was working through the holidays while she waited to take her test for her certifications, then off to get the *big* job.

So, credibility on the following information...I would say is smart, educated, and validated.

Her family gets newspapers from Vietnam and they have direct family still living there.

Vietnam has a trade agreement with China.

China does not like Vietnam very much.

Never has.

China is poisoning the Vietnamese by-way of food they are shipping there to be sold in supermarkets.

According to this young woman, no one is dying, but the people in Vietnam are getting boils on their eyes and ugly rashes.

She said the Vietnam newspapers are reporting this, but no one else is.

She also said that the people there are scared and trying to grow what they need to get on their own, and/or trading locally from people they trust.

I would think a person smart enough to get a degree in bio-chemical engineering doesn't have any need to tell a tale, and would be more concerned about her family and what is happening to them.

With all that is happening in this freaking country and how everyone is just ignoring it like it's not happening, you would think more people would be like *what the hell*!

Why...*why* do we *need*, in the first place, *need*, to send our food overseas for packing... or anything else?

Does anyone see this as psychotic?

—Posted an article titled *'Zika Virus'*—from *Wikipedia*, the free encyclopedia

...while Colombia, the Dominican Republic, Ecuador, El Salvador, and Jamaica advised women to postpone getting pregnant until more is known about the risks.

Isn't this interesting...these are countries who aren't Islam...yet...a virus...that was not much on the radar since the 50s...but since 2014 is suddenly wide-spread...and you think this is natural!?

A virus that forces what Islam wants... Christians to *stop* making babies!

Can we be any more ignorant not to see through this shit?!

~

(February 21, 2016)—*Be with those who bring out the best in you, not the stress in you.*—Author Unknown

To the one who made that *Facebook* pic comparing Adrenal to meth that's going around, and to *all* those who shared it: Please remove yourself from society!

I'm not only speaking for myself, but for every parent who has their child on Adrenal.

I could go into a whole lesson here, but I'm not...stupid is just stupid...and you can't fix that no matter how hard you try.

There is no comparison here...*period*!

All you mothers who have an *ADD* or ADHD child, thumbs up to *you*!

Do *not* let idiots like this put doubt into your mind.

That is the devil...pure and simple.

You have *enough* to worry about!

These are people who want attention because they don't have anything useful to give to society, so they take from it instead.

They lack empathy and sympathy and just plain ole don't give a damn how they make others feel.

All mothers and people on Adrenal... you went to a *medical* doctor, you *have* a prescription for a reason!

You are doing right! Relax. Chill.

You *do not* deserve this kind of *stress*!

Those taking Adrenal with*out* a prescription...maybe, you should do your research.

If any medication is taken without a reason, you are damaging your body.

It's that simple.

Medication...I don't like, but when a patient that *has* a *reason* to take a medication, it's because *there is* a *reason* and doctors *monitor them! My point is made.*

God is great *all* the time.

Comments
▪(*Friend) Literally the only thing separating the chemical composition of adderall from that of meth is three molecules.
▪(Friend) True.
▪(Me) Please send me your research.
I really do want to read it. Thank you.
▪(Me) See my research...from one site...one above.

—Posted an article titled *'Difference Between Adderall and Methamphetamine'*—from *differencebetween.net*

I felt I had to address this because this doesn't just affect me.

It affects those who were on Adderall, including me and my son, and all those mothers who are trusting in this drug.

Adderall: I apologize for my earlier spelling. There are several spellings that I come across.

The spelling with the *n* is wrong and I get stuck on it sometimes.

The difference between Adderall and Meth are very important to those who are blind and really don't care what they say...this is not just for myself who *is* carefully watched by doctors...from EKGs to blood tests every few months because Adderall's an amphetamine, which is a controlled narcotic.

So is most pain medications, even some medications that treat cancer and heart disease!

Amphetamine is also found in common cold medications. Get your facts straight!

Be very careful what you say when it comes to drugs like these.

When Adderall is prescribed to a patient, it is because their body needs help.

I know *how* Adderall works.

For someone *not* prescribed this drug, it goes straight to the heart...causing it to beat rapidly.

For someone who *is* prescribed this drug, it goes to the *brain* first, acting sort of like a bridge...that closes the gap that's missing.

For those who do *not* understand why some of us take this drug, you need to get seriously educated first before speaking.

For myself, I'm carefully monitored by a psychologist and a medical doctor because of this particular drug and fibro.

If you think differently, please take my pictures (I've been taking Adderall since 2008) and compare them to a person on meth for less than a year!

Their outside appearance is nothing compared to what is happening to their *insides*!

This is coming up because [x] is trying to debunk me, weaken my credibility.

He's been doing this for years...telling everyone that the medications I took and take messed up my brain! Hence—*she's crazy.*

Sorry, dear [x]...leave me the hell alone!

P.S...I *am* a narcissist...everyone has a bit of narcissist in them.

All artist of any kind of art are narcissist to the extreme, but...but *get this right*...we are of the good narcissist!

We *have a need* to better *man kind not hinder it*! Did you hear that?

Because I think some ears are full of wax!

You do *not* have to take my word for it.

I've posted videos of a PhD, have his videos on my [video] page...I'd advise you watch them or buy his book because you seriously need education!

The *bad* narcissist denies there is anything wrong with them.

They will do what ever they can to maintain control of their world...tell lies, beat, control, mentally abuse, even kill.

Me...I will always see a therapist because I lived with one for 20 freaking years.

He is still messing with my children's minds.

Me...I'm staying the hell away.

I have blocked him totally from my page, but he constantly goes through other people's pages to see me.

Friends tell me when he post something stupid, even when I don't want to know.

I *have no* desire to spy on him. *None*!

This picture that this post is about was on his page. Still...trying to discredit me.

To [x]: It won't freaking work!

Get the hell over yourself.

My work is about *me* and what happened to me.

Too bad you are [x]...always will be.

You caused this shit.

Apparently, you thought I was dumb! Wrong.

I'm a writer, and I'm writing about my experience to help other people who fall prey to narcissists...the *bad* freaking kind! So, get *over* yourself. Leave me alone.

Stop lying to our children.

My angry arises because you keep lying to them.

I parent.

You apparently don't see the need to understand what you are doing to their minds. I do.

Being a psychopath and being angry are two totally different things.

Believe me, I see therapists to fight all this anger because of the narcissist...you dear [x]!

Get help! That's all I have to say.

Article follows along with website:

Adderall vs Methamphetamine—Adderall and Metamphetamine are both drugs which have a high potential for abuse.

Although used as prescription drugs in some cases, its recreational use can lead to addiction.

The article below will help you understand the difference between the two.

What is Adderall and Methamphetamine?— Adderall, also known as amphetamine mixed salts, is a drug used to treat Attention Deficit Hyperactive Disorder (ADHD) and Narcolepsy.

Narcolepsy is a chronic neurological disorder caused by the inability of the brain to regulate sleep-wake cycles.

Studies show that long term treatment with amphetamines decreases the abnormality of the structure and function of the brain found in people with ADHD.

Amphetamines have also been proven to reduce disruptive behaviors and hyperactivity in children with ADHD.

Children on amphetamines have also shown subsequent improvements in terms of relationships with family members, in terms of attention spans and a slight change in I.Q levels. They become less impulsive.

Amphetamines improve memory and are therefore used as a test taking aid by many students to enhance performance during examinations.

It is also used by athletes to increase stamina and performance.

Therefore, it's common knowledge that recreationally, amphetamines are highly misused.

Methamphetamine, in contrast, is a white crystalline drug, also known as crystal meth.

It is a psychotic stimulant that is used for the treatment of obesity and to some extent for ADHD.

However, it is rarely prescribed because of the high risk involved of being a highly addictive substance.

Recreationally, methamphetamine is used to increase sexual desire, elevate mood and increase energy.

Unlike amphetamine, methamphetamine is a neurotoxic drug, which causes brain damage.

People who abuse the drug consume it by inhaling it through the nose, smoking it or injecting it with a needle.

Some even take it orally and feel like continuing with it because of the sense of well-being it offers.

However, it destroys the life of the user from the very beginning.

Crystal meth is used by individuals of all ages, but is most commonly used as a *club drug*, taken while partying in night clubs or at rave parties.

Difference between their *side effects*: The side effects vary on the amount of drug used.

Adderall impairs thinking and reactions.

The most common side effects include irregular heartbeats, elevated or reduced blood pressure, dry mouth, fast and deep breaths, pain or burning sensation while passing urine, painful erection of the penis, which is a rare side effect, taking more than usual, extreme happiness or sadness, alertness, insomnia and mood swings.

If you are prescribed Adderall and experience any of these symptoms while on the medication, it is important to consult the prescribing doctor immediately.

Methamphetamine is a dangerous and potent chemical that first acts as a stimulant, but, then begins to systematically destroy the body.

Thus, it is associated with serious conditions, including memory loss, aggression, psychotic behavior and potential heart and brain damage.

Loss of appetite, hyperactivity, dilated pupils, flushed skin, irregular heart-beats, hypertension, hypotension, dry skin and dizziness are some of the other side effects.

More serious effects can include insomnia, confusion, hallucinations, anxiety and paranoia.

In some cases, overdose can cause convulsions that lead to death.

An important side effect, which must be made note of is the *meth-mouth*.

The toxic ingredients in methamphetamine lead to severe tooth decay, which causes the teeth to become loose abnormally quickly.

The teeth become black, stained, and rotten, often to the point where they have to be removed.

Summary: Adderall is a salt of amphetamine, which is prescribed for ADHD, narcolepsy and abused recreationally as a performance enhancing drug.

Methamphetamine or crystal meth is a highly addictive narcotic drug with more health risks than benefits and is classified illegal worldwide.

It absolutely must not be consumed owing to serious threat to life.

~Dripping Deeds~

all these things—this past ring
turning me to nothing, or so it seemed
it wanted to deem

inside—burned—these dreams
traditions, situations, *steadifications*
kept me in isolation

in my mind, all these things
keeping me out of *free*
doing something, everything

—just plain ole nothing

years passed—all those things
everyone's ring, except my own thing

I held on—whatever I could
—managed on my own, prices I've paid
Lord†, in this *now*, up against walls
asking *how*

these dreams, now, all these dreams
bursting at seams
at every turn, me—burned
oh! how I yearn

how to get what I so dreamed

age has taken its toll—time—stole
all those things, for me, leaving nothing
dreams to hold

praying—a clean slate
let it not be too late
don't let this *nothing* be my fate

I pray—change it all—take me from fall
I've battled, I've fought—dues—paid
in my heart, this dream
You†, my Lord†, brought

help me find a way
out of this dark swirl, send me into twirl
grant me, I pray—will, determination–
please move this mountain
shower me with love
—on these knees, I pray

open doors
so these dreams You've† given me–
can move forth
so I may, even in the tiniest way
with my mind, hands, spirit
use my gift—use all of it
create, make a better world
for every man, woman, boy, girl

please, Lord†, cast out all strife
with all my strength, help me fight

yes, my precious Lord†–
bring me to pure light
with the fruits of my awakened gift
—live the rest of my life
with the one who sees all my right
who keeps me in the total of *free*
—even after knowing, the truth of me

(March 23, 2016)—*Forget about all the reasons why something may not work. You only need to find one good reason why it will.*—Author Unknown

Never quit. If you stumble, get back up. What happened yesterday, no longer matters. Today's another day, so get back on track and move closer to your dreams and goals. You can do it.—Author Unknown

I have a lot of marketers on my personal page.

I've been reading this magazine *Success from Home.*

There's an article in the October 2015 issue titled '*Life On Your Terms.*'

In this article they highlight—*Five Advantages to Being Your Own Boss—1. Creative Control 2. Pink-Slip Free 3. The Sky is the Limit. 4. Healthier Morale. 5. Plan Your Own Retirement.*

It's a great article.

I know no one wants to hear the negative side of life, but you have to face it anyway.

You *will* face it anyway.

So, why not get it out the way and move on.

Everyone is going after the same thing: Success. It's an admirable stride.

It's also a cut-throat world.

I got into the marketing world and experienced it. No.

Not one on one, but I watched it from afar. Stealing ideas. Pride.

I've learned no one is better than the other.

Some have better skills than others.

Some have gone through the trenches and are trying to teach others how to avoid the falls, then you have some who criticize them for doing it. That's just plain ole silly.

Why would you do that?

If someone's gone through all the bad, and, then takes the courage to show you how *not* to do that, then listen, they aren't doing it to mock you.

Sure, if they are in a program that if they sign you up, and you follow them, they do get a money gain.

So, they will help you get a money gain, too. All win. Why whine about it?

We all make mistakes.

All of us who decided to be *our own boss* have our own reasons and they are *all* good reasons.

A lot of us, God made the choice for us.

A lot of us are creative people.

Okay, what has that got to do with it? A lot.

Most are creative minds...now this is *born* creative minds.

(To prove this fact, just take any person who is a creative person and who's past the age of 40 and look at their resume.

There *will* be, at least...*at least*...15 or more jobs on there. Why is that?

Because creative minds like to explore.

They get tired easily, or rather bored, and they are moving to their gift...the reason behind their creative mind.)

The rest, just got tired of building someone else's empire.

Oh, there's a small few who might have gotten a bit in trouble with the law and, they have a record (which that is a law, I believe is in the works, of changing on job applications), so it's hard for them to find decent employment.

So, for one reason or other...online marketing becomes a choice...or a must.

As I click on the accepting of new friends, which has become an every-day thing these days, a lot of them are around my age or older. I see the connection in a way.

We are at that stage in life where we have raised our families and now we get to finally...finally chase that dream that's been buried in the back of our minds for as long as we can remember.

I think it's a wonderful thing.

This is not the only reason *"Dripping Deeds"* bled on the page this morning.

I've been reading so much on my *Facebook* page.

I've been talking to my close friends and family a lot lately, that all these emotions have been twisting inside me so much that last night at midnight, after a long hot bath, I got dressed and went to the local park and went swinging. I'm such a kid at heart.

Going swinging in the middle of the night is one of my *escapes*. The air in my hair.

The rush of the fall when the swing brings me back down.

The feeling of almost being a bird in the sky. Have you ever had a flying dream?

I used to have them a lot when I was a young girl.

Well, swinging is as close as I've come to that dream.

It's the feeling of *free* and staying young as long as I can.

Many people my age don't dare get on swings anymore and I have to ask why?

Who says you can't still be young?

"Dripping Deeds"...all those mistakes we did when we were young, all those sacrifices we did for everyone else, putting aside all those dreams we had...now at the middle stage in life, we find ourselves alone, single.

Maybe, God is saying—*It's your time.*

If you are having a hard time finding a way to make that dream happen, maybe, you are doing it wrong.

I know when I got back to my writing, I kept going round and round.

I kept repeating everything and not getting anywhere.

It took going through self-discovery, learning my truth that led me to knowing where exactly I fit in, in the great scheme of things.

I'm still not exactly sure where I'm headed, but neither did Macy or Hershey, both I've written about. Look them up.

They lost over and over again.

They didn't win until way after their *middle* part of life.

This is the stage in life where our *beginning* really begins.

We have to trust the journey.

A simple thing to do is to support each other.

I get deterred when people question what I'm doing. Why do that?

Just let me follow my heart. Support me.

I'll support you and let the chips fall where they will. After all, faith is the best way to go.

Those who had the most faith in themselves and what they believed in were the ones who succeeded.

Those who listened to others were the ones you never hear about.

I guess you can just believe what you want. I tend to see things for what they are.

After all, when I pick up a Hershey's *Kiss*...I picture, in my head, that young man pushing a cart down the street yelling—*Candy!* without one dime to his name.

That man who no one believed in.

Today, everyone knows what a Hershey's *Kiss* is. Isn't that something?

Believe in yourself.

So, I leave you with a prayer, print it up, tape to your desk, read it every day, remind yourself that your past is the past.

Ask the Lord to move those mountains, open doors, pave your way.

I just feel He sent these words to me to pass to you, to help you build your strength.

Use it. Don't. Entirely up to you.

The fruits are waiting. Do your gift.

The end part of *"Dripping Deeds"* I added on for those who are wishing for that special someone to share the fruits with.

I know I am.

For me...I would like to bring someone along for the ride, be there when the Lord awards me the fruits, but, of course, that's for Him to decide, now isn't it? Faith.

All things come in His time.

We just have to trust. Amen.

*—How to create miracles: Step 1—Pray, Step 2—Believe, Step 3—Receive—*Author Unknown

When you're in battle, you have to say—*Nope, you don't get to win!*

That's my take on things.

As per my earlier post, I'm sitting here thinking, laughing. I had such a good day.

I really need to share...a bit of my private self because when God's testimony shows, it out-weighs that evil whore's crap every time!

I had a trip into town.

On my way home this thought kept going through my mind—*Go see your sister.*

I wanted to.

I've had so much crap going on and the confusion so much that I just wanted to cry... all of it taking me from the work I need to do.

I argued inside my mind and took the exit to home.

I kept this up until the next road to my sister's house came and there I go, turned down it.

Next thing I know, I'm pulling up in her drive. It felt good.

We had a very good visit, then my niece shows up, then...this...this is where God is truly doing His thing in my life.

I'm not bragging...I'm showing you that if you stick to your faith, He comes and that evil whore (the devil) comes to fight.

I got my car this week.

I prayed for an answer and that was it.

You may not think so, but after all I've been through since last August, it's an answer! I've been missing my sweet daughter.

A lot. I worry. I'm a mom, give me a break.

My niece suddenly says her name, then, out of the blue, there she is!

She lives [five] hours away and there she is standing right in front of me, and she's got herself a car, too!

It's the same as in 2014 when we were so damn broke and we both got jobs the same week! It gets better.

My son walks up the drive. God!

Of course, as in my earlier post, you see

how the devil came in and tried to break in.

That's not all...my oldest son sends me a video of hail that took place for 40 minutes way up in Northern U.S., then I began writing this here post and my lights completely go out.

My life is never boring for very long I can tell you that.

I thought I'd share this little piece before I got back to work.

You know, you can be private about a lot of things in your life.

God's testimony, you should share because He's that great. He's working in my life.

I feel it. I see it.

I see what Joyce Meyer talks about when she talks about how the devil comes in and tries to steal our thunder.

I have said many times I'm a sinner.

I have also said many times I'm one hell of a stubborn child, and this...God surely knows!

In silence, I took people's crap, and it led me to abuse.

I think some out there think that it's, maybe, a weakness that they can take advantage of.

I think God is showing them that—*No, my dear children, it's not.*

I've learned that He has a funny way of showing us how He handles things.

He uses us for His purpose.

When the devil comes in the mix, He uses us a little harder.

You have to stand up for those who are too weak to stand up for themselves.

If you don't, then who will?

I had a very good day. Nope!

It doesn't win.

God wins because no matter how weak I may seem, I am never that weak to let go of my faith.

Remember that when you are faced with something that just doesn't seem right.

I love.

You can love, too, but you can't let the evil come in and steal your thunder.

I saw my sister's beautiful smile today... that was worth all, and, then my children and niece...well...that was all the icing I needed for the most perfect day!

Believe, then you receive.

God is great all the time.

All the time God is great!

Yes, indeed, I said that out loud...and, you can bet your ass, I'll say it again! Amen.

~*Unformalize*~

it attacks you—you cry out
but before you didn't guard the door
why ask—*what for*

when you did nothing to detour
all this blood and gore

you have all the power
–stop this crying and howling
why has your heart grown sour
–have you forgotten
who stands on the tower

you are bitter–
maybe you should reconsider
–instead of sitting in a church
on some comfort's perch
–maybe deep inside
open your heart—search

just to say His† name
won't give you fame
sorry, to Him†, that's just lame
all those silly cries—wasteful moans–
you did that on your own

you let that evil whore
into your inside core—its barren waste
like fine wine you joyfully taste
without considering, it's the wrong way

He'll† give you a better glass–
that'll kick that evil whore's ass

are you up for the task
damn! all you have to do—open up—ask

all this blood—guts—lying in streets
while you sit in fine seats
getting ready to eat
–you moved all out of *free*
your lies, betrayal, deceit
not caring who's blood seeps

shame! shame!—hear Him†, hear Him†

He† pleads for you to see–
before you too
that evil whore—out pours
your blood on streets

(March 24, 2016)—*Realize that everything connects to everything else.*—Leonardo da Vinci

The world will not be destroyed by those who do evil,

but by those who watch them without doing anything.—
Albert Einstein

Hear the word of the Lord, you rulers of Sodom; listen to the law of our God, you people of Gomorrah! 'The multitude of your sacrifices—what are they to me?' says the Lord. 'I have more than enough of burnt offerings, of rams and the fat of fattened animals; I have no pleasure in the blood of bulls and lambs and goats. When you come to appear before me, who has asked this of you, this trampling of my courts?

Stop bringing meaningless offerings! Your incense is detestable to me. New Moons, Sabbaths and convocations—I cannot bear your evil assemblies. Your New Moon festivals and your appointed feasts my soul hates. They have become a burden to me; I am weary of bearing them.

*When you spread out your hands in prayer, I will hide my eyes from you; even if you offer many prayers, I will not listen. Your hands are full of blood; wash and make yourselves clean. Take your evil deeds out of my sight! Stop doing wrong, learn to do right! Seek justice, encourage the oppressed. Defend the cause of the fatherless, plead the case of the widow.—*Isaiah 1:10-17

~

(March 25, 2016)—Say it for what it is: *Crusade!*

XM Radio...interesting concept and on my first long trip today I listened to all this news on the icicle people.

They labeled it over and over *The World War on Christianity*...I'm currently listening to TV...this is *why* I don't have TV...do they really sit back and listen to how evil they sound. Does anyone remember *God*?

Does anyone understand His power?

Does anyone understand the reality of *evil*?

I'm really in wonder if there are really any adults left in this world. It's a very sad reality.

Abuse.

That's only a tipping point to what's really going on in this world.

You have forgot what truly matters, and His head is bowed and the tears are rolling down His cheeks. It's Good Friday.

A reminder that He, in body form, was denied.

He is still being denied, even after all He's proven. Hasn't He shown you enough?

When His wrath comes, don't be a hypocrite and cry wolf.

That's all I have to say. Sad.

You won't find my happy ass sitting in some sorry ass church on Sunday.

I will be doing my gift because He doesn't have to prove to me anymore.

He's showed me enough and He keeps showing, even when He doesn't have to.

He just thinks He has to because I whine.

A father babying His child.
My faith doesn't shake.

~

(March 26, 2016)—*Answer me quickly, O Lord; my spirit fails. Do not hide Your face from me or I will be like those who go down to the pit. Let the morning bring me word of Your unfailing love, for I have put my trust in You. Show me the way I should go, for to You I lift up my soul. Rescue me from my enemies, O Lord, for I hide myself in You. Teach me to do Your will, for You are my God; may Your good Spirit lead me on level ground. For Your name's sake, O Lord, preserve my life; in Your righteousness, bring me out of trouble. In Your unfailing love, silence my enemies; for I am Your servant.—*Psalm 143 Selah

It hurts when the truth reveals itself.

It reveals itself in pieces.

I wrote a post yesterday while waiting at the VA on the *icicle* people. The lie.

How blind we are!? The lie.

It's so easy to fool people.

It's just mastery of that evil whore.

It likes to use people as its puppets.

I write a lot about the *self* and our individual *I*. That's really important.

Each heart has to fully open up and reveal its own truth in order to fully know itself before it can help others with anything.

I still don't know my whole truth, but God is sure showing me a lot, and it hurts.

You can preach to me all day about what you think you see in me, you don't see it all.

The reason behind that is because you haven't come to terms with your own truth, even if you think you have.

How do I know this?

Those *icicle* people are still causing havoc across the globe. That's how I know.

What's happening in our own personal lives is small peanuts to what God is allowing to happening on the global scale.

Don't you see. It's His unconditional love.

Free-will. We all have a choice.

We can stand by and just live in our lives or take action.

I see the choices being made so plainly.

You don't. More people are dying.

The trader you *elected* as your leader, what did he do when those people mourned the lost of their country men? That's your answer.

You are blind to the reality.

You are in the denial stage of the five stages of grief and don't even see it.

What do you think I've been writing about all of this time?

This isn't just about abuse on the single, personal level. You are so gullible.

Every time I get buried into my work pushing me closer to my finish line, I have someone coming in trying to change my mind, trying to *privatize* me. Why?

Do you see?

This war going on in this world is much bigger than all of us.

I've recently spoken to a number of people who understood what I meant without me having to explain.

I found that odd, but is it odd?

Why are there so many questions when the answer is so clear?

You have lost your faith in God!

Tomorrow is Easter Sunday.

Jesus rises from the dead.

A lot of you will attend a building.

Pretend you are a church-goer.

A Christian. *Pretend* is the key word.

When you leave that church, you will go to someone's house, your kids will hunt some eggs, you will drink some beer or wine, and eat a lot of food.

Somewhere...someone will be dying because they believe in Jesus Christ!

You will not be thinking about that because you will feel safe.

I guarantee you someone will be dying because they believe in Jesus Christ. Why?

Because a war is going on and you are not paying attention because you have lost your true faith.

Evil is at play and you read, you talk your little talk on *Facebook*, you may discuss it at work as you slave to the government who no longer cares about this country, which was based on Christianity, you may post a few quotes or pictures, but that is the extent of your concern as you sit in your leisure as someone dies because they *are* true Christians!

On the smaller scale, my faith was tested by people who told me they believed in Christ, but their actions proved otherwise.

Psalm 143 ask God to do away with the enemies of the believers, so that the believers can continue on doing His will.

You can't ask God to do the deed if you aren't willing to take on the responsibility.

What are you expecting to happen as you sit in your lazy-boy, flicking through channels?

What are you expecting to happen as you sit there complaining about what you can't do as you allow that evil whore to take over your mind?

What are you expecting to happen knowing those *icicle* people are already here in the United States of America waiting to make their move?

Are you that stupid to think they aren't going to do it? Really? False prophets.

False love.

Those are using God to get to you.

That's how that evil whore works.

God uses you for the good of man.

That evil whore uses you to destroy the good. If you feel something is wrong, it is.

I've been tested and tested.

I chose to ignore that feeling.

I paid the price.

God has taught me well and that lesson hurts like fucking hell. The evil is here.

We are in it. Play your toys.

Bury yourself behind your TVs, your sports, your videos, your movies...the *Penny Games*...it's such a repeating of history and you don't even see it.

Those *icicle* people: They don't want Europe. They want the United States of America. You don't have to take my word for it. After all, [x] did his fair job of making me into crazy and the weak-minded bought into it. You can research all of it yourself. You are in denial. You are bargaining away the truth. The lie. Oh, what a little web the spider has weaved.

They want the United States of America.

God will not intervene.

He's giving you a choice.

You have *free*-will.

That's called unconditional love.

If you can't understand that, then you surely have lost your faith in Him.

You can change *all* of this, but your heart has to open up in truth.

You can ask all you want.

You can sit in all the pews you want.

Without an open heart in truth, He'll just wait with His head bowed. Read the *Word*.

It's all there.

From the *Word* to all the facts in every single civilization after they failed and ended in war and death...it's all that's written down as warnings.

The only element in common...the only element in common...Him!

They lost their faith in *Him*!

It's your choice to make. *Free*-will.

Unconditional love.

Those of us delivering the message can only deliver the message.

It's up to you to listen or not. Choice.

God is great all the time.

All the time God is great!

—It is the Saturday that Jesus is taken down from the cross

He is wiped clean, then wrapped in linen cloth, then placed on a stone in a cave.

Today, we bow our heads and mourn for He suffered so that our souls may be *free*.

A lot of you have forgotten why?

You celebrate when people are hurt, instead of weep.

You make others hurt worse when you should be helping them heal.

You take advantage of the meek, the poor, the mild.

You stand by as others rape, beat, abuse, murder, torture, use the *Holy Bible* as toilet paper...as long as you have a TV, football, beer, a boat, a big truck, Saturdays at the salon...it doesn't affect you. Why?

Where is Christmas as these icicles terrorize around the world?

Do you think you will escape?

Are you so lame?

You were lame enough to put one of these people as head of state!

He has mocked you and you let him.

Still, you don't see it.

Still, you blame something or someone else. Shame. Jesus showed you.

Yet your eyes are still blind. Choices. *Free*-will.

His unconditional love for you, you will never understand.

He loves you so much, He allows you to make the choice! The icicles are coming.

God is waiting for the ask.

You need to start thinking hard about this.

I would start preparing for war.

The devil plays dirty.

God...well, He's going to sit back and watch the show because you people have forgotten what He is about.

They want the U.S., they are already here.

Waiting. Go ahead watch your TV.

Please, don't wail in streets when it begins.

You know what to do.

You are just ignoring Him.

I know that feeling. He's waiting!

Through His Son...amen

~

(March 27, 2016)—*I am the resurrection and the life. He who believes in Me, though he may die, he shall live, and whoever lives and believes in Me shall never die.—John 11:25-26*—Author Unknown

I was asleep. Paige wakes me up. Weather.

Do you see it as rain or do you see it as Him bowing down His head today because of the disobedience of so many across the world?

This crusade against His people...the believers.

You step foot in a building to praise His name...don't look around at what others are wearing or who's there and not there (I won't be there), instead, take a knee and pray with the truest of hearts (He'll know if you're lying) to help the weak, to feed the poor, to be with the sick, to make strong those persecuted for loving Him. This is not a time to be selfish.

If your church ask for money, don't give it, instead, find someone hungry and feed them yourself.

The church is too rich and they lock their doors and their gates so hungry souls cannot enter. Think with your own heart.

Walk in the steps of Jesus today.

He has risen because He sacrificed Himself for you.

Giving each one of us a second chance, a new beginning.

Don't waste it on silly, mindless things.

If you are broke, sell your things, pay your debtors.

Live in an empty house rather than no house at all.

Give the ones who are the weakest the biggest smile, the biggest hug today.

They may not have a feast waiting at home. Invite them over. Share your blessings.

If you love someone, really truly love, go to them, no matter how far, take a gamble, you never know how much love in return you will get.

Life is too short to not carry Jesus with you. See the rain as His tears today.

Don't let evil win. Talk about it today.

You have the weapon of choice to fight it. Use it.

He's waiting for the true hearts to ask.

What are you waiting for?

He will guide you on what to do.

He's time is never ours, but He never falls short when He prepares for battle. Amen.

The Lord, again, has risen!

~

(March 29, 2016)—I share my works and their explanations from my author page here to reach as many people as possible.

I hope they lift you, inspire you, lead you to the light. God is always great.

P.S. We all are on a journey, God is always there, we go astray, that doesn't mean He's not waiting for us.

It doesn't mean that if we say a curse word, we've gone astray...please...I've heard enough of that B.S. to last a life time.

It doesn't mean if we have a tat or ride a Harley or smoke or have a drink, we've gone astray.

I've heard enough of that, too. Fuck you.

It means...if we've lost our truth, if we've lost our light, then we need to find our way back to *Him*. You will know.

Others (messengers) may come in to give you a heads up.

You won't hear them much, but they will plant a small seed, then leave. It's our journey.

We have to ask.

Our lessons are for us *our individual self* to learn something.

When we learn them, He's ready for the next adventure. Plow on.

No one can save you, except for you!

No one can have a revelation about you, so if someone tells you that, they are full of shit!

Only God can tell you that.

Only He can put that in *your* heart.

No one can directly tell you anything from *God*!

Trust me on this one!

Your light is between *you* and *God*!

Those of us who teach, I guess that's what I do, that's all we can do. You can listen or not.

Pay attention to the world, but don't bury yourself in it. Turn off that damn TV...*OMG*!

You need positive! I have some negative. Sure. Abuse does.

It's only the freaking truth of the matter.

Sorry, but all this news and the bitterness...that just breeds more bitterness. That's not God!

Trust in your beliefs and no one else's.

There are *no* [seven] freaking virgins up there.

Sorry. There are no pots of gold. Sorry.

You strap a bomb to your body.

It's going to fucking hurt.

That's all I have to say, then the muck...that's a bit of hell because God...if you didn't already know...He kind of frowns upon suicide.

Like He doesn't like it—like *thou shall not kill*... so just saying...you won't get laid after you blow your silly self up.

The logic of that...I'm still twirling around in my head! So, Listen to your own heart. Evil is evil.

It's so simple it's freaking scary, and...*and*...I shouldn't have to freaking tell you this.

Use your brain. Please.

This is not just in the U.S...evil is evil.

I love my readers. I really do.

I'd love to hear from you.

Make some sense common...how many will get that...have a good evening.

~

(May 20, 2016)—*Why the fuck do employees have to give a two weeks notice, but companies can fire them on the spot?*—Author Unknown

Oh damn...do not give any more [two] week notices.

You want to quit, find a better life, move away...go for it!

I think if enough people took control of their life, these [two]-faced *company* owners would realize that good employees are, actually, hard to find.

Have you noticed the banks are replacing the tellers with machines?

They get rid of the jobs, but they won't get rid of the interest rates or the loans!

Kind of ass backwards!

Screw the notices...leave. Take care of you.

Greed sure the hell won't!

Let's all be online marketeers and keep the cash flow between us.

I bet all bank and huge companies owners would, eventually, have to come to us after we stop going to them.

Makes sense if you, actually, think for a change, instead of buying into the notion that it's your fault. It's not.

Greed just likes to play that card to keep you a slave.

Do online marketing and change the deal.

I so want to see what that hand looks like!

~

(May 27, 2016)—Remember those who have fallen to preserve our *freedom*.

I think a lot of people in the United States have forgotten what *freedom* is.

I think a lot of people in the United States don't really care about *freedom*.

I'm tired of being told what to do about everything.

There's a law now that says if you throw your cig butt out your car window, you get a ticket. There are too many laws!

There are too many people who have never experienced a third world country where there's little to no *freedom*.

Laws, laws, laws...each new law strips away what all those soldiers died for... laws, laws, laws...each new law denies you *freedom.*

When you do something and the government says you have to pay a fine for doing it, then you do not have that *freedom.*

I think throwing trash out the window of a car or dumping nasty garbage on the side of a road is more worthy of a ticket, then a cig butt.

I got a ticket for having my tint too long on my wind shield...$180.

It's not too long where it obstructs anything.

Still...I got a ticket...even though there are people driving drunk and reckless.

I think reckless drivers should get all the attention, instead of the length of my tint.

Laws, laws, laws...rules, rules, rules...I honor those who died to ensure that the *freedoms* left before them remain.

What will those after me do?

It seems they are handing it over piece by piece.

At least, there are some willing to sacrifice their very life for *freedom.*

I know I signed that dotted line just like those who died.

I'm still here to help speak for them.

Freedom is worth dying for.

~*Society in Chaos*~

what is it—saying *fuck it*
just going with it, with no morals to it

a woman doing it–
winning a simple contest
proving it—principles—sticking to it
military, college
wrapping it—packaging—taking it
to the height of it

with society stumping it
for pure hate of it—not seeing *stupid*–
the breaking down of it

drugs being the way of it
altering minds against it
allowing demons to control it

leaders playing with it
not even seeing it

the young ignoring it
–being toys to the adversary of it
following it—like they know it

sad—writing of it

when no attention goes to it
stripping life of it

the humble of it–
I'd rather know it—grow in it
then run from it

in the end, it's me and all of it
acknowledging my actions towards it
–having clear answers for it
is the best of it

life's too precious to avoid it–
the promises of it
then being weighted down
by the death of it

(June 9, 2016)—*The quill is resting, but the poet is restless.*—Author Unknown

Come out of the masses. Stand alone like a lion and live your life according to your own light.—Osho

Parable of Lost Sheep—*Now the tax collectors and 'sinners' were all gathering around to hear Him, but the Pharisees and the teachers of the law muttered, 'This man welcomes sinners and eats with them.' Then Jesus told them this parable: 'Suppose one of you has a hundred sheep and loses one of them. Does he not leave the ninety-nine in the open country and go after the lost sheep until he finds it? And when he finds it, he joyfully puts it on his shoulders and goes home. Then he calls his friends and neighbors together and says, 'Rejoice with me; I have found my lost sheep.' I tell you that in the same way there will be more rejoicing in heaven over one sinner who repents than over ninety-nine righteous persons who do not need to repent.*—Luke 15:1

Do you understand what is being said here? It's really simple. We are all sinners.

That's a given, and those who understand the ways of the universe and that of God know that when we sin, we need to repent...i.e. prove that we are sincere when we say—*we are guilty*...sincere when we ask for forgiveness. This is an individual thing.

No one can help us with this.

Our hearts belong to us and us alone.

For those who truly understand this, the process is easy.

It's like this: If you are smart in math, math comes easy and each problem that is presented is not really a challenge per say because you understand how math works...i.e. you understand the process and solving difficult math problems is not really an issue, hence, no big celebration.

On the other hand, take someone who doesn't understand the process of solving math problems.

They fail so many times, but when they finally get it...when they finally get just one type of math problem and find the solution, that's cause for celebration.

It's the same process with a sinner who really doesn't have faith in the process.

They either have never been taught properly, never been exposed to the ways of God, or they have gone through so much difficulty that they have forgotten how the process works or lost the faith in the process.

So, when they do find their way, which is a lot of times hard, it's a celebration on a larger scale than someone who has either never lost their faith or found their way back to faith.

It's really not hard to understand.

Lately, I've been moving a bit slow settling into the changes I've made in my life.

It's been a bit costly, but I've made a decision after I made it out of the darkness to not waste opportunities that's presented to me because I know they are from God and all I need is to trust in the journey.

So, at this point in the journey, I look at the cost being a way for God to strap me in place for a while...maybe, settling me down for a bit to completely move into that *balance* side of life.

I've always said that I totally believe that all things happen for a reason.

The older I get I see how this is so true.

Everything we do brings us somewhere and it all comes together in a surprising kind of way.

Understanding how the journey works is important.

As I'm settling in, I'm taking all of it really slow and that's been slowing down my editing and writing, which I don't see as an interruption as much as a need for me to regroup. So, I'm going with it.

While I'm *going with it*, I've been reading a lot on *Facebook* which led to *"Society in Chaos."*

I'm at a *wow* on a lot of things happening in our world today.

It pays, sometimes, to bypass the silliness in life and get serious and open our eyes to the bigger picture that's being presented to us.

This past year, I've written a lot about *chaos* such as the lie, which I've written about a lot.

I've written about the narcissist personality and its association with abuse.

I've written about confusion and betrayal and loyalty.

Chaos involves all the confusion we see day to day.

Just scanning through *Facebook* and reading the news as well as seeing the postings that I deem just plan ridiculous proves to me how much chaos we are in as a society in general.

What's with girls prostituting themselves on social networks?

Are these women so desperate that they would stoop that low?

Or, are these women being forced to do this?

I mean women have been prostituting themselves on the streets at night for centuries.

Where I'm from, you don't see them during the day. They always kept a good low profile.

Now, I'm not talking about a huge city.

In today's world, putting that out on social media for all to see? Really?

How low class can these people get?

Kids are on *Facebook*. Hello!

What's with the video with the [two] lesbians?

Kids...social media...no kind of warnings or protection for them!

These people are even doing this sort of thing on [online labor-for-hire site] where you outsource work, and on there, it's not just women! Chaos!

What's with these videos that show how uneducated people are?

Why not just educate them, instead of posting the nonsense to the world?

From my point of view, the idiocy goes both ways: The person in the video and the people making and posting the video.

Chaos!

What's with the videos that are clearly showing violence and no one helping, but they are filming?!

I watched one video taken from a public transportation bus where this guy clearly brutalizes two women, the door is open and people are passing by and not helping.

Hello! Empathy? Compassion?

Why is this happening? Chaos!

All the nonsense with Miss America.

Pure chaos for no reason at all.

I don't even want to start with politics.

There is too much *troubles* going on in this world and not enough faith.

Removing the *Ten Commandments* from a courthouse won't help your cause. Sorry.

It's a statue.

The *Ten Commandments* aren't going away.

You can remove all the reminders that they exist and try and forget them all—you want.

Those reminders are to help you live in faith and not sin.

Taking them away only weakens your strength because, apparently, those who fought to have it removed don't have much strength in the first place, so they are in denial of where they are headed.

Me, personally, I don't need a statue to remind me that the *Ten Commandments* are 10 simple laws passed to us by God.

Here in the United States...the *Bill of Rights* are based on these 10 simple laws.

I guess that will be the next protest... remove the *Bill of Rights*! Chaos!

Idiotism at its best!

I prefer to go against the grain these days and live by those *Ten Commandments,* instead of getting to the end and having to answer for all the wrong I've done because I was just too lazy. The hell with that!

All those who wish to follow the crowd... more power to them.

I think God's way is easier and just plain simple.

Love the skin you're in and don't let others deter you to deviate from the right path.

Trust me.

They won't be there when things go wrong for you.

When you follow God's path, He'll always be there for you. Always.

~

(June 12, 2016)—I'm reading *Cashflow Quadrant* by Robert T. Kiyosaki.

The same author who wrote *Rich Dad, Poor Dad*. Excellent book so far.

Kiyosaki has been around for quite a long time speaking about money and how to become financially *free.*

It pays to listen to the wise.

After all, he's wealthy.

After all, he's educated to the max.

After all, *he's financially free*!

In Chapter 4, he talks about network marketing and business systems.

He writes—*Network Marketing: Also called multilevel marketing or direct distribution systems. Just as with franchises, the legal system initially attempted to outlaw network marketing, and I know of some countries that have succeeded in outlawing or severely restricting it. Any new system or idea often goes through this period of being classified as 'strange and suspicious.' At first, I also thought that network marketing was a scam, but over the years, I have studied the various systems available through network marketing, and I have watched several friends become successful at this form of 'B'. I have changed my mind.*

Kiyosaki goes on to talk about his research in network marketing and how smart it is to invest into an already made system compared to investing in a business you have to build from scratch. A huge difference.

He further writes—*Due to the technological advances in the computer industry, these organizations are totally automated, and the headaches of paperwork, order processing, distribution, accounting and follow-up are almost entirely managed by the network marketing software systems. New distributors can focus all of their efforts in building their business through sharing this automated business opportunity, instead of worrying about the normal start-up headaches of a small business.*

He goes on to say—*I believe network marketing gives people the opportunity to build up the passive income they need for support while they learn to become professional investors. That is why I recommend network marketing to them. Even if they have little money, they can still invest 'sweat equity' for five years and begin to generate more than enough passive income to begin investing. By developing their own business, they have the free time to learn and the capital to invest with me in my bigger deals.*

Kiyosaki talks about systems a great deal in this chapter.

He says that many of us see the business, but we fail to see the system behind the business that actually runs the business.

This is the part that many of us overlook, and then fail at business because we overlook it. Makes sense.

Banks will not lend money to you to start any business if you don't have a business plan in place...i.e. a business system!

Anyone in business also knows *it takes money to make money.*

So, you can go the old way and bury yourself in thousands and thousands of dollars worth of debt without paying yourself and working from wee hours of the morning until way pass midnight all the time for years and years building your own system, or invest less and start with a system already in place, hence, using that time building your team and generating an income for a short period of time. It's always a choice.

Here's a system that's already built.

[I presented a link to a system the *sweet man* markets.]

It's proven.

For only *one* dollar, you can take a look at this system for [two] weeks.

What other business can you do that with?

Can you give [a franchise] $1 and expect to get a gander at their business model?

Hell no.

They aren't going to share their secrets, unless you put in nearly $1 million!

That's just fact.

So, why would you not check this system out. It's entirely up to you.

Live in fear of trying something new or keep on struggling. I prefer to try new things.

After all, people are making money with this. Why let them have all the income?

Why not claim your stake?

Trying something for only $1 is no big deal.

Understanding the education of it and learning to invest and network is priceless.

Your choice.

~

(June 16, 2016)—*Don't let small minds convince you that your dreams are too big.*—Author Unknown

Don't give up. Remember, it's always the last key on the key ring that opens the door.—Author Unknown

What would you do to make a dream come true? How much would you give up?

What are you willing to sacrifice?

Would you simply walk away from a dream because of how others perceive you because of your dream?

Would you let pride and ego override the logic of your very own dream?

How much of *you* are you willing to invest?

I've been chasing my dream since as young as [eight] years old.

The subject of the dream has changed, but the object of it hasn't. I don't give up.

Many have tried to deter this dream of mine...and they have for a period of time.

This dream doesn't rest for long.

The passion of it always has remained on solid ground.

My point: The dream is your passion.

As Kiyosaki writes below, keeping the fire in that passion is what it's all about.

If you do that, then you are sooner or later going to win, hence, your dream will become reality.

Stay focused on what matters...when you're at that place and your final breaths are just around the corner, you don't want regrets.

You want to say—*I did it.*

You want to say—*I didn't give up no matter what.*

If you haven't read any works by Robert T. Kiyosaki and you are going for that dream, maybe, it's time you picked up a copy.

This is a man who went from homeless to being financially *free* because he had a mentor and he listened.

Many of us don't get the luxury of a personal mentor, and he knew that, hence, his books.

Read the following passage from his book about passion and the advice he received concerning his dream.

To me, Mr. Kiyosaki's true gift is passing on this advice and being mentor to thousands who really need it.

The following is from *Cashflow Quadrant* by Robert T. Kiyosaki—*Find Your Passion—'Do you really want to move forward?' asked rich dad. Yes! I said hurriedly. 'Have you forgotten what you set out to do? Have you forgotten about your passion and what caused you to get into this predicament in the first place?' asked rich dad.*

...I had forgotten. So, I stood there at the pay phone, clearing my head so I could remember what got me into this mess in the first place. 'I knew it,' said rich dad, his voice booming over the phone. 'You're more worried about your own personal survival than keeping your dream alive. Your fear has pushed aside your passion. The best way to keep going is to keep the flame in your heart going. Always remember what you set out to do, and the trip will be easy. Start worrying more about yourself, and your fear begins to eat away at your soul. Passion builds businesses. Not fear. You've gone this far. You're close, so don't turn back now. Remember what you set out to do, keep that memory in your heart and keep the flame going. You can always quit...so why quit now?'

With that, rich dad wished me luck and hung up the phone. He was correct. I had forgotten why I set out on this journey. I had forgotten about my dream and allowed my fears to fill my head as well as my heart. Just a few years earlier, there had been a movie entitled 'Flash Dance.' The theme song said something about, 'Take your passion and make it happen.'

Well, I had forgotten my passion. It was now time to make it happen or go back home and forget about it. I stood there for a while, and again I heard rich dad's last words: 'You can always quit. So why quit now?'

'I decided to delay quitting until I had made things happen.'

~

(June 26, 2016)—Has anyone seen a U.N. vehicle here in the U.S.?

I just watched a video with trucks, supposedly, carrying them in several eastern states. These trucks do *not* belong here!

This country *does not* belong to the world!

It seems like it's time to stock up on more guns! Am I the only one feeling this?

~*Strange Occurrences*~

shades of trees, incoming breeze
sudden chills in freeze

raises bumps on skins—squeeze

lights in skies, hides, bringing out cries
why have sighs, why ask why

open—all deeds, given—all signs
by-passed—goes seeds
sown—not to find

all notions, lost in commotions
–gone honest devotion to sly's promotion

mystics in breeze
no more cries of please

(June 28, 2016)—*You are going to want to give up. Don't.*—Author Unknown

Successful people build each other up. They motivate, inspire, and push each other. Unsuccessful people just hate, blame, and complain.—Author Unknown

I'm currently typing in works in the third book of part one *Denial of Self* in my series.

It concerns the history of America and I just finished typing in the works on Thomas Jefferson.

You know—the third president of the United States of America.

I think a lot of people are not really aware of that.

I can say that with honesty after listening to some of those ridiculously videos on *Facebook*.

Ignorance is so rampant these days.

Jefferson was so past his time as an inventor...just his intelligent was remarkable.

He said a lot of things.

Things people today just simply have forgotten.

A lot of things have been put before me in the last couple of years.

They no longer surprise me because it's just history repeating itself.

If you don't know history, then *ignorance* is playing its part in your life.

If you don't know history, then *"Strange Occurrences"* will mean absolutely nothing to you. Shame.

Robert T. Kiyosaki says in *Cashflow Quadrant* to just *mind your own business* because, basically, the government doesn't give a damn about you and neither does anyone else. He's right.

We're living in a time where if you can't handle your own, you are doomed.

Not doomed to die per say.

Just doomed to be unhappy.

I'm in one of the biggest test of my life and

in this kind of thing, it's easier to run, then to stay put and see where God is leading the journey.

It's so easy to just tell someone to *go*, then to see the problem, and then try to solve it.

I see the problems I face.

I'm in that limbo kind of stage where decisions have to be made whether to solve the problem or run.

I told my mother this morning that I just feel like running off to an island somewhere and tune out the world.

She said she felt the same way.

The ignorance is so overwhelming.

The *impersonal* of people is heart breaking.

It just seems that other's *impersonal* makes me want to be *impersonal* too...just *not* care about anything...and that's not a good thing.

That's not how God wants us to be.

He wants us to be forgiving.

He wants us to inspire others to keep on going.

Sometimes, that's really hard when there's so much crap to put up with, so many people who just don't care. Where's the good news?

Why so much negative?

It's just amazing how someone like me can still ask those questions, but I do.

Take care of *you* and don't bother about others. There's so much deception.

If you just take care of you, then all you have to worry about is the truth.

God bless and keep plowing on.

Comments
•(Friend) Been there...still trying to find the good, it's hard when so many people have become so self-centered...a generation has been lost I suspect.

—Believe in yourself and all that you are. Know that there is something inside you that is greater than an obstacle.—Christian D. Larson

I deleted my *GofundMe* account.

It was an idea since so many senseless causes are on there...why not see what's important to people?

I learned...senseless causes!

I believe in my journey, even if I have to believe in it alone.

It makes no difference to me.

I've decided to dedicate my life to what I want to do.

People can rock and roll and spit their crap, but, in the end, it's still up to me.

I will still do it my way.

If you are in the *online* marketing business,

you are on the right track.

I've been reading so much about it lately.

I did make money online in [online business] before the owner became a trader.

Now, no U.S. citizen is allowed in and a lot of people lost money and advertising credits.

I don't believe in deceiving people, nor do I believe in greed.

If you're going to get into this business, be honest.

If you aren't making money, don't say you are just to *try* and make some money. Be real.

There are a lot of people somewhere out there wanting to get into online marketing or trying to learn how to. Don't lead them on.

It's not an easy business to break into and you will have to spend some money in order to make some money.

I'm not going to sugar-coat anything.

If you want something, you have to work for it. Nothing comes easy.

It doesn't matter how many sites you come across with that *easy* term in it. It's not easy.

So, don't believe everything you read.

Talk to people. Do your homework.

There are a few places I'm learning about.

Once I see how they perform, trust me, I will pass it along to you. Believe in yourself.

Trust in the journey.

Blog and website coming soon.

—Owning our story and loving ourselves through that process is the bravest thing that we'll ever do.—Brene Brown

This is not cool in the marketing world as I see it.

If you are going to try and get my or any other person's attention, this is not the way to get it.

This was a conversation in a message:

Solicitor—*So tell me...are you working any online businesses, Karen?....*

Me—*It's on my page what I do. The marketing page is in the works.*

Solicitor—*What's the name of it, Karen?*

Me—*I'm not revealing the names yet. Once I get the website up, I'll announce it on my Facebook page.*

Solicitor—*Never mind. I see where your not properly branded as a known trusted leader so does not matter where you post it. People join you, not your business.*

When or if you get serious about creating [six] figures monthly online and checking your messages, feel free to reply or re-add me as your friend here and I'll help you....

Have a great day!

Me—*I'm sorry. Did I offend you in some way?*

Comments

▪(Friend) And you, Karen, would be 100% correct. If more marketers actually knew some skills, the rest of us wouldn't get a bad name.

▪(Friend) Please call me concerned.
▪(Me) My phone is without service until the first. Will call then.

—Every morning you have two choices, continue your sleep with dreams or wake up and chase your dreams.— Author Unknown

Which choice are you going to take?

My work takes time.

I'm original and professional.

I don't hire-out writing. I write myself.

I'm authentic.

I don't mask using others' work or others' sale's lines. My dreams are my own.

I'm straight to the point with what I want, where I'm going and what I do.

No, I don't get a whole lot of support.

My subject matter scares the hell out of people.

You don't choose what God puts in your heart. So, why fight it?

It's His choice and He made it *your* dream, so go for it. If it feels right, it's right.

It's that simple.

You can talk about your dream or do it.

The choice is always yours.

It's call *free*-will...God's unconditional love. Don't let others block your way.

They are just fools and have nothing else better to do. You...you have a job to do.

Do it!

Enjoy the journey and keep moving forward.

If you suffer pain, turn that shit around and put it to work for you. That's what I've done.

Fuck all that wasted space.

I'm leaving no room for it.

Every single, tiny moment...I'm putting that shit to use. Love the skin you're in.

Comments

▪(Friend) You mean wake up and go to work....
▪(Me) Chasing that dream...those of us who do it...aren't actually going to work. We're having fun!
▪(Friend) Hi. I actually look at each day as if I am on Apollo 13. The destination is the moon. Some days, I make it and most I don't.

~

(July 1, 2016)—Good morning.

I used all of these.

[Didn't record the pic.]

Not bragging, but it's old school.

I received an award...an *award* for putting Army regs (that's books that tell soldiers what to do and in what procedures to follow) in order according to the Dewy Decimal System.

It was normal for me.

It was amazing to the 42nd MP Group.

I accepted the award with a slight smart-ass smile because it was the simple process of *thinking*...go figure!

Love my Army days...then I read years later how there was a drowning because the *electronic* window wouldn't work after a car ran off the road and submerged deep in water...the *roll your window down by hand* was work, but it would have saved a life.

The shoe measure deal...there was actually a person who knew what they were doing and you didn't have to guess and roam a store for hours searching for a size that fit.

They did it for you.

Just the same as the gas station guy who filled the car up, checked your oil and wiped your windshield without asking for extra money.

Or the guy who brought fresh milk to your door in a glass jar.

Or the paper route guy who put your newspaper in a bag, so it wouldn't get wet and you opened your door and there it was waiting to be read. Times have changed.

I think not for the better.

Quality things meant you didn't need to constantly replace things because things were built to last because *people* took pride in what they did.

Those were the times to appreciate...and we did.

It's a pity the younger generations won't ever understand this concept.

Times today are not better.

They are consumed by greed.

Make things cheap so the consumer will spend more money.

I envy those who still own a homemade ice cream maker!

~*Rhythms of Motion*~

don't walk straight
–missed fate, brings too late

walk the curves, learn a little swerve
life isn't meant to be heard
–it's meant to be served

piece by piece, gives and takes–
you start to feel *ease*
when you let go—societal dis-ease
just feel that breeze—not in safe
that's *not* the swirl, you want to twirl

stay back from flows
your *what-da-fuck* moments—unfold
let it all roll

that *bold*—go ahead—sow
take that chance—dance
change—so good à range

yes, don't do roads in straight
power—you hold—be in *blessing's* state
let them hate—you'll be in *go*
–that *one*, all comes to rate!

(July 9, 2016)—*I'm not a stubborn girl. I'm an independent woman.*—Author Unknown

Like the air you breathe, abundance in all things is available to you. Your life will simply be as good as you allow it to be.—Abraham-Hicks

You can be bold or you can be cold.

It's up to you. What will it be?

I'd rather be bold. Hell *yes*!

Some say that's arrogance.

Laugh my ass off.

I call that trusting in the journey and knowing if I deliver, so will my Mighty Warrior. That's faith right there.

Everything you desire is yours when you believe and let God lead the way.

That's truth right there...added to that is you are *never* too old to learn new things.

Hell, all this computer jargon like CTAs, VSL, CRM...oh my favorite: FOMO which stands for *fear of missing out*!

I'm sooo glad I live with a techno guy!

Fear of missing out...that's a mouthful right there...but the kicker is that you shouldn't fear anything. I'm in no rush.

I'm letting the magic happen as God let's it happen and...trust me...it's happening!

I'm not really interested in being rich.

I'm interested in seeing my dream *be reality*!

All else that comes with that is just blessings from God for doing what I'm supposed to do. Isn't that something!

Keep plowing on...if you are chasing that dream, think of all those who saw that tiny vision in the back of their minds become a reality. There's plenty to choose from.

I've written about a lot of them: Hersey, Macy, Amazon, AOL, Apple, Microsoft...the list is endless...and you know what...they failed first, they were poor first, they lived on a budget, they gave it everything they had while fighting for something only themselves believed in

Can you imagine that? I can.

I was sitting nice and comfortable for a while there, then this guy comes back around and tells me for the 100th time...*what are you waiting for?*

Having someone believe in you is so

important.

Having someone willing to sit on *poor's* seat along side of you while that dream is coming to life is like having a million in the bank. Nothing truly compares to having that!

Your dream is the lottery.

Yes, what's the lottery up to now...like over 100 million or something like that?

That money is the same as your dream... only your dream requires backbone, cold-hearted sweat...after all, it won't become a reality without you being present.

Being present isn't about sitting there on your ass thinking it's going to do itself!

It won't. Trust me on that one.

I've been through hell. So. Hell's over.

The future is now here.

The building of something that was never there, but because I thought of it, dreamed it, because I had faith, it's now here happening!

What are *you* waiting for?

Anything worth having takes time, patience, work, sweat, drive, determination, a backbone, a will, God...*you*!

So, stop waiting and do. You are worth it.

Always. Love the skin you're in.

~

(July 2, 2016)—*Whatever your 100% looks like... give it...*—Author Unknown

Busy these days learning so much...those ebooks look really inviting. Don't they?

I started my marketing education about 10 years ago...that was way before building websites were so easily done for you.

No, I was teaching myself to build my own.

I was learning about niches and shit... even self-published [seven] books through *Amazon's CreateSpace*...I taught myself *Adobe Indesign* and was teaching myself how to set up ebooks on *Kindle* way before it became easy and common...that was all way before the hell entered my life and halted everything. There are reasons for everything.

All that was lost to me is being replaced by the reality of a dream that was placed in my heart I believe at birth! I'm not just a poet.

I'm an inventor. I writer. A creator.

I'm bold to say it so *loud*!

Do you know why? God.

I did a *Google Keyword Planner* test on my titles of my books.

Those titles came out of last year's week-long prayer session, which gave me insight on a lot of things including the titles to my books, how to put them together, and what was coming if I adhered to the vow I made that I would finish the books, which God gave me the strength to write and publish them.

That *Keyword Planner* shocked the fuck out of me! It shouldn't have.

God is great *all* the time. Do you hear that?

All those titles are right on the money!

Keyword Planner revealed to me things in the niche groups about each title that only God knew and I only learned this year.

I was so floored over that.

If you doubt what God put in your heart, you are a damn fool!

That's like judgmental and shit, but I really don't care because He has shown me, so much. Open your eyes and pay attention.

He is talking to you.

If you think it was easy to break apart over 100 small chapbooks (that was already formatted in *InDesign*) and put them in the order in which I was told to (which is about [eight] longer books) and do that formatting shit *all* over again (which has almost taken me a year!), you are crazy!

More judgmental shit, but it's true.

That was a lot of work.

A lot, but I put my life in the Lord's hands when hell entered my door.

Tell me what to do?—came out of my mouth through pouring eyes of rain. He lead me.

He's awarded me when I needed a little more assurance. I'm not bragging.

This is all been about my testimony.

I believe, and all this that is taking place now reveals the truth of who's in charge of this ship. Will my books sell?

That part belongs to God.

Do you know why I say that?

Because the voice that I hear says—*Just write. They will come.*

That has come to me over and over for years! So...I write.

Now, I'm being led down this road of discovery that is revealing how *they will come*. It's not up to me.

My part is the vow I made, the joy in my heart, the gift. Did you make a vow to God?

Do you have a gift?

Does something pull at your heart so hard that you just know that it's right?

Why are you still sitting there thinking

about it? You are supposed to *do* it.
   That's why the gift was given to you.
   That's why that pounding in your heart is there. That gift. That pounding.
   That's the return on *His* investment!
   He's the bank.
   He gave you life to do His work.
   I so wish everyone would watch *Holy Ghost*...you'd really get it after that.
   Love yourself. Show love.
   Strip away all these fucking differences.
   What's all that shit for anyway?
   God wants love.
   Just do it...at least, the shoe people had it right! ☺

~*Riches to Give*~

his aged hand
pulled back a sheered curtain
letting in sunlight–
its glory—glistening, bright

your coffee's ready, sir

a voice came
just out of his vision's sight

by the window, he continued to stand
out there—flowers, trees
manicured, teased, shaped to perfection
–so much dedication
hired hands, money sunk in sands
–for watching from where he stands

his eyes passed from the view
down, slowly down, his own hands
opened palms—facing up–
clean, manicured

his heart began to pound
zero—all around—sound
emptiness—only found

his eyes—slowly, slowly—moved up–
that view, from this angle, he only knew

breakfast is served

the voice rattled his nerves

silence again came, as steps turned to go
procedures, routines—all the same

staring at the view, a tear began its due

enjoy it

words—stopping a slow exit

pardon, sir

he turned, his heart in yearn

enjoy it—so much you've earned

the younger man—taken off cue
his arms falling straight to his sides–
perfect statue—in a uniformed suit

the elder man
slowly, quickly—walked to him
–standing eye to eye
a tear almost in dry–
but clearly seen, in each wrinkled seam
–a face absent of lie

I missed something–
lost to money's ring—it's not in here

moving to the side, facing the view–
through the windowed pane
his aged hand raised
his fingers—straightened

it's out there–
the other side—from where I hide

he turned again
looking in the young man's eyes
that tear began to cry

I've missed something

the young man's body relaxed
he understood that—an aged heart laxed
while building to be taxed

it's a beautiful day, come, I know the way

his arm bent slightly—at his side

the elder arm slipped
in the welcomed bend

together, a walk in purpose
leaving traps of locus
for the light's focus

(July 3, 2016)—*Sometimes, the secret to getting what you want is to give it first.*—Author Unknown

Before you are a leader, success is all about growing yourself. When you become a leader, success is all about growing others.—Jack Welch

Building a business is hard work.
Wanting to make that money.
Wanting to prove you can do it.
Wanting to be bigger, better, richer.
Hearing all of this as I do my research on building an online business and marketing, I wonder if some have forgotten what's it all for. No. I'm not preaching. No.
I have nothing against building wealth.
I believe everyone should achieve their

dreams, but...always a *but*...along the way, we do tend forget a few things...a lot of times, not by choice.

We just get caught up in the excitement of it all.

There are a few scriptures that I was led to this morning.

Not by accident because I have been seeing so much about getting rich quick and making all this money to get all these luxury things, I've been bothered about the true goal.

Maybe, I'm just thinking of myself when these thoughts cloud my head, but they are actually for everyone if you understand the words Jesus said.

In a combination (*Matthew 19:16-22, Mark 10:17-22, and Luke 18:18-23*) this story comes to life—*As Jesus started on his way, a man ran up to him and fell on his knees before him. 'Good teacher,' he asked, 'what must I do to inherit eternal life?' 'Why do you call me good?' Jesus answered. 'No one is good—except God alone. You know the commandments: 'Do not murder, do not commit adultery, do not steal, do not give false testimony, do not defraud, honor your father and mother.'' 'Teacher,' he declared, 'all these I have kept since I was a boy.' Jesus looked at him and loved him. 'One thing you lack,' he said. 'Go, sell everything you have and give to the poor, and you will have treasure in heaven, then come, follow me.' At this the man's face fell. He went away sad, because he had great wealth.*

What would you do if that request was asked of you?

There are many people in the world today who heard God's voice and that request.

It would be interesting to know the state of those today...after they've followed the request and after they denied the request.

Another combination (*Matthew 19:23-26, Mark 10:23-27 and Luke 18:24-27*)—*Jesus looked around and said to his disciples, 'How hard it is for the rich to enter the kingdom of God!' The disciples were amazed at his words. But Jesus said again, 'Children how hard it is to enter the kingdom of God! It is easier for a camel to go through the eye of a needle than for a rich man to enter the kingdom of God.' The disciples were even more amazed, and said to each other, 'Who then can be saved?' Jesus looked at them and said, 'With man this is impossible, but not with God; all things are possible with God.*

Yes, *all things are possible with God.*
Greed is not one of them.
Lust is not one of them.
Jealousy is not one of them.
Following the instructions of God is not easy. Neither is unconditional love.
Neither is being honest.
No one said *good things* are easy.
In all my experience, the better something

is according to how God wants me to live, the harder it is.

There's no formula to *getting rich quick.*

When you hear of someone making a whole lot of money at one time, trust me, it wasn't an *over-night* thing.

It took them years of failures.

It took them years of learning.

It took them years of hard work.

It took them years of honoring their gift when everyone else gave up on them.

They just sucked it up and kept plowing on. An example would be J.K. Rowlings.

She had the first [five] books in her series written before being published, and so many publishers rejected her! Did she give up?

Nope.

She lived in poverty while writing them.

She lived in poverty while being constantly rejected. Did she give up?

Nope, and for that...she was rewarded!

All that money she received...trust me... if you added the hours she spent working through all those years (I believe I read it was 10 years)...you'd see that her *big payoff* added up correctly.

When we do our gift, we are rewarded.

You may condemn some who do their gift.

A lot of people condemn Ms. Rowlings about her subject matter.

Witchery...etc...I find that a bit amusing.

Why? That question amuses me, too.

It's the same for myself when I say *fuck*...it doesn't matter which way God's message gets through as long as it gets through.

Have you ever asked yourself what does the *Harry Potter* books teach you?

I'm guilty. I didn't read the books.

I did watch every single movie more than once.

From my opinion, I see several things it taught: Friendship, teamwork, love, good sportsmanship...that's only a few.

Older people and extremist condemned those books, but guess what...the result is still the same: The younger people read those damn books!

Did wealth change Ms. Rowlings?

I don't know.

I never met her, but I did read in many, many articles that she gives a lot of her money away.

I'm sure I read that she was a billionaire, but not anymore because of her generosity.

I like that.

In the marketing world, if you don't stay on top of the game, you quickly fall behind.

Sure, that's a good thing when building your online business, but have you noticed which direction you are seeing the sunlight from?

Building wealth is nice, but it can lead you in the wrong direction.

This is where *"Riches to Give"* comes from. I have a goal. I have a dream.

In order to make that dream come true, I'll have to build wealth.

In order to make that dream come true, I've already spent years at my computer learning, writing, etc.

I've been called *obsessed, miss know it all,* etc., etc.

I know what it takes to chase a dream, but in order for me to keep that dream alive, I can't lose focus of it.

That is really hard to do when you see all these *get rich quick* schemes, when you see all these ads and videos about luxury and money, money, money.

God does want us to be rewarded for our hard work.

Letting those rewards overcrowd what's really important is *not* what He wants.

The ultimate goal of building wealth is not to get luxury, but to help others better themselves.

The ultimate goal of doing our gift (writing, building, singing, painting, etc., etc.) is to make a better humanity.

For those who haven't yet received their gift or haven't yet understood what their gift is, so they condemn those who have, your bitterness will keep holding you back.

For those who have been rewarded for their gift and not helping others achieve their goals, the rewards will disappear.

This is not something I've made up.

This is living on this earth for 47 years getting educated, reading, learning, and paying attention.

The world works a certain way and God's in charge of it all.

It's up to you...and only you to fucking pay attention. Money will only get you so far.

Once you have it, if you don't show your appreciation for it, you'll be old before you know it...living without any justification for all that work you've done.

Peace and happiness is the ultimate payoff.

You'll know which way you're going by paying attention to how you feel in your heart.

It's very revealing once you learn how to listen to it. Enjoy life. Work hard. Play hard.

Stay in truth. Jesus told you how to live.

So, why aren't you paying attention?

It's so easy when you do.

It's also so easy when you never stop learning...that's the ultimate gift by the way... knowledge and the ability to receive it.

Love the skin you're in. You are worth it.

~

(July 4, 2016)—Hope you are enjoying the 4th! For those outside of the U.S. of A.

This is the celebration of our Independence from England a very long time ago.

For those living in the U.S. of A. and fight every *freedom* by pushing for more laws and rules, don't...just don't celebrate this day.

Don't pop one firework.

Don't tell one person Happy 4th of July.

Don't even smile today.

It's because of you we have less than what these men so long ago put their lives on the line for.

Read a little bit of history and you would understand why we called ourselves the *United* States of America.

We have a choice if we, as an individual, want to be safe or not.

It's not up to some other person to sign a bill behind our backs and force us to be safe.

Congress was never meant to be a career.

Our President was never meant to use the office to better his friends' positions.

History is very important.

The funny thing is...it always repeats itself.

I have a choice to start my own business.

I didn't make the choice for the government to take all my money without my permission byway of taxes.

I learn something every day.

In your county, weed maybe legalized.

In the next county, maybe, right across the street from you, it may not be legalized.

So, if you order it, and it crosses that county line, you could be arrested anyways.

Sounds much like prohibition, don't you think?

I also learned in some areas, if they legalize it, like Louisiana, the people won't have the right to grow their own, it's got to be grown in a lab or greenhouse. Why?

Adding chemicals to something natural?

Sounds a lot like prohibition.

Freedom...it doesn't mean the same thing that it did when all those men got together so sick and tired of how England was treating them...so many freaking taxes (Boston Tea Party...guess they don't teach that much these days)...so they threw a party of their own byway of the *Declaration of Independence*.

Go read that document...I bet many young and *liberals* have never even seen it.

You've got to stand for something, or you'll fall for anything.

I raised my children to buy as many guns as they can. They have that right.

I raised them to speak their minds because they have that right.

They have the right here in the United States of America to be *free* because some good ole boys who done had enough laid their lives on the line and made it so.

Their ancestors earned the right for them... some with their very lives by *dying* for them.

They just have to keep it.

Happy 4th to all those who still believe in *freedom*....

~

(July 5, 2016)—Posted an article titled *A home that looks perfect, until bigotry rears its ugly head*—by *washingtonpost.com*

I was reading through my emails when I came across this article.

We were talking about this type of thing just last night.

I went to the track by the Dome night before last to do my power walk and there was a group playing soccer.

They were Middle Eastern.

I had a strange feeling in me that I didn't like and I stayed away from them.

They were just college students enjoying the air as I was.

As I'm editing my work back in 2009 to 2012, I write a lot, in first person, about the political noise of our country, of our world.

I had begun, at that time, feeling this same noise. I felt it and I wrote it.

I wrote about the history of our country (U.S.A.) and how all this *noise* seeped its way into our world. I judged.

So did, and many do, judge.

How are we to feel when all this killing is going on?

I watched a video of a *Muslim* woman at an airport. How many of you seen this video?

She was arrested.

She had a very backwoods view on what exactly God is about.

Thou shalt not kill—is one of his primary commands, but this *Muslim* woman thought it was good to kill, to rid the world of *U.S.A.* citizens. How is that not judging?

How is that being in the same like as God?

Seeing this sort of stuff all the time, how are we to not judge this group of people?

I think fear is playing a major factor in all this. Know...I know it is.

These *backwoods* people who have an ideology that's way off the beaten path have to answer to God.

Denouncing everyone who are Middle Eastern is just wrong.

I was wrong when I was writing about it, but it's written, it tells the state of affairs that was happening at the time.

I have not written anymore about it because the essence of the world has not changed for the better, it has just gotten worse.

That's too much darkness to write about from one single person.

You have to look in your heart and find the answers.

Fear and hate will not give them to you.

It is only that evil whore, as I refer to the devil, who instills fear and hate.

God only instills love.

No...He doesn't *instill* anything.

He gives us unconditional love.

It *is* up to us, individually, to *instill* what *we* decide to feel in ourselves.

No one can make you hate.

No one can make you love either.

It's a choice...and it's only for you to make...no one else.

All this race-war B.S...that's not God.

All this killing...that's not God.

He does want us to protect ourselves or else we wouldn't have guns.

The *Bible* talks about wars and killing.

The *Bible* talks about the better of mankind, not the destruction of it.

There is a time in the *Bible* when God just had enough of all the B.S. and washed it all away. Do you not think He will do it again?

Just curious. Go on with the hate and fear.

It's not easy to wash away that when all

those who are listening to that evil whore are killing because their man-made religion or political agenda is backwoods.

When we are called to protect, we will know.

Let them backwoods people be ignorant.

It's not our job to educate them.

It's only our job to make the right choice.

How wonderful it would be to have people take the responsibility for their actions.

How wonderful it would be for people to talk about love, acceptance...God, instead of killing and anger.

(If you feed something good all the time, then their bad will starve...I learned this through the love of another person...the best lesson ever taught to me.)

I don't like the way society makes me feel about my fellow brother and sister in the open air.

I like marketing because all those marketing pretty much feels the same way I do...we like to see others succeed and have a good life *free* of killing and shit.

Just saying....

~*Amongst Many*~

words we need, videos we see

moments caught—events saw
without *knowing* brought

he said, she said

accusational entity
without being part of the journey

hate breeds hate

learned cue, from personal ensue
you can't say *you*
without knowing every clue

seeing *live* doesn't mean it's a lie
seeing with a naked eye
doesn't mean there's a connive

people in hide—always face God†
He'll† judge all the fudge

adding to the jive, leaves out *alive*
–just anger in sigh, frustration in deny

it's a failing *win*, carrying others' sins–
–seeking attention by-way of commotion
the oldest intention for any validation

social society's breed makes it easy–
false windows in believe

playing on passions, leading ratifications
to avoid–
inside responsibility's justification

*don't believe: what you hear
half of what you read, half of what you see*

actions, facts—the only deeds
to hold accountability

all the rest, leave to God†
it's His† test—not for others to protest

how you handle the quest–
honors your best
leaving out unnecessary personal stress

~

(July 7, 2016)—Post a video about the F.B.I.'s findings involving the Hillary Clinton scandal.

I can understand the emotions that the F.B.I.'s decision will have, but if you are a person who fully understands what he's talking about at the beginning of this video, then you know that he's factual and not making this up.

He's also right about the F.B.I.'s decision.

In our system of justice, the law works *free of passion*...just because you don't like a person doesn't mean they are guilty of *intent*.

This is the most honest and *free* of passion announcement I've heard, thus far, concerning this matter.

What he is saying, basically, is that her emails weren't necessarily direct treason (intent), but normal conversations without intent.

His conclusion, as an F.B.I. entity and recommendation, is that the *conversations* aren't basis for criminal charges, but...but it *is* the basis to have *all* of her security rights stripped from her.

Anyone who's ever served in the military or worked for the government in any way and had a top secret security clearance, I have, knows...*knows* what you can and cannot talk about.

She was in the position to *know*...she was having conversations without thinking... basically...that's the bottom line.

His recommendation to having all security rights stripped...remember this is only the F.B.I.'s recommendation coming out of a very thorough investigation...only the Justice Department can make that final call...but the F.B.I.'s recommendation, basically, says this woman cannot be president or even considered as president of the U.S.A.

He's saying, according to the evidence they uncovered, that if you tell her a secret, she's reckless enough to tell it.

Basically, she can't keep her mouth shut.

The President of the U.S.A. has...*has* to be trusted with the U.S.A.'s most secret of secrets.

We can*not* have someone in the highest office of our country who is known to have a *loose* mouth!

Justice in the U.S.A. has...*has* to be *free* of *passion*.

So, stop for a minute...strip the hate and your *personal* passion out of your system... and think about that...,*free of passion*.

Clinton can't keep her mouth shut.

She can't keep secrets.

She is *not* a person we want heading our country.

No matter what the Justice Department's final say is.

The F.B.I.'s investigation, if you understand his technical terms, was thorough, and to say she should have all security rights taken away...well, that's major. Really major.

This is just about the *emails* at hand.

Any further investigation to what she loosely said in those emails is another matter.

Did what she say, without thinking, cause criminal acts?

That's another matter and that is for the Justice Department to decide or for an addition investigation.

So, just remember this particular investigation was to uncover what was said in the emails and to make a *recommendation* to whether there was *intent* or not according to the law.

If what she *said* in the emails led to criminal acts, then there's reason to consider persecution.

If you know anything about the justice system, these matters take a lot of time.

They can only move one step at a time.

It doesn't matter what comes out of Clinton's mouth or any other mouth.

That's just talk.

They *have* to look at the *facts*.

So, let those investigating do their job.

It's the same in every single case of misconduct, criminal acts, etc.

Spewing hate because you don't understand, doesn't make the matters get done any quicker.

Here...the bottom line is that Hillary Clinton can't keep a secret, doesn't fully understand what it means by *top secret* or country security.

That's a person who can*not*...*not* lead this country.

Just because she's a woman doesn't lend any...*any*...justification to campaign for her to lead this country. That's just common sense!

~*Natural Light*~

making wrath—won't add like math
–it's only sass, faithless blast
consuming *easy's* laugh

it's a simple task—just ask
–nature's craft, without tags in hash

stop talking trash—it's just a trap

travel a different path, re-route the map
–use simple rap—don't bash
–add some flash
around all—love—please wrap

it's an open-door lab
–common sense—in zap!
God's† rhythmed tap, a dare in *pass*

–fall into love, leave *hate* in burn—crash
then see how fast
then see how long—it all last

God's† love—so vast, brings *easy's* laugh
without even having—to fast

(July 11, 2016)—*Success isn't just about what you accomplish in your life, it's about what you inspire others to do.*—Author Unknown

You should never lose heart. God is merciful and kin. He has endowed you with the best gift—smile, which can make millions happy.—Mother Teresa

You are not just one person, you are one person God created with purpose. So, yes, you can make a difference.—Trent Shelton

After my *Facebook* readings and postings this morning, I sat to write.

I haven't been writing every day because of all the work to be done on these books I'm working on, but today, like the other days lately that I'm compelled to write, I picked up my *Bible* first.

In the *Bible* I use (for all you new comers) is *The Daily Bible...In Chronological Order 365 Daily Readings...New International Version,* which is easier for me to read and follow.

I've read it several times completely, and, then when the poetry writing started, I just sit and asked—*What am I going to write, Lord?* then open it up. This morning I was led to *Isaiah*.

These are the titles of the passages the compilers of this particular *Bible* had on these pages (902-903): *'Obedience of a Servant,' 'Captives Must Trust God,' 'How Abraham was Blessed,' 'Restoration of Ransomed,'* and *'No Need to Fear.' Wow*!

I say *wow* because of what I posted on my personal page about peace and love coming out of all this racial B.S. across the U.S.

I read all of these passages, but I kept going back to *'Captives Must Trust God'*—... *Who among you fears the Lord and obeys the word of his servant? Let him who walks in the dark, who has no light, trust in the name of the Lord and rely on his God, but now, all you who light fires and provide yourselves with flaming torches, go, walk in the light of your fires and of the torches you have set ablaze. This is what you shall receive from my hand: You will lie down in torment.*— Isaiah 50:10,11

Everyone who reads this passage, as every passage in the *Bible*, will come out with a different meaning.

The *Bible* tends to speak to us on an individual level.

Many times a passage will mean something one day, and then mean something totally different the next day.

That is really powerful.

Today, after reading my news feed, this passage spoke volumes to me, hence, *"Natural Light"* bled on the page.

This is my translation of this passage today: If you have faith in the Lord, you don't need any other light because of His unconditional love for us.

If you breed hate, then walk in your hate...accept the chaos that you caused.

I say it many times...God does *not* bring on hate! That's that evil whore.

If you are constantly being egged on by all this B.S. you read on *Facebook* about these shootings, then you are allowing that evil whore in.

You have holes that you need to plug!

It's that simple. I've been through that shit.

I see it over and over in my writings.

It was a fight to get through all that.

Only God helped me through it.

I couldn't fight that whore on my own.

Are you nuts?!

I don't have that kind of power, but my all Mighty Warrior does!

Facebook is an avenue to breed hate!

If you let it!

You have to be honest with yourself.

It's an individual thing.

If all people decided they want *good* and refused to spread *hate*, then guess what?

All those out there trying to instill *fear* in us...they would disappear. It *is* that simple!

When I saw that article about those countries issuing warnings about visiting the U.S.A., that really pissed me off.

That is *not* what our founding fathers intended for this nation. Are you hearing me?

I have several books in my series about the U.S.A. and how it came to be as well as the people involved.

It is sad to me to learn how those we put in leadership positions allowed the adversary to change what this country was meant to stand for. We can fix that. Yes, we can.

It won't be easy.

Nothing good is ever easy, but...with faith...it can be done. You just have to want it.

It's the same all across the world.

We are all people.

Doesn't matter what race, color, belief...we are *still* people...human beings.

You may not believe in God or that evil whore the devil.

They exist...except it or don't.

How do I know that?

Because once you turn your life to God and prayer...you see *good* happening, instead of *bad*. That's a big thing!

That's how you start to see that God is real...even if you believed before...nothing compares to going through the darkness, then coming out with the hand of God on your side and He shows you, straight-up!

I'm telling you...there's *nothing* like it!

Love...yes, love, overcomes all.

You just have to want it to.

If you are constantly watching all these *hate* videos, constantly reading all this *hate* race-based B.S., then you are not moving with God.

You are in-line with that evil whore.

You can argue all you want...I'll just let your face turn blue!

You may just be perfect with that shade of skin! Who knows.

Me...I wouldn't look so good being the color blue. I just go with God. It's easier.

It's simple. It's real.

I've done accepted the fact that blame is blame.

You want to blame me for your crap...go right on ahead.

You want to curse me, shun me, condemn me...that's your fucking right.

I'm pretty easy...I have God protecting me.

I know when He's testing me.

It took a long, hard road to see how He does that shit. I've learned.

His love for me is unconditional.

Unconditional.

I have the right to choose. I choose *Him*!

I choose *love*!

I choose my country...not politics...my country...yes, there's a difference!

What is the difference...*freedom*!

After all, God revealed this land when He did for a reason...or else, it would have been discovered way before it did.

That's just common sense...but, of course, common sense is *not* so common after all.

Be a student of history.

Be a soldier of love, then do *you*.

Don't follow the crowd. Don't breed hate.

It's just not worth it in the end.

Love the skin you're in because you are worth it. You are beautiful.

Trust me...you are!

—*Diversity*! There's a word!

[Didn't record the quote.]

History is *so* important!

This guy is just a blessing in so many ways. It's not about Trump.

It's not even about politics!

It's about being an American and what constitutes that. Learn history. I beg of you.

Stop all this race stuff.

It's just not worth it.

All...*all* of us...no matter from which boundary our families emerged from...*all* of us created this great country.

Stop letting outside fears consume that.

Open your eyes to the *real*...we *all* suffered during this emergence...but look at who we are today!

Stop and think about that for a minute.

Instead of hate...shouldn't you feel *proud* that our ancestors...no matter what race or color...went through what they did, so that we have what we have today.

I know my French and Indian ancestors suffered...thank you for suffering for me because now I'm *free*!

What homage are you paying to that suffering if you are going to let outside influence take that away?

Was their suffering done in vain?

What honor are you paying to them by letting outside influence destroy that?

Because of all our races...we have what we have today! Don't you see that?

If you were born on American soil, you didn't get that privilege because of money.

You got that privilege because someone a long time ago had to suffer to gain their place here.

Remember that when you turn on your lights, or enjoy sugar, or take the train, or do anything else...someone a long time ago suffered in order for *you* to enjoy the fruits.

Thank God they had the courage, they had the will, their blood was spilled...because of them...I am here!

—Posted an article titled *'Three Countries Issue Travel Warnings About Visiting The U.S.'*— huffingtonpost.com

The U.S. embassy of Bahrain, a tiny Middle Eastern island nation, on Saturday urged citizens via twitter to 'be cautious of protests or crowded areas occurring around the U.S.'

This is what I wake up to this morning! Really!

Don't people read history anymore?

Acknowledge who's *causing* this mess!

As I see it...it's not black or white...it's both!

As I see it...it's not being caused by the American people. What do you see? Hate? Racism?

Take a look at the people who aren't allowing *fear* to shake them up.

This country is *not* about black and white or any other color anymore.

Those on the *outside want* you to believe that it *is*. Who are you going to believe?

Scandal...diversion...hocus-pocus...one big circus to cause chaos...that's what I see!

All of you out there falling to this B.S...are you going to church? Are you with God?

If you say you are, where is His love...that would be God's love.

Look at your own life before falling to all this chaos. Question your own self.

History lesson 101: Bring a country down... Instill *fear* of the authorities or peace keepers! *Bam*!

Well, that can be scratched off the list of *How to's*.

Warning: You have let the adversary do its job without even trying to fight it.

Now that the *how to* has been accomplished according to the world...now the next on the list can take place.

Infiltration!—the peace keepers are there to help us when that happens.

According to the world...we are no longer capable of that!

~*Acting Deeds*~

faith alone does not stand
–hear me—understand

crying to every man—*I believe*
does not withstand
the wrath of God's† hand

the good deed brand–
a call's marching band
the *I give a damn*–
a *will's* welcoming fan

this spreading, contagious strand–
fully understood by the Lamb†
one single hand–
then another, another, another
soon stretches throughout the land

turn *yes, you can*, into a *united* clan
up—take that stand
show don't tell—then bam!-
heart's no longer having to cram
you're *free*—of God†—a true fan

(July 15, 2016)—*Before you are a leader, success is all about growing yourself. When you become a leader, success is all about growing others.*—Jack Welch

—*You are what you do, not what you say you'll do.*—Author Unknown

There's been a lot of anger going around on *Facebook*. Why?

The *Book of James* talks a lot about this particular thing...not necessarily *anger*, but about that *practicing what you preach* sort of thing.

It reads—*Was not our ancestor Abraham considered righteous for what he did when he offered his son Isaac on the altar? You see that his faith and his actions were working together, and his faith was made complete by what he did. And the scripture was fulfilled that says, 'Abraham believed God, and it was credited to him as righteousness,' and he was called God's friend. You see that a person is justified by what he does and not by faith alone.*—James 2:21-26

The *Book of James* talks about this...a lot!
You see that his faith and his 'actions' were working together....
Makes you think, doesn't it?

I have been going through a personal struggle lately and it involves just what that tiny statement says.

I've written a lot about *action over words*...for me, my actions, in all actuality, are in my words...to write the words that come to me and talk about God and the goodness that He delivers on here (my *Facebook* page until I get my website and blog up and running), and then compile it all in books, and then publish them.

It may not make sense to you, but it does to me.

I've done a lot more than just write words to prove my actions, but I don't need to talk about that.

That's just my heart and God knows my heart.

I spoke to a dear friend last night about this...about our good hearts and how people are so easy to take advantage of that.

Even though in the past I've cursed those who hurt me, called them out, I didn't have to.

God sees all and He deals with that sort of thing. We don't have to.

Only our selves can please God.

We can't please God through others.

God brings good to us as individuals not as a *group*.

When that heart is filled with joy...that's Him.

When that anger enters our world and we fight with one another, we brew hate and envy and all those other crazy thoughts...that's the evil.

Do you know how to fight that? Pray.

It may seem too simple, but all you have to do is pray and ask God to help.

He, eventually, shows us the way.

Remember: His time is not our time!

I've been through a lot of tests this past year.

I often say that when we get closer to doing what God wants us to do, the tests will get harder.

I wasn't joking...not even to myself.

It's not just the tests that have been harder, but it's the things I'm witnessing that are, I think, even harder.

Since last August, I've been betrayed by people who I thought were my friends and I even betrayed a friend.

I paid my karma and I prayed.

It was a hard lesson for me on a very personal level.

It's the most oddest thing in the world how God handles such things.

It's like He says—*Okay, my child, if you are sincere in your heart, I will give you the benefit of the doubt, but I will put you in a situation where you are going to have to prove your sincerity*—and He has.

The tests are hard, but...but He's my Father and I'm His child.

He already knows my heart.

He wants *me* to know my heart.

That's a twist in itself.

It's sort of like that movie years ago *Karate Kid*...where the young boy goes to the old man to learn to fight.

The old man doesn't teach him how to fight, he teaches him to trust his own self!

That's what I'm learning.

God is showing me *me*...He wants me to trust my own heart.

He wants me to be sincere in what I feel, not in what I say.

I can talk about my faith all day long.

I can talk about God all day long, but if I'm not living it...what's the point?

I have to ask myself with the truest of hearts...how can I help other people be strong, if I can't help myself first?

How can I help others survive the darkness and began a new life, if I can't do it myself?

Those are very honest questions to ask one's self. I trust in God. Yes, I question.

I'm human, but...and there's always a, but... we have to grow and get to that point where Abraham was when God sent the ultimate test...to kill his own son.

He had to totally trust in God...not himself...not his wife or friends...*God*!

Do you see where I'm going with this?

Many questioned me when I made the decision to enter the journey I'm now on.

I even questioned myself. I shouldn't have.

I feel relief that I only questioned.

I feel relief that I *acted*, instead of just talked about it.

It doesn't matter what others think...my family, friends, children...it is what God thinks.

I really had it in my heart that those I loved would continue to dislike this decision I've made. I was wrong.

I'm starting to get support...that's God.

My journey hasn't been easy, but I see how this particular journey is leading to the ultimate goal of my entire journey...help women who suffer from abuse...tell my story.

I'm not alone on this journey anymore.

I prayed for that...to not do this alone.

God has answered me, but not without testing me.

It's all a matter of surety in ourselves, in God and in those around us.

Are we honest with who we are?

Or are we going to follow the ways of man?

It states in the *Bible* that being friends with those on earth is not being friends with God.

It is only in our actions that puts us right in the eyes of God.

It doesn't matter what we've done in our past. It matters what we are now.

What we do now! Do! Actions!

Words are just words if we don't actually live by what we say. Trust me on this.

Actions over words in God's eyes is pretty damn powerful. Love the skin you're in.

You are worth it!

~

(July 17, 2016)—Network marketing. Workplace.

To the *AOL* news (whatever!): Journalism is supposed to be *free* of bias.

An article (that would be *one*) I just heard (it was read out loud) about Trump and his chance-taking with online marketing is just a piece of propaganda and the words *article* and *journalist* should *not* be attached to this kind of thing.

I just finished reading Steve Case's book and I think (seriously) he wouldn't condone such B.S.

(If you don't know who Mr. Case is...maybe, you should read.)

I don't care who you are...rich, poor or in between...everyone in the world has a chance to get into marketing.

I think Mr. Trump is pretty damn smart.

Are you going to argue with me?

I think he surrounds himself with some really smart people.

Are you going to argue with me?

I think he's not a coward.

Are you going to argue with me?

I think it's pretty great that he's put his hands in online marketing.

He's not the only billionaire I'm sure doing business in our camp. Isn't that something!

Hands up Mr. Trump.

To the people *reporting*...(stating their personal bias as articles), go back to school... you need it. Thank you.

~*Shores of Definition*~

walls won't come down
–beat, stump, slam—won't matter
when you stay the clown
–those walls, they'll remain in surround

diversity won't come in surety
'til overridden–
color with talent—individuality

anger, hate won't be of yesterday
without breaking clay
all bodies—together
lived places—this way, that way
can't be changed—rearranged

but today, engraved creativity-
higher mounds, all are bound
laugh without frowns
building networks—sound

taking all passed down
building around, instead of tearing down

using the drivings of hate-
update a better way

diversify—don't ask why—just fly
my talent, your talent—combine
–out-do our family line

what a better way to say
to those of yesterday
who paved our way

it's not race—ethnicity
that gives me audacity
to say *I can* with certainty

it's clarity—those of yesterday
through blood, hope, tears, fought fears
so *I* can live in sincere
so *I* can choose my *own* career

thank you
from whatever shore, opened the door
I'm now the *core,* of what came before

(July 18, 2016)—*One of the greatest gifts you can give someone is thanking them for being part of your life.*—Author Unknown

Here's to the past.—Author Unknown

A lot has driven the words of *"Shores of Definition"*...a lot I've been hearing, reading, seeing on social media, in the news, through broadcast. Do you know what I see?

I don't care if you don't give a fuck about what I see, I'm going to tell you anyway.

Hate! The breeding of it. The joy of it.

The encouragement of it, and...*and* I have to ask...? I don't care what color your skin is.

We all came from some type of oppression.

It's part of *all* our history, but, here in America, we are here, but, in other parts of the world, you are there!

Yes, there is still suffrage taking place. Do you know that?

Not the kind of suffrage as we experience here in America.

I will call the suffrage people are experiencing here as *self-induced*...sorry...if you can't see that, then you are embodied... body and soul...with hate.

In other parts of the world...suffrage... killing, murder, starvation, rape, slavery, human trafficking...I want to cry because ignorance and hate has shield eyes to this... the real meaning of suffrage...something that *is* happening...not something that *happened*!

I'm sorry that your ancestors had to endure slavery. Mine did, too.

I'm sorry they suffered. Mine did, too.
The French. The Africans. The Indians.
The Irish. The Mexicans.
The Middle Easterns.
I'm sure I've left some out.

We have *all* come from family lines who suffered and because of that...we are *here*!

Why aren't you grateful? I am.

Letting what happened to our ancestors eat our souls 100s of years after doesn't change anything.

What it does do is steal our happy, our peace.

Many yell and scream...it's still happening! No. It is not.

It is anger that breeds from something that happen over 100 years ago that still exist.

Let it the fuck go!

I sit, sometimes, and imagine I'm there... back in the pass talking with someone who's been a slave or an Indian or a Frenchman and I see the sadness in their face.

All that they suffered and we don't appreciate it. We don't honor it.

Being hateful and angry because of the color of your skin is downright foolish.

Our ancestors didn't suffer so that we may continue to live in the past.

They suffered so that we may have a better tomorrow. Suppression. Oppression.

Those are two strong words.

There is bitterness all around. Too much. Chaos.

Keep people in chaos...to control their emotions and passions.

That's from an ancient reading I had to read during my college years.

I can't remember the author, but he was a philosopher who detailed how to bring a country down to its knees. Suppression. Oppression.

One more key factor...fucking fear!

Keep them in fear!

The only way anything or anyone can keep a human being in fear is if that human being let's them. You are letting them!

The emotions we have are very powerful.

Anger and hate are two of the most powerful and they breed off each other.

I can talk until I'm blue in the face.

You won't fucking listen.

Stubbornness is another emotion that barricades our hearts.

A lot of times those barricades don't come down until the stubborn person is faced with reality head on through something tragic.

I don't want any tragedy to happen.

I wish those barricades would just come down without any hell to pay.

I do thank my ancestors: French, Indian, Irish, African...for suffering.

I pray for them, but I already know they are in heaven. They suffered, so that I may be *free*.

I honor them.

I don't disgrace them by fighting with others who are different than I.

That's not why they suffered.

I documented a lot of this hate in my writings and I've learned this: Only love...*love* can overpower those other emotions!

Just saying....

~*Re-Training Window*~

minds in re-train–
it's to obtain, if you have a brain
without going insane

mastering c.t.a.'s, ways of the n.r.a.
without enemies to rave

write it in emails, keep your clientele

better yet, try a v.s.l.
–the difference will tell
it's all about c.r.m.'s
–old-school retail, but with a d.i.y-rail

coming together—spiders in a web
s.e.o.'s, e.s.p.'s, c.m.s.'s leads to an m.a.
bringing customers your way
night and day

–object of the game—getting that r.o.i
by-way, a mastered domain–
splash pages, leads, sales
–traffic ingrained

so many sites giving incites
for the f.o.m.o.—pieces of info
others already know

what's true, what's not

it's all up to you—the brain in re-train
without going insane
or sinking your dream, down the drain

(July 19, 2016)—*Time for change.*—Author Unknown

Success is not just a measure of how big you can dream...it is also a measure of how much you can do.—Author Unknown

All my work posted here are first drafts. Did you know that?!

Why do I post them here first?

It's simple really.

I enjoy it and it keeps the flow going.

I'm an artist.

It doesn't matter if you relate or not.

It's about doing the gift and passing it along. Do I make money from it?

I'm not ready to go there yet.

As you can see in *"Re-Training Window,"* a lot goes into building a website and a brand.

It's all possible.

If anyone tells you it's impossible, ignore them please.

Things happen if you make them happen.

Things happen if you don't give up.

In the past five years, I've been through a lot. I didn't stop.

I've moved residence like five times since my divorce...no...not crazy...just keeping it going.

I don't plan to settle back down until I see my dream turn to *real*...that's the way of it.

I wasn't trained in all this online marketing stuff.

I was trained when computers first were

available to the public.

I had to laugh to myself when I read Steve Case's *Third Wave* because he puts it into prospective...*wow*!

How time flies and *how* much has changed in such a short period of time!

My darkness set me back a while, but only for a *while*...you can't sit there and dwell in your self-pity because while you are doing that...the world keeps going, keeps changing.

When I came out the darkness, even though I was writing the whole time, technology jumped so far ahead that I had to re-learn!

Did I mention how long I was in my darkness? Three years!

That's actually a bit abnormal.

It takes a lot of people more years than that to get through all the stages of grief.

I had my work and some dear friends pulling me out.

In today's world, you can't bury yourself for too long in order to heal, but...always a fucking, but...you can't force healing either.

It's almost a catch 22!

If you are stuck in the darkness...don't give up, don't quite.

Keep plowing forward even while those tears are blinding you...just keeping going.

I would have never dreamed two years ago that my work would come together like it has or that I'd have so much to include in my work.

I had no idea that a company...a *company* would take shape, but it is. How? Why?

Because I didn't quit.

I had to take moments to re-group, but I didn't quit.

I ignored all those who said I was wasting my time, that I'd never make it, that it's impossible. I ignored all those hurting me.

I got pass those ignoring me because they didn't believe in me.

I still have a long way to go.

I put everything on the line and struggling financially because of it, but I've learned once you make that decision, make that big move to start...you really can't stop.

Building an online business takes time, a bit of money, a whole lot of learning.

It helps to have a team.

I'm working on that.

It helps to have support.

The biggest, most important piece of advice I'd give anyone heading down the route I'm going: *Read*!

Not just articles online...*books*.

Read books by people who have traveled the road already.

When you do that, you'll see that your struggle is not at all unusual.

Read work by Robert Kiyosaki.

Read Steve Case's *Third Wave*.

Read inspirational books.

Read verses from the *Bible*.

Don't limit yourself to just the net.

Not everything on the net is true.

Not everything on the net is objective.

Reading bias articles is kind of the worse type of reading.

You don't want that kind of influence.

You want to be able to make your own decision about things.

That's why journalism is supposed to be objective on every matter. Be smart.

Don't be ignorant. Think.

That's the biggest thing I stressed to my students when I taught high school. *Think*!

What the hell kind of person you'll end up if you can't think for yourself?

Think about that! Love the skin you are in.

If you are interested in contacting me about my work or partnering in some way, feel *free* to contact me.

(The *Third Wave* has everything to do with partnerships!)

If you are interested in using any of my work, feel *free* to contact me...let's talk.

There are a lot of goons out there stealing people's work without consideration of copyright laws. Don't be one of them.

I keep all my original work and you should, too.

Copying and pasting other people's work is a crime...and I've been seeing a lot of this going on.

If you are offered material that includes copying and pasting long works, be sure that you have the first serial rights.

If you don't, that piece is being forged... stolen.

A small lesson on copyright infringement: The moment someone writes something down...it is copyrighted!

Getting it into the Library of Congress is just further protection.

I know...I have six books registered.

You may be excited about money made, but a simple copyright infringement lawsuit will wipe all that plus everything else you own out. Just saying....

Comments

•(Plantation) You sound good, Karen. Maybe, even...positive? Hope so!

Might wanna consider an audit of the fact-checking in the last paragraph; it's a bit erroneous...very easy to fix.

Holla if you need help with the legal and biz ends of publishing. Best of luck. Take care.

•(Me) That's nice to know. Nice you're following me.

Indeed, my V.A. issued ten's unit returned or I'll have to file a police report in order to receive a new one.

I'll also include the $100 in shrimp and bottle of medication stolen as well. If you need help with that, give me a holler.

You have [two] weeks to bring it to my mother's...that's when I'll be returning to ---- Parish to file the report. No need to respond.

(I don't have problems with stating the true facts or who I am. Call it drama if you'd like.

I call it being real since you felt compelled to add your drug-induced opinion to my page.)

P.S. All who read me know these are first drafts...not book finals, and that last paragraph is *fact*!

Addicts have trouble with facts, so don't look for me asking you for assistance.

Maybe, it's best for you to stop the substance abuse before commenting on people's pages.

—These comments are in regard to a video that circulated around about a speech given by Melania Trump, Republican candidate for U.S. President Donald Trump's wife.

The video showed her giving a speech that paralleled (word for word) a speech given by Michelle Obama.

The video was originally posted on one friend's page, which came my first comment, then shared on another with my name tagged, which led me to reposting the comment and adding to it.

Many may disagree with what I have to say, but what is said in cyber word remains forever.

Comments

•(Friend) It's all a show no matter who you support.

I never place my opinions on here about politics.

I find the video amusing.

•(Friend) I agree about wanting better candidates.

•(Me) You know me...I'm just going to say it!

Hope all is well on your end.

•(Friend) It's all good ☺ hope you are well, too.

•(Me) Thank you, but the comment I made didn't follow the post.

•(Me) Here's the comment: I would say a point has been proven that not one soul is acknowledging...the President stole dead Presidents' speeches during his first [four] years!

This was reported in several magazines, newspapers and I detailed it when I had my political, website which will be turned into a book. This is hilarious at best.

Obama could do this, but this woman can't.

[What] I really would like to know is Michelle's speech was actually original. This is all theatrics at best.

I think Trump has proven his point: The political machines own everything and our vote doesn't matter as well as you can screw up the country, but as long as you go out with a bang...all's well on the home front. No one takes into account the facts.

They propaganda over it at every curve. But who am I?

My opinion doesn't matter.

It's how many lies can be covered and how much show can twist up the people and make them see what's not and never has been there: Loyalty to the U.S. of A. by its own leader.

My personal opinion: Of all the people who are highly educated in this country...better candidates could have been chosen, but it's not for the people to decide anymore.

It's what the political machines want....

•(Me) I would like to add to my comment: I've done work using a bunch of sources on the Presidents of our country...I've used facts as well as included my own thoughts on these matters.

I can't and won't take credit for the research because the research was already done in a sense because those who wrote the books I read went through thousands of articles and documents to get the facts accurate.

I just added spirit to their work by putting their hard work into

rhyme in order to hopefully one day get students to enjoy learning about their history because all of this work of mine took a lot of time and reading, I'm not talking out of thin air.

No, you don't have to trust me.

God leads my way on this part of my journey, but...from all of this writing...I've learned that the political machines, which I'm referring to above have been in existence for a long time.

Some Presidents have gone against these machines...some were killed, some died mysterious deaths, some had attempts made on their life.

Those who found this country, warned against establishing parties... which would separate our country.... Fact: That was their warning.

Tell me I'm wrong: Their warnings have come to pass.

Influences that had no interest in what the *Declaration of Independence* stated are the responsible parties for all this mess we see today.

You have to understand our history in order to see clearly what is happening today.

Many think understanding history is a waste of time. I don't.

Many very smart people agree with me.

When I was stationed in Germany, many were laughing at the Clinton administration. Laughing!

We were a joke to the outside world who weren't influencing decisions. Republican...Democrat...it doesn't matter!

It's who is behind those parties that is making the decisions.

You can argue all you want. Facts are facts.

I'm currently typing in my work on McKinley...learn some history.

It's amazing to me how just the powers that be during McKinley's two terms have affected how things are now.

History says: You either do what we (political machines) want or we take you out!

Here's a small point: If you are going to go to school, if you are going to further your education, you might as well pay attention to what is being taught, you might as well pay attention to how outside influence is reshaping this country and not for the better, but to improve their agenda.

How many people who graduated from school in 1987 or before had the words Muslim or Islam in their history books?

My youngest son who hasn't graduated yet had those words in his history books, but we are not supposed to be teaching religion in schools...yet he was being taught about these so called religions.

So, I question everything being said in the media and what's now being taught to our students.

I've heard it too many times that history books lie!

They don't tell the truth.

I guess that would be said by those who haven't stretched their learning to books other than school books.

In doing so, reading books by people who have done a ton of research before publishing their books, people who write these books to understand the truth, will give you more...more of an incite of the truth of our history.

Plagiarizing any body's work is actually a federal law which I, personally support 100%. I don't care if they are alive or dead. They said it or wrote it. Not you.

If you can't come up with your own thoughts, then you shouldn't be writing or speaking before people you want to help or better. It's that simple.

I'm a very outspoken person when it comes to certain things.

My generation is at the age that we have to voice our thoughts with intelligence, with knowledge.

Our parents did it when we were young.

We have to face it that we are now standing on the plate that they once stood. If we don't do our duty as U.S. citizens, then all is lost... What I mean by that?

All that those who fought for us to have this great country.

We have to throw our pride out the window and use our voice.

Study all the events that took place during and after the writing of the *Declaration of Independence*.

Only then can you fully understand our duties as a citizen of this country. That's opinion and...and pure freaking facts.

I thank the teachers I had in high school and in college who taught me with passion.

If you're too lazy to read history books, then hold on...I wrote about it in a more entertaining way...the books are coming.

The teacher in me will never go away because of disabilities.

As long as my mind is intact, I will teach. It's your choice to learn.

—Why *Bat Cave*?

[Referring to the name of my publishing company and the logo.]

Before my divorce, I had a very large study

and I spent a lot of time in there learning my craft.

I tended to the daily chores in sun light and at night...this room became my haven.

My oldest child began labeling it the bat cave.

When throwing around ideas for a name, this one came up and the emotions went wild!

The logo...is very fitting for my first set of books that are coming, which I personally wrote.

It's about the woman *freeing* herself from abuse, divorce, heartache and surviving the five stages of grief.

The added wings...out the *cave...darkness* she flies...goes well with the covers that were designed for this series.

This is our first attempt at putting a solid bond on the brand. I love it.

It may change later...only by getting better if that's possible, but it's the beginning of seeing a dream come true.

~*(Untitled)*~

I have a beer, my dear
let me sit here, on my rear
chase away—all my fears
while I think about my career....

~*Hands to Hold*~

you come at me, you're not discrete
bold—unsure
maybe, there's a gun in my hand
maybe, I've some contraband

or maybe, I just like hands in pocket
or wearing my earphones in my car
so I can answer this here phone
for this car absent of bluetooth–
protecting me and you

or maybe, you're angry, having a bad day
I pass your way
through your veins runs hate
so I become your play

I'm just like you–
generation after generation
passed through without obligations
to changing the view

–it all seems like voodoo
we both, not really having a clue

–taking it upon ourselves
get off that dusty shelf—change the view
so our kids, won't suffer too

maybe, I do have a gun
–anger raging in stun
do you see inside of me, my hard history
maybe, my hand shakes
though you can't see—you're so angry
not seeing, what's at stake

maybe, I did some drugs–
stopping the pain
keeping from going insane
but soothing, I didn't gain
all looks like a game
emotions—adding to more pain

then you come along, thinking I'm a thug
you want to cut me down–
stump me like a bug
without knowing, the deal at home
why I'm here—a gun—all alone
maybe, don't yell
talk—love—let it swell

instead of jail, lead my soul to help
without making me hate myself

I, too, want peace
between you and me

maybe, instead of arrogance–
show understanding, compassion

I don't want a *free* ride
just a reason—inside—not to cry

I am tough—I've got muscles, tats
my life has been rough
–crazy and all that
it doesn't mean—I'm just stuff to pluck

a handshake, a hug
–that just might be enough

I'm a human being, I don't mean to sting
just a little bitter, please, your anger–
could you reconsider

look at me for me—God's† child
making my way—like you
through the miles

–the past is gone—this is *now*
together, we can make it all
worth while, if we just remain calm—
approach each other in mild

without death coming in fowl

(July 20, 2016)—*I alone cannot change the world, but I can cast a stone across the waters to create many ripples.*—Mother Teresa

At the end of our lives, we will not be judged by how many diplomas we have received, how much money we have made or how many great things we have done. We will be judged by 'I was hungry and you gave me to eat. I was naked and you clothed me. I was homeless and you took me in.'—Mother Teresa

You don't have to read this. Ignore it.

It's okay.

I'm used to it, but, like Mother Teresa, I won't stop. It's my choice.

It's your choice to ignore.

I still choose to love you.

I still choose to pray.

I still choose to speak of God's message in the voice that He gave to me.

I still choose to hope that others will see truth and stop falling to lies and deceit...that, too, is a choice. I choose truth.

I was led to two works this morning in the *Bible*.

One was *1 Chronicles 29:10-20* and the other *Psalms* 5.

Both are excellent and enlightened my heart, but *Psalms 5* really caught my attention the most.

Give ear to my words, O Lord, consider my sighing. Listen to my cry for help, my King and my God, for to You I pray. In the morning, O Lord, You hear my voice; in the morning, I lay my requests before You and wait in expectation....

All around us, we seem to be forgetting what really matters.

All of this mockery on *Facebook* and other parts of the internet seems to just keep going and going.

Here, the author of *Psalms 5* says to begin the day with asking...*asking*...for what we desire, then wait. God's time is not our time.

He doesn't rush in and answer on demand.

Sorry, He just doesn't work that way.

...You are not a God who takes pleasure in evil; with You, the wicked cannot dwell. The arrogant cannot stand in Your presence; You hate all who do wrong. You destroy those who tell lies; bloodthirsty and deceitful men, the Lord abhors....

God only wants love, but He gives us a choice.

That's true love...unconditional love...*free*-will. You have a choice.

You can either love or hate.

You can either do the right thing or play evil's game.

God doesn't say if that man insults you, you have the right to shot him or kill him.

The above passage says that—*You are not a God who takes pleasure in evil*—enough said.

...But I, by Your great mercy, will come into Your house; in reverence, will I bow down toward Your holy temple. Lead me, O Lord, in Your righteousness because of my enemies—make straight Your way before me....

When I read about *house* or *temple* (now this is just me), I think of *self*...what's inside of me.

I say this because I don't ever feel God in a building. I feel Him inside of me.

His temple for me is in my heart.

So, I read, in this part of *Psalms 5*, that if I allow God into my heart, He will give me the strength to deal with those who bring evil my way. Does that make sense?

You may disagree. That's okay.

That's *free*-will.

In my eyes, no building is going to come and give me strength, but God...inside of my heart..*wow*! how the strength comes.

Think about that.

...Not a word from their mouth can be trusted; their heart is filled with destruction. Their throat is an open grave; with their tongue they speak deceit. Declare them guilty, O God! Let their intrigues be their downfall. Banish them for their many sins, for they have rebelled against You....

Psalm 5 is, basically, a prayer for protection of the righteous.

I've looked up the meaning of *righteous* and there are many meanings.

What defines a person as *righteous* is an individual thing.

You can't argue really with that.

There's a prostitute that is spoken about in the *Bible*, then she became *righteous* in God's eyes. How?

She shielded some people, gave them a room to sleep for the night knowing that that simple act could have gotten her killed.

She could have turned them away, but she didn't.

She went from a sinner to a righteous person in God's eyes.

Today, (my opinion) if you're not bleeding the exact man-definition of the *Bible* from your veins, then you don't have a righteous bone in your body.

I think that's a bit of hypocrisy because that's man's judgment.

In the above passage, the writer is asking God to banish the evil, to take the evil out of their life.

In today's world, this is an every-day prayer.

Instead of us doing the banishing, we should ask God. He directs the path.

Instead of carrying around hate, we are told (and it works by the way) to give it to God.

Let Him deal with it.

...But let all who take refuge in You be glad; let them ever sing for joy. Spread Your protection over them, that those who love Your name may rejoice in You. For surely, O Lord, You bless the righteous; You surround them with Your favor as with a shield....

So here, in the same breath, he's asking for God to protect those who do right.

That's love, if you didn't get that.

I have this page in my *Bible* paper clipped.

It's been that way for about [five] years now. There's reasons for everything.

Psalm 5 has become very important when you look at all that is happening around us in the political world and in our communities.

The spread of hate through constant aggravation, of constant history reminding, of constant hocus-pocus...watching from the sidelines, it's all just a show to breed evil.

People are getting killed. People are dying.

People are pointing fingers...judging.

The truth hurts. I felt that anger.

I pointed fingers.

I have over [six] books that tell my story through the darkness...a lot of it I'm not proud of, but it all led me to God, to learning how to forgive myself and others who hurt me.

It all led me to understand what God wanted of me and how to read the words He sent to us.

You have to let go the hate and anger in your own heart, and then you have to stop breeding it. Hate breeds hate.

Love breeds love. It *is* that simple.

You may question my knowledge here.

I don't care.

Here's the facts: I grew up in South Louisiana...----- Parish.

I went to school at ----...go Mighty Mustangs.

I ran track for two years.

The student-body *relationship*...from my eyes... we were all just human beings trying to get the hell out of high school, but enjoying every moment we could...together! I joined the Army.

For over [four] months, eight women shared a room with me...[one] white, [one] Cajun, French, Indian, Irish (that would be me), the rest of color.

I went to Germany where I worked with the MPs...we didn't see color there either...we partied,

had fun, complained, bitched, prayed, laughed, worked, trained, experienced a war...together.

My best friend whom I'm sharing my life with... he's of color...like me all mixed in race.

We have our differences in views, in ways...took a while to get used to living together, but we know how to make each other smile.

Color, race...does not matter. Why should it?

All of this above led to *"Hands to Hold"* this morning.

Why are you still seeing differences?

Why are you still holding grudges about things that happened so long ago that wasn't in our control?

We all know that if something like that happened today, we wouldn't tolerate it.

So, why breed the hate of it now?

Things need to change.

Continuing to carry these burdens on our shoulders is doing one thing and one thing only: Leaving God out of the equation.

God's time is not ours.

Our ancestors leaned on God heavily.

God answered them.

They had to suffer first.

Do you ever think that God was testing them? I believe that. I think they passed.

Do you? We are *free* because of their faith. Jesus suffered.

Do you fully understand just how bad He suffered.

They whipped Him until the flesh fell from His body! He did that for us.

In turn, our ancestors suffered for us, too.

They gained for us the right of passage to *freedom*! We are *all* children of God.

There *is* evil.

It's talked about in the *Bible* over and over.

There are false prophets.

That is talked about over and over in the *Bible* as well.

I was told years ago to pick my fights that are worth fighting...the rest just walk away.

Pride, ego, lust, greed, gluttony...read about the *Seven Deadly Sins*. Learn them.

Avoid them.

In the end, it's you and God...all else won't matter.

That's just fact...all those marks on your heart...you will have to answer to them one day and there will be no court of law, there will be no guns, no home-boys or fellow cops to help you with the answers...it will be just you. What will your answers be?

A point to keep in mind: God already knows.

Can you turn it around like that prostitute in the

Bible?

It's also helpful to acknowledge that all those whom Jesus asked to follow Him: A lot of them led unrighteous lives.

God *is* forgiving...He truly is.

Love the skin you're in...you are worth it minus the color.

—I was awakened early this morning.

I've been sleeping until noon because I stay up pass midnight.

This morning, it seems God had something for me to say. Done. This is what I do.

No. I'm not a preacher. I was a teacher.

I'm a writer.

I'm slowly developing my brand.

I changed my author page appearance a bit. Things are taking shape.

I don't do this for money, but soon I'll have to start making some money in order to get my work out there to as many souls as possible.

I don't have a lot of likes on this author page. That's okay.

A lot of my readers are silent.

If you traveled the years...my work on my author page, you'll understand why.

I am about many things, so please don't put me in one category. Sorry...I just won't fit.

If you are struggling with something, just maybe, I can inspire you to keep going.

I want you to keep going.

Note: On my marketing...sorry, if you don't like it, just ignore it. I'm an entrepreneur in the making.

In today's world, we have to be...us artists.

There's no getting around that.

You can join me if you'd like.

It is quite a fun world to be in. Have a great day.

Off to work now...in my PJs!

—Winning Wednesday. 1. Don't rehash an old story. 2. Think 'bigger' than before. 3. Step outside your comfort zone. 4. Don't listen to negative 'mind-talk.'—Author Unknown

Good Morning America!, and *all* my friends from around the world.

Do you see the first thing on this list: *Don't rehash an old story*...take that advice please.

Today is a new day...*a new day*!

That evil whore is at work...working overtime to keep the chaos going.

We can fight this...it's called love!

Step outside that comfort zone and share a whole lot of smiles today ☺ ...just do it without expecting anything back.

Pay *zero* attention to negative...*zero*!

Think *outside* the box.

Don't egg negative...smother it! Be nice.

If someone is not doing the same in return, be nice anyway...it's not about them...it's about *you*!

Every *you* who can pull this off today, guess what?, a little bit of the world changes for the better of man kind.

That evil whore (the adversary) wants your happy. Are you going to give it up to it?

It's always a choice...and it's yours to make.

After all, *free*-will and unconditional love was given to each and every one of us without God having to think twice.

Do you think you have it in you to do the same?

Do the best you can today, then tomorrow and the next day and the next, it just gets easier. Love.

Hey...they don't write poems and songs and stories about that for nothing!

(Double negative intended!)

Share some love...

~*S.T.E.P.S. to Success*~

success—afraid
doesn't bring together days in paid

fade—play—sitting in wait–
only delays success's desirable weight

hard—steady work—you *must* flirt
–getting out that *pro-longed* surf
does—dawn a better shirt

changing your mind-set–
a few steps—as simple as *simple* gets:

s...tart the way——don't halt—stay
–drop fear away
no time like today—changes—do make

t...o become greater, won't come later
while being a hater or a disbeliever
rise above the deceiver–

–getting out that comfort zone
you'll soon be thrown
a different sortà bone–

becoming the receiver, so much better
than being stuck forever, just a dreamer

e...levate your life—bring it all in sight
with ease—peace

don't fight, turn it to blight
loosen up—walk in the light

what you desire–
quickly *becomes*—outright

p...ersonal height—building step by step
–a ladder to climb
an *always*-growing vine

...fast but don't show you're fasting....

the *bible* says in kind

–live within means
but don't demean what can be seen

read the signs—they're all around
showing where you're bound

s...elf must relay a better way
–to stagnate, leaves minds in sedate–
lost in fears—hate
not seeing clear—a journey's sway–
keeps you in yesterday

put *stubborn* on a shelf–
cover it with a quilt

take ego, pride—wrap them tight
in an old, worn piece of felt–
–push that too, further back on the shelf

then around, turn your *self*
walk away——move forward
towards *best*, without following the rest

take these steps—like forces of a jet
–but in ease, flow with the streams

your solemn face, from frown to gleam
no need to race
door after door, open, walk on through
–dreams to reality—your words to beam

soon you'll see exactly what I mean
you won't ever have to say—*please*
you'll just receive
but—first—you *must* conceive
believe, to truly receive!

(July 30, 2016)—*Think big and don't listen to people who tell you it can't be done. Life's too short to think small.*—Author Unknown

I wish you great success. Stay focused. Keep moving forward. Don't let anyone hold you back.—Author Unknown

What is 'your' definition of success? I think for everyone it is different.—Author Unknown

Call me crazy, but I love to see people happy and succeeding...life's a journey, not a competition.—Author Unknown

In Amy Morin's *13 Things Mentally Strong People Don't Do*, she talks about Herb Brooks.

He was a hockey player back in the day.

He landed a position on the 1960 U.S. Olympic hockey team only to be cut one week before the games.

The team went on to win the games.

As Morin writes, Brooks said to his coach after they won—*Well, you must have made the right decision—you won.*

That's what you call looking past hate and anger. Brooks didn't give up. No indeed.

He made the '64 and '68 Olympic teams, but no wins came.

He went on to become a hockey coach.

Here's one for you: Because of his perseverance, he was hired to coach the U.S. Olympic team!

The year was 1980. I was 11 years old.

My family was doing our traditional hog butcher and there was a lot of activity around the house.

I couldn't peel my eyes from the television that year, getting on my mother's nerves constantly because during a butchery, every hand is needed.

I was never a hockey fan until that year.

Brooks took his team to the Olympics as the underdogs. The Soviet Union ruled!

Ruled! with six golds out of [seven] Olympic games.

The U.S. beat the Soviets 4-3. that year.

Everyone's heart was pounding.

That didn't give them the gold yet...they had one more match!

I think everyone in America was holding their breath.

They took to the ice...Finland...it was a *slam, bam, thank you ma'am* and the crowd went wild!

I could see every American jumping up and down in their living rooms.

Yes, it was that exciting.

During the ceremony, every single player on the 1980 U.S. Olympic Hockey Team stood on that little round platform...the *gold*...the *winner's* circle!

That was an extraordinary thing to see!

Brooks did not stand on that platform.

He left not wanting to steal his teams thunder.

Morin concludes his story with a quote Brook's told his players (which later became one of his most famous quotes)—*Write your own book, instead of reading someone else's book about success.*

Morin writes——*...living an authentic lifestyle is essential to anyone who wants true success in life.*

I read a book by the Dalai Lama and he says the exact same thing.

You can follow others who are already successful, try to piggy-back off of them by trying to mimic what they are doing.

People do it all the time.

Notice how those people never really reach the same level of success as those they are following or piggy-backing off of.

Do you know why?

Because, even if they never, actually, admit it, they resent the more successful person.

That *resentment* keeps a person from ever achieving their full potential.

I had a quote by a well-know publisher taped to my computer for the longest time before all my moves and it got lost in transition.

It said, in so many words: Do your own thing because imitation is suicide.

I've lived my life accordingly.

At the end of Morin's chapter titled *'They Don't Resent Other People's Success,'* she gives some very good *helpful* tips to follow:

1. Create your own definition of success.
2. Replace negative thoughts that breed resentment with more rational thoughts.
3. Celebrate other people's accomplishments.
4. Focus on your strengths
5. Cooperate rather than compete with everyone.

Read that list several times, then read the following list of things that Morin writes that are *not* helpful:

1. Chase after everyone else's dreams.
2. Imagine how much better everyone else's lives are.
3. Constantly comparing yourself to everyone around you.
4. Diminish other people's achievements.
5. Treat everyone like they're your direct competition.

Do you see the difference in these two lists?

This is where *"S.T.E.P.S. to Success"* comes from.

I've read many books throughout the years...many, many self-help and inspirational books.

One message kept coming through all of them: *Be you!*

If Brooks would have quit and gave up because he *didn't* make the final team back in 1960, he would never have had the success he did 20 years later.

That's interesting, isn't it?

Success comes when we don't give up.

Success comes when we get *out* of our comfort zones.

Success comes when we can conceive... that means we have a dream; when we believe...that means we truly believe we will succeed.

Conceiving and believing something I think people get confused with.

If you haven't watched *The Secret* or read the book, you should.

In order to received something we truly want, we first have to believe it's ours.

It doesn't matter if other people don't believe in you.

It only matters that *you* believe in *you*.

Something that the speakers in *The Secret* said over and over again was that if you *live* like you already have it...then you are putting it out in the universe and, sooner or later, it becomes reality.

This is also stated in the *Bible*.

So, if you live like you already have success...I'm not talking about living beyond your means...I'm talking about as the *Bible* talks about *fasting*...in today's world...live thrifty, but fashionably.

Trust me...this is *very* doable!

Building your dream should be fun not stressful. Think about that, then do.

Don't hold your own *self* back because of tradition or beliefs in ideologies that aren't designed to better the *common* man.

Trust me on this.

I proved this theory after I was divorced and moved. I was so freaking broke.

I didn't live in *broke*.

It was a struggle, but I lived like I was already *free* and independent.

One and a half years later...I *was* totally *free* and independent, then...then I was taken back around on a journey showing me how even people with money can't move forward if they don't better themselves, and people without money won't get out of the situation they are in if they don't better themselves.

The bottom line and the *most* important factor I see in those who are successful...I mean truly successful (financially and in happiness)...they constantly better themselves, they are constantly improving their individual *self*...and...*and* they do their own thing!

Love the skin you're in.

~

(August 1, 2016)—Over 400 *new laws* that we did *not* vote for...read them.

They passed a law saying we *can* wear pink to hunt. Really?! Give me a break.

Who gives them the right to tell us what we can wear when we hunt?

Go read some of these ridiculous *rules* that we *did* not vote for! Over 400!

Who made these political feed-off-the-taxpayers blood-suckers *God*?

If I want to wear blue while hunting, I'll wear freaking blue. Yeah, I said that.

Yes, the judgmental side of me...there's your socialist nation.

Welcome to the new America.

~

(August 2, 2016)—I saw the Rock and his song last night, then I wake up to the following message in my in-box.

I took out the spaces, so it wouldn't be too long.

I love my marketing friends and they have their own little way of saying things to market their product. I appreciate that.

I know Trump got into marketing, but to market the presidency by giving away a *free* book! My vote is not for sale.

There are no candidates that I appreciate enough to cast it either.

(One can't be trusted period with national secrets and one seems to be just theatrics!)

I really don't think my vote matters.

The electoral college makes that decision and they (whoever *they* are) makes sure they line the pockets of *whoever* is on the *electoral college,* which is illegal anyway.

By illegal, I mean unconstitutional, but our *Constitution* doesn't seem to matter anymore anyway from all the things I'm reading, so... in my personal opinion, which is not that big anyway either, after all the things I've read in history, this campaign is beyond mockery of what this country stands for.

If you don't voice your opinion about it or stand for *something,* then you are bought no matter how you look at it.

If you voice your opinion, then you get arrested in one way, shape, or form: Either they literary put cuffs on you or they slam you in others ways with fines, charges on your accounts that you have to fight, they spread shit about you on the web, so if you have a business, guess what... not anymore...or they send people to your area to make your life a living hell and your head is spinning so fast that before you know it, your life is in shambles and you have not one clue how the hell it happened.

If you don't believe me, ask others.

Oh, I forgot...like the Clintons and the current administration...they just see to it that you don't live!

In body or business...it doesn't matter!

It's all the same!

I think I'll just stick with God.

He knows the history. He knows the future.

He warns not to trust in leaders who don't follow His way.

This goes for other countries as well.

The new America I guess belongs to the world now.

So, marketeers, Steve Case has it right, the *Third Wave* is an individual thing, which moves into partnerships with like-minded people...my thrown in meaning: I really don't think countries matter, but each country will try to stop your progress by implementing more and more rules on how your hard-earned money is handled and how much they (each country) can take.

If you stay neutral on the political spectrum, you'll fair well until you realize all that hard work is gone or slammed with taxes because big companies support politics and policy...*policy* (*rules* and/or *laws*...it's all the same) controls the little people and they *want* you to work hard, so that *you* make *them* all the money, then they slam shut the door when you figure out how it all works.

P.S. It's all just a game.

The money goes to who plays well with others.

By the way: That seems to be a forced deal.

You play the game or don't play at all.

That's their (the big boys) motto.

Don't take my word for it.

It's the facts all the same.

—One of Trump's Marketing Emails:

From: Donald J. Trump (contact@gopteam.gop)

This message is in your junk folder because you don't seem to want mail from this sender.

Sent: Tue 8/02/16 10:06 AM

Karen, I've spent over four decades of my life making successful deals, and as your next president, I will make great deals that finally put[s] America first!

I've written all about my history of making successful deals in my best-selling book, *The Art of the Deal*, and now I want you to have a signed copy with a campaign contribution of $184 today.

Karen: *The Art of the Deal* is now out of print, so this is a very limited edition issue and only available through this special offer, through my campaign.

Nothing gets done in Washington because we have too many politicians who have zero experience solving problems in the real world.

When I'm president, I promise to change the corrupt culture that has led to gridlock, out-of-control waste, and massive bureaucracy that hurts working Americans the most, but first I want you to read about the unique leadership and business acumen I will bring to the White House in my best-selling book, *The Art of the Deal*.

Get your signed copy of *The Art of the Deal* with a contribution of $184 today.

Thank you and God bless you, Donald J. Trump

P.S. I'm signing copies of my best-selling book, *The Art of the Deal*. Get yours with a campaign contribution of $184 today.

~

(August 3, 2016)—*Anti-vax*...that's a mouthful.

Small pox...polio...oh just those diseases that killed or crippled thousands of people.

Vaccines that were designed to prevent them are now being denied to children by ignorant parents! Really?

So...because of all these ignorant people, the rest of us will have to suffer when there lies enough raw, unprotected meat for these viruses to resurface because that's how viruses fest...on meat...that would be human beings.

So, enough unprotected people start the virus, then all this sickness goes around many other pathogens that didn't exist 50 years ago...bam!...the creation of a new virus strand none of us are protected against!

Way to go anti...*vax*!

Your unrealistic look at life could very well be the primary reason for that coming plague many scientists warn us about!

Genius!

~*The 'S' of It*~

instant gratification—resist
remain steadfast
values, morals, objectives–
place emphasis

your goal's consist, be an optimist
don't forget the premise–
solid foundations
behind objectives to accomplish

to yourself—promise
every temptation:
to be dishonest, to be a pessimist
to be a defeatist—a racist
or an extremist, or fall into malaise–

resist, resist, resist

each reached milestone, be the enthusiast

–celebrate in bliss

do not desist over some exhibitionist

in your own world–
practice, practice, practice
be a learning opportunist
show me that, show me this
insist, insist, insist
become the specialist

don't tread the surface
dig deep in patience
over every obstacle—persist

be an industrialist
expectations—be realistic
immediate results—don't exist

anger, frustration, disappointment–
all part of the process
–don't just dismiss from them–
be an escapist

like a nonconformist–
for each crises, formulate solutions–

instead of falling into a false crevice
of a propagandist
putting you in paralysis
with their false hypnosis

be the controversialist
persist, persist, persist
keep focus, build your edifice
brick by brick—with substance

being a little modest in your quest–
brings finesses, leading to progress
up the ladder—step by step

resistance, experience, attendance
diligence, intelligence, persistence
consistence, insistence

all leads to the zest of success

(Written August 6, 2016)—From *The American Heritage Dictionary:*

Resist: to strive or work against; oppose; to withstand
Consist: to be made up or composed; to be inherent
Inherent: existing as an essential constituent or characteristic; intrinsic
Intrinsic: belonging to the essential nature of a thing
Constituent: serving as part of a whole; component; empowered to elect; authorized to make or amend a constitution; one represented by an elected official; a component
Insist: to be firm in one's demand; to assert or demand vehemently and persistently
Assert: to state positively; affirm; to defend or

maintain
　Vehemently: characterized by forcefulness of expression or intensity of emotion; ardent; marked by vigor or energy; violent
　Ardent: characterized by warmth of passion; emotion; or desire; passionate; glowing; fiery; burning
　Vigor: physical or mental energy or strength; strong feeling; enthusiasm or intensity; effectiveness; force
　Persistently: to hold firmly and steadfastly to a purpose or undertaking despite obstacles; to continue in existence
　Premise: a proposition upon which an argument is based or from which a conclusion is drawn

~

(August 7, 2016)—Posted an article titled *'The True Story: Donald Trump Did Not Mock a Reporter's Disability'—catholics4trump.com*

My journalist professors taught me to be objective.

Though in my darkness...objectively was lost to my inability to care really about no one, but myself.

In my healing years, that changed and I regained ground, although when writing, because of my personal experience, I tend to fight for the good God-fearing woman over the good God-fearing man.

I apologize for my shortcomings.

The attached article is excellent.

The media has not been objective, instead rather deceiving and manipulative for over [nine] years now. It disgust me.

I read this story years ago about this man who pulled over to fix a flat tire.

When offered money, he refused.

The man in the car was Donald Trump.

Trump paid off the man's mortgage.

This was years before he ever announced and probably even considered running for president!

What does Trump have to lose by mocking anyone? Not one damn thing.

Unlike anybody who's ever run for U.S. President, Donald Trump is a billionaire!

He makes more money *not* being president!

I would reckon he is losing money by running and will lose more by actually being President. Lies.

This article shows you how the media is lying. Why?

I can tell you, but you would not believe me. Sarcasm intended.

~*Stuck*~

staying in stuck–

there lies a flapping duck
digging in mud—a self-made nut
–all ends, carelessly tucked

waiting for others' cuts
–not your own buck, depending on luck
leaving you in lonely's hut
drown in muck

get off your butt—have the guts
all temptations—pluck
stop being the bug or passive's cub

there's no lanterns to rub
there's no flying rugs

getting out of stuck–
a self-motivated *self*, filled with love
takes the plunge, doesn't go nuts–

all doubt—unplug
all those fears—in—suck

determination—in—plugs
doesn't wait for another to nudge
knows the way
pulls the plug, on being stuck

even after being fucked
move forward—like a speeding truck

(August 20, 2016)—*Never let life impede on your ability to manifest your dreams, dig deeper into your dreams, and deeper into yourself and believe that anything is possible, and make it happen.*—Corin Nemec

~*Mistakes Teach*~

set pride aside, look inside
–see answers that hide

each venture—see the adventure
–not the failure, but the answer

it's all before the eye–
instead of asking *why*, ask *how*
–improving *I*, always propels the tide

be an evolving creature
then become the teacher
–your worse dents
become your best features

mistakes drive—each—every try
pushes high, high—that direction in fly

(August 9, 2016)—*If you want to change, you have to be willing to be uncomfortable.*—Author Unknown

What constitutes getting uncomfortable?
How about putting all your money into your business and having that extra to pay

rent, phone bill, the internet (can*not* go without this!), the utilities, car note, car insurance, and letting everything else go, so you can eat!

If you want something, you have to go get it! It's that simple.

I'm not going to tell you getting it will be simple.

That's the hard part and the exciting part if you look at it with your goal in mind.

It helps to be around like-minded people as well.

As a regular reader of me, you know I'm not going to sugar-coat anything. So, I won't.

Doing *you*...doing your dream will be hard work. Can you handle that?

Not giving up won't be easy.

There will be people who will get in your way until you get them *out* your way.

There will be haters.

There will be obstacle on top of obstacle.

Are you strong enough?

It will cost you money.

Can you give up some extras today, so you can see your dream come true tomorrow?

Can you? Trust me.

My dream has been inside of me most of my life. I'm 47 years old.

I'm not slowing down.

I'm speeding up, and to see that dream actually taking shape after all this time is like watching a baby being born.

I never stopped to look at my work as work. I just always did what was in my heart.

That moment when you realized you started from a dot!

That's a *wow* kind of moment!

That dream lingering there in your heart, it's not going to get itself done.

You've got to get up and take action!

Trust me. I know what this means.

For over 30 years I've been writing, editing, writing, reading, writing.

It's a lonely profession. Was it worth it?

Yes. Has it made me any money?

When I went for it, yes.

I self-published my first novel in 2004.

I pushed. I advertised. I did interviews.

I did book signings. I made t-shirts.

I made fliers.

I made everything I spent on that book back. In 2004, there was no *CreateSpace*!

I wanted to buy more books, so I borrowed $1,200 from my mom.

In less than a month, I walked into her house and handed her the money back.

She looked at me in surprise and said—*I thought you needed it.* I told her I did.

I sold enough books to pay her back with a little left over.

That didn't happen because someone walked up to me and handed me money.

Nope. I had to work for it!

Work and you get the payoff.

That's the fruit.

After all the hard work, you get the fruit.

Does that make sense?

During the process, you have to be determined. You have to be resilient.

You have to be persistent, and...you have to know yourself.

If you don't know who you are, you back track over and over again. Trust me on this.

I've done it a time or two. *Uncomfortable.*

That's a mouthful.

That's what it takes to make that dream come true.

Do you want to know the really odd thing about *uncomfortable*?

Once you decide *this is what I want* and you start putting everything you've got into it, you get use to that *uncomfortable* feeling and it becomes *comfortable*.

You might not think so, but it does happen.

It's just like if you've been through the darkness. Was it comfortable? No indeed not!

I can vouch for that, but it took that *uncomfortable* feeling to push you into the healing direction. Right? It did for me.

It is the same when you decide you are going to make that dream come true no matter what. You are not changing yourself.

You are improving yourself.

During the *uncomfortable* period, it may not seem like it, but it's true all the same.

Do *you*.

Get used to giving up things in order to build yourself and your business.

You are supposed to be happy with what you already have.

Once you do that, you get the fruits.

One more small piece of advice: It pays to be around like-minded people.

Those kinds of people will tell you like it is.

It won't matter if it hurts you (your pride that is). They are going to be real with you.

They are going to push you to places you never thought you'd go. Trust me on this.

I have a few of these that have never given up on me, and, sometimes, what they did or said hurt.

It took a while for me to see their point of view. *Wow*—That's what I say.

They were right all along.

I was the stubborn one. Get uncomfortable.

Get comfortable with the uncomfortable and plow on no matter what.

It's what you leave behind that matters most.

It's what you *turn* your *uncomfortable* into that matters.

~

(August 11, 2016)—*Doubt your Doubts.*—Author Unknown

Where ever you go. What ever you do.

Some won't support you.

Some will try and change your mind.

Some will stab you in the back by talking their talk about you, by trying to disrupt your credibility, by diminishing your character.

Some of those will be your closest friends and your family. Let them.

Don't...don't let that *some* put doubt into your head about what you have set out to do.

That *some* will do what they can to bring you down because, simply, they can't do *you*.

That *some* does *not* make up your whole!

I have had my fair share of these that I've grouped in *some*.

I have been one of those *some*.

It doesn't matter what others think.

It doesn't matter what mistakes you've made because God has a plan for you and it's going to happen anyway.

So, really, why bother?

I know what I have to do.

Just because I've written a bunch of books doesn't mean I'm going to be rich.

That's not the real purpose of you doing your dream. The purpose is the *doing* part.

The objective is the *finishing* part.

I know I may get interrupted here and there.

Some get interrupted for a year or more.

As long as you and I find our way back to our path, and don't worry, we will, it's all good.

It's how we handle ourselves during the interruptions that teach us the most.

I don't fear the interruptions anymore.

I just live life simple. I do get excited.

I do have goals to accomplish.

I do know that I will accomplish them.

I do know that I will die one day.

That's just the natural order of things.

So, why waste time with that *some* who don't want the best for you.

Haven't you spent enough time wanting the best for others? Get rid of the doubt.

You *are* going to make it.

You *are* going to see it through.

Even when it gets hard, you *will* overcome.

You *will* succeed.

Replace doubt with the surety of *knowing* it's going to happen! ☺

Comments
•(Friend) I love you, Karen! Keep your dreams alive!
•(Me) Love you, too, [friend].

*—Every successful piece of non-fiction should leave the reader with one provocative thought that he or she didn't have before. Not two thoughts, or five—just one.—*William Zinsser

That's all you need to accomplish in each book.

~

(August 12, 2016)—Posted a video of a guy swimming and playing in a flooded Louisiana ditch.

The comments on here are just OMG!

There's always been bacteria.

Media...seems to be using every agenda, every means to instill fear.

If people would use vaccines, go to doctors when they have something just not right on the skin...pay attention, just maybe, you wouldn't get so sick.

We all did this as a child.

We would dawn old shorts and run and slide all over the yard.

Ants would bite us, who cared...we had a blast!

Now, everyone has put fear in everyone's brain that they are so scared to go swimming!

They blame the water! They fear the water! Source...solutions!

Does that not ring a bell with anyone?

No, it's easier to blame the water.

Just like it's easier to blame the victim.

Why not just take responsibility like the adults used to do and look for solutions?

The comments here are absolutely childish.

These are adults saying these things.

Fear is not having faith.

Sorry...and it's spread by those who rather blame, then be an adult.

One more observation: You want that heat and air conditioning.

You want all that processed food.
You want all those clothes you wear.
You want all those houses and cars.
The list goes on and on...but you complain that water and such is contaminated.

You watched the news when Japan was hit with that big wave...what was that again?...sass intended...and a nuclear what? was kind of messed up, then the scientist gave the predictions, based on their expertise, which doesn't hold much water these days according to the geniuses who refuse to vaccinate their kids, and you didn't listen.

They did the same thing when Mount St. Helen was going to blow...no one wanted to listen. A week later...she blew!

Double standards...so tired of this.
It's the same with the Trump deal.
He said what everyone's thinking.
Y'all bash him.

Yet the government, which he's not yet a part of, is funding terrorist nations.

Where's the logic?

The government, which he is not yet a part of has how many Moslims working for them, yet Moslims hate the U.S.A.

Misspelling intended.

This is the most confusing *religious* order I've ever studied.

I think the Mormons don't even come close. You know what I see?

I see my parents in the 70s and 80s who have worked all their life for what they have struggling to pay for medical while people who never worked for anything getting everything, which they didn't earn.

I have some neighbors here who live like pigs...I can bet you that they are here illegal! and nobody cares...they pay their rent, so it doesn't matter...they go to the hospital and I pay the bill! the taxpayer. That's serious.

Yet, you complain and criticize a man having a ball in a flooded ditch.

This stuff just amazes me.

I read on a social media marketing site that marketeers don't want to work with negative people. They only want positive.

If you are speaking up about issues and debating, you are considered a negative person. That's dictating to me.

Have you ever looked at videos concerning the *dark web*?...maybe, you should.

There's more to all of this than what meets the eye and gullibility is rapid.

(I would stay away from *all* bitcoin programs if I were you).

Maybe, I'll end up dead...a mysterious death suddenly...I mean the political machines here are just the start...anyone who speaks up seems to be cut short or condemned.

Y'all call this man stupid for swimming in a ditch.

Y'all call Trump stupid for calling it as he sees it.

A billionaire suddenly losing his mind.
I don't think so.
Hitler's play book in action.
It's really amusing to watch. You know me.
I'm going to say it. Amusing.

Maybe, more should actually read the *Bible,* then they'd see what hands they are falling into. Just saying....

P.S. History tells the story: Credibility is everything.
Credibility changes the course of history in every kind of form.
It's easy to ruin a person's credibility.
The *Bible* says to leave it be.
You don't have to defend stupidity.
Karma comes back around.
You can't educate fools. Illusions are so easy.
Manipulation is even easier.
Hitler did it and didn't have TV or internet.
I would start looking a little harder at what you are, actually, reading and looking at...the obvious is always right in front of your nose.
Me...I've always been mistaken for the fool.
It's easier to be dumb, then smart...meaning smart people are constantly challenged by stupidity, so it's easier to just act dumb, so you don't have to keep explaining shit to people.
Anyone who lives with an above average IQ understands this statement.
I'm celebrating this guy.
There's ants in that ditch.
Anyone from south Louisiana knows that.
Yet, he's swimming anyway. Hurray!
You're only given one life, then God judges us.
Screw what others think. Who are they to judge?
We live, get sick and die.
Fleshing eating diseases...they had plagues, too, spread by fleas. I bet you blame the flea!
Just saying....

~*Breaking*~

who are you, questioning words sent
who are you—His† meanings bent

with every message
see the carnage, see the suffrage

hell in the mix–
what He's† given time—us to fix

the fight is on, staying up 'til dawn

as seeds sown, for each's own

He† awaits the break, then He'll† take
—it's not fake—He† will awake–
His† power won't just make
—but earth, He'll† shake
for good to retake—life in His† wake

~Joker in History~

in history, it comes around
–in abundance—found—then disappears
playing like a clown

under the ground—safe and sound
'til man's hunger steps out of bounds

blame shifts, looking within themselves–
guilt never found, killing each other off
one by one, 'til nothing but tips—found

the joker inside the clown
never totally leaves
–just waits around—'til balance
once again found

~Selfish Sways~

taking for granted–
each thousand years, hopes die
in dry beds—cry

same ole, same ole

the wild card under the yard
suffers the bleeding heart
–slowly drifting a part
as man loses sight—it's true fight

things, things, things
stuff, stuff, stuff

clear messages sent—out ears—went
from common sense, sways the cent

earth protects from birth
dry dirt—a cent's worth
when greed—man does flirt

~

(August 20, 2016)—An interracial couple
is sentenced to prison in 1958 for getting
married in the [first] trailer for *Loving*.
Starring: Joel Edgerton, Ruth Negga, and
Michael Shannon.
Really? This was in 1958!
What the hell is wrong with you people?
Really!
Y'all go to church and you carry hate!

That's why I stopped going to a church
because I couldn't stand the hypocrisy
anymore.
I was raised in a strange place when it
comes to all this.
I had fear and didn't really know what that
fear was about. I do now.
Now, I see the hate when people speak up
and talk...i.e. say the damn truth.
Never forget...the truth never changes.
Lies evolve. It's amazing.
1958 and they got put in prison for being
in love because they weren't the same color?!
It seems like common sense isn't so
common after all!
Here's a pointer: Jesus wasn't black.
Jesus wasn't white.
If you want to argue that point, then you
need a geography lesson.
Why don't you start there?
Get the color of Jesus right, then you might
be able to really figure out what your hate is
really about.

~Times in Chaos~

it all seems surreal
this break-in-chaos deal

–staying in stability, what's the ability
when all seems missing from reality

it eats away time, it ain't nothing kind
–no where's to draw the line
it just keeps it's whine

round and round—there it goes
just as soon go in flow, whatever the sow
that hand doesn't stop
–even when things flop

age creeps on in—it's not your friend
when you can't bend

why worry, that just halts your story–
paying homage to those
who'll never say *sorry*

life—live and die
if it's allowed, chaos steals
missing goes time
–can't get it back—that's just fact

let it go—all that chaos
talk it out—flow
life continues, whatever the menu
it's not a race—time is time

round and round, there it goes

let it eat you, or just enjoy the view
live then die
how you live shows how you die
it's up to you, enjoy the view
or let times in chaos finish you

(September 28, 2016)—*You want me to do
something...tell me I can't do it.*—Maya Angelou

Take a leap of faith.—Author Unknown

*But who am I, and who are my people, that we should
be able to give as generously as this? Everything comes
from You, and we have given You only what comes from
Your hand. We are aliens and strangers in Your sight,
as were all our forefathers. Our days on earth are like
a shadow, without hope. O Lord our God, as for all this
abundance that we have provided for building You a
temple for Your Holy Name, it comes from Your hand, and
all of it belongs to You. I know, my God, that You test the
heart and are pleased with integrity. All these things have
I given willingly and with honest intent. And now I have
seen with joy how willingly Your people who are here have
given to You. O Lord, God of our fathers Abraham, Isaac
and Israel, keep this desire in the hearts of Your people
forever, and keep their hearts loyal to You.*—1 Chronicles
29:10-20

Yes! Yes! Yes!

I can't say these things better than David
can, but I can say that God is always with
us in good and bad; and I can say that with
surety. I wrote *"Times in Chaos"* August 27.

It was a bit of a shaky time in my heart.

My mother and sister both had surgeries
scheduled and this affected me.

The world in which we live, with all its
issues, affected me. My dog is sick.

"Times in Chaos."

I wasn't going to comment on this work or
post it here, but, then things do change.

A good *Facebook* friend contacted me after
being absent for a while.

He reminded me that I'm not the only one
going through chaos. Indeed, I am not.

In the *Chronicles*, David speaks of God's
blessing.

If it weren't for God, the people who built
the great temple would not have had the
resources they needed in order to do so.

I still see piles of debris all around where
I live.

There was not enough attention on this
great flood down here in Louisiana (that's the
United States).

I don't think people really understand how
devastating it was.

I do understand that people around the
world suffer from atrocities.

We have, here, too, but not like this.

It rained for a few days only, and...and...
the water!

(Enough to fill [three] football fields if you stood
them up! That's a lot of water!)

This flood was not caused by a great storm.
Just rain.

This flood was not caused by anything
expecting. None of us had a clue.

Not even an iota of a guess that that rain
would cause so much lost.

Over 40,000 homes were flooded.

I know a lot of my audience are from other
countries.

Here, when I say homes, I'm talking
footage...in the area of 1,200 to 4,000 square
feet of house. That's a lot of house!

They do big here, and they do small.

These are solid houses.

Some have been in families for a very long
time. Some were completely paid for.

Some were owed a lot on. Devastating.

I got word yesterday that insurance
companies aren't moving in a timely speed.

Some families couldn't afford insurance.

Some thought they had flood insurance,
but found out they didn't. The price.

When we feel down, when we feel like we
can't cope, think of atrocities like this one
here in Louisiana.

At the beginning of 2014, there were some
Monks from India who were traveling around
the United States. It was a hard year for me.

I was lucky enough to be able to sit one on
one with an elder of the Monks who told me
through this ancient reading that I *think* too
much. He was, and is, right.

He told me that a good way to calm my
mind was to think of women and children
in third world countries who didn't have a
home, barely any food, who hardly had water
to bathe.

He made me picture this in my mind and
it has stuck to those over-thinking waves of
mine like glue. There are earthquakes.

There are massive floods.

There are hurricanes.

There are volcanoes...and the list goes on
and on.

When you are fighting for your place in
this world and things aren't going so great,
think of people who have suffered more.

Think of Jesus! He suffered. Greatly.

For you! We all have trying times.

It's how we cope that means something.

The prevailing part is...well...just the prevailing part. Why do I say it that way?

Because the prevailing part *is* all about how we coped.

It's not a celebration about us making it through.

It's a celebration about *how* we *made* it through.

We don't always *do* that coping thing well.

I know I failed at it and still do here and there. It takes a lot of courage to cope.

To deal. Don't worry baby, God has us. That's right.

He won't give us more than we can take even though it seems like it. Trust me.

I know this feeling well.

He comes through for me in the most unlikely ways. He will do that for you, too.

Just trust. Keep your faith. Plow on.

The best...the best thing to do in times of difficulty is to keep it moving forward.

You can't do anything about flooded waters.

You can't do anything about the economics of the world.

You can't do anything about your boss being a *dick* (pardon the language).

You just can't. What can you do? *You!*

You can still smile, can't you?

Even when all has been taken, you *can* still smile. I know it's hard.

You have to force it, and you can, too.

I had a 2,400 square-foot house filled with things...all the joys of my children and my life. I have two small storage units left.

Yes, everything is in storage.

My children are living their lives with not much time to sit and talk with their *ole* mom.

I had 2.7 acres of land...a beautiful home and yard, flower beds and gardens.

Not any more. You keep going.

You don't let the adversary get *one* tiny ounce! Not one! You cry. You scream.

You throw shit around, then you get the hell up and keep going because, guess what, God gave everything that you ever had to you. He will again. If that is what you want.

Me. I don't want things anymore.

I want to see others really happy because I realize that's not a codependent *self*...that is *God*! I want to see you happy, too.

In all your mess, I want to see you smile.

I cry, too, but I've learned to laugh harder.

There's one more *guess what*: You *are human*! God didn't make you a god.

He made you human.

So, don't beat yourself up.

Live, love and pray.

He's listening...even when you think He's not. God bless you my dear friends.

—Update for family and friends of the family: Mom thought it would be easier letting y'all know here than calling everyone.

She had right shoulder surgery on Friday, there was a little bit complication, but she's a fighter.

Her diabetes count is high and she's moving slow, other than that, she's doing good.

Since she is 70, and it is her dominate arm and other factors, they are keeping her in the hospital for another night, then moving her upstairs to in-house therapy for a week.

She does have a cell phone.

If you'd like to call her, message and I'll send you her number.

Don't leave a message or text her...she has no idea what to do with text, nor the faintest clue to how to check phone messages.

She's old school and really likes it that way.

~Goblets of Man~

you speak of oppression–
do you feel His† devotion
prophecies long ago–
events didn't yet flow

a once-again history, haven't you learned
–this ancient story—a repeating mystery

double-standard window—crashes
when the cock crows
three, three, three—repeat, repeat, repeat
history, story, history

where lands flow—milk and honey
no difference in geography, same scenery

generation after generation
teachings—God's† mystery
His† grace in spirituality
building of loyalty

three, three, three

Father, Son, Holy Spirit†

–slow fading ancestry
false-god atrocity—beliefs

things worldly—separating
what's spiritual and holy

history, story, history

blame becomes the directory
the devil—our adversary
a way out—so easy
without seeing, understanding

God† brings His† wrath
when our *selves* craft
–in our own backs—stab
He† becomes just a fad
–believing we're too good, Him†, to ask

three, three, three

your embodiment of angry
your hate-distorted creativity
your vengeful destructibility
your materialistic vulnerability

all—He† sees
yourself—believe or deceive

His† cup changed before
–man opened *that* door
underestimating His† core

history, story, history—three, three, three
double-standard windows crash
when the cock crows

(August 30, 2016)—*Your mind is a powerful thing. When you fill it with positive thoughts, your life will start to change.*—Author Unknown

Time for Change (A picture with a clock set on [three] o'clock)—Author Unknown

I am me. I don't pretend to be like everyone else. I don't want to be like everyone else, and I will not change who I am just to 'fit in.'—Author Unknown

Don't dig up in doubt what you planted in faith.—Elisabeth Elliot

I've been quite busy lately.
A *stupid* busy...lost in my head.
What do I mean by that?
I haven't been reading the words of God like I usually do each morning, for one, and...I've been paying too much attention to crap. That's right: *Crap!*
I should be totally, 100%, focused on completing my vow.
(You would have to read me to understand that.)
But...a few things have been put in front of me.
One, which has been a direction I've been headed towards for a while, is important.
A relationship.

The other is how I'm to present this material to the public.
Both of these are really important and it's obvious to me how both are intertwined with the vow I've made.
The rest that has caused me to halt my progress...is my fault and my fault alone or so I thought.
I wanted to take a break from posting anymore work and devote all my time to completing my work (I've been here over and over...!), but...always a but...this morning, I picked up my *Bible*, something I haven't done in a while, and Isaiah had some pretty powerful things to say.
I rewrote here the entire verse.
I had to read this over and over, wondering what it was saying to me...then *"Goblets of Man"* bled onto the page.
I'll give you a moment to read the verse itself, then I'll explain....

Awake, awake! Rise up, O Jerusalem, you who have drunk from the hand of the Lord the cup of His wrath, you who have drained to its dregs the goblet that makes men stagger; of all the sons she bore there was none to guide her; of all the sons she reared there was none to take her by the hand. These double calamities have come upon you—who can comfort you?—ruin and destruction, famine and sword—who can console you? Your sons have fainted; they lie at the head of every street, like antelope caught in a net. They are filled with the wrath of the Lord and the rebuke of your God.

Therefore hear this, you afflicted one, made drunk, but not with wine. This is what your Sovereign Lord says, your God, who defends His people: 'See, I have taken out of your hand the cup that made you stagger; from that cup, the goblet of My wrath, you will never drink again. I will put it into the hands of your tormentors, who said to you, 'Fall prostrate that we may walk over you.' And you made your back like the ground, like a street to be walked over.—Isaiah 51:17-23

Since 2011, *three* has been significant in my life.
I began waking up at [three] a.m. every morning for no reason at all.
This became more profound as the years went on and the darkness clouded my whole life.
Now, it's not just [three] a.m., but [three] p.m. as well.
I make jokes about it all the time...*three*!
The power of *three* should ring with significance in everyone's life.
It's sad to see that it doesn't.
I can't preach to you on how to live.
I can't teach you how to live.
Only you can do that.

Only you can see how your life is shaping and only you have the ability to see God and understand what He wants of you.

The one most powerful thing I've learned, without a shadow of a doubt, in the past four years is that speaking the truth brings strife... people are afraid to face *truth*...that *truth* is what's in your heart.

People don't want to know your truth.

They don't want to face *truth* period...it seems.

Of all the things I've seen and read, it seems people just don't even want to face *truth* when facts are there to backup the *truth*.

It seems more and more people seem to prefer to live in this tight little bubble that only serves their *selves* and their agenda, and whoever upsets that agenda just gets stomped to the ground for no reason at all.

I have experienced this in my personal life over and over.

I'm seeing it now throughout the world with all this *race* atrocity.

I see it closely with the break of the family-unit atrocity.

I say *atrocity* because it is.

I have a hard time with this way of life.

God gave me this heart...and it feels everything.

To see, hear, experience this hatred, this *indifference*, this *selfishness* is so heartbreaking for me.

Do you attend a church?

Do you ask Jesus for help when you are in trouble?

Do you hit a knee when the fear of death is near you?

If you answered *yes* to any of these questions, then why do you speak of *race*?

Why do you not feel for those who hurt?

Why do you condemn those who speak out? Why do you have hate?

Why do you have *indifference*?

Are you bowing your head, thinking about your answers?

Have these questions angered you even more? Why?

In the verse above, Isaiah is speaking of something that has not happened yet in this particular period in history.

Do you fully understand that?

The commentators of my version of the *Bible* write—*In all of Scripture, Isaiah's prophecies concerning Israel's restoration and the coming of the Messiah may be the most marvelous, wonderful, comforting, inspiring, optimistic, and encouraging words ever read by a believer—particularly a believer who has either endured great personal suffering or known the despair of spiritual exile. It (Isaiah's prophecies) continues to be a solemn warning to those who would persist in unrighteousness, but it is a refreshing message of hope to all sinners willing to acknowledge their guilt and lead repentant lives in service to God.*

When any book or person says the word *believer*, I'm dumbfound. Why?

Because of all the accounts, of all the miracles...to even fathom that there are people out there who can't feel God, is, to me, crazy. Really! Just saying....

Isaiah *tells* the people that it's not the devil that will cause them grief, but God.

He's telling them that it's up to them (*free-will*) to see their error-ness ways.

He's telling them that God's *unconditional* love gives them a choice.

We're talking about generation after generation during this period in history where *comfort* took over and the people just assumed God's going to take care of them, so they put Him in the back of their minds and just followed the crowd...basically.

They got so comfortable that they only saw their *innovations,* instead of listening to the teachings their parents taught them.

This went on generation after generation until their ways backfired...pretty much they *enslaved* themselves.

Do you understand that?

God didn't enslave them.

The devil didn't enslave them.

They enslaved themselves.

This is just the story of history.

Over and over.

You might disagree with what I have to say.

That's okay, but I'm going to say it anyway. *Man* enslaves themselves.

We are responsible for our own journey.

We have no right blaming others.

I write about abuse.

I blamed [x] for my torment.

Yes, he did wrong, but I didn't keep God in the forefront of my life and I *let* it all happen.

Instead of paying attention to my *self*...I paid attention to everyone else.

If we can't see our *self*...how in the hell are we going to see the truth of others? We don't.

We become followers.

Did you read that right?

We become *enslaved*!

America didn't enslave people from the continent of Africa.

Those people enslaved themselves.

When their own people sold them and they were brought to America, they continued to enslave themselves.

Do you have an argument?

Of course you do.

Ask yourself—*If they were treated so bad, why didn't they leave?*

I've asked myself this question for years.

The same story goes with the enslaved people of Egypt.

In all cases of enslavement...the *slaved* ones outnumbered their *owners*, so why did they not leave?

The answer to this one question has led millions and millions to their death, to ruin, to remain in abusive situations, to forbid change in traditions that go against what they actually believe in, to wars....

The answer: *Fear*! Jesus said—*Do not fear.*

We don't listen. We fear.

With that fear, we draw ourselves in negative mind-talk, which opens holes for that evil whore (the devil) to lead us to self destruction. We do it to ourselves.

We have all enslaved our own *selves* by way of anger, hate, greed, lust...oh! my!...the *Seven Deadly Sins*!

Isaiah's warnings came to pass.

History repeats itself over and over because man refuses to learn. Ego and pride.

It's happening again.

Watch some documentaries on [online].

It's that easy to learn.

Knowledge is everywhere.

I've been struggling.

I've wasted my *own* time.

If I just keep my faith, God will lead my way.

Life is a struggle...that evil whore likes to play us. We let it. We are humans.

We are weak.

Joyce Meyer says it right...I guess it pays just to read her books over and over again.

The mind...we have to keep God always in our arsenal to help us fight all that hate and anger because that evil whore likes to use whatever it can to break us down. No. No.

Having faith in God, and in what He wants us to do should always be at the front of everything we do.

If you are not sure what that means, the *Ten Commandments* is a good place to start.

Thou shall not kill and Thou shall not lie are at the top of that list.

So, if you can't decide which way to go in your journey, remember those two.

Any...*any* entity, organization, person, etc., who celebrates killing and lying...that's not the way. It's really simple.

History speaks volumes. It pays to listen.

God speed....

Comments
▪(Friend) Nice pieces. Thanks so much for giving me this.
God bless you with more life.
▪(Me) You are very welcome.
▪(Friend) Oh my, you are a powerful writer!
So glad I found you here!
Thank you for letting the Lord direct your steps.
I, too, needed that reminder. God bless, keep the faith!
▪(Me) You are very welcome.

~*Closing of Gaps*~

these social media windows
–closing up shadows
connecting lines, without much grind

the language separation, set in motion
an extraordinary devotion
redefining oblivions on time

a typed word—across miles—heard
a recorded video, not needing a studio
across the globe
differences—in—soaked
what does it mean
what's coming—this scene

social media—closing gaps
as it dictates impersonal hats

~*Quietness of Words*~

do you hear them, are they any where
does someone speak them
should we go there

I don't hear them, here or there
no one speaks them, brave, raising hairs
is there too much noise
to hear His† beautiful voice

have we welcomed the drown
–the ringing of His† musical sound

He† won't yell or ring any bells
He† won't cast spells or ring your cell
or even send a post in the mail

His† voice is a whisper

in silence—to capture
if you don't listen, you miss them

is there anyone left, who hears them
or has His† beautiful words been lost
never again to be heard

for an overworked mind
technology's heavy cost
crossing the line–
nature's heavenly sound
when once—He† was all around

(September 26, 2016)—*Music gives a soul to the universe, wings to the mind, flight to the imagination and life to everything.*—Plato

~*Kicking through Doors*~

fighting through nights
hated words, blank looks, cold tones–
it's a right, like a sworn-in knight
say it—see what's in sight

bleeding words of *hosea*
a foreign arena, a returned agenda
replayed cinema—one certain agenda:

incorporation of rejection
ignoring revelations
–already experienced by nations

historical indications–
God's† bold proclamations
man's once-again *revoltation*

keeping in the light—a constant fight
suffering through blight
experiencing God's† might

turning it around, say something sound
as in past stories found
leaves truth—the drowning clown

like centuries before
keep kicking through doors
His† powers—the core
that's what *truth's* for
–leaving hatred—that embedded lore
in the constance of sore

(September 1, 2016)—*Note to self: Sometimes, it's painful for unhealthy people to watch you become healthy, but that pain is not yours to heal. Keep on walking. Stay on your path.*—Author Unknown

The same people who judge you are the ones who aren't doing a damn thing for you. Their opinions don't mean shit.—Author Unknown

If you don't stand for something, you'll fall for anything.—

This is one of the quotes I have taped to my computer screen.

Standing for something is that rock that so many people try to chip away as the years go by.

It's like those who don't have a solid grasp of anything can't stand the fact that you do.

I stand behind my theory that we learn from other people's experiences.

If no one writes about their experiences, then how are we to learn and do better or survive through ordeals that we really don't understand. My writings here are long.

No, I don't make money here.

In fact, I haven't made a dime on my writings. [Referring to Facebook.]

My journey has been directed to this particular path and I have been faithful to my calling, if that's what you want to call it.

These writings are not meant to be short.

That's the whole point.

So, if you have a short attention span...go on...bypass my work...it most certainly will bore you.

These writings have been labeled many things: Drama, trash, bullshit, etc.

That's personal agendas that I am not part of.

These writings come to me when they are meant to come to me. I'm not a prophet.

Trust me...but I pray...I ask God what I'm to write...then I write.

They always start with a piece of poetry.

I go with it and write it. Take it as you will.

If they insult you in some way, it's not the writings, nor is it me personally.

Think about that. I was given a voice.

I use curse words.

That's not a sin, though some see it that way.

If the word *fuck* or *damn* or *ass* offends you, then move along. My style is my own.

Just because 100 people out of billions don't like it, doesn't mean I have to change for those 100 people.

I always talk about the *self* and individuality.

How can I talk about being an individual, and, then not be one myself? I can't.

This is my style. Take it or leave it.

These writings are meant to teach and reveal.

No, you don't have to learn a damn thing, nor do you have to see a damn thing.

It's not meant for everyone.

These writings are meant for those who need them and those who need them know exactly who they are.

They are my *silent* readers and I know... you don't...who these *silent* readers are.

So, if you are not in need...have a good day. For those who need this...welcome.

I opened my *Bible* this morning to *Hosea*.

I've written about his prophecies before and it seems I've been directed back to him because of a little doubt I had in my heart last night.

The commentators of my version of the *Bible* explain the historical points that surround Hosea's prophecies.

The following points are relevant to what I have to say.

(I prefer to write it word for word, instead of paraphrasing it because, well, they write their point better than I can.)

—The foregoing passage [referring to all of his prophecies] is only a brief reference in the historical account, but it is a forceful reminder that after a century-and-a-half as part of a broken kingdom, the people of Israel have not been willing to put away their idols or forget their pagan Baal. If there is anything which, especially, affronts God, it must surely be the sight of men and women (whom He has created) bowing in worship to sticks and stones (which He has also created and which, therefore, have no intrinsic power). This is, especially, true because God has repeatedly and patiently demonstrated His concern, love, and protection to each generation of this nation to whom He has specially chosen to reveal Himself....

For me, personally, as I see it *sticks and stones* doesn't just refer to man-made crosses and statues, but to all material objects.

I included this passage because over and over I experience this anguish and anxiety over the material world and I don't see God.

What do I mean by that?

When people get frustrated over something, instead of stopping for a while and thinking and talking it out with God, they yell or condemn or ignore or blame or cause unnecessary chaos.

It's taken me, during my journey, to *learn* how to do this.

Reading really good books on self-improvement helps a great deal.

You can't do it on your own.

Trust me on this one.

You have to learn to step back and breathe...think about the situation for a moment, be silent for a little while, talk it over with God, and, then listen.

The mind is a *battlefield* as Joyce Meyer writes about.

It's up to us to fight and God is the only *real* warrior on our side.

Material things are just that *material*.

The spiritual part of our beings is the most important part.

When we are in tune with that part...truly in tune...then the rest falls into place.

Money, expensive clothes, cars, jewelry, travel...nothing of that will satisfy you if you are not in harmony with your spiritual being.

They go on to say—*To God, the people of Israel have been as a wife in covenant relationship with Him, and yet their continued idolatry is a constant reminder of their unfaithfulness to the covenant. Each generation has been adulterous in it's wickedness and idolatry, and now the time is swiftly approaching when God is going to put Israel away as an adulterous spouse....*

As the commentators state here, Israel (the nation (i.e. the people)) betrays God like a spouse in a marriage betrays the other (has an affair)... to put it in simple terms.

Looking at this from a broad spectrum... what happened during this period in time is again happening.

My generation was taught about God in school, in church, by our parents.

Removing prayer from schools, football games, government buildings was unheard of when I was a child.

Today's generations could care less.

See the similarities.

This also makes sense on a personal level.

Have you made a covenant or vow with God? I have. I didn't do it on purpose.

This type of thing evolves over time.

Many of us who have made a vow with God have gone through an ordeal that made us see, or rather opened our eyes to the world around us.

To put it short...we were going down the wrong road and that led us to hit a knee and finally ask God...with a true heart...for help.

He helped us, so, in turn, we vowed to return the favor.

My returned favor is to write these writings.

They continue—*Hosea's prophecies against Israel, to which he, sometimes, refers as Ephraim, begin with a reference to his own disastrous marriage and the anger and anguish, which he himself feels. No message has more impact than one growing out of the messenger's own experience that accounts for the power of Hosea's prophecies.*

Many, many...in fact, I believe just about every single person who comes out of their darkness turns their pain around and uses it to benefit others. Tell me I'm wrong. It's okay.

I accept if I'm wrong, but I don't think I am.

The difference with me is that I write in short, instead of long books, on here.

I am turning all of this into books, but it's part of my vow to write in the *immediate* first. Why?

Beats the hell out of me, but I know deep in my heart that this is part of the vow.

Doing something to help others as quickly as we can is what we are supposed to do.

The books that come later are only meant to preserve the effort.

If that makes any sense.

On a personal note: If the books and website bring me fruits, my dream is to use that money to help as many people as I can who suffer from abuse. To me, that's a win-win type of deal.

Hosea 4:1-6a (the commentators of my version of the *Bible* label this verse as *'Charge against Israel'):—Hear the word of the Lord, you Israelites, because the Lord has a charge to bring against you who live in the land: 'There is no faithfulness, no love, no acknowledgment of God in the land. There is only cursing (That is, to pronounce a curse upon), lying and murder, stealing and adultery; they break all bounds, and bloodshed follows bloodshed. Because of this, the land mourns (or dries up), and all who live in it waste away; the beasts of the field and the birds of the air and the fish of the sea are dying...but let no man bring a charge, let no man accuse another, for your people are like those who bring charges against a priest. You stumble day and night, and the prophets stumble with you. So, I will destroy your mother—My people are destroyed from lack of knowledge.*

This verse inspired *"Kicking through Doors."*

I reckon I was led to this particular verse because I'm often ridiculed because of the way I write. I use curse words for one.

When I was first ridiculed for this, I did a total soul-search and a *Bible* search.

Saying *fuck* as an expression is not the same as actually placing a curse on someone.

That's the same with any words we use today that are labeled as *curse* words.

I'm not defending myself here.

I'm simply stating facts.

We use words labeled as *curse* words to get our point across or to express anger.

Do you see the difference here?

Man's version of God's words is often different in meaning.

Man's rules and laws are often different than those of God's words.

Is the *Bible* meant to be followed word for word? Probably not.

The *Bible* is a collection of parables and stories passed down generation after generation.

As my daddy said—*The Bible teaches us how to live and how to die.*

It is not meant to be used for us to condemn others.

Here's a point to be made here: Do you personally know a biker?

You know those who ride motorbikes and are covered in tats and cuss and raise a little bit of hell.

I do.

I also know a lot of military guys and gals like this. Okay. Think of that kind of personality.

Do you have a picture of them in your head? Okay.

Now think of a person who attends church, wears a suit, shakes people's hands and appears to be nice and kind and gentle.

Do you have a picture of them in your head? Okay.

Here's something I've seen: (This is not the case in every situation. I'm not condemning anyone here.)

I've seen the roughest looking guys and gals do more of God's work than guys and gals who go to church and wear suits and nice dresses.

I've seen the roughest looking people treat those they love with kindness and total respect, while watching those that wear suits and go to church beat the shit out of those they love.

I cuss. I have tats.

This doesn't define me as a person.

It only says that I'm an individual and I prefer not to follow the crowd.

It's my personal way of not conforming to the norm of what everyone deems professional. I'm *me*.

Can you say that about yourself?

I'm a sinner. God knows my heart.

I have faults. I'm weak, then I'm strong.

I stand for something.

Can you proclaim that in your own life?

Are you willing to proclaim that in your own life? It's not easy.

In fact, to admit to errors is fucking hard... there's my cussing self.

Are you going to condemn me because I said *fuck*? If so, why?

Does having my own personality and not being afraid to reveal it going against the grain? Guess what?

That's *man's* grain and not God's.

There *are* laws to follow. Those of God.

Writing about my world, my journey...does that make me *trash* or *drama-driven*? No.

It's only that way to those who adhere to *man's* way, *man's* idea of conformity.

You have to release the fear of being who you really are in order to get anywhere.

Fear...halts you. Fear...torments you.

Fear...destroys you.

I know this because I let *fear* do these things to me.

I still have those fears, but I pray and I cry out to God, and, then He returns this to me— *Fuck fear, Karen. Use your voice!*

Need I say more?

God speed to those of you out there that take the time to read my work and use this knowledge to better your own life.

Knowledge is key.

If you don't want to understand something, you just lock yourself into a closed little box without ever feeling the whole of life.

This new technology that we are all experiencing is leading us all to *knowledge.*

What is important about this is to know the difference between good knowledge and knowledge that just brings us fear.

Learning is a very good thing when you learn to improve yourself.

Learning something that just keeps your fears growing is just a waste of good energy.

Just saying....

—You either like me or you don't. It took me 40 something years to learn how to love myself. I don't have that kinda time to convince someone else to.—Author Unknown

I love these strong women pics.

This one says a lot.

I'm [two and a half] years away from being 50.

I do *not* have time to convince anyone of my status in life.

I've done enough and seen enough to know exactly where I stand.

Now there's the menopause factor to include, so I do *not* have time to bother myself with mindless things. I write.

I write a lot.

If you are too steadfast in your ways and in your life to sit and read what's written here, then don't come here.

This page has a specific goal: To reach those who have gone through, currently going through any type of abuse or grief.

It's a journey.

I'm not selling anything currently.

When that happens, this page will change.

I'm not here to set the course of any brand.

If k. e. leger is referred to as a brand...so be it. That's not my objective.

This page is *not* about trash talk.

If you consider this *trash* talk, then you shouldn't be here.

Those who are struggling through grief or the darkness...those are the ones who benefit from what is written here.

You can contact me through this page if you need more than what is written here.

If you are in an abusive relationship, there are resources that can help you.

You are not alone.

I'm still traveling this journey.

If those in my life can't handle the journey, then they can leave.

It's the power of strength and God that helps us through.

The *Bible* is a good place to start.

Thank you.

—Note to self: I am enough.—Author Unknown

Note: Social media set the stage for all of us to be who we are in our very own space.

If we have fan pages, author pages or business pages...we set our own standards on how we brand ourselves.

I'm not after to make a million dollars like most marketeers.

I'm out to talk about silent abuse, its wake, and how to survive the wake.

If you can't handle that, then, maybe, you shouldn't be here.

It's an ugly subject, but it needs attention!

I'm a lot to handle. *A lot.*

I use my own life because, well, that's where the expertise comes from.

If you can't handle that, then, maybe, you shouldn't be in it! I'm bold on this subject.

I will *not* sugar-coat abuse in any way, shape, or form. I know I am *enough*!

You are, too.

If those in your life can't handle that, then, maybe, they *are not* enough. Just saying...

~

(September 2, 2016)—All I see with this race-war issue is attention-seeking B.S.!

Sorry if I offend, but Jesus isn't, wasn't, and has never been about hate, jealousy, revenge, etc.

Slavery has always...always been.

Who the hell gives blacks the right to take full credit for being the *only* race ever enslaved?

You don't see the Jews or Scotts or Indians or Irish, etc., ranting and raving like a bunch of spoiled brats!

Like every race ever enslaved, the world owes you nothing! Sorry.

Go boo-hoo some place else—I don't feel sorry for you.

You want a real excuse to rant: Look at pictures of a woman with her face smashed in after being raped and beat or those African savages who cut a girl's clit off with broken glass and no anesthesia!

You people are not of God period!

Jesus...that's what all of you need!

Being black doesn't give you permission for any special anything!

My hands go up to the black woman...now that there's a gem.

You want to know real struggle talk to her!

Black men...you have not one...not one damn thing to complain about!

~

(September 3, 2016)—Posted an article titled *'Girl stabbed on school bus during fight over social media post'—www.wafb.com*

There you go.

Social media changing the world.

It sure has changed mines.

It's time to just disappear and do things your way when social media dictates how you feel about another person...so bad that you insult, halt your relationship, allow it to rule your mind, hate, and/or kill.

This only tells me that people can no longer think for themselves.

To destroy your life because of social media...wow!

I guess life is indeed ruled by the computer. *1984*...big brother one step ahead!

The individual heart no longer exist!

~*Pillage*~

I've seen this monster
disguising itself in trickster

come—it said—*I'll be your gangster
I'll stand up and fight, guide you to the light*

with nothing to lose, nothing to gain
I gave in—took its hand

it was mighty–
when it wanted sovereignty
not holding me, but enticing me
with uncertainties, never to be

I held to the belief, it wasn't deceive
there was more—way down deep

I refused to see, the constant of defeat
encaged—me to keep

wanting more
with every slamming door

with every scream, sucking in the blame
the living of repeat
me, again, lost down deep

too late, too late
afraid—my words to seep

the pillage of coverage
the robbery, of robbing me—of *free*

(September 10, 2016)—Pillage: to strip (a conquered land) of money or goods by open violence in war; the act of pillaging; booty or spoils

~*Entombed*~

fallen down
bound and bound—look all around
here comes the clown

the jackel is not sound
the hyde is only found

white, yellow, brown
in—always the crown

lift your frown, every entity of a town
you followed the hound–
helped build the mound
suppression—the constant noun
over and over, you allowed the pound

round and round, wound then rewound
you allowed the drown—up then down
lift your frown
you already knew where you were bound

(September 8, 2016)—*When life gives you rainy days, wear cute boots and jump in the puddles.*—Author Unknown

Life is very complicated. Don't try to find answers because when you find answers, life changes the questions.—Author Unknown

Free my people...words from God seem to be a constant echo that *no* one is listening to.

Thomas Jefferson said that the American people have a God-given right to overthrow their government (with arms if necessary) if their government got too big.

He had a right to say that.

He was, after all, there when this country

was started.

He felt the suppression by the British.

He felt the *slavery* of a big government.

This is my opinion: After the British (i.e. those evil people, at the time, who wanted to control the world... read some history, please, and see how much of the world, at the time, they did own and who was in charge of all of that!) could no longer enslave the people in America, those British and Spanish who came here and took over, brought more people (i.e. Africans) to enslave.

If they can't enslave one race, they will find a way to enslave another race...it's all evil trying to win over God's law. It really is that simple!

It is not the flag or the anthem that you should protest against.

There's a big difference between the flag/anthem of any country and its government.

I was led to *Hosea* again this morning.

My, oh! my, how God does speak!

In the passage below, Hosea is talking to, of course, the people of Israel, but...always a but...what he says (now this is a prophecy [prediction of sorts] of what's to come...it hasn't yet happened when these passages were spoken) that the *people* will be held just as responsible as the *leaders* (priests) because they followed.

Isn't that something?!

Because you have rejected knowledge, I also reject you as My priests; because you have ignored the law of your God, I also will ignore your children. The more the priests increased, the more they sinned against me; they exchanged [I will exchange] their [My] Glory for something disgraceful. They feed on the sins of My people and relish their wickedness, and it will be: Like people, like priests. I will punish both of them for their ways and repay them for their deeds.—Hosea 4:6b-9

I read about the students at California State University *wanting* segregation again.

I watched a video this morning posted by *Black Global Village* on all this *Kaepatrick* B.S.

I posted my opinion on the matter as well.

The guy in the video has it right.

Education...i.e. knowledge is key.

I truly believe that Dr. King is rolling in his grave right about now.

Affirmative Action (a mouthful) may have had good intentions, but what it did wasn't.

Political Correctness (another mouthful) may have had good intentions, but it's a true over-kill.

No Child Left Behind and *Common Core*... my God what a twisted stance these are...i.e. the exact opposites!

There are many other programs or rather *ideas* as these...do you see the relation?

They are *all* government...federal-

government-led agendas to hold us all back.

All this *World Order* talk...come on now... there would be no such thing if the people of the world stood up for what they truly believed in without fear.

This is where *"Entombed"* comes from this morning.

We entomb ourselves by buying into all this crap that governments are feeding us.

Do you realize how easy it is to suppress a nation? Knowledge is key.

Can't you see why it is so hard to break out of *poor* and get an education?

Oh, you can do it. I did.

They don't outright tell you because they *want* to suppress you. It's so simple it's scary.

We entomb ourselves because we developed this *you owe me* attitude.

No one owes us diddly-squat.

If the government is bothering us so much, then why is there only a few stepping up to the plate?

The flag and the anthem isn't your problem, but you take it out on the flag and the anthem and the pledge.

Strange deal there. It's the leaders.

As Hosea says, you follow the leader, then you pay the price.

God holds both responsible and will punish both.

So, you can keep following the leader or you can, actually, step up, instead of just talk, actually, take your rights back.

This leads me to a soldier who signs the dotted line without a gun to their head and says: I will fight for *freedom*. I will die if I have to.

You don't degrade a soldier.

You go after the cause and that *is not* the soldier. It's the government. I was a soldier.

We didn't make our own rules.

The government sends down orders and we have to follow.

Do you know that the President of the United States is the Commander-in-Chief of the military...all branches?

That means whatever orders he gives, soldiers have to follow.

So, you appoint...that's right...*appoint* a president with zero leadership skills in matters of war and guess what?

This is not just our current leader.

This is all leaders in our past.

So, why complain? You made the call.

You entombed yourself by setting the

lowest of standards for yourselves.

You sit at home and refuse to work because the government gets all your money byway of taxes. Who's the blame for that? *You.*

You allowed the government to pass all these laws to take your taxes while you sat there doing absolutely nothing!

You have no right to blame anyone, but yourself.

Do you realize how many laws have been added to the *U.S. Constitution* alone that *you* as a citizen did *not* vote for? Do you?

And now you complain?

You followed the leader!

Free my people is written over and over in the *Bible*.

God didn't voice those words for just one race. *All races* are *His* people.

He hates slavery, and that's slavery of any kind...including that of money, governments, people...suppression at its finest!

A revolution took place on these *United* States lands. A Civil War, too.

It's the same in other countries.

Much blood has been split over those words *free my people*.

The adversary works against this fight.

Don't you see?

That evil whore (the devil) wants *you suppressed*!

Its war against God will never end because *you* allow it to keep going.

Call my *bluff* anytime. You will lose!

Not because I'm arrogant or anything of the sorts, but because there isn't a *bluff* here... only truth. You *suppress* yourself.

You *allow* your own self to be encaged by money, by government, by propaganda, by people.

So, don't sit there and blame it on the color of your skin or anything else. You *allowed it*!

Free my people...all people not just a color or race. Get that right.

The message is already written in the *Bible*.

If you can't read and gain knowledge and understand what exactly God meant, then don't sit there and protest against *yourself* because that's what you are doing!

Suppress me if you want.

Come at me with your dogma.

My hands are extended in the air as I praise *my heavenly* Father.

Some say to be careful what I say because they will go after my family, even kill them to hold me back. Really?

Is that what happened to the Russian President? The *world order* went after him?

Did they kill Michael Jackson and Prince because they spoke out?

Are they going to poison me, rape me, stab me, shoot me, cause me to have a car accident?

Are we to live in fear because of their propaganda or are we going to listen to God and *free his people*?

That's a *common sense* kind of question by the way. Suppression is nothing new.

It's been around since the beginning of time. The people *let* it happen.

Give me a break. Our minds are weak.

We allow all this fear because we see it, hear it and lose faith because manipulation is a matter of brilliance.

So, go on and suppress me.

It'ss not like it hasn't happened to me before! (Double negative intended!)

Point: You allow suppression to continue to control *you* or *you* take control of it!

God sees all.

You entomb yourself or break the chains of bondage and be *free*.

You would think after over what 2,000+ years we'd all get the message. Nope.

Round and round we go!

—Posted a video proving that the electronic voting is rigged.

Politics. No...they say...don't get involved. It's bad for business.

I could not take my eyes off of this video. Our votes don't count.

This step is before the Electoral College, which is totally unconstitutional in itself.

To me...this says that the people who run all the offices in our country weren't elected at all. They were placed!

I'm leaving this public.

Everyone should look at this.

Every citizen in the U.S.A.

—Posted an ABC video

With all the craziness going on around us like the new evolved segregation, the *medical* chip they want to force on us, etc...this is worth seeing.

~*Internal Exposure*~

get it out–

that ingrained lesson in your head

stop! suppressing it—instead—shout
–you are *not* dead

don't worry about—green or red
stand out—too many, already bled
for you to shrivel in dread

don't quiver, beg—you *do* have a choice
redefine what's been fed
rewire that *inside* voice

female verses male–
look who's already led
down, down, down—the bottom of a cell
–on the surface, why do we still tread

slogans they spread

find a good man

–what happens, after *I thee wed*–
dreams—cave-on in
while *man* elevates in win

pretty little mommy—
on lists of *craig*, might as well list—

'held back' little mommy

–tuck her—nice and sweet—in her bed
advancement's common thread–

smart like daddy
t-shirts read—propaganda of *j.c. penny*
–analogies deeply bred

she's just a *girly*
words, over and over, said

follow the creed, every line—in the 'reg'
–you're a 'she'
be a teacher in ed or a nurse for ned
forget going into med
forget running for the leg. or even a pres.
–don't you see, for this, you need a third leg

words, buried in the head
advancing, common avoidance
leaving girls in dread
hanging their intelligence on a peg

I'll say it—what others said

get out of your head

go out, lead, forget the man-ego clout
don't be misled
don't listen to *internal's* doubt

bypass labels—*bitch, bossy*
–ambition is not damnation!

but a reclassification—recondition
of old worn, torn traditions
–here's some jubilation:

it's okay—go red
save green for those babies you wean

you can do both—let that—in—soak!

it's okay to be a queen!
expose that internal dread
in front of the crowd, be in the lead
–hire someone to clean
forget all those slogans said–
you're a woman–
removed from by-gone's *dead*

be heard, seen—never again–
hiding behind tradition's thread

let another make that bed–
dawn those heels, paint those lips red
rewrite those *unwritten* regs
that wrongly imposed–
man's ego-driven creed

(September 9, 2016)—*A woman would rather struggle every day of her life than ever give someone the pleasure of degrading her with words like 'you wouldn't have had that if it wasn't for me'.*—Author Unknown

Never underestimate the power of a determined woman.—Author Unknown

If you are new to my writings, here's the gust of it: My writings take you through my personal journey through silent abuse, then the five stages of grief, then the gaining of strength to *not* be afraid of being a *free*-thinking woman in today's society. I post here bits and pieces of that journey.

The *whole* of it is being compiled in over 11 books.

I have been ridiculed greatly for these writings, for being so out-spoken.

It did affect me at the beginning, but once I learned how to gain the strength needed to move forward, it became easier and easier, and that is the sole purpose of the *why* behind all of this writing.

I often stress that reading self-help books and books written by women help us move forward during this *strengthening* process.

I write a lot about the books I've personally read.

I'm not paid to promote anybody's work.

When I find a book that has me taking notes, highlighting, underlining, shaking my head *yes*, I write about them.

These are books worth my time.

[I will include all of these books on my blog in case you'd like to read them yourself.]

I'm currently reading Sheryl Sandberg's *Lean In.*

[Before becoming the chief operating officer at *Facebook*, Sandberg was vice president of Global Online Sales and Operations at *Google* and Chief of Staff at the United States Treasury Department.

That's not all of her resume.

You can get her book to learn more about this fascinating woman.]

This is one of a stack of books that I bought last summer before I entered the most pivoting moment of my healing process—the acceptance stage of the five stages of grief.

Of this huge stack of books, Joyce Meyer's *Battlefield of the Mind* was the only book I was able to read last year, and I read that book several times!

[In 2014, I read one book as well, a John Gresham novel.

I started a few, but could not, at the time, finish them.]

(If you read me regularly, you know as an educated woman, I'm a serious reader.

A small recap: Before the darkness hit me, I was a 30+-book-a-year reader!

This year is a huge turning point for me, especially, since June.

It's a *milestone* if you want to call it that...I'm pass the 10-books-read mark!

On my personal journey, this is how I know that the metamorphosis of my *self* is moving forward and not backwards.)

The first few pages of Sandberg's introduction had me so hooked that I immediately started underlining and putting my little stars on passages that struck me to the core, which inspired this morning's writing *"Internal Exposure."*

Sandberg writes—*We internalize the negative messages we get throughout our lives—the messages that say it's wrong to be outspoken, aggressive, more powerful than men. We lower our own expectations of what we can achieve. We continue to do the majority of the housework and child care. We compromise our career goals to make room for partners and children who may not even exist yet...My argument is that getting rid of these internal barriers is critical to gaining power.*

This is a powerful paragraph because it *is* what I write about before, during, and after surviving the five stages of grief.

Sandberg boldly states that—*Some, especially other women in business, have cautioned me about speaking out publicly on these issues.*

Wow! I have been cautioned over and over as well about the exact same thing.

People have gone as far as deleting and blocking me here on *Facebook* as well as totally disregarding me as a human being, and dismissing me as a friend and relative outside of the internet!

Sandberg goes further—*I have heard these criticisms in the past and I know that I will hear them—and others—in the future. My hope is that my message will be judged on its merits. We can't avoid this conversation. This issue transcends all of us. The time is long overdue to encourage more women to dream the possible dream and encourage more men to support women in the workforce and in the home.*

That is *just* in her introduction! No.

I don't plan on quoting her entire book, but these few passages are so profound that I had to include them in today's message.

I'm *not* alone when it comes to my thoughts about the world in which women live today.

Sandberg's book is not the only book I've read with this same message, and...*and* these books I've read *after* all the writings I wrote myself about this very same subject.

I agree with Sandberg when she says that it seems that, no...women *are backsliding* as she refers to it. Her research is thorough.

Her notes at the end of her book prove this.

I saw all of this as I made my way out of the darkness. I didn't see this before.

Or, maybe, I did and just ignored it. Nope. That's not it either. I did see it.

I know this because of the work I wrote before 2012.

I wrote about the suppression as a woman that I was feeling.

In my first book, *The Denial and Isolation of Self: Guiding 'Self' Straight into the Hands of Silent Abuse,* you'll find that I'm very subtle with the admittance of this suppression.

When I first entered therapy, I learned about the *denial* stage in the five stages of grief.

It is a depressing thing to learn about yourself, but it also leads you to a place (it takes a while) that strengthens that part that you suppressed.

I grew up with all these *traditions* that's been passed down: A woman's place is in the home. She is to be *seen* and not *heard*.

She is expected to take care of the home, the children, the man, the yard, etc., etc., then the added burden of having to work *outside* the home as well; and...I have to laugh at this...men, now-a-days label women as *crazy*...etc., etc.

As an over-forty divorced woman, I hear a lot from divorced men who are looking for a relationship.

The constant of *crazy* is all over the place!

We aren't *crazy*. We are fed up!

We gave, most of us, over 20 years to a relationship...did all that was *required*...according to tradition...plus the added bonus of *working outside the home*...only to be left because we hit pre-menopause with that mixture of that *empty-nest* deal, financial stress, a body-shape issue because we didn't have time to take care of ourselves because we were devoted to family, job, house as well as illnesses all human beings experience after their 40s...which all adds up to anxiety and stress we don't want.

A woman has so much more to deal with than a man. You can argue all you want.

This is pure fact.

Many women want a career, too.

We want to shine just as much as our men counterparts do.

I know I put myself through college while dealing with house, husband, children (babies at the time), and working at the same time.

I know from my personal experience, I was stretched so far that it was difficult to hold it all together, but I was *expected* to; then after *all* of that, I had to face the [x] not wanting *it* anymore!

I'm not the only woman who has gone through this. I won't be the last.

The message here as well as the message from every other woman who is bold enough to talk about it is: We *have* a right to be a leader in any kind of business.

We have the *same* kind of mentality that a man has.

We may use our way of thinking in a different light, but our end results are the same.

We are no less able than a man.

I'm not a *woman activist* in the sense that I think women should be on the front-lines of a battlefield during war, or that a woman's body is equal to a man's body. No.

I was told that in federal buildings, a woman is *not* allowed to ask a man for help.

It's okay for a man to *offer*, but she is *not* allowed, according to *written regulations*, to ask for help. This is absurd to say the least.

I guess I need to explain this a little bit: If a woman works in a federal government building in the U.S.A. and, say a desk needs to be moved or a heavy box of computer paper needs to be moved from the material room to the office in which she works in, she can't...by *written law*...ask a man to help her!

Excuse my language, but that's fucked up!

In my opinion, many women are stepping back from the *ambition* part of life because of this constant treatment of always considered the little *girly*! I know I get this all the time.

I also believe this is happening because of the music industry. Why do I think this?

Have you watched some of these rap videos or listened to their lyrics?

I'm not condemning their art forms...and that may sound a bit mixed up, but it is what it is.

I think the messages sent down from these *pop* stars to young girls is a bit off-key because they are selling the message that—*being sexy and bowing down to your man*—is a woman's role when that is not the case at all.

Those messages are not only in music, but in movies and reality TV.

This has been going on for years and a lot of women get the brunt of it when they try to excel in the work place.

I know I've experienced it.

In 1991, I was asked by an attorney, during an interview for a job, if I planned on getting pregnant.

I was asked this same question when I joined the National Guard after exiting the Army.

I did get pregnant in 1999 and had my baby in 2000.

I was homebound for a short time, then laid off after working for a company for three years and being successful in what I was doing. The reason given: Lack of money.

The real reason: I had a baby.

I know this for a fact because I wasn't the only woman who had been laid off by this company after their baby was born.

They stay inside the guidelines of the law (time-frame given by law to a woman to stay at home with her newborn baby).

After that time is up...laid off!

It's the same when I sit down to write. No.

I'm not making a buck yet. I know I will.

It's all a matter of timing.

Any artist knows this.

This is what I got when I was married—*You are lazy!* That's right.

I completely taught myself *PageMaker* and *Adobe Photoshop,* then *Adobe Indesign*.

I wrote a novel...formatted it and published it myself.

I wrote five chapbooks, formatted them, and published them myself.

I did all of this when I became sick and

couldn't work outside the home for a while.

I spent many days and nights teaching myself about the internet and online marketing and publishing.

This was all before 2011.

This was all before websites were made for you...etc., etc.

What do I have to show for all this self-study and hours upon hours at the computer?

Over 15 books, which I'm going to publish myself!

There's a reason for everything...and it's not *lazy*!

Why did I spend so much time learning all of this on my own? Because of tradition!

I couldn't work outside the home at the time, but I was expected...*expected* to bring in an income!

I was doing, but I couldn't get any *man* to help me.

When I had to get a computer *guy* to come to my house to help me with my wifi, I was treated like a child, even though I had my entire 2,400-square-foot house wifi'ed, except for a minor glitch...the cable people (a couple of men) didn't secure my ethernet cable under my house, so it kept being ripped out by critters who took refuge under the house!

All my time spent at the computer to learn all of this was labeled *obsessed* because I wasn't doing the *traditional* role of a woman (i.e. cleaning house, cooking supper, etc., etc.).

I couldn't and still can't get anyone to help edit my work.

I'm shunned because of the topic I write about (saying out loud what everyone wants hushed!).

I also wasn't moving on *man's* time frame!

Because of all of this, I'm divorced and ostracized...as if I have a scarlet *A* tattooed to my forehead!

To top that, I'm labeled *crazy*, *lazy*, and *obsessed*. Go figure!

The story is the same with sexual harassment, men being advanced over women because they are part of the *boys* club, etc., etc.

In order to break this, more women need to talk about this issue...use their voice.

I can't stand this *hush-hush* society.

It is time to open the gates and say what's on our minds as women.

I personally plan on continuing forward with my journey...ridiculed or not.

To me, it's worth it!

~*'Right' Prevails*~

all this n.f.l. hoopla
over shadowing *truth's* agenda

what!—am I out of bounds!
or is hard-love now found

–it's only throwing a ball
wrestling bodies to the ground
more, more money—above all
–you won't give up throwing the ball!

–behind scenes, wives scream
rape and beat—crowds stomp their feet
wave flags, clap hands, win or defeat

corporate hum, go on—beat that drum
same, same—all around

science and game
the common—constant lame
money's fame, genetically altering flame

make us angry—violent scenes
as illness, death—lives in green

pharmaceuticals, politicians
–play some ball—lies in communication
void of principles–

it's slavery—all the same
just disguised as a different name

there's higher words to sound
hearts in right, stay in the light

it's your call, after all–
to stall, backwards—fall

or bypass the hoopla—rise up
in Jesus'† name, fill your cup

money and greed
–to words in prophecy—heed

those enslaved—oh my! oh my!
always triumph, at the end of the day

for their trust and faith
stayed in the grace of God†

(September 12, 2016)—*You don't need religion to have morals. If you can't determine right from wrong, then you lack empathy, not religion.*—Author Unknown

People are often unreasonable and self-centered. Forgive them anyway. If you are kind, people may accuse you of ulterior motives. Be kind anyway. If you are honest, people may cheat you. Be honest anyway. If you find happiness, people may be jealous. Be happy anyway. The good you do today may be forgotten tomorrow. Do good anyway. Give the world the best you have and it may never be enough. Give your best anyway. For you see, in the end, it is between you and God. It was never between you and them anyway.—Mother Teresa

The political agendas have become amusing at best.

Too bad it was already written about thousands of years ago, and *still* it's not being paid attention to.

The NFL...part of the *penny* games... to keep you amused and entertained, while governments slaughter their people behind closed walls; while governments sneakily steal their people's money right in front of their eyes.

The act of illusion always happens right in front of your eyes or didn't you learn from Houdini?

After all, he *was* a master at fooling people. The NFL is just a distraction!

You watch it on TV or pay your good, hard-earned dollar to attend a game like all the other sports...*penny* games.

You spend thousands of dollars on crap with your favorite player or team's name written all fancy on it, and it sits there collecting dust!

The corporations keep getting bigger, while your bank accounts keep getting smaller. Funny how that works. Isn't it?

You watch gangsters, rapist, abusers, thieves play sports.

You pay thousands and thousands of dollars to award them, then when they want to honor people who died, the corporations want to punish them because *corporations* want the people to *forget*.

It is just the same as the Holocaust.

Same ole. Same ole.

Just different players on the field!

Here's another kicker...the corporations are paying big dollar for politicians to keep the anger of slavery in the forefront of everyone's minds.

They are paying top dollar to keep color an issue. Why? Breed animosity.

Breed war because war and hate bring in big money to those who have control of the money, the guns, the drugs, etc.

Do you really think all those drugs are coming into your country because some small-minded *business* genius found a way?

Lame.

It's your government doing it to control you!

Mindless games that have been around for thousands of years, and you still have not learned a damn thing!

Do you really think this is all happening out of the blue?

If you are, you are dumber than a pig waddling in mud!

For those who are angered by all this. Why?

God's already promised you His grace.

Are you doubting Him? You go to church.

I see a lot of post by people who *say* they believe in Jesus and in the total of the Holy Trinity, then I turn around and see the same people post hate and anger. I'm no different.

Never claimed to be. God did promise.

He has never, *never* broken a promise yet.

Read history. Tell me I am wrong!

I was led to the *Prophesies of Zephaniah* this morning.

This section in my *Bible* is titled *'About The Day of the Lord.'*

These sayings took place 635 to 625 years before Christ! They all came true.

Are you going to call Zephaniah a liar?

In these prophesies, he is talking to Israel.

If you read them over again, you'll see the exact...exact same thing taking place today.

I see a repeat of history.

Same ole, same ole.

Lessons taught, but never learned from.

We are in the year 2016...that's two thousand and sixteen years *after* Christ!

(*Note*: If all those who *say* they don't believe in Christ really *do not* believe in Christ, then why... *why* does every single person on the *face of the earth* use the same calendar? Answer me that.

Oh, you don't understand what I just said.

Today is September 12, 2016. That's 2016 A.D.

Do I need to explain further? Okay.

A.D...stands for After Death.

That's after the death of Jesus Christ!

Stupidity at best, and they stay they don't believe in Jesus Christ!

In my opinion, I just think they are deathly afraid of God's power! I know I am.

B.C. and A.D...i.e.

Before the birth of Christ and *after* his death.

Every single person denotes their time in this manner. Oh, tell me I am wrong! You can't!

Further note: If Islam truly believes in their prophet whom they claim has written *their* bible, then why does their calendar not follow his birth and death?

I believe he came 800 years or so after Jesus.

Hummm...interesting at best!)

The authors of my *Bible* state—*In one sense, the day of the Lord is coming rather immediately for Judah (Israel), when it will be destroyed because of its sins. The day of the 'Lord' is also coming for 'all the nations' which have 'oppressed God's people.' In another sense, the great day of the Lord is coming at the time when God will bring judgment against all the wicked. In each sense, the day of the Lord will be accompanied by salvation of God's faithful remnant....*

Zephaniah says in verse *3:18-20—The sorrows for the appointed feasts I will remove from you; they are a burden and a reproach to you [or I will gather you who mourn for the appointed feasts; your reproach is a burden to you]. At that time I will deal with all who oppressed you; I will rescue the lame and gather those who have been scattered. I will give them praise and honor in every land where they were put to shame. At that time I will gather you; at that time I will bring you home. I will give you honor and praise among all the peoples of the earth when I restore your fortunes [or I bring back your captives] before your eyes.—Zephaniah 3:18-20*

Why do you fear?

All citizens of the United States of America came from people who were *oppressed! All!*

What makes a Jewish human different from an African human?

What makes an Irish human different from a Scottish or French human?

What makes a German human different from a Native human?

[I didn't leave out *all* other races for spite...I just mentioned the common...*all* races matter!]

All of us who have native rights (at least, [one] full generation of naturally born blood) have all come from oppression.

What gives one race more privilege than another? *Not one damn thing!*

Those of you who *think* you deserve more privilege are the worse enemy because you are a hypocrite...which tells me you preach, but you are too much of a coward to practice!

This is where *"'Right' Prevails"* comes from.

Those of you who talk out of your ass... yes, I said that, don't know or understand the lessons that are taught in history.

You talk, talk, talk, but have zero iota of what you are talking about. Amusing at best.

I saw a video about the NFL this morning.

The guy had it right.

These NFL players and in other sports organizations as well, rape, abuse, etc... nothing...*you* as the fan make zero effort to punish or take a stand and say—*That is wrong. You don't deserve my time.*

And then they don't honor the flag and you protest! That's what's wrong with our country.

I watched a *Netflix* documentary on Saudi Arabia...appalling at best. Surface! All of it.

I don't give a rat's ass about how much money anybody has.

A human life has more value than any gold on the planet.

Saudi Arabia...1945...look those two things up. I think you will be a bit surprised.

They are Islam. They control everything.

Watch the Dakotas here in the United States.

The Government reprieves itself and gives all natives land.

These natives are given full authority to control their land, then big corporations come in and the government changes its mind.

Really? Money over human lives. Really?

I watched a movie last night...I love movies based on actual lives.

It was about genetically altering seeds that we plant, genetically altering the chickens that we eat...etc.

According to the remarks at the end of the movie, the United States is the *only* country who does *not* force these huge corporations to warn us on packaging labels that their food is from chemically, lab-rat tested (90 days or less) seeds! and everything else we eat!

Corporations...greed.

That's what it is all about.

Did you see the war attacks on the corn fields...I forget the country?

Just because this particular place is standing up to the evil owner of most of the world's banking.

Do you really think these big corporations care about human lives?

Insurance companies...pharmaceuticals... seed industry...banks!

Holy watermelons Batman!

We are all made to believe that *we need them*! We are the customers.

Their job is to make *us* happy...*not* the other way around.

The world...that's right...*the world* has forgotten that simple point.

We are the common!

We are the customers!

If we continue to *allow* them to get their way, guess what...we are stripped of our consumer rights. We are no longer valuable.

They get over on us every time because we tell them we *cannot* do without their product!

What if the world came together and said— *Fuck you!* to the corporations?

Do you know what will happen? I do.

They will shut down the internet, so we can't communicate with anyone.

Third world countries like Saudi Arabia already beheads anyone in their country who speaks out. It'll come to the United States.

Hell, hanging already took place.

What the hell makes you think it won't happen again?

Read *The Turner Dairies...1984* has already taken place...*big brother*...there are cameras every where and the governments of the world...lead us to believe it *is* for our *own good*!

I read an article about the *medical* implant that *is* supposed to be put in every American's hand by 2017.

They say it's for medical reasons.

So, when we get in an accident or have to be rushed to the hospital, they'll have our records right there. Right!

Here's a bit of the bigger picture: Years ago, I was at a drug store fulfilling a prescription.

The lady in front of me was asked to swipe her *driver's license* before she paid.

I am a nosy little bitch and I am not afraid to admit that.

The cashier told me that that new strip that they have put on our driver's license includes *all* of our medical records!

Okay...that didn't sit well with me. I let it be.

A year or so later, I'm buying some boots at a workman's clothing store.

They didn't sell any kind of medical anything.

I paid with a check.

That's a paper deal that we paid with, instead of cash years ago.

I was asked to swipe my driver's license.

I was offended. *Why?*—I asked.

They said they could *not* accept my personal check until I swiped my license. Medical? Really! No.

It was the first step to the forthcoming *medical chip*!

After that strip on our driver's license, the debit card came along.

Hardly anyone is accepting the paper check any more. They say it's for our safety.

No one is asking questions about this.

We are just accepting it!

After all, it's for our *safety*! Really?

Read *The Turner Dairies*...everything that professor who wrote that book in the 1960s (black-listed by the government) is coming to pass!

You still believe that this medical chip is for medical purposes.

That leads me back to the *penny* games... all this pokey man crap, football, computer games, online everything is to keep your mind off what the governments are doing, and you buy into it. My voice is loud.

Maybe, they will come kill me, too or put me in jail or erase my work.

I wouldn't put it pass them...big corporations!

How about the *under world* of the net... maybe, you should do more research.

We are called *scare mongers*...for a reason!

All this Hillary crap!

I posted a video on my personal page about how this electronic voting works and you still ignore the facts. Why? Fear that's why.

I think I'll stick to Jesus and His words.

All this man-made ideology...for greed.

There's a reason why royal families and billionaires exist...they feed off of you!

They take your money, and you just give it to them.

The IRS...they rob you blind, and you don't care. You gladly hand it over.

After all, they have a right...*right* to take your money electronically if you don't want to hand it over willingly.

They have a *right* to put you in jail.

Where does this money go?

Do you see all those rich people in D.C.? Need I say more?

You are losing your country.

Third-world...here we come!

Saudi Arabia wants this country.

You are gladly handing it over! Fools!

God sees all.

He will take care of business, but not until you've lost what He has given you, and you will.

Over and over again, it has happened in history. You will ignore this.

You will be lazy and bypass all these words.

You are now a product of the *penny* games. Congratulations!

You haven't learned a damn thing!

Welcome to your life.

The repeat of history.

If enslaved...the worst of it...doesn't happen in your life time, I promise...it will happen in your child's.

You handed your child over on a silver platter.

P.S...they will be the ones who will shackle you by the way. That's history, too.

It's already happening around the world.

So go on continue to protest against mindless things like the NFL...it won't last.

You will watch the Super Bowl.

Nothing will change because your mind has already been enslaved.

It won't be long before your body is put in-line with that. Yes, this is my say, my opinion.

It's fact all the same.

God speed to those who continue to spread the truth.

A big *God speed* to those who continue to add to the chains that bind us all!

Their date with the devil is coming.

Oh, by the way, God promises that.

He never breaks His promises.

God is great *all* the time!

—I am oblivious to numbers.

As long as you get the message...it's all cool with me. I'm not after popularity.

I'd rather save a life. You are important.

Yes, *you*! You deserve the best.

My author page.

I write for my readers...those who speak out...those who remain silent. I love you.

Why? Because you are *you*!

You can walk out that darkened place.

Trust me.

It's a hard walk...but you can do it.

I've got one of your hands.

God has the other. Don't worry.

You will fall here and there.

You *will* get back up. How?

You don't need to know or understand...just have faith. He will lift you.

Love yourself. Cry those damn tears.

It's perfectly all right and normal.

You are not crazy. Trust me.

You are *just* human!

You can come like my page or not.

It's okay. Read. You can review me or not.

Read anyway. Trust in your journey.

Keep faith. I'm regathering my momentum.

God has had me on a different kind of journey lately.

Learning love in its truest form, I think is the most difficult lesson I've ever learned.

I'm grateful for the tough of it.

Loving family is different from loving someone with absolutely zero ties to you.

To experience that...is worth every bit of lonely. Don't give up.

God has something and someone waiting for you.

If that person hasn't come, you are not ready. Trust in God's work.

He is making you strong.

He knows what He is doing. Love yourself.

That person on his or her way to you...will teach you some of the most valuable lessons you'll ever learn. No matter your age.

Plow on....the light is coming.

Love the skin you're in.

~

(September 13, 2016)—*You will never go broke from investing in yourself.*—Author Unknown

Invest in yourself. Invest in your friends.

I've been sending friend request out... making my rounds.

Thank you to all who've accepted my invitation.

I'm busy, so I don't have much time to chat, but I spend time reading posts, getting to know y'all that way.

Getting to know people is a good way to invest in ourselves.

We are in a perfect time because we can learn from each other and help each other easier than ever before.

Investing in ourselves byway of others helps us to grow.

When you read someone's status and they sound a bit negative, maybe they are having a bad day, maybe, if you give them some words of encouragement, you can improve their day.

I'm learning all about the online marketing world, have been for a number of years now, and I find this one of the most fascinating of worlds.

So many connections with liked-minded people is, to me, close to being in heaven.

So, welcome to my world.

A world of a lot of little things that add up to everything that I like.

~*Stereotyping Zit*~

don't sit there
let it grow—pop it—have a fit
it's not a conflict
m or f—don't check it
white, black, hispanic—just forget
–leave it to idiots, to deal with it!

break, smash, dump it–
this stereotype threat
–do the math—take the bet
let them talk about it, put on your swag–
see them drop a lip, have a hissy-fit

demand relationship's

true-balancing mix
parenting, working
–the win-win kindà hit

take a risk—bypass—*shut up*—*sit*
overthrow tradition's
seen-not-heard trip

a common guessing

I don't know how does she do it

–let them take a whiff

over that board-room table—slap it
be that *bad bitch*
standing up, to that man-chauvinistic pig

be the it, that can say it–
fuck it—I'm woman—the *roar* of it

~

(September 22, 2016)—Posted an article titled *'Venezuela Crisis: Sterilizations Soar as Couples Count the Cost of Children'*—by *theguardian.com*

A *largely Roman Catholic* country, and the women being forced to sterilize themselves because of lack of food?!

I see something a whole lot greater going on beneath the surface than a failed government. Do you?

~Brazed Annihilation~

condemning the throne
won't fix what's wrong

live the seeds sown—enjoy the mix
pack your bags—go home

words—just a drone
a quick fix 'til it's all overthrown

go ahead, celebrate the clone
right-wrong mix
don't be surprised—your cover is blown

~Death in a Box~

it's all a hoax—this carrying-on cloak
just one big joke
covering up secrets in float

blaa, blaa, blaa

manipulation's game—it's all the same
–each scenario's trying of tame

go ahead—gloat—appearances do soak
truth seized–
smothered in a deceiving moat

win, win, win
losers constant in drain—truth remains
lies always change
depending on the range

study island of oaks
so easy—build that hoax
death comes in notes
as tales believed—bodies float

it's all the same
a loser's winning game
always some to tame
just to build a flame
for nothing more but fame

~Game of Wrongs~

it's called abuse
it's condemning—cruel
no matter what tools used–
whips, fists, hands
words—anger, hate, silence

someone before us, made the rules
in this game of wrongs
keeping us in control
keeping us feeling confused–
without comfort of a home

it doesn't matter
the decade, the century, the millennium–
in all its forms, it's the same chatter
leaving bodies in splatter
without a reconsider

(September 23, 2016)—*There comes a time in life when you have to let go of all the pointless drama and the people who create it and surround yourself with people who make you laugh so hard that you forget the bad and focus solely on the good. After all, life is too short to be anything but happy.*—Author Unknown

Life is too short to stress yourself with people who don't even deserve to be an issue in your life.—Anon

Some people won't love you no matter what you do and some people won't stop loving you no matter what you do. Go where the love is!—Author Unknown

Sometimes, the hardest thing and the right thing are the same.—Author Unknown

What do you see when you look in the mirror? Do you see black, brown, white?

Or do you see just you?

I see and hear about all these shootings.

I read about all this political *need*.

Do you really think you make a difference by ignoring truth?

Do you really think this will all go away

just because?

All of our families have been enslaved at one point in time.

I don't think any of this *hate* has anything to do with *slavery*.

I think it has everything to do with the simple fact that we are different and still have not learned how to deal with that.

Labels. White. Black. Mexican. Caucasian. Jewish. Catholic. Etc., etc.

Why do we have to check these boxes on forms?

Why are we still separated by these differences?

Haven't we learned anything from the past?

In the *Bible*, God got fed up with all this *difference,* so he, on purpose, divided the world by language barriers.

He left it to us to figure out how to live in peace.

It could have been easy, but, no, those who came way before us experienced the same shortfalls...differences.

So, He just made it more complicated for us.

We created this complication...the matter of *different*. He didn't.

He just gave to us what we wanted.

It's been two thousand and sixteen years since the Lord died.

Still, we have not learned.

I have but one difference: Evil. I see the evil. No, we are not to judge, but as it was pointed out to me, God also said that we cannot stand by and let evil prevail. What is good? What is evil? That's the questions here.

Evil is killing.

Evil is wanting to destroy peace and all that God made.

I can only think of one sort of evil on this earth.

Everything else is just product of this one evil.

If you have to ask what this evil is, then you are not paying attention at all to what truly matters. There has always been killing.

Today's world just puts it on the internet, so it becomes instant news.

It has always existed.

All this brutality, all this she-said, he-said is just part of a bigger plan.

It has nothing to do with being enslaved in the past.

It has everything to do with being enslaved in the future.

If you can't see this, then you are missing the boat entirely. Abuse.

I write about silent and physical abuse in relationships.

The one thing I missed, well, not completely, is the wider definition of *abuse*.

Abuse is about control, keeping a person confused, disorientated, mixed up.

Abuse is stripping a person of their pride, their joy, their happiness, their peace.

Do you see it? Abuse is in *all* relationships.

Everyone is guilty of abuse.

I know I am, even if I didn't mean to bring someone down, I did. You did, too.

God judges, but we are to protect His assets.

In Detroit, they are parading pictures of a beheaded Jesus. Really?

And you are fighting among yourselves over the color of your skin.

It seems some priorities are mixed up a bit.

I watch all these wonderful hugging sessions and talk of peace and love and God, yet, they are in Detroit exploiting a *beheaded* Jesus.

Don't you think Jesus suffered enough for us?

Those who are parading these pictures... that's your enemy not those who have a different color of skin.

The fight over fresh water has begun.

The fight over new land has begun.

The rise of hatred, prostitution, slavery, deception has begun.

How long do you think God will allow this to go on before He's had enough?

Can you rightly say the names of those you trust completely? Can you?

How do you know?

The *Bible* warns of deception over and over.

I was deceived and my world fell apart because I spoke the truth and continue to do so.

How far do you think you are going to get by speaking the truth?

You have to act upon it.

You have to protect God's assets.

Talking back and forth he-said, she-said... bla...bla...bla never really got the innocent out of trouble in the past.

What makes you think it will now?

I read *Facebook* and the news.

The destruction of Venezuela...how all

those young *Catholic* girls are sterilizing themselves. The uprising in the Carolinas.

All this political mumble-jumble.

How much of it is propaganda?

How much of it is caused by the one true evil in this world? Do you really know?

Do you? Deception.

The sure thing to keep you in chaos all for one thing: Control.

This is where *"Game of Wrongs"* comes from. Can you see a lie from a truth?

Can you?

~

—Posted an article titled *'Who's Behind the Riots: 70% Arrested in Charlotte Have 'One Thing' in Common'*—by *thefederalistpapers.org*

Hey my former political blog readers, didn't I talk in debt about G. Soro?

Well, well, well I fucking hate knowing so much crap.

That *new world order* I wrote about back in 2010...well here it is.

I knew there was a common thread in all this.

I would place a bet that all those school shooting that killed all those *kids* and all those *crazy* people responsible for all those street shooting, which didn't provoke us and now being replaced by cop on black shootings was all sponsored by dear old Soro! Go figure! I had it fucking right!

—Posted a video of Syria.

We go in and fight places where there's genocide. Isn't this genocide?

So why don't we go help them?

I wonder...is it because they don't have anything to offer in return?

Just wondering...if all us don't want these refugees, then why not go help make their home safe? Where's God in this attitude?

Priorities in this world are fucked up!

Watch the documentary and tell me I am wrong.

—Posted an article titled *'Be Very Careful at the Supermarket'*—Hot Springs News & Breaking Information—by *hotspringsdaily.com*

If 200 million North Americans refuse to buy just $20 each of Chinese goods, that's a billion-dollar trade imbalance resolved in our favor fast! The downside?

Some Canadian/American businesses will feel a temporary pinch from having foreign stockpiles of inventory.

Just one month of trading losses will hit the Chinese for [eight]% of their North American exports, then they will at least have to ask themselves if the benefits of their arrogance and lawlessness are worth it.

Start now and don't stop, and tell your friends.

Start *reading* labels more closely and buy *American,* even if it cost a few cents more.

—I am furious right now and I trying to be peaceful.

I read another controlling deal about NMU making it a reason to expel a student from the university if they talk about suicide thoughts to their friends...oh brings suicide bombers and [seven] virgins to mind.

Can't say prayer in schools.

Can't say the Pledge in school.

Oh, Mr. President, you need to be impeached for you anti-American policy.

I call for impeachment of the United States President. We are *not* a Muslim state.

We *are* a Christian state and our Christian ways are being pushed to the max!

We are to protect God's assets.

What are you waiting for?

When they start spreading this around the entire country?

American people, your government is dictating to you.

I pledge my allegiance to one nation under *God*! Because she's *free* for now!

—Posted an article titled *'Obama Signs Executive Order Banning The Pledge Of Allegiance In Schools Nationwide'*—by *ABC News*

If this is true, then Omg.

Taking God out of all our lives.

If you don't believe in God...delete me!

Don't follow me. Don't anything.

~

(September 24, 2016)—I've just watched *The White Helmets* and my emotions are mixed.

This atrocity is for a reason.

In this film, there are *no* women.

The mother of one of the *Helmets* is briefly shown, but her face is behind a black cloth.

If those in Syria get to read this, there is a message here.

To understand fully God's law, you must understand the role of the woman.

She is *not* to be hidden.

She is to be celebrated as equally as man.

Whatever the reason behind Syria's regime

and Russia, the true reason is to open up completely to God.

Everyone prays for the Syrian people.

I can't express myself more clearly.

You can't choose only part of God's word.

You must choose all of it.

Celebrating humanity means *all* of humanity.

This, to me, is an atrocity in itself when man can openly celebrate their journey, but hides the most important journey to *all* of mankind...that of the woman.

Take the veils off of your women.

Bring your women to the forefront of your world. Let her make her own choice.

She is what God wants revealed.

See that and you are truly open to God's word.

Fail to see that and the strife will continue as it will here during this *race* atrocity.

We cannot discriminate: Man, woman, white, black, brown.

We are *all* part of humanity.

This message was put into my heart during the watching of this film.

Sorry to offend, but the truth is the truth.

You rescue all, but you must reveal all as well. May God be with you.

May God bless you, and may you see truth and reveal it.

~

(September 26, 2016)—*My open letter about racism and abuse:* All the same thing.

Here's your problem *and* your solution.

Controversy: I couldn't sleep.

As I sit here and write this, I wonder how much more *drama* can I take.

In my personal life there has been so much and it's blamed on me because I *chose not* to be silent.

Yes, I *chose* because of that decision, my life has turned upside down.

I'm told I have to take the blame for my part.

Not like I have...out in the open!

Still...I am to forget. No.

It's rather hard to put *abuse* of any kind behind you. Am I right or wrong?

Controversy: I spent the day learning that those who do the abuse *can* put it out of their mind.

They *can* go on to live *normal* lives. The victim. Hmmm. Oh, the sweet little victims.

They have to bury their pain, so everyone else can move about *freely*, so everyone else can *forget*.

It is *mighty* how this particular system works.

Controversy: I couldn't sleep because of that, then all this *police* violence stares me in the face and I feel I'm to choose sides.

I am in a mixed racial relationship.

I'm in the deep south.

When I first began falling in love with this man, I had to put all...*all* those *racial* traditions on the table. I had to be honest.

That hurt him, but I had to do it because it wasn't fair to him if I wasn't.

It was a lot of pressure. Why?

I always taught my children there was no such thing as color.

I taught them that it didn't matter what color skin they fell in love with. Love was love.

It's not that easy, I've come to learn.

Controversy: I can't rightly introduce this man I love to my family because of color. That hurts.

I want him to meet them.

If you think it is easy to go around with your head up with racism staring you down, you are wrong. I am French-Indian.

My father was discriminated against when he first started school. He couldn't speak English.

Hate is taught early.

In school as a young girl, it was put before us by the adults.

I graduated from ---- in 1987 and we weren't allowed to have our senior prom as a class because of race. It wasn't our decision.

It was the decision of the parents! Tradition!

Controversy: I came across Tommy Sotomayor's video and began to read the comments because my guy was fast asleep and I didn't want to disturb him.

It had been bothering me lately that he has been constantly looking at all these videos posted here on these police shootings.

It's hard to blend when deep in one's soul the scars from experiences are different.

For him, I will try to understand.

Controversy: The thread of comments I was reading was good until *those* came into play.

On each major comment there were hundreds more.

The likes on these major comments or first comments were in the thousands.

I shared this video on a page, but the thread didn't follow. I can't find this video any where else.

It was said in the comments that *Facebook* has been deleting this Tommy Sotomayor's videos.

I have to ask why?

Controversy: There was a particular part of this long thread of comments that really caught my attention.

There was a woman (her *origin* I'm not sure of, but she wasn't black) and there were those commenting on her comment (they were black).

I am putting color in for only one reason: To say my point.

The woman's comments were very educated... to the point, as a former teacher myself...I would assume she's academic.

The others...not so much.

Here's my point: History books: Before self-publishing came into play, there was what we called publishing houses that published your book.

They still exist.

In order to get any kind of historical book published, you'd better be sure your facts were backed up and noted (what we call a bibliography).

The competition to get a book published back then was maddening.

The facts *had* to check out extensively or you didn't get published.

Plagiarism was out of the question, and still is a federal law.

So...on that point...anyone who comes out and says history books lie, I have to question.

I'm not speaking of today's history books in classrooms of high schools.

I'm talking about history books put out by individuals who put their name and academic reputation on the line (that's their careers) in order to publish their research.

These are the kinds of books we study in the higher academics (i.e. colleges and universities).

These are the kinds of books that *real* journalists use! They are not filled with lies.

Point: These books are individual.

Meaning that each history book looks at particular events in history.

You can't just read one and say you've read history. No. That's not how it works.

In some of these comments, I think that is what is happening. It was absurd.

One little fellow looked to be in his early 20s was arguing with the more professional woman, whom I can say knew her history, calling her a liar and things like that, then an older woman called this woman a *nonbeliever* in less than colorful words.

I use these words (some of them), but I wouldn't use them to curse out someone online and expect to be taken seriously.

It is one to use such language to get your point across in a general setting, it is another to use such language in an argument online where all can see. That is not Christian.

Stay with me: I've been in that mind-set to use such language online directed at another person.

I know where the mind is. It is in hurting.

It is in anger.

Double Standards: You can't have them.

In character or personality, you are in pain or you are not. Does that make sense?

You can't pretend to be strong and righteous, then turn around and belittle another with foul language if you're not in pain.

You can't deny your pain, then belittle someone else and expect to be taken seriously.

Point: From personal experience, you can't.

Controversy: People have told me over and over through the past [four] years to let go my pain.

It is not easy, then I turn to *Facebook* or the news and see others who have not let go of their pain and live their lives in anger all the time.

I don't want to be like them.

So, I wonder what makes these people, so *animal*-like in their behavior if they want others to take them seriously?

Controversy: Tommy Sotomayor has it right. He's speaking from a black man's point of view. (You can watch the video).

From a white woman's (I hate to be called white, so that's a biggy for me) point of view, there are white men who behave in the manner in which Sotomayor speaks of black men.

I was a high school teacher.

I saw the spectrum from both sides.

I also worked for law enforcement, the *scumbag* kind were of equal color. Guns don't kill.

People kill.

Controversy: From my personal experience, in all that I've seen from living in the deep South to being in a foreign country in the Military from going through a war from being a teacher, going to college and having my own children, this isn't a black and white issue. This is a government issue.

The people shouldn't be turning on themselves.

They should be forcing people out of office.

You don't need to take my word for it.

The facts speak for themselves, and I won't sit here and dictate numbers...you can look that up for yourself.

Affirmative Action. No Child Left Behind.

There's two big ones for you.

I know what they did.

If you're not out robbing a store or sitting around with your drugs and guns and a big chip on your shoulder, you should know, too.

Those are policies handed down by the government. Not by your neighbor.

Not by that nice white guy at the grocery.

By your government, and it appears it doesn't matter what color skin they have!

If you want to show your ass (pardon the language), then go to D.C.

Why start riots and stuff like that in little towns?

If you are so big, then why not tackle the problem head on?

What are you so scared of?

I'm so tired of seeing the guy I love have to remember things that happened in his past because of color all because he's doing his work and has to constantly see all this *crap* over and over online.

It's not fair to him or me.

Look down at your skin.

You are affecting those of the same color.

That goes for blacks and whites.

Don't you see that?

You want to do something that will actually make a difference, then why not just do it big and get it over with?

Why make men like the one I love suffer?

Solution: Get rid of big government.

I would say that all those people who state that history books lie, should have read the beginning of them at least.

Those who founded this country...i.e. those from Europe who came here, because they refused to bow down to a king, at least I know the French did, stated and wrote it down that if the government got too big, then its people had the right, *the right,* to overthrow it, with arms if necessary (hint: The reason behind the *Second Amendment*).

They knew what would happen.

They had been through it.

They knew what a dual-party system would do. *Grow*!

They gave the power to the people to *control* it!

That was a bunch of smart men there.

They warned you way before it would happen.

I would say that those *white* men gave a damn about you!

Don't go all *slave* on me.

The bottom line is even though all of our ancestors went through some hell to get to this point, we are *here*!

All of us are part of the *Constitution*.

That means that *all* of us have the same rights to stand up against our government as a *united* people.

Seems you want change, but you are too afraid to go get it the *real* way, so you take a knee and hold protests and riots, burn stuff down and steal other people's property...oh, let's not forget scream and yell injustice!

I say if you are man enough to hold a gun in your hand and do all the rest of the above, then you are man enough to hold the *right* people accountable!

Those who fought for this country to be *free* of Britain gave you the *solution* before... way before...the problem came, but you don't get it.

You are too busy arguing and yelling and cursing the educated out that you can't see the *simple* in anything.

You are too busy worried about getting your drugs and weapons and blaming that you have forgotten what *all* of our ancestors have died for. We *all* come from slaves.

Black or being poor does not give you anymore privilege than the rest of us have.

Period.

The gust of it: Liberals pushed for this and for that, then when it got out of hand they created racial tension.

Let *all* people come to America, and we have.

The door's wide open. Now *race* wars. No.

That's not the answer and won't solve anything.

Solution: Get rid of *big government*.

You live in a *free* country.

You might not see that because you are so into *they owe* me. No.

No one owes you anything. You don't steal. You don't lie. You don't kill.

You don't abuse. You earn!

We *all* play the same game. *Earn*.

If you can't earn your way, then try a third world country.

Do what you are doing here there and see how far you get.

This, too, you forgot to read in the history books that you say are lying. There.

I had my say.

I'm in a *free* country where I can. Or can I?

Tommy Sotomayor seems to have a hard time keeping his pages up.

When I spoke out on abuse, I was casted out.

Seems our *freedom* to speak is slowly going away. Hmm....

Let me give you head's up on this: *All* that I've been seeing on these videos is *abuse*.

I'm a woman in the deep south.

Abuse goes hand and hand with marriage down here.

If you think you are oppressed, try being a freaking woman!

I've learned if you want to be taken seriously, you have got to act seriously...especially, in a *free* country.

Politics today is our enemy. Not our friend.

Appealing to a politician is like getting water out of a dry well.

You won't get anywhere!

Ending: I gave you the problem.

I gave you a solution. Time is ticking.

The *Bible* gives you the exact same thing, and the *Bible* should be the first history book you should read. For myself, I want truths.

I want peace for myself and the man I love.

I want to go to the doctor and the doctor shakes my hand and *his*.

All this *different*...God didn't see it that way. So, why should you?

(Any errors are mine and mine alone.)

~*Tradition's Backfire*~

they said

you're just a girl—this is a man's world

messing with my head
holding me back—in their dizzy twirl

I tried to push ahead
but *esteem,* they made me lack
on my butt, they'd just slap

ignoring my educated snap
  –putting me in dead
all those words they said

but I don't go down like that
my mind—I discovered—sound
so much world all around–
I bounced back, learned a few facts

I got over their curse
learned new adverbs
set it all up—for a reverse
when they came at me in their attacks

they said

*you can't put it out like that
you're too bold—too negative
you, no one will respect
they'll drop you as a contact
–see you as an 'old crab'*

much more than that–
from all sides—came their attack

my professional swirl–
downgraded to *just a girl*

my mothering cap–
smashed to the ground
with a raging man-ego trap
stripping me of those I gave birth

my christian-wife-giving perk–
crushed into dirt
as hands—around my throat—grasped

my daughtering burst
my sistering worth–
taken, stripped, clasped
as man-driven pride submersed
fist to head—stripped 'til I was dead

I couldn't go down like that
my mind, put in the back–
lost from sound
so much world all around–
on a different-leveling track
I bounced back, met their crap with crap

in sexual immortality, I did flirt
around edges of freak
I certainly did skirt
–screaming, yelling, cursing
I explored my worse
–from the depths of dead
completely lost in my head
over and over rolling–

those words they said
–all those lies fed—I did the *dread*–
around every corner, I did tread

but I don't go down like that
my mind, I discovered
much more sound
so much world all around–
I fell in their trap
but it's just fact, I bounced back

into a dim light, I emerged—ready, able
put up my hard-core fight
as the light moved to bright–
breaking their holding-down trap
unveiling their curse
–I moved into rebirth, learning my worth
what truly sets my turf

I am a woman, not just a girl
my looks—just a perk
on my body, let your eyes flirt
–all this framework, aids my intelligence
(the likes of brilliance)

yes, on my face, a slight smirk

out—I reemerged
this butt, yes, try and slap
see if I don't call out your crap

this mind, try to trap—I'll come at you–
out of this cave—like a bat

yes, it's like that
don't like it—down—sit back—sap
for I've learned my worth
bridges, I'll easily burn, say *it like it is*
this right, I've readily earned

and...I don't go down—just like that
my mind, I know
clearly—positively—sound
all this world all around, I am bound
for, indeed, I bounce back
with the resistance of a cat

it's just fact—you, I'll come straight at
I'm 'all' that...and...that's just that!

(September 28, 2016)—Traditions. Lies.
Stories. What's real? What's not?
It's hard to tell these days with so many
websites putting up fake information, with
so many people, like the underground
web, *Photoshopping* and manipulating,
specifically, to deceive us.

In order to survive through all the mess, we have to know who we are inside, our individual truth, and we *all*, individually, have to stand for something, and that *something* has to be a good something *free* of anger and hate.

I read all these articles concerning race.

I have to ask—*What the hell?* I'm a woman.

I write about abuse not because it was my life-long ambition, but because it was an experience that altered the entire course of my life!

I decided after going through so much of other people's drama that if I didn't take all this negative and turn it around, it would consume me. So...I plowed on.

I have to ask another question—*Why aren't the people questioning why police all around the country are suddenly on a seemingly killing spree?*

Okay. I have more questions than that.

Why aren't the people questioning why the police all around the country are suddenly *seemingly against* the people?

Why aren't the people questioning themselves to why they are falling into this aged-old trap of *racism*? I know racism.

I wrote an article on my personal page about racism and abuse.

The two go hand in hand.

I can't write from a black woman's point of view, although I've seen their struggles as a teacher and a person growing up in the deep south.

I can write from a pure woman's point of view. You want to know what suppression is?

Ask a woman.

I'm currently reading *Lean In* by Sheryl Sandberg, Chief Operating Officer at *Facebook*.

She writes in the first chapter titled *'Internalizing the Revolution'*—*...In addition to the external barriers erected by society, women are hindered by barriers that exist within themselves. We hold ourselves back in ways both big and small, by lacking self-confidence, by not raising our hands, and by pulling back when we should be leaning in. We internalize the negative messages we get throughout our lives—the messages that say it's wrong to be outspoken, aggressive, more powerful than men. We lower our own expectations of what we can achieve....*

Wow...I bought this book back in 2015 when I sat on a course that changed so much inside of me beginning with Joyce Meyer.

It is only now that I've picked this particular book up and started reading.

That is a strange course for me because what Sandberg writes about is exactly what I've been writing about, so I wondered why I didn't choose this book earlier.

I watched the movie *The Shift* by Dr. Wayne W. Dryer put out by Hay House.

I related so much to this film because it is everything I've been discovering for the past ten years.

I've read the book *The Secret* and saw the movie.

Everything Dr. Dryer talks about is basically what *The Secret* talks about.

God is the *universe* and everything we have in our lives, we attract.

To make our lives better, we must first start with *self*.

I always say that everything happens for a reason.

I am smiling because, indeed, everything does.

When I bought Sandberg's book, I also bought about [eight] other books.

The first book, of course, that I picked to read was Meyer's *Battlefield of the Mind*, which literally changed my world.

All the things Sandberg writes about, I've experienced on a different level.

Being smart, being pretty, being a woman...the perfect recipe for strife and drama!

These ending paragraphs in Sandberg's introductory chapter had me shaking my head with a crocked smile on my face—

...Some, especially other women in business, have cautioned me about speaking out publicly on these issues. When I have spoken out anyway, several of my comments have upset people on both genders. I know some believe that by forcing on what women can change themselves—pressing them to lean in—seems like I am letting our institutions off the hook. Or even worse, they accuse me of blaming the victim. Far from blaming the victim, I believe that female leaders are key to the solution.

Some critics will also point out that it is much easier for me to lean in, since my financial resources allow me to afford any help I need. My intention is to offer advice that would have been useful to me long before I heard of Google or Facebook and that will resonate with women in a broad range of circumstances.

I have heard these criticisms in the past and I know that I will hear them—and others—in the future. My hope is that my message will be judged on its merits. We can't avoid this conversation. This issue transcends all of us. The time is long overdue to encourage more women to dream the possible dream and encourage more men to support women in the workforce and in the home.

I, too, was heavily criticized when I began speaking about abuse and the *traditions* I was raised with out loud.

I live in a constant *hush-hush* society.

I have been shut-out by family and friends who couldn't handle my extreme, sudden open side.

I had got to a point where I refused to be quiet any longer.

My hope is the same as Sandberg's: That more women stand up for themselves and go after their dreams without being condemned or shot down by both men and other women.

The woman world is very *catty* from my point of view.

Other women don't like *smart* women.

They sure as hell don't like *smart, pretty* women, and the worse is being *smart, pretty, and thin*! That is just the worse curse.

Or, so I thought.

I look at the books that I chose to read first compared to the ones I've read in the last few months.

Those first books were all about rebuilding *self* and making *self* stronger in body, mind, and spirit.

These books I've turned to now are all about *empowering* the self.

I truly think that I didn't read these books first because my *calling* is to write about the *authentic* self in the immersion of strife: The entering into, the fight to get out, and the surviving of.

Everything happens for a reason.

Isn't that amazing?! Empowering of self.

My eyes truly opened up back in 2012 to abuse and the results of it, the *secrets* of it.

Not much has changed since I began my journey through the five stages of grief.

I still see all around me women who bow down, who hide abuse, who live with it.

I am also keenly aware of the racism issue as everyone else is. Racism. Abuse.

Same damn thing!

If you are a black man, think of all those moments when you felt belittled *put in your place* condemned harshly in subtle words... that's what abuse feels like. The silent kind.

The most dangerous kind.

Women of all races experience this at one point in their lives. It's a given.

There's no getting around it.

This is what my work is all about.

This is where *"Tradition's Backfire"* comes from this morning.

You can't make others see your point of view. You can't change anyone.

You can let all that hate and anger and manipulation destroy you.

It almost destroyed me.

Or you can learn from it and turn it around starting with *self.*

How we deal with things determines how others will treat us.

If we allow them to make us anger, then they have control.

I can say this today that [x] doesn't control me as a person.

What still angers me is that it doesn't seem to bother anyone that he said he loved, but clearly he lied.

Meaning: This man could do what the hell he wanted without suffering the consequences.

He could unravel the lives of [four] people and still be considered a *good* guy, and I, the one who suffered his wrath and sudden change of mind, am considered the *bad* guy.

No, I'm not stuck on the past.

I'm stuck on a society that breeds that it's okay for people to treat others with cruelty, as long as, that *people* is a guy, and that's the gust of it.

I've spoken with so many women in the last [four] years and over and over again I get the same message: Women really don't have any say-so.

I even get this from other women, and that has been the biggest shocker of all.

Note: As I've said many times, I have, but one [x]. Sorry, that's just the facts of it.

So, my experience with that [x] is all I have.

I have no intention on writing about something I do not know about, so using my personal experience is going to happen... like it or not, and just because I use my experience does not mean I'm *stuck back there.*

With that said, using experiences that we do not *actually* experience is not really being totally factual because we can't speak about something truly truthfully, from the heart, that we have *not* personally experienced.

It becomes a matter of hear-say: *She said, he said* sort of thing.

I say that because of all the articles I've been reading on slavery issues which no longer exist.

I have to ask the legitimacy of the anger expressed in some of these articles.

If you weren't actually there, then how can you actually express your anger in truth?

You can't.

I have to ask, what is *your* experience *now*?

Then you have my attention, and that's what matters now, leading me to the articles I've read and the videos I've watched about what a black man or woman actually experiences today.

Appalling, but it doesn't stop there.

There are the articles and videos about how women are still treated today. Appalling.

Hello. Earth to Mars. Mars to Earth.

Houston we have a problem!

Videos. Wow!

When we were children and we took a cookie without asking, that was considered stealing and we got our hands slapped.

This may have to occur a couple more times before we learned that we must ask before taking a cookie.

Hint: May I have a cookie, please?

I'll use the police as an example.

Call it racism or whatever you want.

It's abuse all the same.

One or two police shootings, that would be a police person shooting an unarmed person recorded on video and put before the world would have me saying—*Something is just not right here.*

As any captain in any police department across this gigantic bitch of a country, I would damn well be sure that safety meetings are held pronto, that retraining takes place weekly, psyche evaluations occurred regularly and without warning as well as drug testing, that *all* ammo is accounted for and that every police officer on my force had *working* cameras everywhere and they are constantly being examined to ensure the safety of the public, and I wouldn't do that to save my officers' asses.

Hell no, that would be just to save *my* ass!

One or two policemen from across the country showing unnecessary force towards another person who *is not* endangering their lives, the same action would be taken, but with a vigorousness that would *ensure no* police officer on my force mistreated *any* civilian. *Period*!

I would also hold conferences on the television, on the radio and on a public *Facebook* page (because every body is on *Facebook*) and ensure the confidence in my force that no civilian should *ever* fear my department because we take *all* precautions to *ensure* their *safety*! Oh, that's just me.

Did they even watch *Beverly Hills Cop?*

As in domestic abuse, after seeing how many videos on *Facebook* where police officers from around this gigantic bitch of a country brutally attacking people, holding people without cause, arresting people for no reason, you would think eyes would be further opened, then this is *every* department around the country, then you have to wonder the *real* reason to why domestic abuse still exist in *this* country!

Which leads me to this: Domestic abuse. In any form. Relationships of *all* kinds. Racism. Etc., etc. has been around forever!

People like little ole me speak out and get slammed! Ignored! Shut the fuck down!

Labeled *drama* starters and every other name in the book! Bullies continue their B.S.

Now it has escalated to policemen...those that take an oath to uphold the law and *protect* the citizens of their districts!

You would think there's some kind of *outside* influence going on here!

So, where does it stop? Abuse, I mean.

What has to happen to open the eyes of everyone, not just the victims?

So, where does the anger stop, the hate?

Small. That's right. Small. *Self.* Family. Friends. Community. State. Country.

All with God in the forefront.

It's that simple. Hate breeds hate.

The more hate shown, the more hate attracted, but take it the opposite direction and see what happens!

Posting all these videos isn't doing what you think it's doing.

The captain of each department all over this entire great big vast country...why isn't anyone putting them on camera?

A good question. Don't you think?

A group is as strong as its leader.

Meaning: Take for instance a military unit. I can write about this because I have experienced it. Each unit has a leader.

The morale of that unit is a direct link to the morale of its leader.

Take a school and its teachers.

Take a business and its employees.

The atmosphere. The morale. The spirit.

The anger. The hate.

All...*a direct link* to the leader!

Take the country. The same goes here.

What you see going on in the country is a direct link to its leader. Need I say more.

Back down to the basic: The most intense...

the morale or disposition of a woman in any relationship is a direct link to the man she is in relationship with.

It's really simple.

What goes around, comes around.

Treat people bad...sooner or later it backfires on you! That's a given.

Not a promise, but a fact.

Treat people good...sooner or later, you're going to get a bag of Hersey's kisses and shit.

Trust me on this. God is great *all* the time.

You can take that statement to the bank!

~*Unleveled Grounds*~

how sure to ever be
pictures—fighting for *free*

born in places, hatred in faces
differences in colors
still loving our mothers

round and round
goes the merry-go-round
all arguments sound
still, peace—never really found

how sure to ever be—pictures, videos
hatred bred in film inches
pieces, pieces, pieces
control enabled—cyber stitches
fighting for *free*
playing in the hands of God's† enemy

~

(September 29, 2016)—Posted an article titled *'FDA Approves Tranquilizer Dart Guns that Puts Kids to Sleep'*—by *itsjustme.mobi*

Cops should use this, instead of guns.

To use it on kids, you should be condemned to hell.

—*Note*: As a veteran, I still feel it is my duty to fight for the *freedom* of America.

Election day is quickly approaching.

Through all the methods of control: Education, race, death, politics, economics...all that plays on our emotions, there's the adversary doing its part.

That evil whore knows how to manipulate us.

It has done its homework. Have you?

Personally, I will continue posting what I deem the truth in all matters.

I don't care if you don't like it. Delete me.

Ignore me. I'm bold and brave.

I wouldn't have been a soldier otherwise.

I have been condemned by enough of man to know that I don't give a damn, I'm going to say it anyway.

Like Father Orsi says, we *are* under serious attack. If you can't see it, then you are blind.

I'm a United States citizen. Born on her soil.

I have native blood. I stood the wall.

I raised my children here. No place else.

I was silent for too long on many issues.

Not anymore. I write. I market.

I stand as an individual along side my fellow comrades to protect foreign as well as domestic enemies!

Our political system is a mess and is *not* standing on its own for us.

We the people must decide which side we are on: The right side or the wrong side.

This country began because of God.

There have been much strife for all her people to be able to stand on our own.

Democracies have never endured because of economics and power-seekers.

We, the American people, have a chance to prove this wrong!

It is only in the power of *the people* that a democracy survives.

When its government becomes corrupt beyond repair, when its government becomes bigger than the *people*, then it is in the power of the *people* to take back their control.

This is not about the President.

This is about Congress. Period.

Who's putting the money in their pockets.

The Rothschild guy (he looks like he's the enemy's child) or the American people who slave all day long in the hot sun or the drug dealers who live life in luxury, while their product is killing our children or the Saudi's who can't even care for their own people because of their greed or the Islamic (the enemy's instruments) who slaughter anybody who believes in God as a Christian?

Who is it?

Are you too afraid to acknowledge the real truth? Are you too scared?

I have but one person to answer to, that is *God*. Who do you answer to?

Maybe, you should pay attention to how many Islamic people are in control of the U.S.A.'s government.

Maybe, that will wake you up a bit!

All the things I post here isn't for some crusade.

It's for education, and a lot of the American people are *not* properly educated.

When the younger generations have no idea what the Civil War was about, there's a serious problem.

When the younger generations are spewed by hate because of black/white issues, there's a serious problem.

When the younger have no idea what socialism is and demand it, then there is a very serious problem.

Lack of education is a serious issue in this country, but guess what, this is the number *one* agenda of the enemy: *Dumb down America,* then they strike.

I started my political education forum back in 2009.

I slacked a bit because of strife brought to my personal life. I won't stop again.

This isn't a crusade. This is facts.

This is truth. You just refuse to face it.

The enemy is at your door.

Boom, and they laugh.

Don't believe me, go review the celebrations after 9/11, then come back and tell me I am wrong. Read. Education.

Take your own action. I still stand a wall.

Not with a gun.

Oh, my, with something a little more powerful. A pen...i.e. a keyboard!

How are you going to take a stand?

If you missed your moment of serving as a soldier, maybe, you should serve another way. Make a damn difference.

Take it out on D.C.!

Comments
•(Friend) At last, a person and a lady who speaks great sense and has not hit the nail on the head, but *smashed it.*
Fantastic post and all very true...yes, I read it all...no it's true I'm not American, I'm from the U.K., but it's happening all over the world... and, yes, that day I watched dumb founded in the U.K. at the TV as all that devastation happened live in front of my eyes. ☺
I thought should I rub my eyes, is it April fools day, this is a film trailer...what the hell is happening, as [one], then [two].
We know the rest.
A massive *respect not only for your brilliant words* and explanation, *but for serving your country, too.*

~*Not A Man*~

if you want a man, get a man
–I 'm not a man

if you want intelligence, I can withstand
if on my two feet, you let me stand

if you want practical, I'll do what I can

–listen carefully—I'm not a man

I don't hang a penis in my pants
boobs, to me, God† did hand
so suck it up buttercup–
you'll be disappointed
in what, you don't understand

if you can't handle emotion–
then move on, 'cause I can

I'm not a man, I am a woman
if you don't get my strand–
you were bred to be the *man*
this, I understand
around your circles, I already ran
now, I just don't give a damn

I used to slip in the sand
behind—stand
be the mothering, *hush-hush* little ant
listen to all the *you can'ts*
while leaving myself in a trance

things have changed–

call me strange—against me—gang
again, I don't give a damn

I am patient–
waiting, that perfect circumstance
putting together my band
–that smooth mixture in my pan

when it's time to dance–
then you'll understand
why I didn't jump on each, every chance

oh! I am so woman—not at all a man
'til you understand, always, there's a plan
filled with intelligence–
a basket full of emotions
to the right clan—undying devotion

–no longer slipping in sand
before anyone else
my *self—I've* become a fan
if you see me just as contraband
so easy for me—you—to ban

get it right—understand
I won't just sit at the table, raise my hand
–on my feet, I plan to stand–
with only the expression on my face–
make you feel bland
as—on my hips—lay my hands
make you want to study—cram
by your nightstand
–hoping to outmatch my *I can*

save your troubles–
–you can't—for I am woman
the *different* strand
you were taught to withstand
in the back, make her stand

they forgot one piece, of that plan

slap her down, pity her frown
treat her, over and over, like a clown
things—come back around

remember: she's not a man
–when a sincere woman finally stands
her roar—loud, loud over the land

−no chance, you stand−

she doesn't need you as her fan
her faith, stronger than any brand
for God† designed her–
mixtures of intelligence
emotions and heart
after all—His† mighty hand
made *her* mother of *all* man

get the plan—do you *now* understand!

(September 30, 2016)—Read the following statement closely, and then think really hard:

...If a woman pushes to get the job done, if she's highly competent, if she focuses on results rather than on pleasing others, she's acting like a man. And if she acts like a man, people dislike her....—from *Lean In* by Sheryl Sandberg.

Read it again if you need to.

Did you think really hard about this statement? Can you relate?

If you are a woman who has pursued a career, raised children, taken care of a home, etc., pretty much every woman on the planet should relate.

Sandberg goes on to say...in response to this negative reaction—*...we temper our professional goals. Author Ken Auletta summarized this phenomenon in 'The New Yorker' when he observed that for women, 'self-doubt becomes a form of self-defense.' In order to protect ourselves from being disliked, we question our abilities and downplay our achievements, especially in the presence of others. We put ourselves down before others can....*

In Sandberg's book, the following statements stand out for me:

1. She is *very ambitious*...is not a compliment in our culture.

2. Aggressive and hard-charging women violate unwritten rules about acceptable social conduct.

3. ...many women *still see ambition as a dirty word*.

4. When a girl tries to lead, she is often labeled *bossy*.

5. Young women internalize societal cues about what defines *appropriate* behavior and, in turn, silence themselves.

6. ...the fundamental assumption is that [men] can have both a successful professional life and a fulfilling personal life.
For many women, the assumption is that trying to do both is difficult at best and impossible at worst.

Most women—*...feel fraudulent when they are praised for their accomplishments. Instead of feeling worthy of recognition, they feel undeserving and guilty, as if a mistake has been made. Despite being high achievers...women can't seem to shake the sense that it is only a matter of time until they are found out for who they really are—impostors with limited skills or abilities.*

If a woman is competent, she does not seem nice enough. If a woman seems really nice, she is considered more nice than competent. Since people want to hire and promote those who are both competent 'and' nice, this creates a huge stumbling block for woman.

Does any of these statements hit home for you?

How many of you have suffered from that *fraudulent* or *imposter* feeling?

I self-doubt myself all the time, especially, when others won't give me a time of day (i.e. ignore me).

Or worse, when people tell me that I shouldn't write about what I write about.

I hate that.

One of the most interesting statements I get is that I shouldn't use the word *fuck* in my writing.

Worse, I shouldn't use the words *fuck* and *God* in the same sentence.

I think this is just a method of control that's been put on us, especially, here in the south, since birth!

The following are some of the things I grew up with and/or taught by either my parents, religion class, school, other adults in my community, teachers, and/or my peers:

1. Don't say curse words.
You're are not Christian or a lady if you curse.

2. Tattoos are bad.
You are a slut, whore, gangster, or a criminal if you have a tattoo.

3. Don't show your boobs by wearing low-cut shirts or show your ass by wearing short-shorts.
You are considered *loose* or a slut or whore if you do so.

4. Too much perfume or makeup, you are considered whorish, easy, low-class.

5. If you have a baby out of wedlock, you are condemned in the community, make the family have a bad name, and/or you're whore material and not wife material.

6. Don't talk out of turn.
It makes you look uneducated.

7. *Do not* argue with a man. Period.

8. A man is *never* wrong.

9. A woman can *never* show her intelligence in the presence of men in public!

10. A woman is to be subtle with her knowledge and never, *never* make a man look bad in public. *Never*!

11. Don't disrespect a man.
They have to get respect first if you expect to be respected.

12. Don't undermine a man.
What a man says is right, before what a woman

says.

13. It's okay for a man to discipline his wife.

She's *his* responsibility, so if she *misbehaves* in public or makes him *look* bad, it's okay for him to degrade her, and even hit her to *correct* her behavior.

14. The woman is considered *the wife* not *my wife* as if she is a possession that can be easily traded in.

She *is* made aware of this in tone, actions and such.

15. A woman *is* the *sole* person responsible for the children and the *man* in the household.

She *is* to cater to both.

16. A woman can take charge in the household, but in public, she is expected to bow down.

17. A woman can make financial decisions on small levels in the household, but *all* major decisions are finalized by the man no matter if her money is involved or not.

18. If issues arrive due to money, it's always her fault!

19. She is *expected* to put her family first.

If she goes back to school or tries to have a career and things don't get done around the house or she has to miss a child's event, she is neglecting her family.

20. She can work all day in the house, take care of kids, work outside the home, etc., but in the afternoons, *she* has to cook supper, wash clothes, etc.

A man works at a job, then comes home and it's perfectly okay for him to relax and do nothing... after all, he's *worked* all day.

21. She *is* responsible for keeping her man happy above herself!

Ex: If the AC is on 65 because she is hot, but he is too cold, the AC gets raised no matter what!

22. What happens behind closed doors, stays behind closed doors.

So, if a woman is degraded, treated with constant disrespect, is cheated on, etc., etc, she isn't supposed to talk about it. (The *hush-hush* mentality.)

Family do *not* get involved.

You, the woman, who *is* responsible for keeping her family together (i.e. her man happy), is responsible for the problems and a failure, and is totally blamed for the divorce (i.e. she is never totally accepted again by the family or her friends).

His family completely casts her out like she never existed!

23. *Divorce* is a *dirty* word, and if you divorce, you disgrace your family.

Yes, this is what I was raised to believe.

I learned different when I moved out at the age of 18, but when I returned, these lessons were quickly reinforced.

I returned as a single mother and because of the stigma placed on having a baby out of wedlock, I had to struggle to gain my *place* back in the community and family (i.e. I had to struggle to make ends meet on my own without help, I had to prove myself, so even if I didn't have much food to eat or couldn't make my rent, I was given *zero* help).

I was also expected to find a husband.

When I did, I had to pay for the entire wedding! This is reality.

I am a lot like my father: A take charge, intelligent kind of person.

I was allowed to exhibit my *intelligence* to an extent. We are raised to *showcase* the man.

So, that is how I behaved, taking no credit for the things I could do or the things I've accomplished.

In my experience, a woman can be very creative and talented, but if she is, she has to do *all* the work to make whatever she does make money. The man does not help.

If she spends a lot of time and money on her craft and does not make money right away, then she is condemned, she is *ridiculed* for wasting the family's money (i.e. *his* money), and she is told she is wasting her time, that she will *never* succeed, but if a man has a talent, etc., she *is* expected to help, and she *is* expected to be patient and put out the money to encourage the project no matter what.

When I finally had enough of all of this, I was called *lazy*, accused of wasting the family money, a liar, a *drama* starter not just by [x], but by family and friends.

I was totally expected to accept that I was abused, accept that [x] changed his mind, accept that I had suddenly become the *enemy* and move on without a fight, *and* without verbally expressing my anger. No.

We don't have to accept anything of what we don't believe in.

We don't have to bow down because of this *traditional* expectation.

We, as women, have a mind of our own.

It is perfectly okay to feel all that we feel.

We were designed that way by God.

It's taken me a lot of therapy to see this clearly.

I did feel like I'd done something wrong.

I did feel like a fraud and that all the things I'd written during this period of my life was just made up (i.e. *all in my head*).

It took a lot to come to terms with the fact that I was right in expressing myself, that I was right telling the truth about what happened to me, that I was right in feeling all that hurt, and expressing it the way that I did.

I finally learned that *no one* had any right

telling me that *I couldn't* do what I was doing.

Sandberg nails it when she writes—*I feel a deep and enduring sense of gratitude to those who have given me opportunities and support. I recognize the sheer luck of being born into my family in the United States rather than one of the many places in the world where women are denied basic rights.*

I recognize the fact that my family may have had traditional ways, but, still, I was born in *free* where I can, sooner or later, express myself with an open mind without being put to death or imprisoned.

With that being said, I also recognize the fact that many others are not as advanced in thought as myself, so they will condemn me, they will makeup stuff about me in order to discredit me, they will ignore me, they will bash me. So fucking what!

I learned to stand on my own two feet without that *traditional* way of thinking held over my head.

Breaking *free* from all of that nonsense is the best thing that ever happened to me.

I owe that to God.

I also am very grateful that I've been given the gift of words in order to share my experiences and show young girls that they are just as capable as a man to stand on their own two feet.

It is also my responsibility as a woman to explain to these young girls that their ride will not be easy because, even though we do live in a *free* country, there are still stigmas placed on what a woman *should* be.

These stigmas are not just from men.

Women who aren't ambitious and are buried in this *traditional* way of thinking, also place these stigmas on those women who stand on their own two feet.

It is up to us women to empower young girls and other women, and let them know that they don't have to play by *man* rules.

A woman was created different than a man.

She was given that natural gift of nourishment, but she was also given the gift of knowledge and the ability to think outside the box. She is creative and full of emotion.

None of what she is naturally should ever be held against her.

In today's world, people in relationships should work together so that the woman and the man *can* have that family unity and those careers. It is *never* a competition.

There should be support on both ends.

A woman shouldn't have to *act* like a man in order to become successful.

She is *not* a man and no matter how you see her, she'll never be a man.

Hence, *"Not A Man"*!

Ladies: If you know a woman who has an ambitious mind, cheer for her.

Don't put her down because you can't be as ambitious. She's not arrogant.

Think about that particular woman, then replace her in your mind with a man.

Would you still consider her arrogant?

I don't think so.

You think she's arrogant because she's a woman.

The stigma of what a woman *should* be is deeply ingrained in your thoughts because of years and years of teachings from *traditional* ideals that aren't at all accurate.

The woman was not put on this earth to be silent. Sorry. That's man pushing that issue.

She was also not put on this earth to cater to man. That...again...is a man-pushed issue.

Success depends on if you can withstand the hate and the stigmas put on being a woman in a *man's* world.

Any woman can do anything when she puts her mind to it.

Don't let man's agenda-driven ego stand in your way. It's okay to speak up.

It's okay to say what's on your mind.

It's time to open up these discussions as Sandberg says in her book. It *is* time!

Note: I support all women in the world.

I don't support anyone who lies or uses manipulative tactics to advance themselves in anything.

I don't support using the body for advancement either.

I don't support anything that goes against God.

~

(October 1, 2016)—I'm on the line with [phone company].

Big Corporations really have us by the balls, don't they?

[One and a half] years ago I had to *buy* a [phone cable] system for over $100 and they promised that I wouldn't have to buy another system and I was only paying $19.99 a month. Always and completely.

Now...my system is no longer valid, so I have to get the $50+ taxes and surcharges and they so easily say that I don't have to purchase the equipment.

Well...that's right because they've included the price of the system in my bill *and* I have to return the system.

Big corporations, and I *have* to make a year's commitment.

Boy, do they know how to sucker us into the marketing schemes!

I need a marketing make-money-easy like that of [phone company]...that's a guaranteed $50 per person monthly income...man are they making a killing!

~

(October 3, 2016)—Approaching my infamous [three] a.m.

I have engaged on all this hoopla going around and I have to say *bla bla bla.*

People love drama and will believe anything, as long as, it fits their little closed up world! No surprise.

On politics...we're fucked!

The [two] main choices have made a mockery of our country, our honor and our integrity.

I listened to both sides and though my tiny little opinion doesn't matter since, in my opinion, my vote doesn't either, I am going to say it like it is. We are at war with Islam.

Face it. We are losing.

Bla bla bla celebrities bask you in their made-up world and steal your money.

They are no better than politicians.

All this clown bullshit...all this cop bullshit...all this black/white bullshit...it's all Islam! Sorry to cut to the chase.

That's just evil.

That's fact and it is happening no matter how you look at it. World government.

Now that's a concept! Not for me.

I am sticking to my vows and will complete my work, love the man who decided to stay, honor my children by being who I am...*me*, and bypassing all this bullshit.

I served. I ask for what?

So some damn raper can continue to make a mockery of truth and honesty, while all the young kids, who were so dumped down that when given a chance, will put all us old folks in old people jail and pray we die a fast death.

Or for some lying politician who is using our tax dollars to take his family to foreign lands, while we stay broke watching the same fucking walls day in and day out.

Or for some greedy selfish prick living a life of yachts and expensive cars, while his company saves him money by sending our food to freaking China to get packaged where there's no regulations so people are getting parasites in their bodies.

Or for some dumb ass liberal who decides they know more medicine than years and years of research and refuses to give their child vaccines not at all thinking what a vaccine is really for.

We have lost the country we know.

I prefer to make a little money, ignore the pansy asses of this world, buy more guns and pray I don't need them. Stupid! Ignorant!

Uneducated! Poor advised! Hotheaded. Haters.

All products of the one thing it appears so many can't exercise with common sense: *Free*-will!

I am an individual thinker.

I would rather leave something of value behind like helping others make it through strife with a sane mind...letting others know it's okay to be angry and sad and there is a way to happy again minus the bullshit spread by Islam and liberals who can't recognize the love of Christ! Take a knee for that!

~

(October 5, 2016)—*I'd rather have bad times with you, than good times with someone else. I'd rather be beside you in a storm, than safe and warm by myself. I'd rather have hard times together, than to have it easy apart. I'd rather have the one who holds my heart.*—Author Unknown

I am responsible for my own mistakes and failures. This I can do.

I take the responsibility, then I correct it, then I move the hell on.

I cannot correct other people's mistakes and failures.

Lord knows I have tried in the past.

It doesn't work that way.

Everyone is responsible for their own mistakes.

If they don't correct their mistakes, then they just stay stuck in the same ole rut.

I can encourage and inspire, but I cannot get them out of their rut.

Lesson learned: People don't want to help themselves get out of their rut.

They want to blame someone, and take a handout and will do unimaginable things to get it.

I don't live off any handout.

I worked many, many years...working until I couldn't anymore.

Trying to please people is just too damn exhausting.

—I think we benefit from expressing our truth, talking

about personal situations, and acknowledging that professional decisions are often emotionally driven.—from *Lean In* by Sheryl Sandberg

~*Wasted Hours*~

sitting many hours, waiting for *ours*
instead of looking at *mine*
–let time slip in kind

pondering the *hours*
while cleaning a house—turned dreams–
the *searching-for-the-cheese* mouse
left empty—without clout

sitting more hours
feeling casted out—zero house
–scared little lonely mouse
years spent thinking about
all those hours, losing more hours
searching—screams and shouts

living in so much doubt
fighting, clawing out
to sitting there, trying to figure it out
still—more hours
still no more clout than started out

all these wasted hours
still fighting the cringe–
self-induced doubt
as the world moves about
–moving fast, in forward's shout

(October 6, 2016)—*The first step towards getting somewhere is to decide that you are not going to stay where you are.*—Author Unknown

Define success on your own terms. Achieve it by your own rules, and build a life you're proud to live.—Anne Sweeney

Sheryl Sandberg wrote a line in *Lean In* that had me staring at it for minutes before moving on with my reading.

The line is—*The cost of stability is often diminished opportunities in growth.*

I read this one line over and over again.
Wow! How it hit home.

There have been so many times during my pushing through the five stages of grief that I was told that I wasn't *stable.*

You're too unstable for me—I've heard over and over.

Stable: able or likely to continue or last; resistant to sudden change or fluctuation; reliable and steady, as in emotions; resisting physical or chemical change (*Random House Dictionary*)

Sandberg writes just before the above line—*As they had been all along, the men were more*

interested in new and, as we say in tech, higher beta opportunities—where the risks were great, but the potential rewards even greater.

Note: Sorry, I couldn't help but relate this line to the thought of why men cheat. Seems obvious.
New. Risk. Rewards.
Doesn't that fit a man who cheats?
I'm kind of banking on love and devotion.
It exist. I know it does!

Back to being stable.
So, men don't like stable and women do, but stability costs. It does.
I settled down when I was 24 wanting that career, but also wanting the family and house thing.
Of course, through the entire 20 years I was married, I also had a disorder that was affecting me a great deal, but didn't know what that was until 2010.
It is sort of strange fighting something and not knowing what that *something* is.
It's worse when you discover that all those years of your personal fight, it was being used to manipulate your world and you didn't know it.
Check out my books when they come out to see how this played out. Not a good thing.
Anyway, it was a lot of work to maintain a home, raise a family, do school and a career.
All at the same time.
You have no idea, but I did it and I did it with an underlying disorder that kept me fatigued 100% of the time, and it was easy to put me in confusion to where I'd get agitated, but I maintained. I had no choice.
I maintained until I got sick and watched as so much I worked on, and for, went down the drain.
I realized that nothing worked unless *I* worked it.
I was called *unstable,* but the reality was, and still is, I keep things stable around me, and when others faltered, then I'm the one *unstable.* Does that make sense?
When you are walking the walk, it makes *straight-in-your-face* sense!
Sandberg brings in a word: *Averse.*

Averse: strongly opposed or unwilling; the verb form, avert: to turn away or aside; a ward off or prevent.

She writes—*…there are times in life when being risk averse is a good thing; adolescent and adult males drown in much greater numbers than adolescent and adult females. But in business, being risk averse can result in stagnation. An analysis of senior corporate management appointments found that women are significantly more likely than men to continue to perform the same* *function, even when they take on new duties; and when female managers move up, they are more likely to do so internally, instead of switching to a different company. At times, staying in the same functional area and in the same organization creates inertia and limits opportunity to expand. Seeking out diverse experiences is useful preparation for leadership.*

Maybe, you should stop and read that one more time! She hits the nail on the head!

That paragraph can also be applied to a relationship big time.

Men who cheat don't try to improve *internally*—hell they move all sorts of ways with this one and that one, destroying the *internal* business of it all.

They are applying the business world to the marriage! Damn straight.

Women stay *internally,* wanting to improve their relationship, forgetting about the external of it. Funny how that works.

Back to business: If more women thought like the men who cheat, damn, they'd be great in the business world!

This is where that damn word *unstable* falls into place. I know a lot of creative minds.

Every single one of them live *unstable* lives.

It's when, like me, we lean to that *stable* that never really fits, our lives fall apart.

Creative minds can*not* be in a stable environment.

Stability leads to self-doubt and wasted hours, hence, my work *"Wasted Hours."*

There's something else that Sandberg talks about: The *Tiara Syndrome.*

I nearly fell off my chair when I read that.

Literally. I dropped the book!

I know exactly what this feels like.

This is where women—*expect that if they keep doing their job well, someone will notice them and place a tiara on their head.*

When you do all the things a woman does and you don't get recognized, don't worry, you aren't alone.

No one will come and celebrate us because we can pop out a baby and wash dishes an hour later. Men just don't understand.

This has been going on for so long that it is natural for a woman to just go on like having a baby is the same as washing dishes.

It's not.

We all know it's not, but who really gives a shit? Surely, men don't. Why is that?

Logically speaking...they have never...ever, in the history of man, been able to give birth to a baby! It is that simple.

Their brain can't even fathom the notion of what it must feel like to give birth to a human being, so they don't worry about it.

They have never, ever been that in-tune to another human life, so they can't even fathom the pure definition of *nourish.*

Women are different!

Damn straight, and we *do not* have a choice! No one is going to hand us anything.

Trust me...I've waited and waited for someone to really care about what happens to me, to really care that—*Oh, she can't breathe...give her a moment. It* doesn't happen.

I've watched my mother suffer with migraines all my life.

No assault to my dad, after all, he was doing what he was raised to do.

He'd come in the house during one of my mother's migraine moments and turn on the damn lights and yell—*What's for supper?*— without any consideration to my mother.

She would squint her eyes, take the cold pack off her head, get up, and fix the damn supper, crying the whole time.

She was doing what she was raised to do: Care for the man, instead of the other way around when she is ill.

Man. A strange beast that one is.

Man doesn't have that nourishing ability in them. They see black and white.

Woman sees all the gray.

You can't change that.

Sandberg says—*Hard work and results should be recognized by others, but when they aren't, advocating for oneself becomes necessary.*

Most men don't have to *prove* themselves.

They get jobs straight out of college with hardly any upset.

A woman...she has to *prove* herself!

When a woman doesn't move up as fast as the man or sees that she will never be treated on equal grounds to a man, she starts looking for a husband. *Fuck it*—that's what she thinks.

She'd rather get a husband and sit back and relax at home having those babies because the fight is just too exhausting.

(Isn't it amazing how we are, indeed, exhausted during these baby-making years, but we don't equate that to working a career!?)

Then, and I can speak this with pure experience, later in life, she realizes what a mistake she has made because she really does want that career, then she sees how she's given up her whole life for *him*...the man!

It doesn't end there.

When she does began her *mergement* into

the great big world, man still puts on brakes.

She's spent an entire life reading and learning, while sitting back there taking care of the family.

Sure, she wasn't in the workforce entirely, but she wasn't dead, either.

So, when she does start showing her stuff, those around her can't comprehend that she does, indeed, know her stuff, plus their stuff as well! I find this so amusing.

All those damn wasted hours on mindless people who can't sit at the same table, disgusts me to no end.

Why in the hell did I waste so much time? Tradition. That's the answer.

Sandberg quotes Alice Walker—*The most common way people give up their power is by thinking they don't have any.*

Yes, indeed!

Men believe that abusing a woman strips her of her power.

What they don't get is that it actually builds her power.

Have you ever met a woman who survived abuse?

You can't say *no* because you're reading me. You have met one. Speak up.

If you see something not right and you remain silent, it remains not right.

Love the skin you're in.

God is great all the time.

—I dare you to stop making excuses.—Author Unknown

I'm registered to vote. I'm not voting!
Facebook asked me—*What's on your mind?*
Plenty, *Facebook*, plenty.

Here's the gust of it: What the hell are you voting for? Do you know?

As long as there is electronic voting, count me out. I saw this years and years ago.

Did you see the video they made proving that the electronic voting does *not* work? Well....

Donald Trump can say all that he wants. Damn.

He already knows the outcome of this election. So do I.

If you think it's decided by your vote, you are really blind.

I'm gonna say what I'm gonna say as much as I can say it, *and I can write all freaking day long*!

We do *not* decide who wins U.S. *Presidency*!

Donald Trump is proving facts to you that you should already know.

Fact: What he says has all of you up in fumes.

People are hating on people because of what he says. Did he *do* anything? Nope. He's just talking!

Laugh. Laugh.

Obama *did* things and you aren't raising hell or anything about that!

Trump is a billionaire, and, even though he's been married several time (which doesn't matter to anyone anymore...morals out the window just like Christ in our schools), he has a stand-up family.

All his children work for a living.

I believe most if not all hold a college degree.

Damn, the man gains nothing from running for President! He's just talking.

Point: Has Donald Trump caused anyone to die? Well, has he?

Hillary Clinton caused many people to die because she failed to act!

There have been more mass killings during Obama's [eight] years in office, then the history of the U.S. combined (I'm not counting 9/11 and I think you are smart enough to know why). Oh *my God*!

Does that even matter?

I can't get over the stupidity raging in this country.

What are you thinking?

The man is just talking and you are outraged.

Has anyone paid attention to what Obama, who is the President, has said in his [eight] years. He advocated for a world government.

Does that *not* lift your ear?

He advocated racism, abortion, saying our *Constitution* is old and should be replaced.

WTF?

Clowns seen everywhere and you dumb-asses are scared? What is that about?

You have a gun. You have a 911.

You have a car. *Use it.*

Hello, seeing these videos of clown sightings and people running away like little bitches.

I have to wonder if they aren't staged.

Yes, they are I have to only guess.

Idiots!...then all this racism with people brutality. I have to wonder about that, too.

All to take the heat of the politics.

Penny games.

Donald Trump is proving that this is *all a game* and he's getting under *your skin*!

Really! The hell with politics in America.

Donald Trump is a billionaire.

He's got a fine ass wife.

He is a businessman.

He built businesses here in America and put you dumb asses to work!

He knows the tax code. Jealousy.

I wish I were him. Damn straight!

Did you see his penthouse?

His children fucking respect him. Damn.

Yet, you don't look at his accomplishments as an American citizen.

You only pay attention to what he says.

He knows this.

He's not a billionaire because he's dumb.

No. He's really smart.

He's doing the penny games.

He's seeing how foolish you really are, and he's proving his point. I'm not voting.

I do admire Trump for saying what's on his mind and not playing the political game.

If you really don't know what that is, read Sarah Palin's book.

Her remark about soccer moms...remember that.

That was her line and she got scolded by the Republican party.

They dictated her every move to the $70 stockings she had to wear.

Remember that soccer mom speech, the jacket she wore. That was her jacket.

She did that behind their backs, too, because she felt herself in her own clothes.

She got scolded for that, too.

That was her best speech, then they brought her down.

Do you know what she did for the state of Alaska? You are so freaking dumb!

She's the best person for the job hands down and you fucking hated on her. Idiots!

Yes...there's my judging self.

I'm prepared to pay my dues for that!

Why?

Cause I have the freaking balls that most men don't! Stop making excuses for yourself.

Donald Trump has you in an uproar because people are not actually listening.

They are hearing, but not listening, and you are getting high blood pressure because you don't take the time to actually understand the process, let alone educated enough to cast a vote that counts because you don't even see that the people's vote doesn't count anymore.

Ask around and see how many young people are actually voting, are, actually, registered to vote.

You will be shocked at the number.

I'm not.

They aren't educated about U.S. history.

They don't understand civics because civics is now downgraded to an elective for one or two semesters!

They are dumbed down people, and they are out there screaming B.S. that they know not a damn thing about.

Oh, but they will take on every damn cause out there including not vaccinating their children and killing babies!

That's *all* okay for them!

Seriously, *Houston* has a problem!

Note: Our country is not a damn *cause*.

Grab the damn clowns, wipe off their makeup and put their faces all over the internet.

Stop getting mad over what someone is *saying* and pay attention to their record...their actual actions.

Stop judging people because you are jealous of their status.

Stop playing the race card and become colorless! Yes, do it!

If someone comes at you with a racist attitude, go back at them with grace and God-like love! Straighten up America.

Damn, you are so playing into the hands of the adversary and you don't even see it!

Get a damn brain and plow the hell on!

Be the Trump. Be the Gates.

If you're an Obama fan, hell, be the Obama! Damn, you can do that.

P.S. If it so pisses you off, don't vote and shut the hell up or, better yet, educate your damn self, then go out there and change the damn system!

Be like Trump: *Not a damn politician bleeding the pockets of american people!*

P.S.S: Oh, there are plenty others running the race.

I guess you're not educated enough to know this.

I did post the list! What about them?

Don't they matter.

Who the hell says republicans and democrats matter only? If you don't want it, change it!

Freaking all talk and *no* walk, but you can slam Trump! Oh, he's walking...forgive me!

He walked himself up to billionaire status!

Get a life and stop riding your anger on other's walk!

At least, Trump has the balls to put himself out there knowing your dumb ass will criticize him.

To me, that's the most courageous thing I've seen in years. Go Trump!

You are the man of the hour.

~*God's*† *Agenda*~

she's made that way
don't try to out it—play
she's the mother—every single *other*
she'll hover, she'll protect—cover

she's the nourishing flower

her mind—always in split
don't worry, she knows how to blend it

she's made that way
her womb's journey—paved
she wants it, too, just like you
a career's view, added to the menu
God's† cue—just for you
so don't force the delay
don't downgrade her pay—just to say

I'm better than you

no, no young man–
she, too, that career's cue
–can—and—and—raise a baby, too

don't stand in her way
don't block words, she has to say
she's a miracle in rays
beauty—mind and body
God† made her that way
her—don't try to understand
you, she gave birth to, too

~*Saved Soul*~

it is not up to you, to decide *who am I*
it is not up to you, to ask why

forgiveness—it is written
God† removes poison
it's not your decision
pay attention—learn the lesson
don't breathe words not written

acceptance—it is so written
you cannot move forward
if you're going backward

it's not up to laws—yours
it's up to His†—which opens doors

you can't save souls stuck in old
their argument stands no more

anger grips their heart
tearing lives apart
–look back, look at the chart
God's† already dealt with their darts
–no need to agitate—sort
His† time—not yours to bark

do—do your *I*—without asking why
only in God†, can you truly fly
anger, hate—just brings souls to die

(October 7, 2016)—*The second you limit yourself is
the second you fail.*—Author Unknown

The phone rang early this morning, waking me.

The VA discussing an email with me that I sent yesterday.

I talked loud, forgetting I wasn't alone in the room. My mind still a bit hazy.

The call ended.

I laid there feeling a bit strange.

I had a dream, but it's like the call forced the dream out.

I know this sounds strange, but I felt a bit of awkwardness like it wasn't a very good dream and I laid there in a haze for like a minute and where ever I was seemed to be coming back. The phone rang again.

The VA making an appointment.

Again I was loud.

The blanket ruffled a bit, reminding me I was not alone. I lowered my voice.

The phone call took a bit longer, fully awakening me like I wasn't meant to go back to where I was.

It wasn't meant for me to remember.

I got up, closed the door behind me, as I left the room, made me some coffee, then sat at my desk.

I checked email and went to *Facebook*.

I hid a post I made yesterday.

Something felt awkward again like I was in a daze.

I turned my head and there, lying under some papers was my *Bible*.

I picked it up and *Hosea 2:14-23* came into view.

...therefore I am now going to allure her; I will lead her into the desert and speak tenderly to her. There I will give her back her vineyards, and will make the valley of achor [trouble] a door of hope. There she will sing [respond] as in the days of her youth, as in the day she came up out of Egypt.

...in that day,' says the Lord, 'you will call Me 'my husband'; you will no longer call Me 'my master [baal].' I will remove the names of the baals from her lips; no longer will there names be invoked, in that day I will make a covenant for them with the beasts of the field and the birds of the air and the creatures that move along the ground. Bow and sword and battle I will abolish from the land, so that all may lie down in safety. I will betroth you in [with] righteousness and justice, in [with] love and compassion. I will betroth you in faithfulness, and you will acknowledge the Lord.

...in that day I will respond,' declares the Lord— 'I will respond to the skies, and they will respond to the earth; and the earth will respond to the grain, the new wine and oil, and they will respond to jezreel [God plants] I will plant her for Myself in the land; I will show My love to the one I called 'not my loved one [Lo-Ruhamah].' I will say to those called 'not my people [Lo-Ammi],' 'you are My people'; and they will say, 'You are My God.'—Hosea

2:14-23

I read this several times, fixed me my coffee and set off to write.

"Saved Soul" filled the page.

The word *bigot* kept coming into my mind because it was mentioned to me yesterday in reference to my strong emotions about Moslems.

Bigot: a person who is intolerant of any creed, belief, or race that is not his or her own.

This bothered me.

I looked in my *Bible's* table of contents for the word *bigot* and didn't find it.

I was quickly led to another part of the *Bible*. I think you'll find this very interesting.

...woe to him who builds his palace by unrighteousness, his upper rooms by injustice, making his countrymen work for nothing, not paying them for their labor. He says, 'I will build myself a great palace with spacious upper rooms.' So, he makes large windows in it, panels it with cedar and decorates it in red.

...'does it make you a king to have more and more cedar? did not your father have food and drink? He did what was right and just, so all went well with him. He defended the cause of the poor and needy, and so all went well. Is that not what it means to know Me?' declares the Lord. 'But your eyes and your heart are set only on dishonest gain, on shedding innocent blood and on oppression and extortion.'—Jeremiah 22:10-17

Jeremiah began his ministry around 626 B.C.

This was a time of chaos: Nabopolassar rebelled against Assyria and established the Babylonian Empire, bringing Babylonia to world supremacy.

Jeremiah's prophecy (above) about Jehoahaz (Josiah's son and the new Judahian king) comes to pass.

Interesting.

I flipped back to where I was before in my *Bible* and this is what I get—*...when the Lord began to speak through Hosea, the Lord said to him, 'Go, take to yourself an adulterous wife and children of unfaithfulness, because the land is guilty of the vilest adultery in departing from the Lord.' So he married Gomer daughter of Diblaim, and she conceived and bore him a son.*

...then the Lord said to Hosea, 'call him Jezreel, because I will soon punish the house of Jehu for the massacre at Jezreel, and I will put an end to the kingdom of Israel. In that day, I will break Israel's bow in the valley of Jezreel.'

...Gomer conceived again and gave birth to a daughter. Then the Lord said to Hosea, 'call her lo-Ruhamah (not loved), for I will no longer show love to the house of Israel, that I should at all forgive them. Yet, I will show love to the house of Judah; and I will save them—not by bow, sword or battle, or by horses and horsemen, but by the Lord their God.

...after she had weaned lo-Ruhamah, Gomer had another son. Then the Lord said, 'Call him lo-Ammi [not my people], for you are not My people, and I Am not Your God.—Hosea 1:2-9

...yet, the Israelites will be like the sand on the seashore, which cannot be measured or counted. In the place where it was said to them, 'You are not My people,' they will be called 'sons of the living God.' The people of Judah and the people of Israel will be reunited, and they will appoint one leader and will come up out the land, for great will be the day of Jezreel. 'Say of your brothers, 'My people,' and of your sisters, 'My loved one.'—Hosea 1:10-2:1

Hosea's prophecies took place during Jerobuam's reign between the years 780-775 B.C.

That's 154 years between what God told both these men. Interesting isn't it?

I did a search in the middle of writing this for pictures of *Biblical* Africa and Europe (the parts that are mentioned in the *Bible*).

I've included my findings here.

[I left the maps up on my author page on *Facebook*.]

I posted a very harsh post on my personal page yesterday (I locked it), and, then had a harsh discussion about what I think about Moslems and the world today.

My thoughts on all of this don't come out of thin air.

It comes out of years and years of reading and studying and working on my political blog.

During that period, the feelings that I felt about all that I was learning, all that I was being shown and the reality of my personal world brought my health down, but I did what I was supposed to do.

I wrote in-depth through poetry and commentary everything that I was shown.

All this took place way before all this mess we see today.

A lot of my writings during this period were about what was to come. I find that odd.

When I read the prophecies in the *Bible*, it seems odd there, too. No, I'm not a prophet.

Not even close, but I know what I've written.

I have learned that when we open totally to Christ. He opens up to us.

When we close our world off to His light, He steps back until we are ready to acknowledge Him again. *Free*-will.

I'm not a bigot or a hypocrite.

I write about what I see.

I make my decisions on what I'm going to say out of years of study.

I don't breathe truth into something that is a lie. It is what it is.

If you pay attention to the maps I've

included here, you'll see where all this that we are experiencing comes from.

There's no use in blaming this group of people and that group of people.

All people came from the same people.

If that makes any sense.

In the *Bible*, there's passages that use Israel and Judea interchangeably.

If you study the few maps I've put up here, they once were until a separation came into play. Do you see it?

I've included a map of Africa.

In the far upper right hand corner of that map, you see Egypt.

Notice in the maps labeled *Old Testament Nations* and *The Holy Land Then and Now* and notice Egypt again.

Egypt is part of Africa (then and now).

There is a beltway between the Middle East and Asia.

Notice the continents of Asia, Africa and Europe and how they are connected.

Do you see that?

Now look at the continents of North America, South America, Australia, and Antarctica. Do you see that?

Are you getting the same picture in your head as I am.

There was a reason God came to us in human form (i.e. His son Jesus) to that particular part of the world.

It has always been in strife.

That particular part of the world brought strife to the rest of the world.

I've included pictures of the equator.

Again notice the rose giving N, S, E, W and the separation of Africa itself, then look again at the old maps at the places Jesus came to as well as the places mentioned over and over in the *Bible*.

Can you connect the dots?

Notice how small Israel is today.

Notice how large Africa is.

Notice how large Asia is.

I've included a world map as well, so you can see the size of Russia.

Notice that Russia, which is a country, is on two continents. Do you see that?

Do you see the size of Russia?

Got all that?

Now, look at the size of Europe, which is not really the West, but actually the North East, and the size of North America, which is in the West. Do you see it?

Ask yourself why would the citizens of the *continents* Asia and Africa want to constantly come to North America?

Look at their land mass. It's huge.

When you can figure out the answer to that question, then you can understand the strife going on today.

History always repeats itself.

It's always best not to focus on the little things, but on the wider scale of things.

The Untied Nations doesn't have their main headquarters in these bigger places.

It's in New York City. Did you know that? Think about that.

What does North America actually have that everyone seems to want?

I think both men that I've written about here today says it all.

Greed is the root of evil.

Again look at the world map that I've included here...really look at it.

Which places on this map are *free*?

Pay attention.

Really pay attention before you make your decision.

If you can't see it, then you are sleeping, and I don't mean that as an insult.

Freedom comes at a price.

Where does the land of milk and honey truly lay?

If you can't answer that, then all hope is gone.

I thank God that I was born in the United States of America. Just saying...

~

(October 8, 2016)—Absolutely well said! [Didn't record the quote.]

Bravo [friend]!

Everyone does, indeed, have their opinion.

I, myself, am frustrated to see the judgment all around, myself included a time or two during this race. What are we kids?

Don't we have any common sense?

Saying it like it is brings me down to tears at times because a woman's opinion is less than a man's...but I'm going to say it anyways.

My whole entire character gets attacked when I use the damn word *fuck*! Come on.

I want to remain *free* thank you very much.

I *want* the right to say it like it is.

Tearing each other apart over all of this is not even worth it.

I'm not a hypocrite for talking about God

and using the word *fuck*!

Who came up with that rule?

All this arguing and griping, and, then to stab someone in the back for something they said in private over 10 years ago!

That's just crazy and school yard games.

I wrote about these games in 2012.

Still...they go on. Adults. I have to ask.

Where are all the adults? I'm 47.

I am acting my age.

I'm tired of all this childish behavior.

You are adults. Act like it.

What [friend] here says, hands down is the best I've seen so far. Think. It's not that hard.

Let all that anger in and it will consume you.

Vote out of intelligence, not hogwash you see on here! Thanks [friend].

The following was[friend]'s post

This is a little long, sorry.

My $1.02 contribution...what can I say... inflation...and, again...if you disagree...that's fine. Post your own opinion on your page.

Just know, I still love you.

I still consider you a friend.

—Where there is mankind, there is always opinions....

I said this. Made it up all by myself. ☺

So, someone decided to record something Donald Trump said eleven years ago.

So, let me just start off by talking about the guy who illegally recorded a private conversation—*What a great fucking guy he was*—this guy actually not only plotted and recorded this, but held onto it this long, just waiting for his opportunity to *get his*.

I ask you—*How evil do you have to be to do something like that?*

But, yet...no one, nowhere is talking about him.

Another self-serving social-tard hiding in the shadows just waiting to make his mark?

What did he think this would get him?

Paid, perhaps? Hmmm...I'll leave it there.

So, Mr. Trump is a man.

He participated in a conversation that some would say is inappropriate, vulgar, piggish... yeah, okay. It is.

I'm betting 99% of the men out there, beginning from age [nine] (of course now, that's debatable) till...death (hence the phrase, *dirty old men*) has had some version of that conversation more or less in all course of situations...golf courses, locker rooms, high school lunch rooms, for that matter, middle school lunch rooms, soccer games, football games, bar rooms and clubs, bar-be-ques, crawfish boils, the parking lot at church, and even at grandma's house for Christmas dinner; and it's not just Christian nations, it's all over the world.

All those *macho men* (do we still use that phrase?)

Some even text this crap back and forth to each other, just so they have a record of all their so-called *manly* achievements.

Ah, cell phones...all that technology...the inevitable doom of mankind.

Some, even take pictures or videos of the event itself and pass it on to their friends, believing it adds some sort of additional credit to their *manhood* somehow, and, low and behold, it's even in three of the best-selling books available nationally.

Hell, we see worse than this at the movies, [online], etc...shit, Donald Trump could take a lesson from *Game of Thrones*.

Cersie and Tyrion Lannister could teach him more in fifteen minutes than anyone at the *Playboy* mansion ever could, but, America *loves Game of Thrones*...(Oh, yes, I love me some *GoT*).

Look, Donald Trump is not the first and only person to ever speak that way.

I have friends and family members who could make anybody blush on a Sunday morning over coffee.

No problem, but off course all those hard-core, high moral, *good Christians* morons would have you believe we're the devil's advocates, and then, they'll point the finger at me for writing this, of course...*so, what does that say about you, being around all 'those kinds' of people?* My answer...*real*.

My life is so much more enriched for having known them.

Real life is not what you see on TV.

It's not scripted. It's not words. It's choices.

My choices, and if you're going to judge me over these 651 words, what does that say about you?

I'll wait while you go look in the mirror....

So, does all of this excuse Donald Trump?

No...by no means, but, the entire country is going to hold a man deviant for something that was believed privately said and illegally recorded eleven years ago?

Why aren't they doing that for the seven

years of Obama? Eight years of Bill Clinton?

Even the thirty-five years of Hillary has produced greater sins than this...fifty-fold.

All of these bought and paid for major media outlets are all clawing at any information snippet they can twist and contort to their favor and have you believe Trump is the devil and the Clintons are the saviors...what a shame...sheep.

You don't want to vote for Trump.

Fine, but, have a legitimate intelligent reason not to, but, do not vote for him just because these fools on the media are telling what he said eleven years ago.

Oh and by the way, if Trump would have simply added some beats to it and released it, he could have received an *Emmy* award for it because this is the same thing most artist today call music.

~

(October 9, 2016)—My comments during the 2017 Presidential debate.

—She's for the *Second Amendment*...but...but... WTF!

She just told us she will control our *Second Amendment* rights! Do you not see this!?

—Mr. Trump has his issues, but he is raising questions we all have.

You can't be a hypocrite and not see this!

—She's for killing unborn children!

Is that a Christian? Hell no! That's a psycho. *Thou shall not kill!* Hello. Christ anyone?

—Bill Clinton left a [two]-million dollar surplus! What planet does she live on?

—She has not made this country better. WTH!

—Were those Latino's she registered to vote in Texas legal?

—What about *America*? Don't we matter?

—What the hell does the icicle people have to do with the election of the U. S. Presidency?

—The debate is going on.

Has there been any police shooting or white on black crimes? Just curious....

—The debate is going on.

Where's the clowns right now?

—*It takes a village to raise a child!* What about that?

How much damage this policy has done to the family unit! To children in schools.

OMG...no responsibility taken!

—Hillary just said I and all national guard and first responders around the country have health insurance because of her! WTF?

She did nothing for me! Nothing!

She did nothing for me because I am a woman! Who the hell she thinks she is for saying this?

~

(October 10, 2016)—I am not defending anyone.

I have heard men talk like this so many times. OMG! This is 11 years ago.

He's bantering like normal guys.

I don't see rape. I don't see crime.

If this is a crime, then every guy I have ever worked with should be arrested.

Girls do stuff like this, too.

I have heard married men talk like this!

Banter does not give intent!

What the hell!

You people need to get a life.

I am not voting! Period.

Read my page before you make yourself look stupid.

The man wasn't a presidential candidate 11 years ago!

I am so embarrassed about my country right now.

People are starving and dying and you are debating banter that happened 11 years ago!

—Here's some voice for you: I am a Christian.

You will have to pull the trigger before I renounce my love of Christ.

With that said, here comes God's hard-headed child: There's this thing called *Freedom of Speech.*

Have you heard about it?

Ratified in the 1800s by some good ole boys who thought it would be best for us to be *free.*

All you people bad mouthing Trump for talking dirty...you best repent because you are gonna go to hell with that kind of bigotry!

I am a woman in the south.

I have heard men talk worse than that all my life. I was raised in a Christian home.

It didn't matter!

I went in the service where this was normal behavior as well.

I taught high school English.

In 2003, I taught at a high school.

[Ninth] grade.

Do you know what game the ninth grade boys had going on?

How many blow jobs they can get by the end of the year.

I caught boys with actual list of girls who already performed the act.

Fast forward to 2014 and *Anaconda.*

The music video, and you attack a grown man for saying a lewd comment!

With singers fucking on stage.

Movie producers having their actors actually have real sex in movies when we bogusly celebrate them for *acting*...give me a break! You are hypocrites.

Look in the damn mirror! You yourself!

Are you a saint?

Who gives you a right to judge?

All you people yelling about a past that's over with, don't dare go into that Baptist church and sing your glorious music on Sunday. Don't you dare!

God says to forgive and live in peace.

You are a hypocrite if you are yelling fowl play over something that already happened.

Throw that damn *Bible* in the garbage because it will serve the dump better than it is serving you.

All you white men...especially over 50... get a life!

I am sick of seeing this age of white men treat fellow human being like dogs.

You are nothing but dirty old men and the women wouldn't behave as such if you didn't beat her into submission. Lunacy! All of this!

Everyone should be shame of yourself.

You need to get right with God.

Those trumpets are coming.

The white guy exploiting the young black woman...from the comments I couldn't tell if she was a prostitute, but in any way she didn't deserve that. You are a pig.

[Referring to a video that circulated exploiting a young black woman in a not-so-good way.]

If I knew where you were, I would go get you, tie you to the back of a truck and drive!

Yes, this makes me so mad. Pigs!

What have we become to behave so ungodly?!

~*Trials*~

push through—don't let it destroy you
its simple test, no time to rest
bringing out worse—best
attacking this quest, making it a conquest

it's a strange occurrence–
the surfacing perseverance
seeing yourself in deliverance
singing your own cadence
instead of sinking in forbearance

push through—don't let it destroy you
in its deepest crest, don't dawn its dress
in its wake, remember–
you're only a guest

don't be modest, be its pest
–in all its stress—it's all a game of chest

suck it up, digest—with self, be honest

it's just a test, perseverance in harvest
you're not its apprentice
yourself—express—don't let it oppress
strength—you do possess

it's just a test, a little bit of mess
–beat your breast—God's† love—caress
through the endurance—
your strength, you'll be able to profess

(October 11, 2016)—*Accept what is, let go of what was and have faith in what will be.*—Author Unknown

—*This is the meaning of love, to give until it hurts.*— Mother Theresa

I wrote this several days ago and with all this mess with the politics, I thought I'd post it this evening.

I was led to the *Book of James* before I wrote this, particularly James 1:2-4—*Consider it pure joy, my brothers, whenever you face trials of many kinds because you know that the testing of your faith develops perseverance. Perseverance must finish its work so that you may be mature and complete, not lacking anything.*

Everyone talks about the *Revelations* and, frankly, I'm starting to listen.

Many, many things happening today also seem close to the *Revelations*, maybe, more than ever in history. Why?

I believe because the language barrier has pretty much been broken.

The very first reason God put the barrier on language was because those living at the time didn't get along, so God just made it harder.

A little bit of hard love for His stubborn children.

With the internet today, things have changed. So has the ability to easily deceive.

We want to believe all these stories.

We want to put logic to everything we see and hear, even without researching to see if what we are seeing and hearing is accurate, because it's, well, easy to believe what others say, instead of taking the effort to research, even though just about everyone on the planet has a computer in their hand.

For example: Lincoln is suddenly black. No. He wasn't.

You can't just pull things out of thin air just because someone posted some random picture on the internet.

If you truly studied the period of the time when Lincoln was President, you'd understand why he couldn't possibly be black.

That's just history.

You can't change what has already

happened.

He was considered the *black* president because he started the Civil War.

(I have a complete book written on him. Yes, I did the necessary research.)

We're standing all around the world holding computers in our hands, scrolling, scrolling, *wanting* to get all the drama, and add to it, that we aren't actually paying attention to the things we are letting in our minds.

We aren't even questioning what we are seeing and reading.

Instead, we are pronged to argue to the point of destroying relationships with people we truly care about, to the point of raising our heart rate up and having our palms sweat over things we can do little to improve by just arguing about it!

We are just accepting, and this is not a very good thing.

As a journalist student, seeing this type of thing happen, before the internet made it big, was scary enough.

That was when this thing called newspapers was the primary tool to get information.

During this period, if someone got a fact wrong, what we termed *sensationalism* spread like wildfire, adding just enough juice for the *tabloid* to be a major money-making racket. What is a tabloid?

Ever heard of *The National Enquire...* the articles were based on pure gossip and hearsay...basically, lies!

The internet, today, is basically a combination of *The National Enquire* and solid news, so it is very difficult to decipher through all the B.S. being put out there by people who aren't researching enough to ensure the facts are right.

The days of the journalists being the ones to ensure the public gets accurate information are long gone.

Now, anyone can claim they are a journalist and have the authority to write articles, and this is even scarier.

While we are scaling through all this B.S. on the internet, we aren't paying much attention to what people actually do.

This really came to light for me in 2012.

Everything that I had done as a wife and mother, a daughter and sister...all my 43 years on this planet didn't matter.

What mattered? What I *said*!

I was so angry and hurt over the betrayal that I lifted all the breaks and let everything just fly. I mean every single thought.

I didn't care what I said or who it might hurt. I just *said*.

Four years later, still, not a damn thing about me in my first 43 years matters.

It's what I *said* in the last four years.

Do you see what I'm getting at?

We live in a visual world where communication is massive.

Anyone can put anything out there and bam! we believe it. Trust me. We do.

What have we become?

It seems that if the *Revelations* are here, then more and more people would take heed, but they are not.

It seems like more and more people are pulling away from God, instead of walking to Him.

You hear people like me screaming [for others] to hear Him, yet they just walk away.

Why is that?

Is it because of the ones He's chosen to speak for Him?

Is it that you don't believe that people like me are actually speaking for Him, but we are speaking for ourselves?

Trust me, I want to be doing something else, but I am in awe at what I've been chosen to do. I don't argue with God.

I've been there, done that.

You can't bargain with God.

It doesn't work that way.

I've learned my lesson over and over.

I'm currently in another tough lesson. No.

The lessons don't get worse, but they don't get terribly easier either.

Learning to listen is key.

The second verse that I marked off was James 1:5-8—*If any of you lacks wisdom, he should ask God, who gives generously to all without finding fault, and it will be given to him; but when he asks, he must believe and not doubt, because he who doubts is like a wave of the sea, blown and tossed by the wind. That man should not think he will receive anything from the Lord; he is a double-minded man, unstable in all he does.*

If the first verse didn't strike a cord, then, maybe, this one should.

The tests that we go through are meant to strengthen us.

I like when the first verse says that if we persevere and finish the work God wants us to finish, then we become complete.

That's that peace I talk about.

I know deep in my heart that if I don't finish the work I have to do, then I'll never be at peace.

I also know that when others interfere in my work, they are removed from my life.

Why?

Heaven only knows and it hurts a great deal, but I have come to accept this, too.

In the second verse, we are told to ask, but we can't have doubt.

That means if you want that car you've been eyeing and you pray about it, you have to be totally sure you want that car or else you'll just keep on wishing you had that car.

If you want that relationship and you pray on it, you can't second guess yourself all the time or it will never be right.

It is very hard to have zero doubt.

We like to play the *what if* game...admit it...you do it! Everyone does.

Our faith is as strong as our will.

That devil likes to come in and play with those holes. I tell you this all the time.

You have to get right with yourself.

Sit back. Take the stress out of your life.

Breathe, then really have a heart to heart with the man upstairs.

All this anger going around, and I've been reading so much news-feed that I'm sick to my stomach, and I'm floored by what some are saying. No.

Step back before you speak, please.

You can't place a logical argument with only half or even [a forth] of the facts.

Everyone is upset about so many issues that I'm surprised *one* issue gets anyone's full attention.

If you want to solve problems, then you have to see the problems first.

Not the surface problem, the root of the problem, then you need to see all that affects this particular problem, then decide which to deal with first in order to fix the problem.

With all the problems this country is facing, that's a lot of deciding that's going to have be done. Take the problem with race.

That's an extraordinary problem that is very clear throughout the entire world.

You will never fix or even come close to minimizing this problem with name calling and yelling.

If you want to change something, you have to actually get involved. Run for office.

Join an organization that actually has some kind of impact.

Take your *Facebook* page and make it a problem-solver, instead of a problem-maker.

Don't go searching for threads that you get to argue on. That will not solve the problem.

Just think if everyone took a stand to fix this issue how much could actually get done.

The second verse also says that without being totally with the Lord, you ain't getting a damn thing! Well, you're not.

Do you ever, actually, sit and wonder why you are stuck where you are in your life?

Well? You ask God, but you doubt Him.

You do or you wouldn't be stuck.

In 2014, I was *so* broke.

I have fibro and a deteriorating spine and neck. I took a job at UPS slinging boxes.

The night shift. I hurt so bad.

Every morning when I got home, it was a hot bath and icepack, but I had to do it. Why?

Because it felt like if I didn't prove to God that I could stand on my own two feet, then He wouldn't help me anymore.

He'd already lead me to a vehicle of my own and an apartment.

He brought people to me to help us move.

I was divorced, hurt, lost...barely could I think on my own without going into a rage.

He led me to where I needed to go.

So, I had to show Him my gratefulness, then I needed...get that word...*needed*...to show Him that I was willing to work, too.

I really don't think He would have helped me if I had continued to sit on my ass like I did in 2012 and 2013 just waiting and praying.

After that first job, another came, then another.

I allowed myself to open up to each job sent my way and, believe it or not, at each job there was a message for me.

The year 2014 was my depression stage in the five stages of grief and in order to break this horrible affliction, I had to help myself.

God isn't going to give us all the blessings at one time.

He's testing us to see if we are worthy of the next step in our journey.

We can make it hard or we can make it easier for ourselves. It's a choice.

If you want to keep going round and round, go ahead. I had enough of that shit!

My last job that year was teaching.

It was *so* stressful. A *D* school! I endured.

I pushed through and my reward was my first disability settlement that took me through the year and most of the next.

It wasn't over.

Trust me, there's going to be something else. It's just another test.

I had a long line of them. I pushed on.

In the middle of 2015, I received full disability.

I could finally, completely support myself.

I felt it to be one of the ultimate awards for what He wants me to do. I'm not bragging.

When all of this happened to me, I had no way of knowing where I was going.

I lifted my hands up and let go.

I cried a lot.

I'm not going to sugarcoat anything. Depression fucking hurts.

Moving into that acceptance stage, with still a bit of anger, with the depression, doesn't help either. *Perseverance.*

That's one of the most powerful words ever! I'm still here.

I have a lot less material things than when I first left my home behind.

I've moved [seven] times since dropping off a little here and a little there because it became easier to let go of the material world.

I could move [seven] more times.

I'm not kidding.

I don't want to be stuck ever again where I feel unwelcomed or unwanted. I'd rather ride.

I still have trials. They are hard.

I'm not giving into the devil's little games.

I've gained a lot of strength from all of these trials. I still cry.

I'm a *girly* girl inside, but I can also be tough.

God set a path for me because I gave everything to Him.

He's awarded me, even when I had doubt.

For example when I got my car, I asked Him to just give me a little sign that I was on the right path.

I said to myself—*if I get this car, that's my sign*— (because it was next to impossible for me to buy this car). He made it happen.

This is where *"Trials"* comes from.

You keep pushing, then you preserve over all your hurdles. Some people won't like you.

That's okay. In the end, it's you and God.

Unless you're so bold that you are going to take that chance that God doesn't exist.

Your gamble.

Deep in my heart, I have felt His power.

I can easily bet you right now: He does exist! Love who you are. Stay in the light.

If you are fighting, don't give up.

There is a light coming.

You may just have to go through a little darkness first. Hold on. You will make it.

You are wonderful, beautiful and worth everything. Love the skin you're in first.

—Watched *13TH* [online video site]

Thirteenth!

Thank you to the producers of this great movie.

You want to know what *free my people* means. Watch this film.

Thumbs up again and again.

Maybe, this will help you to decide that we are [one] nation under God and, finally, move away from the hypocrisy of saying you believe in God, yet you are selective on which part of His word to follow.

I watched this movie with [*sweet man*].

Early in the week he called me a bigot concerning some of my beliefs about moslems. I argued. Stomped out the room.

He was right. I am and vow to change.

I vow to change because through his beautiful heart, he showed me that my truth is only truth if it's totally seen through eyes that see Christ in everything not just part of everything. A human being is a human being.

It's time to actually mean what we say when we say we are Christians!

Unshackle those fucking chains.

Rewrite the *Thirteenth Amendment* to the *U.S Constitution*! Demand it!

All this B.S. happening in D.C...no.

We can't let this continue.

We as a country can't stand on God's ground without totally being on God's ground. Amen.

—I think if some would actually think before commenting or even speaking, then there wouldn't be so much ignorance.

[Former *Facebook* friend] didn't appreciate me putting all white men in the same category.

Well...what about everyone putting all black people in the bad category?

Oh, did I misread you [former *Facebook* friend].

I guess you don't really understand the

irony in what you wrote.

I guess you are perfect and have never ever said a curse word or engaged in the taunting of a woman!

I remember your way before you allowed God in. Seems you forgot about that.

I guess you escaped the certain of common that has been a part of men since the dawn of time.

Don't come at me with that kind of hypocritical kind of thought.

I already know how you feel about me saying *fuck,* yet you are still here.

The truth of our selves always brings on anger when it's put in our face.

Finding God doesn't mean you are God.

It means you understand right from wrong and vow to live right without the judgment of others.

You should read my work today, and to the second commenter, I do appreciate your recognition of the *First Amendment,* but, maybe, you should read what I wrote several more times.

I don't think you actually understood what you read. I will tell it like it is.

I won't sugarcoat or make up shit to make you feel better, and you can't take your sins out on me.

I am not the one you have to answer to!

P.S. I wasn't far off about the big robbery in Paris. Now was I?
Clowns are a symbol of ignorant.
Or haven't you caught onto that yet?

~*Rituals of None*~

a childhood mixed in loot
a constant voice and view
hate bred—now in review

always feeling a different cue

*your traditions—mixed values
are not mine, too*

how did I separate myself from the coop
how did I see a different ritual
than those in the vestibule

in school, mix all colors
through and through
at home, messages construed

no color'ds can visit you

the constant blame, the constant ensue

you're a white girl

*no black boys will bother you
they'd better keep
their filthy hands and eyes off of you*

in bred macho attitude
I didn't ask for the fortitude

a kind smile, pleasant remark
compliments—through and through

a white boy demanding on cue–

what you looking at, who you talking to

butting in—for what revenue
I never had a clue

I just knew
talking or friending a black boy
he would turn into a toy
or some kind of amusement to enjoy

stay away, stay away

one look and I knew–
reasons—away to stay
expectations on cue, no words to say
just in the shadows—fade

so many thoughts, so much confused
a young white girl
caught in a southern balloon
leaving no room for her self in true

away, away, away—I just flew
living in mixes of colors
feeling selfish and lost
–all those mixed views
what's my own, what's my view

separate—far away—learning truth
I'm white, I'm black
who cares—we're all soldiers too

then back there, I again flew
but with a different view
still, half mind, trapped in tradition's cue

struggling—this different view

why haven't you changed too

acting all nice, with kindness too
then behind closed doors
the old ritual review–
you can be kind, but inside, there's a line
unspoken signs
those looks, innuendos—not hard to find

voicing opinions
leads one in cooked roux

an expectation to agree in lieu
caught up in this loo
brings a mind in constant review

what's false, what's true
so easy to bring up, crimes black boys do
everything else—out windows—flew

so much heat—confused, opened up fuse
so many ways–
feeling used, totally abused

tradition's valued little loot
turned away from rituals–
not my own view
knowing—yet not having
a sincere point—to place my finger–
letting God† lead my avenue

I'm not revenue, but a person too
–rose-colored glasses were due

minus tradition's ritualistic menu
leading me into a barless cube

oh well! love for me—God's† direct root
–a strength inside, I can openly toot

for your view was not mine's too

(October 12, 2016)—*Sometimes, people try to expose what's wrong with you because they can't handle what's right about you.*—Author Unknown

Question everything.

People will hate on you because it's easier than accepting their own shortcomings.

It's not about you. Question everything.

You don't have to accept anything, and you don't have to agree with everything.

You are entitled to your own opinion.

To remain *free*, you have to be able to stand up for what you believe in.

To lose *freedom*, you easily blend with a society you don't agree with.

Comments
•(Friend) That's what I'm talking about...speaking truth.
•(Friend) Amen, Karen.

—To admit your truth is to admit your lesson.

Some come at me with their new truth without acknowledging their change and or lesson.

I have seen this so many times in my own life that it has become normal.

The flip-flop society. So be it.

I prefer not to take part in others illusions.

I have enough on my hands figuring out my own journey.

Learning from my own tests (i.e. lessons).

I don't open myself up for public judgment when those can't look at themselves first.

I will leave it at that.

—Posted an article titled *'Hidden Cam: Democrat Admits Election Is Rigged, Millions Are Shocked!'*—by *usapoliticstoday.com*

You decide if you matter.

The Rochells (however you spell that) and the Rockefellers...who gives a damn about them.

They don't matter.

We the American people do.

The Trump thing is a set up!

All to get Hillary in there.

Vote for Johnson.

We can test this system out this election!

—I placed options here on my page.

Don't sit there and label people when you clearly don't understand the role of an American President.

For those who do know, you have many options.

An American citizen has the option of choice.

No one should dictate to you that you *have* to be a party.

That's the republican/democrat control created many, many years ago to control American thought and dictate the vote.

Why do you think there's the GOP and no one else is allowed in?

These are machines controlled by big corporations and politicians who take *your* money and build nice fancy houses and send their kids to private schools, and go on expensive vacations, and buy the best of everything.

Where do you think that money comes from? You. *You. All them taxes you pay*!

Do you get it?

The system was never designed for that.

You make the choice to keep following the crowd or finally take a damn stand.

You don't like racism, damn! do something about it, instead of constantly yelling and spreading drama.

Take the power away from the republican/democrat machines. Just do it! Yes, you can!

—Posted an article titled *'2016 Presidential Candidates (Presidency 2016)'*—*politics1.com*

You have a choice.

No one...absolutely no says you have to vote republican or democratic.

That's B.S. if you believe that.

Get out of your traditional ways that are not accurate and think for yourself.

You are *not* throwing your vote away.

You are voting for whom you deem fit to be the leader of the *free* world.

You want a change, then stop barking and take action.

Clearly no one likes Trump or Clinton.

Make a difference and stand for what you actually believe in, instead of following the crowd.

—You really don't always have to be super nice. Sometimes, you have to show your bad side, so that you can sort out who can accept you at your worst.—Author Unknown

Our bad sides always come out during election times. Remember that.

Don't allow the anxiety of differences when it comes to this election destroy what you built in your personal lives.

It's not that serious and God always works it out. We do learn ourselves, don't we?

Hold tight. It's almost over.

True friends always accept you no matter how you see issues.

Comments
•(Friend) I agree with you cousin.
We are all entitled to our own opinions.
This is America where *Freedom of Speech* is part of our way of life.
My opinions are strictly my own.
Right for me, but not for others.
I respect all of my family and friends who agree or disagree with me. Love them, no matter what!

~

(October 13, 2016)—Posted an article titled *'The Clinton Body-Count—What Really Happened'—whatreallyhappened.com*

I posted this last year. It's been updated. You decide.

~

(October 14, 2016)—*Whoever selling this [weed] just got trapper of the year.*—Author Unknown

I constantly hear people asking—*Anyone got fish for sale or shrimp?*

I am waiting for—*Oh hell!*

I will ask it—*Has anyone got weed for sale?*

~

(October 21, 2016)—I don't condone either republican or democrat.

I am a registered voter and if I do vote I will vote independent. I am a woman.

I am bitterly ashamed of Clinton.

I was ashamed of Mr. Clinton whom I served under.

God help us all if this sad excuse of a woman becomes the first female President.

It will be a total embarrassment, not only to women, but to this country and all that it stands for.

It will also be a disgracement to every soldier to have her as commander and chief.

~

(October 22, 2016)—Posted an article titled *'Report: Eating Raw Weed Prevents Bowel Cancer, Fibromyalgia and Neuro-degenerative Diseases'—organicandhealthy.org*

The U.S. federal government is ate up!

If this plant can help me, then why is the feds keeping it from me with the surety of jail if I get it to help myself?

Answer: Greed!

Big corporations who don't give a rat's ass about people!

The U.S. federal government should be ashamed of themselves.

They are keeping us sick for money! Really?

I am so ashamed of my government right now.

If anyone can get me in touch with anyone who grows this plant, I would be most grateful.

I am sick of being in pain, and to think there is a natural way to make my life more bearable and my own government is preventing me from getting it all because of money, you can bet your ass God *will* deal accordingly!

~*Broken Hands*~

empty in mind halts time
rages in unkind
when there's no even line

how to properly dine
over red, delicious wine
–lacking of dimes
seizes time, drawing unwanted lines

over and over, same's unintended chime
ringing its unwelcomed rhyme
leaving zero time to relax—unwind

oh! crocked, crocked lines
remove eyes in blind
open vastly—lights in shine

take hands from bind
stretch them straight—in divine
opening all window blinds
to happier, peaceful times

let it be joyfully kind
fill glorious minds with cheerful chimes

welcomed in rhyme
with plenty time in pleasures–
meals to dine
mixed in the finest of wines
minus worries—lackings in dimes

(October 23, 2016)—*Turn your wounds into wisdom.*—Oprah Winfrey

Have faith. When you step outside your comfort zone for your higher purpose, the universe supports you in every way.—Author Unknown

On Judgment Day…God will not ask you about me! Thankfully, He's well informed and needs no assistance from you.—Author Unknown

I am willing to work for 'everything' I prayed for.—Author Unknown

I have been at a blank lately, then yesterday morning, I went into my spare bedroom to get my exercise mats and I received a wake-up call.

It's wonder how things happen unexpectedly to get your attention.

My exercise mats were against the wall behind some rolled up rugs.

I have a bed frame that I do not need, so it's in pieces and the headboard is propped up against the wardrobe sideways.

Some how I stepped on the bottom portion of the headboard and the top came slamming down on my forehead. Ouch!

It hurt like hell, but I take Adrenal in the morning, which mask the pain of fibro and I also take a natural supplement for pain, so I didn't bother with the pain for long.

Later last night, oh my, did the pain resurface.

I don't handle this kind of intense pain well and I tend to take it out on whoever is around.

Trust me, I've been working on this weakness of mine, but when you are in the depths of intense pain, you can't really focus on the control you'd *like* to have.

I directed all my anxiety on [sweet man].

He was the only one in the room.

He fired back of course, which made me cry. Give me a break. Pain is pain.

You don't want to cry because of it.

You don't want to let others know about it.

After so many years suffering from fibro and the lack of understanding, I've learned it's best just to hide all of it as best as I can.

So, over the years, I adapted this fierce personality to mask the intensity I'm feeling, so, I don't appear weak.

I can't tell you how many times it's backfired because the person on the other end of this fierceness takes it totally personal when it wasn't meant to be.

What gets to me isn't their anger towards what I do or say, but their lack of understanding towards the knives and hacksaws piercing my body.

If you can understand that, then may God be with you every day for your heroic efforts in masking your own pain.

After several intense hours of agonizing pain, which kept me from laying my head down, the pain finally subsided.

I had to take three nerve anti-flammatories, which I only take when I absolutely need it, and two more supplements. He gave up.

I slept in another bed.

It took a while for me to fall asleep and during that time, I prayed.

Why am I telling you this?

Because, sometimes, during our most dreadful hours is the perfect time to connect with God.

I began my prayer session with the *why* questions, then I just said, the last thing I remember—*God, just show me.*

I woke up in a daze.

He was at the door worried about me.

I was still upset that he didn't fully understand, but was I upset at him or me?

It's hard to live in a world where there's this pain your body feels, but no one else fully understands it.

You have this disorder, this dis-ease that is invisible.

I can't tell you how many times in my life that I've been accused of *faking* it to get out of something.

It has happened so many times that I began to think I was imagining it. I'm not.

For me, when I hit my head in any way, because of the disc issues in my neck, my entire body is affected.

I don't think I need to go into detail about the way I felt this morning.

It does make me question the *why* of this kind of cross.

Dealing with an invisible illness makes us all question so much in life.

It's not fair—is the ultimate!

I met his gentleness and worry with my aggravation.

He went to his end of the house.

I stayed on my end. I laid down. I got up. I drank coffee.

I peddled around, then I was compelled to write. I had no idea what to write about.

It's been this way for more than a week with me only producing one or two works.

"Broken Hands" poured out of me.

I wasn't quite sure what it meant until about half way into the work, then I saw it.

I typed it up, then opened the *Bible*.

Ezekiel. I turned the page. More Ezekiel.

I began to read. Wow! I thought.

At the end of this commentary, I included the entirety of the passages I read.

We all tend to look at our lives in blind truth.

We get lost in the rat-race and forget about ourselves in the process.

I've always looked at the pain that I suffer from as a reminder that I am alive.

When it gets really intense, I cry, blame, hate, get angry, but, in the aftermath, I see that I am still a part of this world and that God has a purpose for me.

When we suffer from a disorder or disease, it is the same type of misery that someone feels when they are suffering through the five stages of grief...all the elements are the same: Hate, anger, depression, bargaining, denial, accepting.

So, some of us just have this part of life as a continuous journey and we just have to find a way to deal. It's hard to deal at times.

I've read in so many places (articles, forums, *Facebook* groups) about people's experiences when they are dealing with an invisible animal like fibro.

Of all that I've read, about 10% have their family supporting them.

The rest are left to deal by themselves.

They are labeled with titles such as *unstable, crazy, delusional*. They are not.

I understand this.

There are about 30% who have their illness used against them. I understand this, too.

All of those who suffer from an invisible illness seem to be used as Ginny pigs giving this medication and that medication.

They are all searching for a *natural* way to make their lives easier to manage.

I'm one of them.

I posted last night an article about the usage of marijuana and how it can minimize the pain and even cure certain illnesses.

I was sick to my stomach when I read that.

They legalized medical marijuana here in Louisiana.

I spent over an hour talking about this with my therapist.

She told me not to hold my breath.

It will take between [two] to [five] years for the universities who have the right to make this marijuana medicine to get it right.

What the hell?!

The federal government of the United States (my country) holds the patent on marijuana and it's ability to help people like me.

They have been holding this patent since the 1970s!

They have known about this plant's ability all this time. They patented it to control us!

That's my take on it.

While millions of Americans are suffering from diseases and illnesses that keep them in pain, their own government holds the key to helping them and has made it illegal to obtain this *miracle* plant!

It saddens me when I think of the stigma that we have all grown up with when it comes to marijuana.

We were brain-washed to believe it is *bad* and that anyone who uses it is *bad*!

Millions of people are sitting in prison because of this plant.

They are rotting away because of a natural plant God gave to us to help us! Control!

I have read so many papers on marijuana in the past several years that I'm now a full-blown supporter of anyone who uses this plant. I have tried it.

I have felt the benefits of it.

The U.S. government reveals its true self when it comes to this plant.

In order to promote their greed (the benefits of pharma *big-business* corporations), they are so willing to sacrifice its own people.

The hypocrisy of all this is astounding to me.

How many people in our government have used the services of a prostitute?

This is off my subject, but bear with me.

I did a impromptu speech in college about legalizing prostitution.

I have a very good argument.

I lived in Germany for three years.

It is legalized there.

There are less, if any, sexual crimes.

Those in the prostitution business, after all it's their bodies, their choice (seems to go hand in hand with abortion, don't you think?), so they get to decided on price.

Their government ensures the safety of the public (from disease) by requiring them to carry a medical card that proves they are *free* of disease because their chosen line of work is legal, they don't have pimps beating the shit out of them or stringing them out on the actual bad drugs like heroin and cocaine.

They are taxed. Legal! Everyone benefits.

[The *moral* implicitly of prostitution is a personal choice.

Again, hand in hand with abortion.]

Here in America, prostitution is illegal and the person paying for services and the person offering the services get arrested, and...at the same time, you have D.C.

U.S. government people who have employed these laws and push the enforcement thereof soliciting prostitutes!

It's all about greed!

How many in the U.S. government have used and/or using marijuana or wish they could?

The same goes here concerning the illegalization of prostitution. Hypocrisy.

Three Presidents of the U.S.A. have said they used marijuana: Bush, Clinton, Obama.

Go figure! It's all about greed.

The *Seven Deadly Sins*: Wrath, greed, sloth, pride, lust, envy, and gluttony.

In my opinion, The U.S. government has taken on the precedent that they are God!

In the state of Louisiana alone, government this year passed over 500 laws that the people did not vote on.

They assume that they are responsible for our health, welfare, and livelihood.

They have taken it upon themselves to regulate what's right and what's wrong, yet they are removing *God* from everything.

Hypocrisy. Playing God!

Yes, in our most deepest of agonies, God reveals (if we are listening) the importance of our lives. I've been slacking.

I'm too busy worrying about the little things, instead of what I'm really supposed to do.

I look at that bed post smacking me in the head as a wakeup call.

I've been waiting to be *comfortable* in my surroundings, so I can continue my work when God is saying—*What the hell for?*

Point taken.

In the following passage, God is speaking to Judah.

He is attacking their unfaithfulness (i.e. the portrayal of the adulterous wife).

I included my notes that I wrote in the margins back in 2007.

When I was reading this passage for the first time, I clearly saw the United States as Judah. It strikes me how right I was.

The United States government has lost its way.

It concentrates on too many little things, instead of the most important.

It's a total waste of energy and money to have simple things like prostitution and marijuana illegal.

If the government can step in and say in *Roe vs Wade* that a woman has a right to choose what happens to her body when it comes to a human being (i.e. baby), then why can't she have that same choice when it comes to the whole of her body?

That goes for marijuana as well: A natural plant that can actually help people in so many ways.

If a woman has the right to *kill* another human being, then all should have the right to choose if we want to use our bodies to profit from and if we want to use a natural plant, instead of lab-made drugs to help our bodies.

The United States government is a hypocrite in so many ways.

God doesn't miss much.

You can count on that.

The *Seven Deadly Sins*: The U.S. government and everyone involved in it...that means every single person that collects a federal and state government paycheck is guilty of all seven of these sins. That's not judgment. That's just fact.

In the end, we all have to answer to God.

For me, I'm glad the rose-colored glasses have been lifted.

Woe! Woe to you, declares the Sovereign Lord. In addition to all your other wickedness, you built a mound for yourself and made a lofty shrine in every public square. At the head of every street you built your lofty shrines and degraded your beauty, offering your body with increasing promiscuity to anyone who passed by. You engaged in prostitution with the Egyptians, your lustful neighbors, and provoked Me to anger with your increasing promiscuity...then you increased your promiscuity to include Babylonia, a land of merchants, but even with this you were not satisfied....

[I wrote in the margin in red back in 2007—*This would be like having a government without God's laws. They all worshiping the state or country and not God!*]

...How weak-willed you are, declares the Sovereign Lord, when you do all these things, acting like a brazen prostitute! When you built your mounds at the head of

every street and made your lofty shrines in every public square, you were unlike a prostitute, because you scorned payment. You adulterous wife! You prefer strangers to your own husband! Every prostitute receives a fee, but you give gifts to all your lovers, bribing them to come to you and from everywhere for your illicit favors. So in your prostitution you are the opposite of others; no one runs after you for your favors. You are the very opposite, for you give payment and none is given to you....

[I wrote in the margin in red back in 2007—*This sounds almost like the U.S. always giving money to other nations, but getting nothing in return.*]

...Therefore, you prostitute, hear the word of the Lord! This is what the Sovereign Lord says: Because you poured out your wealth and exposed your detestable idols, and because you gave them your children's blood, therefore I am going to gather all your lovers, with whom you found pleasure, those you loved as well as those you hated. I will gather them against you from all around and will strip you in front of them, and they will see all your nakedness....— Ezekiel 16:23-43

[I wrote in the margin in red back in 2007— *History will repeat itself!*]

~

(October 25, 2016)—Posted several articles about votes being changed by the machine.

I did post the test that was done that proved the machines are rigged/flawed... whatever. Something's just not right.

~

(October 28, 2016)—*It might take a year, it might take a day, but what's meant to be will always find its way.*—Author Unknown

Back to my working self.

Thought I'd take a moment and release some love.

If you are one of my marketing friends, this is some of the best advice ever.

Don't quit.

There are a lot of programs out there and a lot of ways to get into your zone.

It's not an over-night thing, but it *is* a thing.

Watch all the videos you can.

Ask tons of questions. You can do this.

We are. You live and learn.

Trust me, you will make some mistakes.

Hey, that's the spices of life.

Think about this: If we did what we wanted to do and never made mistakes and just made it to the top, they'd be no excitement.

Mistakes are a part of living.

That's when you make the most memories.

Didn't you know that?

Keep plowing ahead.

Not every program is for everyone.

You have to find the right program that fits you. You got this.

If it helps, throw something across the room, break a few dishes, just don't take it out on your partner.

After you throw whatever, look at your partner and just laugh.

That's one less frustration.

Now, continue on my friends.

Remember: 1,000 light-bulb mistakes before the right move counted.

Comments
▪(Friend) Amen.

~*Outré*~

they yell for independence day
they yell black—white's race
—forgotten along the way
her decisive play—left behind–
save for mother's day

she's better off—they say
the fiancée, a lady in wait
cooking—making *frappés*
as he enjoys, a *served* thanksgiving day

she seems passé—a mere cliché
–dawn her in a negligé
yell *laissez le bon temps rouler*
twirl her around then enjoy a *café au lait*
as the boys quietly sauté
last night's entrée

never mind her résumé
she's forgotten on labor day
–left to the risqué
to dine with in a café, over some rosé

she seems a chance in *bullraé*
a forgotten matinee
entangled in dismay

here, go buy some lingerie
touché, touché—I hold the attaché
don't worry your pretty little head
this isn't your forté

setting her aside, in a bit of wordplay

to him, she's an awaiting pompeii
to be cased away, at a moment's delay
a bellyache to be cured, until another day

back to front, front to back
goes the sway
–even sideways—over and over
goes the ricochet
from his missed portray
to a woman-to-woman forestay

her skills, see the light of day

–succumbing to april fool's day
a little clever cashé, to the boys—obey
hand-to-hip protégé

then the quiet in-house communiqué
another *she*—she can purvey
as long as she doesn't out-weigh

it's an uneven betray–
an on and on gainsay

she's bound to the exposé
–the little nurturing pâté
only a *few* can parlay
the rest—behind—must stay

(October 29, 2016 (Not published on *Facebook*))—
Owning one's success is key to achieving more success.
Professional advancement depends upon people believing
that an employee is contributing to good results. Men can
comfortably claim credit for what they do as long as they
don't veer into arrogance. For women, taking credit comes
at a real social and professional cost. In fact, a woman
who explains why she is qualified or mentions previous
successes in a job interview can lower her chances of
getting hired.

As if this double bind were not enough to navigate,
gendered stereotypes can also lead to women having to
do additional work without additional reward. When a
man helps a colleague, the recipient feels indebted to him
and is highly likely to return the favor. But when a woman
helps out, the feeling of indebtedness is weaker....

...There is little downside when men negotiate for
themselves. People expect men to advocate on their own
behalf, point out their contributions, and be recognized
and rewarded for them. For men, there is truly no harm
in asking. But since women are expected to be concerned
with others, when they advocate for themselves or
point to their own value, both men and women react
unfavorably....—from *Lean In* by Sheryl Sandberg

—I get *The Daily Advertiser* a local
Lafayette, Louisiana newspaper.

Inside of this newspaper is a section titled
'USA Today'...the pictures of the articles,
which I've included are the three *headlines*
on this page in the order in which you see
them! WTH? What kind of world are we in?

The first article states *'FBI Review'*...
referring to a U.S.A. Presidential candidate.

Are you serious?

No candidate running for the office of the
United States President should have an article
on the front page of any newspaper about
them with *FBI* and *review* in the *headline*,
then the second most important thing
according to *USA Today* is people who can't
accept who they are! Really!?

The U.S. Supreme Court (the *highest* court
in our nation) is wasting tax-payer dollars on
deciding whether or not people who don't

like who they are can use any bathroom they
want?! WTF?

I think the U.S. Supreme Court needs to be
under review for even considering this grade-
school B.S.

I really do believe that there are *more*
important issues to be considered like
legalizing marijuana because it can help
people more than those greedy corporations
can, or how about all those people rotting
in prison because the government decided
to patent marijuana, so they can control
people and support greedy corporations and
these people are victims of that injustice, or
all those incident people rotting in prison
because shady lawyers can't do their job
because they haven't a clue that color does
not determine a person's innocence, but
instead actual facts; then *flying freaking cars*!

The third most important thing going on is
UBER! OMG.

Who the hell can afford fancy cars these
days much less fancy flying ones?

I guess they are telling us to buy those
greedy corporations' vehicles, and, then turn
around and become a taxi cab in order to pay
for them.

No big deal, as long as, the greedy
corporations get their money.

A corrupted politician who has made
her living off taxes paid by the people and
disgracing everything that successful, honest
women are trying to build, the Supreme
Court using tax money to decide if people
with dicks can use a girl's bathroom because
they don't like their dicks and people who
wish they had dicks can use a boy's bathroom
because, well, they wish they had dicks; and,
flying cars so greedy corporations can get
more of the people's money are the...*the* most
important issues today?

I guess dumbing down America is paying
off. Congratulations!

—Women matter!
Question for any law enforcement officers
working or retired: How are these videos from
police cams getting into the hands of the public?

Reason for question: The Criminal Justice
Department has rules set in place to protect the
innocent.

Every time there's a shooting from an officer's
gun, there's a case.

So, everything that happens from the moment
that police officer answers the call to when the
police officer turns in his/her report becomes

evidence in that case.

So, wouldn't it be a destruction of justice when evidence becomes open to the public before the case goes to trial?

Would this be considered tapering with evidence, which could lead to change of venue because a person can't get a fair trial?

Or the whole trial becoming a mistrial because of this?

Further: All these *police* shootings, why aren't we seeing the trials on here (*Facebook*)?

If we see the shootings, shouldn't we also see the trials.

So, if we are *all* acting as judge and jury, shouldn't we get the *entire* case put before us?

Everyone is making all these assumptions and *uneducated* guesses and that's find for discussion if you intend on writing a *fiction* account of it, but if we are only getting *part* of the story, how can anyone in their right mind make a solid, fair decision or judgment?

I mean do you *know* how easy the eyes can deceive you. There are tons of studies done.

Anyone hear of the test a law professor performed with an auditorium of students?

He had a man run through the room wearing a red shirt.

The professor, then asked students what they saw.

You would be surprised at the answers.

Many couldn't even tell what color shirt he had on!

Further: If I'm constantly told to put my 20-year marriage and deception behind me and move on, then why is all this racism still being put before my face?

That's a bit of hypocrisy...*no*...that's *all* the way hypocrisy.

Further: If you are going to praise the Lord, then why are you so easy to raise hate and not see clearly what the adversary is doing?

You go to church, dress all up in your dresses, hats, and suits, sing rocking praises to the Lord, yet you are constantly spreading hate.

How can you say you love the Lord and continue to raise these race issues?

If equality is what you want, then why have separate this, separate that (i.e. *Ebony Magazine, Jet Magazine*, etc., etc.)? This is so confusing to me.

Should every race single themselves out to make their point?

Further: If you are so hell bent on making injustices against blacks an issue (i.e. black lives matter), then how come you don't make a bigger issue out of *domestic violence*?

Do you want to know the answer because I have it for you?

Answer: Because every man on earth has, at some point in their life, been a part of *domestic violence*. They either did it.

They either witnessed it.

They either covered it up.

They either knew of someone who did it and did

nothing! That's just fact.

(The same goes with women!)

Oh, my God, black lives matter.

How many of those screaming out that beat or just hit or just degraded a woman?

How many of those screaming that B.S. raped or sexually abused or insulted a woman?

How many of those screaming that B.S. didn't pay for child support because they were too lazy to work or abandoned their families because of another woman or drugs or both?

How many of those screaming that B.S. use their children for money or sympathy while downgrading or lying about their mother?

Black lives matter no less than a woman's, but women aren't considered important enough to have signs drawn up to protect them. How about: *Women Matter!*
Or No More Domestic Abuse!
Or Mothers Are The Most Important! etc., etc.

I'm sick of all this black lives matter B.S.

Do you know how the Islam (the adversary's prized instrument) treat their women?

Women are beat, raped, and have to cover their bodies including their faces at all times!

If she accuses someone of *domestic abuse* and no one admits to it, she can be beheaded!

You are fighting the *wrong* enemy and you are being *played* by the adversary and you don't even see it. *Women matter*!

End of story!

~

(October 30, 2016)—I don't want my sons to have to fight a war on their own homeland.

You people in D.C. need to open your mouths about what the hell is going on over there.

The President should know better and should have fired Hillary himself.

I hold him responsible if my children have to fight here. He will be the blame!

He is the reason we have these two sorry personalities in the front running position.

He is our commander and chief and he is not protecting this country from strife.

Hillary will be on his head. Now.

I have said what so many are thinking.

This isn't about color B.S.

This is about *my homeland*!

—Posted an article titled *'Flashback: Bill Clinton Cheered 11th Hour Indictment that*

Doomed Bush Re-Election'—washingtonexaminer.com

Another must read.

Appears the Clinton's are known to throw exaggerated content to the public to win an election. Runs in the family

—Posted an article titled *'Democrats Should Ask Clinton to Step Aside'—chicagotribune.com*

I think you can say the *Chicago Tribune* is a pretty reputable news source.

This is about a presidential candidate under investigation for selling governmental influence and leaking national security information.

This is like Richard Nixon all over again.

The people can't be serious about even considering this candidate just because she is a woman.

She denied all those women her husband messed with. She didn't stand up for them.

She isn't standing up for those acclamations concerning her husband's so-called son by a woman Clinton denied as if she didn't exist.

She is an embarrassment to all women.

I believe one day a woman will be president, but this is not the woman.

~*Free-For-All*~

so it goes, so it goes

history playing its role
a hitler-beat-the-world bowl–
lack of communication
leads to easy dictation

open—straight-up indication
à heading-backwards verification
à lacking common-sense clarification
–internet's world-wide unification
its playful satisfaction
its mind-boggling integration
false/truth manipulation–
keeping *thought processing*
bound for declination

deny, deny, deny

oh! how easy to control–
keep that guessing-game in roll
history proves—it's just so

a little lesson manifesto–
in case you didn't know
which way that wind really blows:

easy's *label—inevitable*
coined *free-for-all*–
power's rolling of the ball
a chess game of stall
waiting for *that* moment's call
leading to nothing at all

horizontal, vertical mergers
–a bet in wager
(the absolute of comical)
–by the people
seen as economical, avoid of principle–
more disguised as *wireless*
adds up to just less
without understanding
history's purposeful quest

a past blanketed in kind
open communication—easy to find
after masses led willingly
to gas-infested showered vines
–cutting off family lines
oh! so welcomed–
land of lines—strung along power lines
incorporating party lines
–wealth building in streams of fines

adding to money's sucking-up grime
a little wiggle–
more things *entertainable*
keeping things unstable
through prices in cable
–never mind—pockets of the people
putting corporate bank accounts
in greens of favorable

oh the whine, oh the whine

signs of times or basics in redefine
a *penny-game* intertwine
keeping eyes in blind

*we can control—just move slow
it'll hit them before they even know*

pay attention how this ball rolls–
building wealth in acquisitions
stealing earnings and health
downgrading knowledge
through dictated education–
holding back—truth's verification

oh my! oh my!

perfect little web of lies
manipulation—through fine little lines
a world to *unify*—way up high

satellites beyond the sky

brilliance in terms
their mission confirmed
world-order interim—
network—inserted little germ
ringing in the ears
spreading world-wide ignorance–
forgotten past years—hitler—so sincere
master controller of fear
knew damn well how to sell
propaganda—the prized ale
throwing millions in dug cells
years and years, without one single yell

*cut communications dear
their lives—you can shear*

cable soon to disappear
wireless—the weaponed spear
–so easy the people to adhere

ring, ring, ring

those satellites go ding
zero bars's sting—a *surety* thing
that phone won't ring
without a land line to sing

boom! boom! boom!

which way the ball to roll
free-for-all
(blindside's little attracting glow)
to just nothing at all
lost in world-order control
perfecting hitler's play-book bling
power's money-hording elites–
the ball to roll for total control

it's just a repeating-history thing
don't worry, you gave them the power
that bell, your permission given to ring

(October 31, 2016)—Support oppression.
Do nothing.

We must reject the idea that every time a law's broken, society is guilty rather than the lawbreaker. It is time to restore the American precept that each individual is accountable for his actions.—Ronald Reagan

I've been led to *The Book of Job* again and if you are a regular reader of me, you know that *The Book of Job* was instrumental in giving me the ability to leave my home after I divorced in 2013.

I have been told many times that each time your read the same passage from the *Bible* at different times in your life, the passage means something totally different. *Wow*!

How true this is.

I started rereading *Job 11:7-9* and ended with *Job 36:22-26*.

Back in '07 when I first read the *Bible* in its entirety, I was so engrossed that I made notes in the margins in red ink.

Since then, I've made additional notes and this time was no different, but my notes were in more detail because I was seeing so much more than I saw before.

If you are not familiar with *The Book of Job*, it's a must read, especially, if you are going through some kind of strife.

Job was a very wealthy man before God got a hold of him.

As the authors of my *Bible* explain, God and Satan had a discussion of sorts.

Satan tells God that Job was only faithful (righteous) because he was rich and that if his money was stripped from him, he wouldn't be so righteous.

Well, if you know God like I do, He does have a wit about Him.

So, God gives Satan permission to strip Job of all his riches.

God does know us, doesn't He?

Job never lost his faith.

He lost *everything* and Satan learned that Job's faith wasn't attached to that *everything*, then Satan tells God that personal suffering would surely reveal Job's weakness.

Yeah, right!

Job never curses God through that either.

Instead, he begins to seriously question God.

Questions like: Why some get punished for their sins and others don't?

Why is there inconsistency in God's distribution of punishments? etc., etc.

Basically, the *why me?* syndrome we draw ourselves in during our self-induced depressive state during the darkness or the times of our afflictions.

During this questioning session, three of Job's friends begin to argue with him.

They try to convince Job of the traditions that they were raised with, with falsehoods like suffering is the results of sin and God always punishes sin, so those who are wicked will always be wicked and there's no hope for them.

They try to make Job believe that he is a sinner, which is why he was suffering and that he is lying to himself when he says he's not.

A fourth friend enters the picture at the end and tells Job that suffering is used by God to teach lessons and to strengthen a person.

Finally, God comes into the picture and questions Job.

His questions are harsh, but Job proves to God that he can't be shaken and that his faith remained.

Job, without a shadow of a doubt, proved that it didn't matter if he had riches or if he was poor, if he was healthy or if he was sick, his faith would never change.

God wants us to live in faith in our personal lives and, sometimes, He calls upon us to do more.

God wanted Job to not just live in faith, but lead others to faith.

Hence, he was spending a lot of time with people who had done wrong, which led gossip that he was becoming a wicked person, too. Nothing has changed.

People are still like this today.

I find the most important part of Job's journey was when he voiced his faith publicly.

Oh, the people did not like that one bit.

All those who admired the Job before this, abandoned him, mocked him, denied him, etc.

His speeches were considered that of a crazy man. Sounds familiar?

It should because a lot of people who speak about God are considered *holy-roly* or *nuts* or some other version of this insanity.

The following passage is quite revealing as in showing how people think when they are not truly living God's way—*He is wooing you from the jaws of distress to a spacious place free from restriction, to the comfort of your table laden with choice food. But now you are laden with the judgment due the wicked; judgment and justice have taken hold of you. Be careful that no one entices you by riches; do not let a large bribe turn you aside. Would your health or even all your mighty efforts sustain you so you would not be in distress? Do not long for the night, to drag people away from their homes. Beware of turning to evil, which you seem to prefer to affliction.—Job 26:16-21*

This was said by Elihu, whom I see as a young, I-know-more-than-you sort of person.

God does not *woo.*

In all that I've learned in life through living and studying, God gives us two basic things that are truly simple: *Free*-will and unconditional love.

We have the choice to love unconditionally or not to.

As God knew Job's heart, so He knows all of our hearts. We can try to fool Him.

Try...is the key word. It won't work.

We can lie, pretend, betray, lie some more, ignore, hide...it all won't work when it comes to God. He knows all.

Which leads me to the work today *"Free-For-All."*

Words and phrases that seem to be everywhere these days: *The adversary, the prince of the earth, the devil.*

All referring to, of course, Satan.

That evil whore wants to win against God.

They have always been in battle.

You and I are the instruments.

We have to decide which side are we on: God's or Satan's. It's really that easy. There is *only* two sides.

There is *no* middle ground.

Thinking that you are righteous in the eyes of God because you are rich and have plenty friends or fans is so down the road of wrong thinking that it's so laughable.

Job clearly explains this.

If you are suffering, that does not mean you are bad or that God is punishing you.

I so had this wrong for a long time.

I tried to blame God for my hurt.

I couldn't even believe my own words.

I knew it was false.

I begged God to just take me home.

I knew that was so wrong, too.

He gives us a choice.

I've explained so many times that this very deal...giving *us* the right to choose...is what unconditional love is all about.

An example: We want to be in the limelight.

Say it's sports or entertainment or politics...that's our dream.

We have this vision in our heads that if we can be either of these things, we would be so rich that no one can tell us what to do.

We can have anything that we desire.

We can do anything that we want.

We can go anywhere that we want.

We wouldn't need anyone because money can buy everything. So, we bend the rules to get there.

We go against what we *thought* we believed in.

I say *thought* because if you can bend your own rules...you never really believed in them in the first place.

So, you are offered this great opportunity and you take it without considering what you are betraying. If that makes sense.

I see it all the time.

People sleep with whomever to get a break and get more money or fame.

People give up their morals to fit the crowd

or group.

Look at *Facebook* or any other social network and see all the shamelessness: Girls exposing themselves...all of themselves, women changing their appearances with plastic surgery to fit in or be accepted, men are doing this, too.

All these people who aren't even sure what sex they *should* be. Amazing at best.

It's *all* personal choices that will affect more than just their immediate moments.

They sell themselves to Satan without thought of consequence.

History.

Everything has happened before, but in a different way.

Think about this: If you lost everything today, would you blame God, yourself or someone else?

In what I read on social media, in newspapers, etc., etc., I see no one taking responsibility for their actions.

We here in the U.S.A. see it every day as clear as day.

Instead of holding those responsible for the injustices, we forfeit our own responsibility and blame others; hence, this political circus we find ourselves in, this constant race-war deal, etc., etc.

Job had it right.

If we are so easily bought, then we aren't really living the way of God.

We are pretenders at best.

Unconditional love means we forgive and move on, we accept those who have done wrong believing truthfully in our hearts that they will find their way to God.

It also means that we take care of or look out for other's well-being.

If we allow others to mislead or manipulate or cause sin, then we are just as sinful as they are.

If we allow hatred to continue to breed, then we are just as guilty as those hating.

It's so simple it's scary, yet the wrong continues.

The *freedom* to choose to do wrong is an individual thing.

There's no one else to blame, except yourself.

You, in the end, will have to answer to your very own choices and no one else's.

History.

Have you ever been in a storm and all the lights went out?

Have you ever been in a hurricane?

When there's a terrible storm, satellites are disrupted and we lose cell phone connections.

It is an unspoken deal on the coast that you should always have a land line because of this.

Landlines work no matter the conditions.

Hitler was able to do what he did because there was a very limited communication line during those times. Today, seems different.

I read an editorial this morning that talks about the merger of *AT&T* and *Time Warner*.

The writer mentions how we all are turning more to videos on the net, instead of TV and everyone rathers the wireless world of cell phones than cable.

The underlining message is cable will soon be a thing of the past. Will it?

Is it easier to live in wealth, then to live by God?

It seems more and more people are turning their lives in that direction.

I guess we'd rather make history with evil intentions, then make history the righteous way.

No one thinks about that...what future generations will think of us when they pick up history books.

Or will they lie in those history books as well.

Sugarcoating seems to be the national pass time these days.

Free-for-all...doesn't end up that way.

It's just an illusion. We all pay for water. Water!

Greed runs àmuck and the sad part is that we let it. Just saying...God bless.

~Jonah~

why complain, why even blame

He† gave decent housing
you brought it to ruin
fit for mouse rousing

why drain, why try to explain

He† gave you money for food
you wasted it—drugs, guns, prostitution
leaving behind, your wife and children
in places—turned to forbidden

why leave stains, separate in domains

He† gave you *freedom*
for you to blend, you didn't hear Him†
breeding anger and hate
instead of standing up straight

He† called on you—you ran—
you were supposed to teach
His† trust—you breeched

passed on anger and hate
nights became your date
you blended—felt it your fate
turning opened gates
to suppression—oppression
separating instead of blend
not hearing, while He† patiently waits

why complain, why even blame

you sold your soul, brought His† light
in darkness—weary and cold

the whale will shoot you from its mouth
once you see what He's† truly about

instead of separate—blend
instead of anger
become the forgiver, a peace maker

instead of *race*, set the pace
–all this waywardness
set a different path to trace

let it shine on your face

then out you'll come—seeing, breathing
truth in Him†—His† blessed son

Appearances
Facebook (November 6)

~

(November 7, 2016)—This morning I read through news feeds and made my comments.

I think everyone wants to put themselves out there without having to prove their point, but when you offer your opinion, they want or rather demand that you prove yours.

Fact is: I don't need to prove my point.

Hell when it comes to the Clintons, just pull up back dated newspapers and magazines.

It seems to me that people don't read anything but *Facebook* and they only show that they have an opinion during an election.

I voice my concerns year round.

I'm at that age when it matters that I do.

All these people supporting Hillary Clinton are not looking at policy at all.

They are seeing *first woman* just like *first black*...well that's not policy and eight years later, look at where we are.

Mass killings galore.

People coming to the U.S. like it's an international gateway for *free* money, *free* health, *free* education, *free* everything and the blood of Americans (those who actually are citizens and have that *right* to vote...*no Obama* you can't vote if you're not a citizen, but you got around that [eight] and [four] years ago! didn't you?) are paying for all this *free* stuff.

Here's one for you, no offense to my African friends, but there's a lottery that takes place every year in Africa (apparently the whole entire continent takes part).

There's a selected number of people pulled in this lottery and guess what their prize is: A *free* pass to the U.S.A. and guess who pays...for everything! Your tax dollars.

Okay, so does anyone get a *free* pass to any country they want if they are from the U.S.A.? I don't think so.

This is a deal made by your dear government *the U.S.A.* without your permission.

Hillary knew about the ambassador that was slain in the street, fucked in the ass by a cattle rod, rapped, beaten and the pictures went all over the internet for his family to see.

He begged her to help him and his coworkers and she denied him!

That's the Clinton/Obama way.

Do *not* come at me to *prove* anything.

Did you see that concert Hillary had to campaign off of? Well, *did you*?

All that sex just proves all the stories about her and Bill...oh, who was in front of the courts in threat of an impeachment for a girl, not his wife, that would be not *Hillary*, giving him a blow-job in the *oval* fucking office! A laughing stock.

That's just some of Hillary's forte... did anyone care to look up their status in Arkansas. They nearly broke that state.

The Clintons and the Obamas knew each other in Chicago.

Guess y'all forgot about that. Conspiracy. Give me a break.

Obama wrote a book before his office of *king* and said he *hated* America.

The Clintons are thieves.

All those mass killings in the last [eight] years.

I guess you people forgot about all those children killed.

Well guess what the Secretary of State is it and the Commander-in-Chief didn't have our backs when all that was happening, and isn't it funny that Clinton was president [eight] years, then comes Obama (remember friends before all this back in Chicago), and, then

Hillary is back in the White House as an appointed figure head. Give me a break!

This is lame as lame can be.

The best damn mystery novel and it's freaking real.

You can't tell me you are that blind to see what is going on?

You people voting for Hillary and Trump. Go on. Fuck up America more.

You have not one once of common sense.

You are voting for a party because someone told you to. It *is* as simple as that.

You have an option, but you are too scared to take it.

The chance to make your move is tomorrow on election day. *Not next time*!

Lame ass excuse to hand over the rest of our *freedoms* to other countries!

Your health bill is about to go up.

Your tax bill is about to go up.

I beg your differ not to sit there and whine like a little bitch because you are bringing it onto yourself. *I am a Christian.*

I do live the ways of *Jesus*!

I can cuss if I want to.

It does *not* mean I go against my values.

Those stay as do my principles.

I see more than half of this country switch their principles like they change their underwear. Yes, this all pisses me off.

I wore a damn uniform and because of that I'm disabled 100% and for what.

For some idiot who wants a *first*...who can't even stand for the *American Anthem* or say the *Pledge,* which they probably don't even know the damn words to.

Those are the ones who will be crying in their beds because their rights are gone!

Me...I'll be sitting with my feet kicked up smoking my cigars with my rum and DP... flicking my matches saying—*I told you fucking so!*

I already picked up my gun, and I'm not afraid to pick it up again.

I read the *Turner Diaries*. Have you?

I am a survivor.

All those acting all big and juicy for Hillary and Trump, a hurricane went their way and they tied up the damn phones dialing 911...that did happen in Jersey if you have forgotten.

I have no time to explain shit...look it up!

Give me a break. Your decision.

I hope you are teaching your kids how to bow and scrub floors because they are the ones who will be enslaved.

You are paving the way for them!

Congrats.

Your last chance to turn the cards around is tomorrow at the polls.

—If you vote third party, it takes electoral votes away from *Dumb and Dumber* and sends the election to the House of Representatives.

From there, third party candidates have a fair chance of being elected, and it takes power away from the greedy.

Don't vote for a party, don't vote for what you think is the lesser of two evils, vote for values and change.

The people have the power to fix this mess and show the world that America is still a great country. We can do this y'all.

~

(November 8, 2016)—Am I seeing that right? The Donald is President?

—I have a good one for you.

I was going to drive down south and vote... was...weather, aches, pain, not happening.

What to do? I wasn't going to vote.

My daughter calls—*We going vote...change your address location online...okay.* Done.

Received the print out. Went to vote.

Got turned away.

I was apparently supposed to know on Oct, 11, that I was going to be down today and not able to drive if I wanted to vote.

I didn't know on Oct, 11.

I didn't know Oct, 11 if I was going to have my apartment here.

So, now a U.S.A. disabled Vet. can't vote because I didn't know I was going to be ill on Nov. 8 on Oct. 11.

How many other people had this issue?

I really feel silly even going over there and trying.

I embarrassed my beautiful daughter because I was so insulted that I couldn't vote.

[Forty-seven] and turned away.

I had the printout with all my information and my driver's license.

It feels like when Jesus was born and they had that census and they all had to go back from where they were from.

All those dead people voted...that's what they said anyways.

Obama said illegals can vote.

He said that on TV, and I can't vote because I didn't know I'd be ill today on Oct. 11. Interesting.

~Came Here~

we came here again—radical, calm
hateful, peaceful
emotions—tied in knots

a system free of passion
doesn't exist in our communication

we came here again—doubtful, hopeful
confused, clear
emotions—separated lots

we awaken, then, again, fall asleep

we came here again
debated, argued—became divided
—media bias, drawing lines
instead of defending

united under God†
they preach it, but don't get it
they put us in a class
as they drink from fine glass

we fall—over and over—on our ass
as words of conspiracy
illuminati, rotchel
plague us to fall undercover

we came here again—to renew
to continue, it's been the same
their endless little game
keeping common in lame
different name—same old drain

freedom of speech—they say we have it
but they'll strip us
this we make a fuss—yell, scream, cuss
turning us to crust, as if we've made it up

we came here again—will things change
at last, from the power gang
move from range

so much killing, so many willing
games of breaking and stealing
greed's evil milling

we'll they keep us together
or separate us forever

we came here again
what's the difference
the same—stays each second

change takes courage
keeping us out of bondage

~

(November 9, 2016)—*Be yourself. If you water yourself down to please people or to fit in or to not offend anyone, you lose the power, the passion, the freedom and the joy of being uniquely you. It's much easier to love yourself when you are being yourself.*—Author Unknown

The older I get, the more interested I am in the *real* of things more than people's sauced-down logic.

Things like leaving a marriage that's poison (it's not a sin because I've learned that God removes the poison); like love and having an open heart and leaving nonsense like race and color out of the equation (it clearly states in the *Bible* that God does not approve of oppression, suppression, slavery, or prejudice; He does hate liars, deceivers, killers, and such.); like the idiocies surrounding *pot* (God gave us everything we need to heal ourselves naturally...*pot* also known as marijuana is grown in the dirt. Need I say more?)

I first tried a puff in 2012...really, [one] puff.

I bought my first bag at age 45 in 2014, basically because stress, sadness, and other strong emotions brings unnecessary pain to my already tormented body and it was suggested that *pot* would mellow me enough to control the pain.

(You would have to read my work on my author page and coming books to understand what was causing all of these unwelcomed emotions.)

At that point in my life, I would have done anything, that wouldn't hurt my body more, to gain the momentum I needed to fight this naturally causing deterioration of what we as humans call *our body*.

(No, I don't keep weed hanging around. It's not legal here in Louisiana. They like to put people in jail here, even though half, if not all, smoke it behind closed doors...and I truly believe that. Why fight against a plant that does nothing more than some of the crazy pharma drugs they give you at the doctor's office? Makes absolutely no sense!)

When I realized how much *pot* helped my pain [I have several major defects caused by my time in service as well as the natural deterioration, which makes me 100% permanently and totally disabled (point: there is no return to where I'm headed)] and left me without people-made side-affects, I was floored.

So, began my interest in marijuana and how it could benefit me.

This was a small battle for me because I'm a Christian and was raised to believe that *pot* was bad. They were so wrong.

I've done quite a bit of reading, since me buying that first bag, and it has floored me to no end how much this plant can help me and the government is putting people in jail because of it. Why?

Money is the only logical answer I've come up with. Greed! The root of all evil.

When I sit and think of all those people in jail (behind bars for life for some of them) all because they possessed *pot* on their person, I want to throw up!

I have *not* read one...not *one* account of any person killing another person or dying because of *pot*.

I have read plenty of articles and reports on people doing so many bad things to other people while on chemically-made drugs like cocaine and you know the others.

So, why are the police and government so hell-bent on convicting people for *pot* when there are far worse things to worry about?

It makes no sense. I'm 47 years old now.

In January, I'll be 48.

I have kept fit for my age.

This last year has been difficult for me and I'm not as fit as usual.

I have [three] children ages 25, 21, and 16.

I don't want to leave my children with *traditions* that aren't correct when it comes to logic.

I want them to know that it's okay to question tradition.

I want them to know that it's okay to take a stand for something they truly believe in.

I was in the dark when it came to *pot* for years, to the point of hating my neighbors who were *pot* smokers. The dark has lifted.

The articles I've posted on my [personal] page are indicators that the dark is lifting from others as well.

There *are* bigger things to worry about than *pot,* which is naturally given to us by God.

Yes, it can be grown in plant pots and the places where people grow them are, at times, called labs, but these plants are grown in the dirt. There are many varieties of this plant.

Some are strong. Some are very weak.

It's an individual thing.

So, making this plant legal (dear U.S. government, throw away your stupid patent...you have no right to control this God-given plant...it's not for you to decide...you are *not God*!), people can grow the variety that suits them.

They'd be less fear. More happy people.

Less drugged-out pharma people...have you ever seen someone on those anti-depressants?

Yes, the pharma owners wouldn't be as rich...let them grow their own plants, too.

They'll need it! Point: I've already made it.

Congratulations to the states that have opened their minds and clearly said to the world and the U.S. government and the pharma-blood-sucking hounds, that they give this right back to the people!

We are smart enough to think for ourselves!

It's our right to decided what we can handle.

Comments
•(Friend) Wouldn't know how to even start....
•(Me) I didn't either. I told my mother how it helped.
She's 70 and she said—*I want to try it.* It's a mind-set I believe. Once you get over that tradition that it's *bad*, then your mind changes.
When I get a chance to have some, I still have that tradition in the back of my mind. Nevada...I have my eye on.
I'd rather be happy, then in constant pain. That's just fact.
It's going to take a lot of people in this state to make some loud, loud noise to wake the politicians up.
So, folks like you and me can benefit from this plant.
Gone would be depression! *Gone!*

~

(November 10, 2016)—As my blog is getting set up (Hurray!), I revamped my *LinkedIn* account.

This is all really cool stuff we're doing.

It's exciting to really see a company being born. Bat Cave Publishing is on the move.

Slow, but steadily moving forward.

I'm still k. e. leger (the author), but I'm now a product of the main source...that would be Bat Cave Publishing.

That blog is my sounding board.

What does that mean?

Well, in order to sell anything, promote anything, establish yourself as an authority in anything online, you need a website.

I've been waiting for months...prayers do work my friends.

I'm posting this on here for I have over 3,000 friends here.

My author page...well...(I'm not complaining) has a little over 300 fans.

I have been knowing for a few years now that *Facebook* wouldn't be my steady home.

Nope. My dream is much bigger.

It's all about moving it forward no matter what tries to halt you.

You just keep it going and support one

another as much as we can.
    I do so support my friends here.
    Can't wait to share my work with you on
a bigger scale...and, yes, I'm going to talk
about it. How else will others learn?
    We need to speak about our paths, our
failures and such. That's how we teach.
    That's how we learn. I *love* learning!
    So, at this point in the game, I'm not
focused on the dollar sign.
    I'm more excited about the beginning...the
birth.
    How can anyone not be excited when
a vision in their head is coming to light,
actually becoming real.
    (I look forward to the day when I'm a
Corporation!)

~Not Walking Close~

trump and hillary
woke up an aged refinery
what's the difference in their cadence–
threaten a revolution
using feces as lotion
stripping naked in streets–
protesting in beats—city to city
paid-off defeats
sending all hiding under sheets

all thinking—inside jobs
foreign flags trying to rob
–just turn the knob
eyes in sob, whining their lot
all claiming america—their homing crop
seems quite a flop, just new-media slop

people here, people there
burning, destroying, killing
soros—his illuminati flair
putting us to the test
ensuring our up-rest

social media *journalists*
pretending *activists*, arising, in the mix

–all just fascists loving socialist
–jokers in injustice

all—*all* playing their card
here's at the heart:

to get better—first—it'll get worse
in every improvement
there lies—a movement

yes, stand up, speak, enjoy *free speech*

actions over words
we're not cattle in herds
we're people—black, white, brown
poor, rich, middle—grounds
schooled, not schooled
hands-on geniuses, common workers
brilliant writers and entertainers
techno junkies, down-right nerds

letting money buy our time
selling souls for by-lines
just rhythm and rhyme
for saudi-backed grime

ambassadors, every where we are
americans, we've some so far
unity—in each sewed-in star

don't be weak
their promised hand-out greed
seeps, seeps, seeps
command, command, command
then back their slowed stand
we, fools—they've bread their strand

careful, careful, careful
watch, watch, watch

they'll yank unity from our feet
ownership—they want our streets

chaos, uprising—they'll steadily deny
–our red, white, and blue
they don't want us to fly

our vast, beautiful land—you see
they want to command
all part of their take-over plan
us, they aren't a fan
they're here to ban—all they can

open eyes—see
let a little shaking, move under our feet
no time to rumble, zero time to stumble
give things a chance
–make those machines dance

push foreign powers out of range

give, give, give....
our homeless more change
our vets, helping hands, our inner cities
remove that steadfast trance
racism—laugh in their little prance
let's build a building romance

fuck the tap dance
it's time to firmly plant

we *are* no longer the middleman–
the go-between avalanche
for the greed and power milkman

we *are* the *minuteman,* we're americans
legal–
birth certificates, social security cards
in our fucking hands

everyone else—live in a fairyland
–taking our land
they deserve a backhand
they're just contraband
we can easily disband

we have unity
they cannot see—we *are* the *homeland*

black panthers, hell's angels
here, there american gangs
even the blood-sucking ku klux klan

it's our damn *mainland*
we show our underpants
then we complain
in streets, we break dance
in jails, sing a chant

we conceal contraband
making our police—fans

we work in plants
have a volunteer army to command

we're a businessman
we're athletes who don't scant

we're nurses, doctors
working all night with steady hands

we're a fireman, a doorman
we drive taxis and trucks–
make way for every ambulance

we're a vulgar, loud rock band
or a peaceful, careful trainman

we have wetlands and quicksand

we like the sun, getting tans
we drink beer from a can

take us as we are or leave our homeland
we get inflamed—here and there
we settle down, we play the game
satire—we proclaim—politics our aim

we get involved
run our own campaigns

fuck you if you don't like our domain
this is how we roll
all your penetrating defame–
all *in vain*, we always remain the same

for you see–
with you, we'll walk streets
–never do we walk too close

cross our line, we close the do'
we *are* americans
birth certificates, social security cards
in our hand, we *can* proclaim!
this is *our homeland*

you, causing the disdain
oh! how we easily can ban

(Written November 12, 2016, but didn't post it.)—This morning in my local paper read the headline *'Trump Song Fallout: UL Coach Apologizes.'* UL is the local university here.

I missed this in the news, but, apparently, some members of the football team made a video in the locker room and it got put on social media, then...then the fans were outraged.

There are two points to be made here: *Freedom of Speech* and being and ambassador.

Freedom of Speech: This is a quote from the coach—*...It's also disappointing that so many people have vilified a few 19-year olds making some immature decisions, and then they were the same ones that voted for someone that has done much worse by grabbing a female in the private areas for the office of the (President of the) United States of America.*

I didn't see this picture.

Meaning: I didn't see any picture of Trump grabbing a female in her private parts.

Did you?

I read countless blogs and posts about this.

I heard all these women coming forth and telling us that Trump did that and did this.

I saw a lot of *mudslinging*, but I didn't see any *evidence* to back this all up with.

I read the information about the *13-year-old* now (I forget how old) claiming Trump assaulted her at a party over 20 years ago.

She first filed it in California without an attorney and asked for $100 million.

She said she had $300 to her name. Okay.

The court threw it out.

Oh, they had a legal reason.

That didn't work out for her, so she sought an attorney, found one *in New York.*

So, she gets on a bus and goes clean across the country to New York and files a new claim, but doesn't ask for any money.

Strange!

I smell a *catfish*...you folks on dating sites should understand that word.

In the new lawsuit (I didn't find any actual charges filed like in a criminal kind of thing), this woman has absolutely zero hard evidence.

It's all he said, she said.

Do you know how many people are in jail and innocent because of such craziness?

This woman is clearly after her five-minutes of fame.

How can I say that so lightly?

Let's use the priest and alter boy cases.

Those claims (many, many were *proven* true) happened...most 15 to 20 years before these guys came forth. Okay.

These are men and something really bad happened to them as young boys.

They were seeking justice, not fame.

None of what actually happened to them made the front pages of newspaper and websites. Do you get the picture?

Something happened to these men when they were boys. Something bad.

We don't need to know the particularities.

We just wanted justice, and furthermore, in all these cases, not just one boy, but many boys came forth and gave their *complete* testimony. Lawyers took their cases.

Cases were won.

No amount of money could have stopped justice from being sought! Back to Trump.

If this woman's allegations are true, then why didn't any of those liberal women attorneys in California jump on this case?

Why didn't they jump on the case in New York?

Why did this woman have to put up money?

And...the big *and*...why...oh! please tell me...why did the courts allow all this content from, supposedly, the court filings be released to the media?

I mean I read some of this stuff and what this woman claimed happened to her, in writing, is a bit disturbing.

Why would the courts allow this information out when they didn't for the alter-boy cases?

I really don't think people are thinking clearly or putting the pieces together.

There is so much being *reported* on social media, but without proper authority to actually write what they are writing.

There are so many sites on the web today who are claiming to be *news,* but aren't news at all, but pure gossip.

I know a lot of these sites aren't even coming out of the U.S.A.

There are sites from all over the world *claiming* to be U.S.A. sites and news sources, but aren't and writing bogus news reports to stir up chaos.

So, again I ask, has anyone actually seen a *photo* of Trump grabbing someone's female parts?

As a trained journalist, I do have to question my sources. I haven't always.

I, many times, allow passion to take over and just posted crap.

I've had friends call me out on it.

I appreciate that a great deal.

After this election, the posts I have read are beyond disturbing.

The comments on pages, absolutely disturbing.

The United States had a Presidential election. One opponent won. One lost. [That would be the political machines by the way!]

This happens every four years.

Eight years ago a black man ran. He won.

I dedicated an entire website to his first [four] years.

I didn't respect a lot of policies he came up with.

I didn't respect a lot from Bush and Clinton as well. I voiced my opinion. *Free* speech.

I'm not an Obama fan, but he was the President.

I wrote a lot of things, as a journalist type of person writing in satiric form about his presidency. That's normal for journalists.

What's not normal is lying to the people.

When I had my political blog, I researched and found more than one source to back my writing up and included the sources in my writing.

What's going on today with all these wanna-be writers is destroying the very art of journalism.

The coach for the U.L. football team further said—*We value and take seriously our role as ambassadors for this great University. The immature actions of this relatively small group will not define us; nor will it overshadow the outstanding body of work of our nearly 400 student-athletes.*

Right on the money, sir.

I was in the Army on foreign soil.

As a citizen of the United States of America, I was representing my country while on that foreign soil.

I was not just a soldier, but an *ambassador*. What does that mean?

It means that how I behaved reflected on my *entire* country, but I wasn't just an ambassador for my country, but also to my state and my family.

Do you comprehend that?

That woman in California who took her clothes off and shit on the street, then picked it up with her hands and smeared it on a pole!

She represented all those in California, then she represented, to the outside world, the *United States of America*!

How embarrassing is that!

At the end of the article, the coach said—
And if everyone that voted for Donald Trump can forgive him and put him in the office of the President of the United States...then I would think they can forgive a few 19-year-olds, too.

This article led me to write *"Not Walking Close."* Do you understand the poem?

It's really simple. *Propaganda.*

When studying W.W.II, this word and what it stands for played a key factor in what Hitler did.

Hitler and his followers killed over [six] million people!

It doesn't matter what race they were, they were human beings.

From all the reports I've read, this Soros fellow, worked for Hitler!

If that is true, then why isn't he in jail?

I don't care how much money the man has. Why isn't he in jail? Money.

A little research for you: From https://en.wikipedia. org/wiki/George_Soros
Soros was born in Budapest in the Kingdom of Hungary to a well-to-do non-observant Jewish family. His mother Elizabeth (also known as Erzsébet) came from a family that owned a thriving silk shop. His father Tivadar (also known as Teodoro) was a lawyer and had been a prisoner of war during and after World War I until he escaped from Russia and rejoined his family in Budapest. The two married in 1924.

Tivadar was an Esperantist writer and taught Soros to speak Esperanto in his childhood. In 1936, Soros's family changed their name from Schwartz to Soros, in response to growing antisemitism with the rise of fascism. Tivadar liked the new name because it is a palindrome and because of its meaning. In Hungarian, Soros means 'next in line', or 'designated successor'; and, in Esperanto, it means 'will soar.' Soros was 13 years old in March 1944 when Nazi Germany occupied Hungary. Jewish children were barred from attending school by the Nazis, and Soros

and the other schoolchildren were made to report to the Judenrat (Jewish Council), which had been established during the occupation.

Soros later described this time to writer Michael Lewis: 'The Jewish Council asked the little kids to hand out the deportation notices.' I was told to go to the Jewish Council, and there I was given these small slips of paper...I took this piece of paper to my father. He instantly recognized it. This was a list of Hungarian Jewish lawyers. He said: 'You deliver the slips of paper and tell the people that if they report they will be deported.' Soros did not return to that job; his family purchased documents to say that they were Christians, thereby allowing them to survive the war.

Later that year, at age 14, Soros posed as the Christian godson of an official of the fascist Hungarian government's Ministry of Agriculture. The official was involved in making inventories of the estates of wealthy Jewish families who were being sent to death camps. Rather than leave Soros alone in the city, the official brought him along and Soros participated in this action. He wrote in 2000 about the Nazi occupation of Hungary, in the foreword to his father's autobiography: It is a sacrilegious thing to say, but these ten months were one of the happiest times in my life.

Granted he was on 14 years old, but he still had a choice.

You can read all about this man on *Wikipedia*. He's rich.

He has so much money that he can control, and he has.

Sure, he's given money to help...but and there is always a *but*...he has used his position to influence entire countries.

Read it carefully, you'll see what I'm talking about.

He is not a U.S. citizen: https://en.wikipedia.org/wiki/Talk:George_Soros/Archive_8

Is George Soros an American citizen?

He *considers himself a U.S. citizen*, but according to the U.S. State Department, officially, no.

If he is, when was he naturalized?

If he is not, what country is he a citizen of?

An answer to a question on *Wikiquestions* says George Soros is not a U.S. citizen.

He has been convicted for a crime: https://en.wikipedia.org/wiki/George_Soros
His insider-trading conviction was upheld by the highest court in France on June 14, 2006. In December 2006, he appealed to the European Court of Human Rights on various grounds including that the 14-year delay in bringing the case to trial precluded a fair hearing. On the basis of Article 7 of the European Convention on Human Rights, stating that no person may be punished for an act that was not a criminal offense at the time that it was committed, the court agreed to hear the appeal. In October 2011, the court rejected his appeal in a 4–3 decision, saying that Soros had been aware of the risk of breaking insider trading laws.

He has poured money into American

Presidential campaigns and other Amercican institutions to promote his *world order agenda.*—http://www.politico.com/story/2016/08/george-soros-criminal-justice-reform-227519

While America's political king-makers inject their millions into high-profile presidential and congressional contests, Democratic mega-donor George Soros has directed his wealth into an under-the-radar 2016 campaign to advance one of the progressive movement's core goals—reshaping the American justice system.

He's not an *Amreican*!

As far as I understand, Americans running for any elected office can*not* accept contributions of any kind for foreigners.

Foreigners do *not* have a right to pour money into anything to influence our government, and this is just George Soros.

There are many other *outside* influences that are shaping our country to fit their own agenda, and we are letting them!

Americans need to step up.

We have enough resources here in our own country to fight these self-agending world-order people.

It's up to us to do something about it!

—Actions prove who someone is. Words just prove who they want to be.—Author Unknown

So, as the quote says, I'm a bit dulled by those who *say* they help people in *all* their news feeds and sell products that *claim* they teach!

Of all the 3,429 people I have on here [*Facebook*], I only got two [two] responses to my *help* post. That's a bit messed up.

So, if you aren't a serious marketer, you're not one of my close friends, and/or you don't have a business you take serious enough... you need to go!

I post my whims as everyone else, but I am also serious when it comes to business and marketing.

I believe we should all help each other, instead of being like the politicians and each is out for themselves, sucking the blood out of everyone else. That's just my opinion.

So...*if you are not serious...delete me,* so I don't have to do it!

Also: Any one of you who is serious and have a good blog, please PM me the link.

My blog is tailored to women: Those who are hurting, coming out of divorce, been abused, lost in the darkness, etc. (men can benefit a great deal as well), and part of my blog will be used to help women find ways to make money to get *out* of the situation they are in.

I will need links to good blogs that are not so technical explaining how to market, build a *WordPress* blog, make money...I mean really make money (the majority of these women don't have a lot of money to dump into something they don't understand yet...), networking, traffic and what the hell that means, etc. I think you get the picture.

I will also be looking for guest bloggers when it comes to inspiration, surviving the five stages of grief, divorce, woman issues (health, fitness, work, relationships).

My blog will start out small and slow, so if you are serious and keep your blog up, it will land on mine. [i.e. I scratch your back, you scratch mine.]

I'm telling you this because I take what I do very serious.

The material I write on is very serious.

I don't need any players, hustlers, or fake people. I think you really get the picture.

Thanks. God Bless.

~

(November 16, 2016)—*Take action! Wanting is not enough; act upon your goals! If somebody was watching your day-to-day behavior, would they be able to see what you're working towards; what your goals are? If the answer is no, fix it!*—Steve Maraboli

I'm *battreasure* on *ebay* if you care to look up what I've got up there so far.

I had 51 items, but took down [four] (combined a few).

I'm messing with pricing and seeing what works right now.

I reviewed these three items that I just posted and I had *international shipping* checked, but it wasn't checked when I reviewed them today, so I have to see why that happened.

I do have *best offer* for all items.

These are only a few that I have.

I'm getting views, but everyone gets views. So far no sales.

I've spent about [four] days total on taking pics, writing descriptions (some need to be revised), pricing (that, too), looking up similar products and figuring out all this shipping.

It's changed since last time I sold on there.

This time more competition.

My blog is still being tweaked and I will have a store, so I haven't decided, yet if I'll just move all these items there.

I've been reading some post about others like me getting into this online business.

You can make money.

I made a good deal with [online business] until they sold out and left the country!

I really enjoyed doing that.

Like I said I've done *ebay* before.

I sold some *how-to* books and did quite

fast. That was about [six] years ago.

Everything seems to have changed.

There doesn't seem to be much bidding going on.

I checked out *Amazon* and they want product numbers and such.

I'm selling personal stuff (lightening the load even more...more on this once the blog is up), so, some of these things are handmade or bought years ago and the packaging has long been thrown out. I'll stick with *ebay* for a while.

Me. I'm not trying to get rich.

I just want to sell some things and have fun doing it.

I think this is practice for me for when I have to seriously market my books.

Yes, those are still being worked on as well. I fly on God's time. Patience.

Something I've learned very well.

Check me out on *ebay*.

I am always open for suggestions to improve my selling techniques.

All of my experiences will be part of my blog to help abused women get out of their situation.

So, if you have any pointers, I'd rather you PM me, so we can talk more open.

I want to find out what works and what doesn't. So, on I go.

Looking forward to hearing from you.

~

(October 2017)—As of right now, I still don't have my blog/website up and running.

I tried out *ebay*, then shut it down.

Not my forte, though it was fun while doing it.

~

(November 23, 2016)—Posted an article titled *'Aftermath: Sixteen New Yorker Writers on Trump's America'*—*newyorker.com*

I have mixed feelings this morning after reading an article by Tony Morrison.

She paints a picture of *whitness* that's both disturbing and a bit embarrassing.

As a writer, I expect class from someone like Morrison. Not slander of a people.

I am a mixture of groups, but my skin is white.

Why do people constantly have to insert color in everything?

Black/white...who gives a fuck?

Do your job, love God, and be damn sure to love yourself!

God doesn't see the color of your skin.

Sorry. It just doesn't work that way.

This racism B.S. is coming from the outgoing President.

Strange how someone as smart as Morrison doesn't see that.

Is it because *color* has clouded her own vision? Wake up. It's not about color.

If you try leaving that out of the equation, maybe, true intelligence will shine through.

Just saying....

~

(November 25, 2016)—Posted an article titled *'Conspiracy: Are 125 Dead Scientists, 72 Dead Bankers, and 3 Dead Journalists Related?'*

What is on my mind?—*Facebook* asks. God! This article is long.

Over [seven] pages. I took notes.

Interesting.

World information not just U.S.A.—world.

Maybe, we all should be paying a little more attention.

Maybe, we will all *kill ourselves* or die suddenly in an accident. Maybe.

God is always watching.

The ones causing these deaths, for those of us living in the light...we know what happens to them.

Me, personally, I would rather not gamble with...*is there heaven and hell...God and devil*. Nope. Not for me. I am on God's side.

I will *be* and speak clearly.

Evil...evil...will burn.

There is *no* doubt in my mind.

Don't be silent. Don't hide your gift.

I would rather join these who honored their gift for the sake of good.

Sorry, those who sit in luxury and bask themselves with tables of food, for if you *pillage* on earth, your heaven is *only* on earth.

Your eternity is only fire.

God is great *all* the time.

~*Looking Within*~

it's not to your treasures, you are bound
look carefully around–
is your heart sound

quantity of possessions
do you measure, your worth
to all your journey's identities–
do you take pleasure
now, from your birth, is *that* the quality
–your only creation

all your roads traveled—of life–
are you still baffled
wishing, you were still in the cradle
wishing, on no experiences to tattle

is it no more a mystery
your *back-there* history

for every lesson, comes a reason
for the next season

round and round
goes the merry-go-round
'til no more—you see the clown
never lost, never found
stuck in between—that round and round
not seeing the lesson
not rightfully sound

'til it comes from within
the *stuck* always in begin
again and again–
so sad at the end, feeling *still* in begin

(November 29, 2016)—The blog is coming...
slow, mind-bogging, aggravating...the books,
too. Who cares! All I have is time.

What the hell's the rush for anyways?!

Live your life.

It's all about being a woman.

It's all about loving yourself just the way
you are.

Anyone who can't comprehend that can
take the bus!

To all you guys who appreciate a good
woman (all of her—emotions, baggage, cries and
laughter, ass-hole family members, etc., etc.), you
are a good man. Stay like that.

There are so very few of you.

Those *other* guys, they are complete
morons.

—It takes no time for the universe to manifest what
you want. Any time delay you experience is due to your
delay in getting to the place of believing, knowing, and
feeling that you already have it. It is you getting yourself
on the frequency of what you want. When you are on that
frequency, then what you want will appear.—The Secret

If you want something, desire something
and you're constantly looking at all the
negatives and seeing all that's wrong, then
nothing will ever be right for you.

All those couldà, shouldà, wouldà's...(even
for myself)...they'll never help you reach your
full potential, what you *should* be.

Do you relate to *"Looking Within"*? Really.
Do you?

One of the best books I've ever read was
The Secret...another book *Proof of Heaven*...
written years later...proves it to be true.

Books *are* good for something.

They help you grow. Look within.

There's too much murder, hate, and evil in
today's world. Too much!

If you say you're this way, but act another
way, then you are just the same as those
creating this hell on earth.

Change starts with you.

One wondrous change brings another and
another...my heart cries for the beauty inside
people who can't see it for themselves.

Look within.

Each time a woman stands up for herself, without
knowing it possibly, without claiming it, she stands up for
all women.—Author Unknown

The Lord does not look at the things man looks at. Man
looks at the outward appearance, but the Lord looks at the
heart.—1 Samuel 16:6-13

Hence, the poem *"Looking Within."*
Positive.

It's really hard to be positive for a lot of us
this time of year.

Especially, those of us up in age and have
lost so much. It's a sensitive time for us.

We don't want to hear what's *wrong* with
us.

We need...*need* to hear what's *right* about
us.

So, when we can't get it from those around
us, we need to do it for ourselves, which,
sometimes, is even harder.

To me, in all that I've learned...47 years is
a lot of learning...I've witnessed the actions
of others and their words (myself included).

When that hatefulness comes through, it's
not about you, it's about them.

You can't change a person.

You only can change yourself.

Meaning, you only can grow in life
through what you do, not what others do.

I like to make people happy...it's my
nature, but I also have this woman side of
me. You know...I am a woman.

I don't think men get this part.

I'm not dumb.

They *do* get the breast and the rest of the
body. The easy stuff.

I'm talking about a woman's emotions.

We were given this really deep-set type of
emotion because we bare children.

We have to be open to these emotions in
order to raise these children.

(I'm very aware of those women who aren't born with this...this is *not* about those.)

As mothers, we teach our children certain values: How to be respectful to others, how to clean themselves, how to do things such as the dishes and such, how to say *I'm sorry* and *thank you*...those really important things that make us into who we are.

I thank God for my mother.

This past week I was faced with the certainty that she, indeed, did her job well.

I will always be grateful for the values she's taught me.

A woman is a very special human.

I've written this many times: She will do anything for you if she's treated right.

She will close the hell down when she's treated wrong. A woman can take a lot.

Her shoulders may be smaller than a man's, but they are way stronger.

A good woman is priceless.

If you don't value her, it's your loss not her's.

She will cry and suffer the loss, but sooner or later, a good man comes along that sees her value.

She's tough like that because once that good man finds her, she's already raised herself up.

She's learned the tricks of the trade.

She'll deal if that value-seeing goes down, but not like before.

Understand that and you know a woman.

Why am I talking about this?

Because, even though you say *women are liberated*, we are not.

You talk about slavery and all that bullshit and want others to feel sorry for how you are treated as a man.

You have no idea how a woman feels.

Still today, she is still being controlled no matter her color: She is still expected to bow-down, she is still expected to follow man's orders (rules), she is raped, beaten, killed, held hostage in human-trafficking...and you turn the other cheek.

You are a hypocrite.

All this race bull, that's about you men.

It has nothing to do with us women.

We are still suppressed!

You can argue this point until you are blue in the face. We are *still* suppressed!

Don't tell me about God.

Don't tell me about Jesus.

I get so many men on my personal page preaching.

I have one guy sending me scripture for some *world* Christian order, and, then sends me a message about dating! Really?

I'm a sinner. I'm not righteous.

I'm not ignorant, either.

Jesus felt deeply for those in pain.

So much so that He suffered ridicule, hate, and was murdered for His *personal* love for others.

It's written in the *Bible* that those who suffer here on earth have a place in heaven because those who suffer learn what life is truly about, learn how to love the deepest.

That says a lot about a woman.

For those carrying your racist bull shit, God doesn't approve of that.

What you mask on the outside does *not* covet what's on the inside.

That's what God sees.

That's *all* that He sees.

You can mask your true self all you want.

It doesn't matter. He sees all the same.

Hate only breeds hate.

Anger only breeds anger.

Stop trying to be rich or popular and start living the *Word*.

That's when good things come, then your ending will be satisfied.

If you don't understand that, then you are still stuck back there.

—Posted an article titled *'Racism.'*

Go on, read this damn page, then delete me out of your freaking kkk-black-lives-matter bull-shit, drama-filled lives.

This is the final of my day's yelling and screaming.

If you can't shake a man's hand because of the color of his skin, you are the biggest hypocrite on the face of the earth, just as much as you not being able to be around a man who can't shake your hand.

Who's the better man? Neither.

If you can't touch a man or woman because of the color of their skin, I don't want to know you. I don't want you in my life.

You have a disease and only you can cure it. Go away from me. Grow the hell up.

Get some Jesus.

(Oh! you might want to re-think that...Jesus' skin wasn't white, but brown...*no*, Jesus' skin wasn't black either...it was brown, and, yes, I'm a miss-know-it-all when it comes to this...region, placement of the sun! Get a brain and read!)

If I did anything good in life, it is to instill in my children there's no color, just people.

What they do with that is on them.

This question...I can answer truthfully if God asks me: It's not the color of their skin, it's the color of their heart.

—Posted an article titled *'Unspeakable horrors in a country on the verge of genocide'*

Here you go.

All you folks calling yourselves African-Americans...your homeland needs you.

Are you really an African?...then your kin are being slaughtered.

Are you going to get on a plane and help them. Read this article. What the hell?

I'm so sick of people saying they are *found,* that they are *God's* children, but at the same time allow this to happen.

The Indians, these Africans...they need help. It's not about money. It's about life!

Go on...call yourselves *African* Americans, while these people are being slaughtered.

Hint: You *are not* an African.

You are an American.

These people are Africans.

They actually *live* on the continent of African.

They are fighting for their lives...literally, while you sit around on your sofas eating cookies and getting fat. Shame.

—Posted an article titled *'Standing Rock Sioux Tribe Cites History of Government Betrayal in Pipeline Fight.'*

This is the history of what the U.S. government has done to these people.

This is not the first time.

The government did offer to pay for some of the land they have stolen only after gold was found on the land.

The Sioux refused to take the money.

It is estimated to be worth over a billion dollars today. It's not about the money.

It's about the land and fresh water.

If one spill happens...*one*...the Missouri river would carry it and all that contamination over half the U.S. through feeders of the river. Greed has to stop!

Has to stop.

Note: Obama went over there and visited. Just visited. I wonder why. Nothing has halted. The governor of this state is not doing anything. I wonder why? *Money!* Line their pockets and they *hush-hush*! These people are not using weapons. These people are protecting this for all of us.

What the hell are you bitching about in your little selfish world?

There are *real issues* going on. *Real*!

—Posted a video titled *'Standing Rock a Dark Reality Must Watch!'*

These are hired...*hired* security by these rich oil companies. They are not police.

They have police on their clothes, but they aren't police. They have no right.

This is not their land!

They have even leveled grave yards!

~*Broken Record*~

its continued game
all the same—so very lame
—really insane

same ole, same ole—the bells do toll
words, roll and roll
that vice isn't sold—just boring—old

can't you find a different vine
to hang your sign—get with the times
your black and white crime
way behind—*real* in times
living in *human* kind

your broken record
has lost its minute to minute second–
choosing color over person
just makes you dumber, stuck in slumber
to God†, you'll have to answer

yep! same ole game—different name

traditions with zero validation

fuck you—fuck you, too
you're black, you're white—damn!
you're fucking human too

loose the excuse
stop the back and forth abuse
up—it's all been used—color isn't in cue
—so long overdue, this view in new
I'm human—so *are* you!

~*Wasteful Breaths*~

are you thinking rapture
or is it just pressure
are you thinking scripture
or is it just exposure

are you really concerned with legislature
it's forever evolving infrastructure
or is it just adventure–
expressing so much displeasure

is all this political conjecture
–false-journaling literature
a sly way to rupture

free speech's measure

so easy—the manufacture
deceptions through pictures

so easy—the sculpture
changing scenery, texture
facts and figures
–raise that blood pressure
add some furniture, erase a few fixtures
diddle-daddle with exposure
–with a quick move of the wrist
a quick finger-tap
oh! how the insist—viola! a reconfigure

better yet! let's add to the mixture
an opinionated, fabricated feature
–make it a brilliant lecture

bust the core of the imagination
elevate the temperature
all this hoopla—let's nurture

take *freedom of speech*
to its highest investiture
with these minds—easy torture
the smallest gesture sets the course–
false disclosure

oh! what fun they're having–
these amateurs
in their *free*-for-all pastures
minds in seizure—taken, stolen
under attack by vultures
the dark-internet-world fracture
the b-site imposture
penetrating all exclosures
forcing a capture
changing culture—on a whim–
their simple leisure, then disappearing–
their cowardly nature

again, the posed caricature
are you really thinking
a biblical departure
questioning the ultimate architecture
or you just being fooled into capture

(December 6, 2016)—*OMG! You scared the shit
out of me (quote came with a picture of a baby looking
frightened)*—Author Unknown

*Mental Hospital! To all my fellow nuts...I just realized...
we sit and stare at a screen...we talk to ourselves...we have
imaginary friends, zoos, farms, cities, and fake animals...
we cook imaginary food in imaginary bakeries...we play
bingo that gives no money...we poke people and think it's
okay...we even write on walls...think about it...Facebook
is a mental hospital and we are all its patients. Party in*
my ward later...feel free to share this...I just did!—Author
Unknown

Note: This commentary isn't about just one
thing. My commentaries usually aren't.

So, to understand it fully, you have to read
it to the very end.

Clear understanding of things is so very
important in today's world.

"Wasteful Breaths"...I wrote this yesterday
after reading a *Facebook* post about the
Bible's Revelations.

Good...except, whoever posted it changed
some of the words, which changed the
meaning of the whole damn thing!

Yeah, I got two *Bibles* out and compared
them. That would be something I'd do!

Here's my stubborn child behavior...the
one God knows so damn well: A big *fuck you*
to all the men out there who misinterpret the *Bible*
and believe women are evil and/or rewrite passages
of the *Bible* to fit their own ignorant belief of what
they believe, instead of what the *Bible* and God
actually meant! *Fuck you!*

The *Bible* does not say women are evil.

Many of the writers in the *Bible* used the
word *prostitute* to describe how the people
behave in their ways against God.

I can see why they did this because the
chosen people did sell themselves to the evils
of the world, instead of keeping their faith in
God's words and promises (i.e. they didn't trust
in God.).

Notice the third meaning of the word
prostitute below.

The word used in the *Bible* was used in
accordance with *men* and *women*...not just
women!

Whole, entire countries are labeled
prostitute in the *Bible*. Need I say more?

Prostitute: a person, usually a woman, who engages
in sexual intercourse for money; to sell or offer (oneself)
as a prostitute; to put (one's talent or ability) to unworthy use
(*Random House Dictionary*)

Man says women are evil because *men*
fuck women up with their lies!

That's just how it is...from our *dads* to
our boyfriends to our *husbands*...why can't
people just *not* judge and love you and be
freaking honest? Why?

Why can't men just be real?

I've been writing about this for so damn
long that it's become redundant to the point
of *disgustingly* redundant.

A word to men: A woman gives birth.
Do you really understand that concept?
That means: She gave birth to you.

She raised you.

She was given a warm heart (most anyway) to see that you were safe and *free* of harm.

She feels deep.

(I'm really sorry for those men out there who were not given this. It's not *every* woman's fault.)

She deserves respect.

After she raises you, she sends you out into the world.

Whatever happens to you out there in this big ole world happens to you, not to her.

She has her own shit to deal with.

A grown man should *never*, *ever* think a woman still has to *raise* him.

She is only responsible for her life, not yours.

A lot of women have to overcome the shit they have gone through because of men (what my work is about).

So, don't look at every woman as evil.

She's dealing. Just like you are dealing.

Women over 40, just like men over 40, have even more crap to deal with.

Menopause. Empty-nest syndrome.

Mid-life crises. Retirement. Divorce.

Sexual changes. Body changes. Abuse.

So...don't put your shit on her, and don't use the *Bible* as an excuse to blame her for your shit. Your shit is *your* shit.

She's busy repairing herself.

You should do the same.

Just saying...(I should note that this *is* a general observation.)

A word for women: All you women out there soliciting sex and posting all these pictures of your private parts...you are giving all us good women a bad name. You need a *self* check really bad!

All you women out there using your body to get attention, you are not loving yourself.

It's that simple. You have *no* self-respect.

Posting pictures of your butt and all that mess... *zero* self-respect.

Don't be calling men out if they come after you. You are sending the message of *okay*!

If you don't get that, then you are so screwed.

Note: In my opinion, it's okay (in a relationship) to send your other half pictures of yourself, even videos, because it's fun and it's only for them.

Those of you breaking up, then using that against the other...shame!

I believe one state, thus far, has passed a law making that illegal. Good for them!

Off my *man-woman* shit and onto this *Facebook* crap. Do you watch movies?

Come on...do you?

Making movies has been going on for a very, very long time.

Do you know *how* they make movies?

I don't think some of you are catching on very well.

Let me be the smart ass that I can be and give you a short lesson: When you sit down to watch a movie, say it's a [one and a half]-hour film, it's continuous, and non-stop. You understand that?

If you don't, stop reading now!

Well, when that movie is made, it is not filmed *continuous*.

They film it in parts, at different times, in different places...a lot of that film is filmed in a room and they *add* the background like scenery and sounds later. Can you comprehend that?

Any one studied *War of the Worlds* or even know what it is?

It was a play and before TV, they acted out this play on the radio.

This was way before commercial breaks.

Actually, this play was the *reason* we have commercial breaks today.

This play scared the shit out of everyone!

No joke. Go look it up.

People, actually, thought aliens were coming to invade, packed up all their shit and created massive traffic jams across the country.

They had gone mad until some jackass decided—*Hey, I think we should tell them this is only a play and not real life.*

Well, this same thing is happening today, but in a different way.

It's *War of the Worlds* byway of *Facebook*.

In comes the *clip-and-splice* editing process!

Here it goes...you see it, then say—*It's real... look...you can't deny that!*

I can watch any film (movie) and say the same damn thing!

These short *Facebook/YouTube* videos (films) doesn't make it anymore real than a [one and a half]-hour movie!

The *alien* flashing lights!

I watched this great performance the other day with this guy using light to animate his movements on stage.

You should watch it, too, if you truly think those zipping lights in the videos are real.

Sure, there may be something *alien* out there...zipping, flashing lights...big ole machines flying in the sky (i.e. *War of the Worlds* B.S.).

Okay, we have the alien thing out of the way.

Let's move on to the *journalism* blogs and websites.

I have watched the manipulation of words since my Army days.

I was on the *inside* of that news and it was appalling to read the false B.S. that was being reported on news TV channels and in newspapers.

It's gotten worse ever since with the inventions of *Facebook* and *YouTube*.

The media (i.e. newspapers, news channels, magazines), if they say they are *reporting* the news, then they have a responsibility to the *people* to be accurate, *free* of bias.

This isn't happening.

I don't care what the views of a particular corporate-owned syndicate is...they are *still* responsible to get the facts correct no matter their personal passion.

Picking fun of a political candidate is normal.

That dates back to the beginning of newspapers, but to spread full-fledged lies about them is another story. Facts!

In today's world, everyone and their brother thinks they are writers and can abuse the *Freedom of Speech* and put out there whatever they want...fabricated or not, and they are doing it at a speed so quick that they have most of the world believing in their crap!

For me, now those who *do* report accurate information, I question because *what the hell to believe* is at stake!

I'm currently editing my political work dating 2011 and back.

I am appalled even more to see how much worse things have gotten, and believe me, it *has* 100-fold!

Facebook was pretty new back then.

I don't think anyone had any idea what *Facebook* would open the door to.

Freedom of Speech is on the line here.

I see it coming.

The more crap out there, the more worrisome things are getting.

The perfect solution for those wanting control...put a handle on the internet (i.e. [for Americans] *Freedom of Speech*).

I watched an interview with the Dali Lama online. It's there for you to watch.

[Online search engine] has already began this journey of knocking out *Freedom of Speech* on a worldly scale.

[Online search engine]...isn't it an *American* company?

They have made agreements with China to monitor what is being posted about the Dali Lama in China.

Meaning...they are only allowing bad/ fabricated shit about the man, instead of what

he really stands for to be seen on the internet in China!

That's an *American* company controlling speech!

That agreement should *never* have been made! *Never*!

My assumption is that they made that agreement to get the China money.

Oh, my! Greed!

They are willing to give up a *freedom* for the almighty dollar. Hmmm!

So, there you go. That's one *big* example.

Here's a solution: Make it a mandatory rule that those putting out crap must post a disclaimer (clearly for all to see) that their website or blog is *'Opinion Not Based on Fact'*...then everyone will know that they *must* question what these people are writing.

News...*news* sites *must* insure that what they post is *fact*! and not opinion.

Pick up any newspaper and there is a few pages that are dedicated to people's opinions.

It is up to the consumer to decide if they trust that person's opinion or not.

In today's internet world, people are writing crap without any disclaimers stating their site is *opinion* and this is causing chaos across the globe. Tell me I'm wrong!

Now to the videos.

I watched a video of this very large woman running down some street naked as a jaybird screaming and, seemingly, lost out of her mind.

These people in this car filmed her, just filmed her. They didn't get out and help her.

They didn't grab a blanket or something to cover her. They didn't save her dignity.

Nope!

They saw *likes* on *YouTube* and *Facebook*.

They saw *self* and had not one once of empathy for this woman.

Yes, she most likely took some type of drug that made her lose her mind. *So*!

That does *not* give anyone the right to put one of the lowest moments of her life on film and post it for all the world to see, and everyone is questioning why there is so many suicides going on today. Hello?

It's because of your selfish damn ass!

Another video was pointed out to me that totally rocked my world.

There was an accident.

I'm guessing a motorcycle or something of the sorts was involved.

I could not watch the whole thing.

The video clearly showed body parts all over.

The head separate from the body...that's as far as I got.

I was told there were arms and legs separated from the body!

What the hell kind of person would film that for one?...and what the hell kind of evil person would post that on the internet?

Don't you know that that is just *not* something to film or post?

The family has to see that now all over again...and again...and again!

Not to mention people who have seen war!

Do you *not* understand what that does to a person's mind?

Of course, the evil person who posted and filmed this probably does because they are evil!

There is a time to film and take pictures and a time to go quiet!

I've written about this when I was teaching how the younger generations have *zero* concept of empathy!

Narcissist is becoming more of the norm and this is upsetting! Now to Donald Trump.

He ran for President.

There was quite a show.

The racism part was already at play.

Or didn't you notice that?

I wrote about it clearly in my political work dating before 2011.

Now...all around I hear *the prince of the earth has risen. Nope*!

Evil has always been around.

Did you not study history?

The real history...like researched history and shit.

The kind of history books where people actually did the footwork for you.

That means they went into library archives...read the newspaper accounts, saw the actual pictures that were taken during those times, read tons of books on the particular subject they investigate, then write their book.

These are the kinds of books you should read.

These are the kinds of books people who attend a university read.

Pages and pages of it...then we are tested on it. Hello? It's called actual education.

You (I'm talking about Americans) have the tools you need to actually research your candidate, then you are *expected* to make an educated vote.

The voting system put into place was not put into place for you to make a decision based on *Facebook* B.S...but that is exactly what happened. Now the deed is done.

Does it stop there? *Nope*.

Trump hasn't been sworn in yet.

He's been elected, but he is not acting president yet.

Yet, I keep hearing that he's made this move, he's made that move. Really? How?

He's job right now is picking his cabinet.

He doesn't do that by himself.

Oh, I forgot, you didn't know that either. Shame!

I read one post about Trump's wife.

How silly!

I would reckon that when she married Trump...what [eight plus] years ago that she had *no* idea he would run, let alone be elected as President of the *United States*!

She was a model, posed naked (by the way... she had a beautiful body back then, so you should be proud since you all post your naked pictures everywhere these days!)

She can't undo her past, and you have *no* right to condemn her because of it.

She was also born in another country.

Okay, but she married a U.S. citizen.

Do you not know how that works?

She can't be deported!

The lack of education in this country is appalling.

Our country...politically...is in a mess!

The people in this country are losing their minds.

One woman shit in the street in one city.

Took her pants off and *shit* in the street, then picked her own shit up and wiped it on a poster of Trump.

That is so disgusting, then what is worse, someone filmed this event.

They didn't try to help her or anything.

They filmed it and posted it on the net.

Both of these individuals are way out there!

Freedom of Speech is being abused to get *likes*, to get money.

Empathy is being replaced with greed.

People are filming other people losing their dignity, getting hurt, embarrassing themselves without helping...just to get *likes* on the *internet*!

Finally, the *dark internet*...go ahead and view some videos...you like doing that...on *YouTube*. Go ahead.

They talk about this *B* site...this site challenges its participants to post the most ridiculous pictures and videos...byway of *Photoshop* and such.

Their idea is to see who can come up with the most appalling/disturbing stuff or *create* the most absurd/disturbing stuff.

With today's technology, the necessary programs used to create those [one and a half]-hour movies, are now available for everyone to use. Some are *free* over the internet.

People: *Most* of what you see on *Facebook* comes from this site! It's *not* real!

This is a time when you have to question your own mind.

I had a professor (I have a degree in Journalism) say: Don't believe anything you read, half of what you hear and see until you know the facts!

He was right!

There are a large number of people out there (call them trolls) who have nothing better to do in their boring, miserable lives, then to make shit up and see how far they can push your buttons. I know my life. Trust me...I do.

There are reasons for everything I do in my life. I question, then I learn. You should, too.

~

(December 9, 2016)—I am moving to Nevada or Colorado when my lease is up.

Fuck politics.

Why suffer when I don't have to.

Make weed legal across the board.

Screw pharmas and the keep-America-sick B.S.

It's time for *all* to speak up and stump these stupid laws to the ground.

Oh, and *free* every single soul who was put in prison just for weed. That's B.S., too!

~

(December 10, 2016)—*People aren't as beautiful as they look, as they walk or as they talk. They are only as beautiful as they love, as they care and as they share.—*Author Unknown

You are a Badass...How to Stop Doubting Your Greatness and Start Living an Awesome Life by Jen Sincero...for all who suffer from *let-me-take my-shit-out-on-other-people, instead-of-look-inside-of-myself* syndrome, this book is excellent. Go read it.

Scroll down and see the comment by a little old lady who said using the word *fuck* is a sign of a weak person.

I should invite her to walk in my shoes for just one day.

Not to be mean, but I think she'd fall flat on her face within an hour.

In all sense...she said—*anyone who uses a four letter word is weak*—so I guess using words like *love*, *like*, *life*, and such are weak as well.

I'm all of the above and I can still use the *fuck* word when the occasion arises.

The adversary at work in the oddest of places.

This judgmental society needs a *self* check really bad.

I know I *self* check myself all the time.

After all the *shit*...[four] letter word...I've been through, I'm still standing, still able to read and write, still able to love beyond people's differences, still able to smile when others show their ignorance.

That, in itself, is *your*...[four] letter word...decision...to bypass other people's insecurities and live an authentic life.

It's not called *weak*...[four] letter word.

It's called being strong no matter what.

I promote good books when I get my hands on them. This particular book is really good.

Get some warrior in yourself and read a good self-help book including the *good*...[four] letter word...book (that would be the *Bible*).

Life...[four] letter word...is worth living and building.

Hate...yet another [four] letter word...is for the weak.

True...yet another [four] letter word...is for the *real*...[four] letter word...God appreciates that. I know that is the truth.

His *Word*...[four] letter word...is *all* that matters.

So, do your *gift* [four] letter word...and don't worry about those out there who have nothing better to do, then blast people and their truth.

The best thing you can do when that adversary shows its ugly head is to turn it around and use it to better the world.

For me, it always gives me something to write about. Have a beautiful day.

P.S. I got into a heated discussion with *Microsoft's* animated computer support system early this morning.

I bought a desktop and a notebook two years ago at the same time. Both had *Windows 7*.

Microsoft upgraded all of us to *10* last year.

I don't use my notebook all the time and when I have since this nice little upgrade, I get *Activate Windows*...I ignored this little phrase because my windows was already activated, then some deals stop acting right.

Since my first discussion with *Microsoft* last year, they are trying to get me to spend $199 to pay for this upgrade, since I didn't *activate* this new upgrade *right away*.

Those of us who were around since the first home computers were around, are used to the *buy-one-windows-system-and-then-you-could-use-it-on-all-your-home-computers* thing.

It seems greed is now part of the equation.

How much is Bill Gates worth?

So, according to Gates, every home computer in your house has to have a separate product number key or digital license.

If it comes with one system and *Microsoft* gives you a *gift* of a *free* upgrade, then later comes along and says you have to pay for it, even though you didn't ask for it, then that's a lie. Greed.

My notebook has a license and a product key... since they upgraded my system by automatic updates, they are saying my system is pirated!

After several round and round *discussions* with this computer system support deal this morning...I gently said—*fuck you, Bill Gates* and went to bed.

Isn't having only two operating systems: *Microsoft* and *Apple*...in the whole entire world, a bit of controlling the population.

No wonder there is so much anger in the world.

All you geniuses out there...there has got to be a better way.

How about a little competition for *Microsoft*, *Apple* and *Google*? After all, the universe gives when we ask.

So ask!

For the rest of the naysayers who don't know the difference between a [four] letter word and a curse... get some education, then get back to me.

Thanks. Rant over.

Comments
▪(Friend) I totally agree.

~Places Shackled~

He† asked not to forsaken Him†
yet gives a choice–
free-will to accept within

analogies, theological preachings
leads only to leeching
the wrong, deceitful teaching
–a constant arguing of bitching
leaves hungry souls
waiting, anticipating
in places allowing shackling

He's† proven enough for everyone's love

He† doesn't have to do rough
–that's the enemy's stuff
but He'll† get tough

when love's smothered in crud

to push buttons
lead people to suffering
–He's† testing, seeing who's believing
wondering how long
for hearts in changing–
faith begins ringing

amazing to watch, tickings of the cock
deceptions—coming in hot
–evil's little bot
it'll be easy to come in without a knock
as you wage wars—on a dot

careful now, He† understands *wow*
hears every prayer in loud

evil things—He† does allow
waiting for the choice
a hungry heart's voice
in *free*-will—the bow
–without asking how!

(December 20, 2016)—*I am a living witness you can love your enemies and haters, only when you have love and a heart of God. It's truly complicated and difficult to really love in your own strength—it takes God!*—Author Unknown

Stand up for what is right, even if you stand alone.—Author Unknown

I had an online discussion early, early this morning when I posted an article about the inauguration of the President of the United States.

It's amazing how easy it is for people to believe in false stories, to see how easy deception is playing its role.

I ended the discussion, then posted my thoughts of truth on my personal page.

This morning I was lead to *Psalm 11*—... *the Lord examines the righteous, but the wicked and those who love violence His soul hates On the wicked, He will rain fiery coals and burning sulfur, a scorching wind will be their lot. For the Lord is righteous, He loves justice; upright men will see His face.*

Most of what took place in the *Bible* happened on the African continent because that is where Christ was born.

There is no dispute here.

The ancient maps reveal exactly how this all unfolds. Okay.

So, does this mean that Africa is special or needs to be put above all? No.

It means that once all of this particular part of the world was connected and that there was a lot of turmoil that man could not solve on his own.

God cleansed this place once with water.

He promised never to do that again.

They didn't listen.

So, this next time, instead of water, He sent Himself in the flesh.

This guy in the discussion this morning... after calling me a racist because I posted about the *Inauguration* said that Jesus was made up by Europeans. Amusing.

According to him, my whole world is a lie!

Hence, this morning when I opened my *Bible*, which it has been over a week since I did so, I was led to this particular *Psalm*.

There's no argument here what God is saying to me. Deception is amongst us.

Like it or not. It doesn't really matter.

It's how much faith do you have that matters the most.

We all have been lied to...by man.

I can tell you this about my life...I've felt God's love. I don't need to see His face.

At all!

—That evil whore is at it again.

Certain very important (i.e. *used-a-lot* keys on my keyboard quit working).

Microsoft...praise the Lord...added that really need on-board keyboard.

God always prevails...always.

Do you realize how many times we use the *l, ., and backspace keys*!?

Editing my work on the presidential history and my eyes are turning behind my head.

[Four] days 'til Christmas and as the past [four] years, I have not bought one gift.

I wasn't even going to decorate like I did last year. He decorated. This tiny tree.

So sweet.

I'm simple...don't require much these days.

Sometimes...being happy is all that you need for Christmas! God is great all the time!

—Dim...that's all I wrote...*dim*...and got two likes...it was a typo y'all..

Note...if you are a product of evil...delete me. I am a Christian.

Meaning: I believe in Jesus Christ. God, and the Holy Spirit.

I have encountered some odd things in life.

The oddest are the ones who don't believe in Jesus...not a European deal.

I heard that one tonight.

Misguided minds fallen prey to you know who.

Yes...Africa...the huge continent was where Jesus was born.

If you get a map out, you'd understand the geography.

The racist bullshit...don't come at me.

I will tear you up.

Being a deep south Cajun...I have seen enough of people's crap to last a life time, including from my own family.

A black man calling another black man racist...really?

[*Facebook* friend] and I have policy differences. He pisses me off, sometimes.

I piss him off. We debate and move on.

I know we are not raciest.

To me, if you call another black man a racist...you being black...that's a northern thing, or all together not an American thing.

If you do that, you know *nothing* about color differences, not the reason behind it here in American. Nothing! Sad.

Really sad because we are all the same in God's eyes.

I currently don't live in the same country I lived in 30 years ago.

I am less *free* because of the Clinton's and the Obama's.

Read the *Constitution* at any university.

That's all you have to do.

I didn't vote for Mr. Trump. You did.

I read his story.

All you guys that got kicked out of class... he's you.

It's not the color of your skin that makes or breaks you. It's what you do.

You can hate Trump all you want.

He's still President of the U.S.A.

He did the impossible without political machine money. That's impressive.

He said a lot of things.

So would you to get the vote.

Look at any entertainer.

Whatever it takes to get that almighty green.

Shame that some can't see the ironicism in that. I don't like Obama.

I did like him and rooted for him.

He seemed clean and unscathed.

At the time, I didn't know about his book or his learned hatred of a country he, so easily won, then his intentions were released with his slippery pen and teleprompters...a puppet! and we are less *free*.

That's why I don't care for him.
I ask those who criticize any President...are you judging the man or the policy.?
It's the policy, not the man or his family.
Our government was designed *free* off passion. *Free* of passion.
Don't preach your beliefs to me.
My beliefs are my God-given right to have...so far, because I am *free*, I can speak them.
All those radical innuendos...that's just evil fighting against good.
All those saying I was lied to... brainwashed.
You are reading the wrong books.
It's about humanity and God's gifts of *free*-will and unconditional love.
Your hate doesn't live on my page or in my life.
You are the ones who will surely need to read my books. God bless *all*.
Your deity...bow down...it's yours.
That has no place in my world.

~*Lions in Dens*~

my eyes opened to those in weak
how hard to see, those not in *free*

I've lived my life listening
watching, learning
closed-minded, or so it seemed
then this rapture, a part—diving in strife
all that I thought right
teaching my children at night
what wasn't exactly insight
of a true knight

my hands shake
knowing what was coming outright
bearing down—no way of holding tight
what I was to fight

my ears closed
then opened with might
my body—emotions—untied
from a long awaited awakening
—my eyes no longer blind

it came upon me, in a slow fright
during the night—
—three nights, fear gripped me tight
visions, touches—I've seen the blight
—what wasn't right

then it came, things never the same

a direct answer, fog rolling into a ball
—there's no time to stall, you will fall
I've been there, through it all
I shook inside, like never before

no longer—could I deny
this opened door
right before my eyes, an answer I heard
silently like before, over and over
my questioning allure
He† showed me for sure

since then, answering–
me, again and again
directly—how could I bend

God's† power
even through night's of howling
endless prowling
denying what I'm to follow
again and again, I beg—plead
then His† answer bleeds
for my eyes to see

more and more revealed
unlocking of eye's closed—sealed

man's insecurities
their strong-held traditions
embedded vulnerabilities
—no longer a sanctuary to hold dearly

through this pen
write what's already written
plead the forsaken
—they're already forgiven
patiently waiting
He's† here for the taking
sincerity in asking
—change these taught lessons
it's time for love's blessing

okay, okay, okay
my pleading brethren
I'll do what You† command
forsaken I'll be—I fully understand
'til it's all complete
then I'll be totally *free*, to do as I please
—just don't forsaken He†

~*Fields of Purple*~

I have suffered the foes—not like most
but too close not to know
which way the wind blows

I have felt seeds I've sown–

folded, unfolded, unfolding
words of crow, I understand the code

it's not about who you know—
if who you know really don't know

it's not about values you grow—
if they're wrong—so in *no*
stuck in *back there*
traditions so long ago—
allowing them to flow
stuck in fears of letting go

it's not about education
or *I told you so's*—if all that audio—
just brain-washing's manifesto
leaving you naïve and sold
with nothing in the soul to hold

it's not about family-unity's gusto—
if secrets send you to the gallows
—a buried-deep tornado
wanting to explode
but that *be-nice-cajole* breaks down
the heart to hollow

it's not about adhering to motto—
if it's only set up to control
to break all peaceful's widows
to steal joy's beautiful rainbows

it's not about race-driven innuendos—
that's just a plain ole gestapo
using *passion* as an inferno
to twist and entangle—
turning minds into psycho

it's not about ciaos and chaos—
all that political mumbo-jumbo
—if voices from history's echo
are continually buried
in some vaulted escrow
while always wanting a *faute de mieux*

it's just the bases of cammo
—a constant-overlaying incognito

it's not about the
who's-right-who's-wrong fais doe-doe
it's not about the fearless desperado
or the brave heroes
or even the enslaving furrow—
that's been smeared as a *free* throw
for man's undying ego

it's not even about
some government's invented lasso—

thinking they have us
in some kind of sealed bowl

it's *all* about the release of soul—
knowing all hearts are the gold
no matter which way eyes roll—
the country folks, the city rambos
the east, west, north, and south—
each lady and fellow
from the richest châteaux
to every breathing ghetto

there's no promised tomorrow

there's only today's hold
no matter how much dough
in your barrow
no matter what your zip code
no matter who *free*-loads
or the matters of your household

no matter what loopholes
you think through—you stroll
no matter what powers you feel
only *you* patrol
—or you think you have
in some stronghold
—it's all just trolls in the minds to erode

there's only one, single phrase
always *so, God's*† *in the know*
all to Him† will go

you can deny, swear it isn't so
—here's a little flow
for your turned-up nose

today's steady-turning cargo—just ditto—
it's already happened befo'
you're just beating your head—
again, an over and over swinging do'

just so you know, the *bible* tells us so
which way this all goes

enlighten your soul while on earth
you still have the 'go
or sure as the water flows—
flames on your skin—you'll feel the glow

history's repeating manifesto:

learn not from its lesson's code
repeat, repeat, repeat—back around you go

it's all the same, it's all the same

a slightly different scenario
a different looking toad
—same ole libido—*pride, greed, ego*

the constant in grow
'til bam! the massive explode

it's not a tall-tale glow
nor a massive lie told
there's no hidden proviso

no, no, no....

it's the same lessons told—over and over
the tests experienced in hold
but never heard–
just covered up in shadows
–evil's little sucking-in hole

if you truly want to unfold
–a worn purple robe—so long, long ago
tells you what to know
the *bible* says it is so

there's no dreamy baskets of gold
waiting at ends of rainbows
–just words in hebrew code
instructing and teaching which way to go

never promised tomorrow

build fields of purple flowers–
let them breathe
see them sway in a wind's blow
smell their fragrance
as it cleans your nose—feel their peace
as back and forth they flow

it's *all* in the purple's glow
words written long ago
repeating, repeating–
lessons to the turned-up nose
following the wrong road
without listening to the one, single voice
who truly knows
to each individual—those words flow
for the *bible* says it is so–
God† is *so* in the know!

(December 30, 2016)—It's the repetition of affirmations that leads to belief, and once that belief becomes a deep conviction, things begin to happen.

Might not be tonight, tomorrow or the next day...but everything's gonna be okay.

I was in debate about my last message of the year.

Night before last and all yesterday, I paced, joked around, stared at the drawings that are going to be the covers of my books, stared at nothing at all, then back to pacing. I prayed.

I was first led to *Isaiah 40-54:9,10* (more about that further down), and, then last night to the movie *Kill Switch*.

I was still blank until this morning.

"Fields of Purple" filled my empty page.

Isaiah 40:6-8 says—*A voice says, 'Cry out.' And I said, 'What shall I cry?' 'All men are like grass, and all their glory is like the flowers of the field. The grass withers and the flowers fall, because the breath of the Lord blows on them. Surely the people are grass. The grass withers and the flowers fall, but the word of God stands forever.*

All of Isaiah's writing made me think hard...I wrote extensively in the margins!

(That is something you should do, too, when reading the *Bible* because each passage speaks to us differently, and...if you read the *Bible* regularly and continue to add your thoughts about what each passage means, you can actually go back and see your personal growth. That's just a suggestion.)

For those of you who aren't really sure or don't even know, Isaiah is part of the *Old Testament.*

To give a little head's up of the happenings of the time: The years are Ca. 725-585 B.C. (that would be before Christ...that's Jesus...was born).

Israel falls.

Isaiah begins to warn around Ca. 714 B.C. about Egypt and Ethiopia.

By this time, Isaiah has seen a lot, he's well up in age.

There were many prophets before him, but no one is taking heed to the warnings or prophecies.

Okay.

Are you in the mind-set of the time frame in which this is?

To add a small bit of enlightenment... the United States of America declared its independence from Britain in 1776 A.D. (that's after that death of Christ...that would be Jesus!)...that's just 280 years ago!

Again, I have a simple *Bible* that is easier to understand...*The Daily Bible...In Chronological Order 365 Daily Readings (The New International Version, With Devotional Insights to Guide You Through God's Word).*

It's accurate...I've compared it to two other versions of the *Bible* and the only difference is that it puts everything in historical order... meaning...as it happened in time, and the authors included historical data on what was going on at the time these biblical events took place.

If you have trouble understanding the *Bible*...this is an excellent choice.

For more perspective: After Isaiah, you have Nahum's prophecies in 650 B.C., Zephaniah's prophecies between 635-625 B.C., Jeremiah in 626 B.C., Assyria falls and Babylonia emerges between 626-610 B.C., Judah's first deportation around 605 B.C., then the great deportation and Nebuchadnezzar and Ezekiel around 597 B.C., (all during this time, Jeremiah's prophecies are the talk of the town, a lot of rebellion (Israel)...a lot of political stuff going on)...[during all this time, all these prophecies are coming to pass....], Jerusalem falls around 586 B.C...all this leads up to the *Exiled Nation* Ca. 585-535 B.C...all foretold by prophecies!

The last utterance of Jeremiah is about 586 B.C.

By this time, all the great prophecies by Isaiah, Jeremiah and Ezekiel come to pass...then Job comes in the picture...I've written a lot about him.

So, that's a very narrow, brief explanation of the time frame.

There's many years between Job and Isaiah...they pretty much speak about the same things.

For me, Job is more inspiring because of what happened to him.

Isaiah...over [seven]...seven hundred years before Jesus is born is telling us about Jesus!

He tells us where Jesus will be born and how to recognize him.

For Christ's sakes, he tells us the earth is *round*...40:21-26...*He sits enthroned above the circle of the earth....*

He tells us who has put those circles in the fields in Europe...remember those...*42:1-4—... He will not shout or cry out, or raise his voice in the streets. A bruised reed he will not break, and a smoldering wick he will not snuff out....*

Those who studied these circles know how this relates.

He talks and warns about slavery!

Over and over again.

He foretells the Civil War here in America if you pay attention: *43:1-7—I will say to the north, 'Give them up!' and to the south, 'Do not hold them back.*

[Are you going to deny that this doesn't apply to what happened during the Civil War?]

He tells us that the stars and moon and earth work together...that's in *48:12-15.*

That was how many years *before* the world gave credit to a man who probably just understood the *Bible*?!

He says over and over that Jesus (who hasn't been born yet....) *is God!*

Over and over...He constantly refers to *history*...he constantly says to pay attention to ancient days, to look back! to learn from *back there*!

He talks over and over about *greed*!...its evil!

He talks about *lessons* and *tests* and how God gives them to us, so that we may make the choice ourselves.

He talks about leaders not caring for the poor and enslaving people...oh! how he talks about this! Why am I telling you this?

Simple.

You don't listen to what is already told to you.

You remain ignorant and blind for no other reason, then enslaving yourself.

Why do you do that? Why do I do it?

The answer to that is simple as well...fear instilled into us by man! Not God! Man!

There's no guessing to this.

There's no mathematical equation to solve.

There's no ingenious way of looking at it.

You don't need some man-made spiritual leader to tell you. It's already written.

All you have to do is read.

In the movie, *Kill Switch*, Adam Swartz... (interesting that his full name doesn't automatically come up when you type in Adam...it should...and the movie doesn't come up automatically either... for someone who does a lot of research, I find this unusual!...both are buried on purpose)...was 26 years old when he died (I'm sure not by suicide and that's not a guess)...all because he protected a right we all have...*Freedom of Speech*!

Same with Bradley Manning.

These guys aren't criminals.

They are patriots who did their job as patriots. Why am I telling this?

It all interlinks. All of it!

I'm editing my second political book, which I write about the history of America, and from that research to reading the *Bible*, it's already foretold. All of it!

How does that apply to you?

Because it is the same whether it is some political government, or a corporation, or a family, or a relationship, or an individual...it is all the same.

Strife comes in many different disguises, but it is all the same: The devil. Evil. Greed. Pride. Ego...*control!*

If everyone had faith and believed in peace, they'd be no strife.

The power of money is the drive for evil. It is that simple.

Think about the fights you had with others.

All of them...money was the key factor no matter how you look at it.

Many times that demon is hidden very well...but, in the end, it's all about money!

All of this strife puts us *all* in a circle...the five stages of grief consumes us and keeps us in the devil's mix.

Those who have sold their souls know how to use the five stages of grief to their advantage.

They know how to keep us in strife.

It's rather easy, and we let them.

God's great. He is the ultimate father.

He loves us unconditionally.

He gave us the most precious gift of all... *free-will*!

There are only two sides and you have a choice of which side you will bat for.

I thought hard on what I wanted to write about to end this last book of mine in my serious on the five stages of grief.

It's really a universal issue that trickles down to the individual...and it's all the same, *and* we *all* have been already warned about it, *and* what we are experiencing in our personal lives as well as in every relationship, including that of governments, has already happened over and over again.

We just haven't learned the lesson.

So...as I've said over and over...the tests will keep coming until we do learn the lesson and actually move forward.

Until then, we remain slaves.

Free My People...God says over and over in the *Bible*. Who are His people? We are!

Or haven't you figured that one out yet?!

I've learned a lot these past [five] years.

People will lie their asses off to save their own skin.

They will destroy another to hide their secrets.

They will condemn a race to hide those secrets.

They will consume themselves in pride, greed, ego in order to be none other than better than the next person, no matter the price (which they fail to see by the way!), and there is always a price!

There will be no peace on earth.

That is warned over and over in the *Bible* as well.

Man was built with what would seem a fault. There's a reason for that.

What is that fault?

The ability to think for him/herself.

Free-will! God created man.

He's the most of everything.

He knew what He was doing.

Or haven't you learned that either?

Free-will.

The ability to make our own decisions.

The greatest gift. Think about that.

You make your own choices.

If you hurt someone, that's your decision.

That person you hurt, they have to survive your decision.

If you enslave people, that's your decision...that would be heads of governments, owners of corporations... entities like that...right down to parents and husbands and wives (i.e. the individual).

It's your...*your* decision.

How big a decision brings about how big the surviving of that decision, which, in turn, brings about more and more evil...*oh, those holes*...that evil whore likes to penetrate to control us. It's all the same....

God is the only way to close those holes, to stop evil in its fucking tracks.

Without God, strife will continue to plaque your life.

Without God, even if your life seems dainty and cheery...it's not. It's an illusion.

I was told through a comment that I was pushing *my* religion on others. Fuck that.

I don't have a religion. I have God.

I have Him in His *three* entities: The Father, the Son, the Holy Spirit!

That's not religion. That's faith in *all* ways.

I've been folded.

I've been through the unfolded part.

I'm in the unfolding in its completeness.

I thank God every day for this experience.

He's opened my eyes to what it means to have unconditional love and *free*-will.

I chose him...the *sweet man* who stands by my side.

My father chose not to shake his hand because of the color of his skin.

That was something a father's little girl should never see. I saw it.

I saw it at 47 years old when God was ready to show it to me.

I understand what unfolding means!

Love has no conditions.

It has understanding. It has forgiveness.

It has loyalty. It has communication.

That day...opened my eyes to a lot of things.

Particularly, the meaning behind my work.

I understand the journey I was brought on. (Against my will, I might add.)

Everything happens for a reason.

Pay attention. Listen.

Don't just hear...listen.

Perception and patience were my two hardest lessons to learn these past [five] years.

I am grateful for the turmoil in which I had to suffer in order to fully understand these two most precious gifts. Lies.

The illusions of the deceivers. Corruption. Denial. Enslavement.

My...my...my how the world is open to all those holes.

From the individual on up...it's a personal choice to get right with God before that tomorrow comes that we are not promised... after that, it's the marks on your...*your*...no one else's...your heart that tells the tale.

2016 taught me a lot.

I hope through my writing that I've shared enough so that you may learn that you are a wonderful person.

It doesn't matter what others think.

It matters what goes on in your own mind...that determines your perception and patience...which leads you to the only true thing that matters: Love.

May God be with you on your journey always. Love the skin you are in.

Thank you for traveling this journey with me.

You are appreciated more than you will ever know.

About This Book

I included all my political writings from 2012 until 2017 in this book.

I haven't focused so much time on politics this year, but there is still concern in me to which way the people are going.

In any sense, I've learned that the anger stage continues if you continue to be around strife. It's very hard to let the anger go.

More on this part of the healing later in another book.

For now...I keep it moving forward.

There's a posting to the right of my screen that ask: *Do you love the Constitution?*

There are a little over 140,000 clicks for like.

I'm a tad bit disappointed in that number. What the hell!

This is the United States of America, right?

I think I'm in that country...born and raised, as did every single generation in my family extending as far back as [when] the Choctaw Indians began their existence.

I'm a native.

The *Constitution* of this country is very important to me as is the fundamentals of freedoms my ancestors have enjoyed since the inception of this great country.

Note from the Author

(2018)—This is the tenth book of a 12-book series on the topics of silent abuse (showing you, not telling you, what it is and how it turns to physical abuse and divorce; as well as, from this point on, showing you how to survive it), the five stages of grief, and life. It is March and I'm finally going to publication.

The introductions of these books are being re-read one last time, but the manuscripts as a whole are not. I've edited them once.

That's enough of going back there for me.

I've gone over the formatting so many times, my eyes are crossed.

Any mistakes are mine and mine alone.

I do not include a bibliography in my books, so I hope the notations within the text satisfies the masses.

If not, then you'll have to trust me that I have not claimed anyone's original work as my own. If I have missed a notation, then it is my error alone.

I pray that these books end up in the hands that need them.

I pray that you continue your fight through your darkness and stay amongst the living for a little while longer. There's so much of life still to experience.

I pray, in Jesus' name, that you can see that.

Say to yourself—I Am Woman. Hear Me Roar! Say it and say it loud!

Love the skin you are in. You are beautiful and worthy.

Believe that and you are half way there to being a survivor, too.

About the Author

After a tour of duty in the Army (stationed in Germany during a freaking war!), I attended Nicholls State University in Thibodaux, La. and joined the Louisiana National Guard as a photojournalist (where I completed eleven years of military service).

While at NSU, I studied creative writing under novelist Dr. Albert Belisle Davis and journalism under Dr. Lloyd Chaisson, I earned a Bachelor's of Arts degree in Mass Communications (print journalism) and certification in Secondary Education.

I was a teacher for seven years.

My journalism and photography work have appeared in numerous regional publications, and I won numerous awards including the South Regional Award and the Bonnie Toups Wells Award for feature writing, the National Library of Poetry's Editor's Choice Award, Creative Arts & Science Enterprises' Accomplishments of Merit for Outstanding Literary Achievement Award in Poetry, and Lliad Press' Honorable Mention in Poetry.

My poetry appeared in nine anthologies in the United States and the United Kingdom—which all means nothing to you, but, to me, it means a great deal since it all ended because of silent abuse.

I was born and raised in South Louisiana and have three wonderful children whom I adore more than than thing.

I'm also a grandmother, and one day I hope that my grandchild, as well as my future grandchildren, see that their grandmother was one hell of a strong woman.

I am a 100% disabled veteran writing full time, living where ever I want...currently that place is Las Vegas, Nevada